E. W. CLARK.
Originator of the University of Pennsylvania Expedition to Babylonia.

NIPPUR

OR

EXPLORATIONS AND ADVENTURES ON THE EUPHRATES

THE NARRATIVE OF THE UNIVERSITY OF
PENNSYLVANIA EXPEDITION TO
BABYLONIA IN THE YEARS
1888–1890

BY

JOHN PUNNETT PETERS, PH.D., SC.D., D.D.
Director of the Expedition

WITH ILLUSTRATIONS AND MAPS

VOLUME I
FIRST CAMPAIGN

WIPF & STOCK · Eugene, Oregon

Wipf and Stock Publishers
199 W 8th Ave, Suite 3
Eugene, OR 97401

Nippur, or, Explorations and Adventures on the Euphrates, Volume 1
The Narrative of the University of Pennsylvania Expedition to Babylonia in the Years 1888-1890
By Peters, John Punnett
Copyright © 1897 by Peters, John Punnett All rights reserved.
Softcover ISBN-13: 978-1-6667-7301-9
eBook ISBN-13: 978-1-6667-7303-3
Publication date 3/6/2023
Previously published by G. P. Putnam's Sons, 1897

This edition is a scanned facsimile of the original edition published in 1897.

To the Public-Spirited Gentlemen
of Philadelphia
who made the Expedition possible
these Volumes are Respectfully
Dedicated

PREFACE.

No city in this country has shown an interest in archæology at all comparable with that displayed by Philadelphia. A group of public-spirited gentlemen in that city has given without stint time and money for explorations in Babylonia, Egypt, Central America, Italy, Greece, and our own land; and has, within the last ten years amassed archæological collections which are unsurpassed in this country. The first important work undertaken was the Babylonian Expedition. As described in the Narrative, this expedition was inaugurated by a Philadelphia banker, Mr. E. W. Clark. The enterprise was taken up in its infancy by the University of Pennsylvania, under the lead of its provost, Dr. William Pepper. Dr. Pepper made this expedition and the little band of men who had become interested in it the nucleus for further enterprises. A library and museum were built, an Archæological Association was formed, and a band of men was gathered together in Philadelphia who have contributed with a liberality and enthusiasm quite unparalleled for the prosecution of archæological research in almost all parts of the world. Upwards of $70,000.00 have been spent on Babylonian exploration alone; and Philadelphia and the University of Pennsylvania have won a noble and unique reputation, for princely liberality in the support of scientific explorations, wherever scholarship is honored and admired, both in this country and abroad.

These two volumes bear the title, *Nippur*. Before the explorations of the University of Pennsylvania Expedition, that name was known only to a few scholars, and they knew little more than the name of the city and that at an early period it had played an important part in the religious development of Babylonia and, through Babylonia, of the world. We now know that in the times of the glory of Nineveh and Babylon the name of " Nippur " was as familiar to the citizens of those cities as the names of Nineveh and Babylon are to us, and that Nippur exercised on their religious life and religious development an influence as potent as that of Jerusalem on our own. The Temple of Bel at Nippur was to the religion of Babylonia and Assyria very much what the Temple of Jerusalem was to our religion. It was this city, which exercised so great an influence on the religious life of the people that so long dominated the civilized world, and so materially affected and determined the religious and scientific development of both Orient and Occident, and particularly the great Temple of Bel in that city, the oldest temple in the world, which the University of Pennsylvania Expedition explored.

I have called this temple " the oldest temple in the world " We found that Nippur was a great and flourishing city, and its temple, the Temple of Bel, the religious centre of the dominant people of the world at a period as much prior to the time of Abraham as the time of Abraham is prior to our day. We discovered written records no less than 6000 years old, and proved that writing and civilization were then by no means in their infancy Further than that, our explorations have shown that Nippur possessed a history extending backward of the earliest written documents found by us, at least 2000 years

The history of Assyrian and Babylonian research has been full of surprises. The explorations of Layard at Nineveh astonished the world by their revelation of buried cities and buried records, all antedating the earliest Greek and Roman civilization of which men then had any knowledge. The discoveries of George Smith—the deciphering of the libraries brought by Layard from Nineveh—excited even more wonder and surprise, by revealing the close connection existing between Babylonian and Hebrew civilization, legends, myths, and religion. The work recently done in Babylonia, both by the University of Pennsylvania Expedition, and also by the French explorations at Tello, southward of Nippur, have opened to us new vistas of ancient history. They have shown us that men in a high state of civilization, building cities, organizing states, conducting distant expeditions for conquest, ruling wide-extended countries, trafficking with remote lands, existed in Babylonia 2000 years before the period assigned by Archbishop Ussher's chronology for the creation of the world. Our work at Nippur has carried our knowledge of civilized man 2000 years farther backward, an enormous stride to make at one time.

It was my good fortune to be, in a sense, the discoverer of Nippur, as these pages will show, but this was in very truth my good fortune, and not my merit. Our first year's work, which is described in the first volume, was more or less of a failure, so far at least as Nippur was concerned. In contrast with this, our second campaign, which is described in the second volume, was a complete success. The amount of inscribed stones, bricks, and tablets found by us was enormous, not to speak of uninscribed objects, sarcophagi, pottery, stone and metal implements, and the like; but what was far more important, a large part of these objects came from a period up to that time regarded as not only prehistoric, but even remotely prehistoric, antedating all possible history by several millenniums. In fact, we had found the oldest inscriptions ever discovered. Further, we had in large part explored the Temple of Bel, and in doing so had made an important contribution to the history of religion.

The results of the second year's campaign were so satisfactory that it was determined to carry on the work farther, and Dr. J. H. Haynes was sent out to conduct the excavations on the lines laid down by the first expedition. His excavations extended over the years 1893-95, and were eminently successful He explored the Temple farther, and found almost double as much inscribed material as had been unearthed by me, much of it of the very earliest period. But his excavations, by their very success, only made it clearer that all the immense mound of Nippur should be explored to its bottom-most layers. The public-spirited gentlemen of Philadelphia, so far from abandoning the Herculean task, raised the funds to send out still a third expedition to take up Dr. Haynes's work as he laid it down. Unfortunately, the person chosen for this work allowed himself to be turned back, after he had reached the field, by the report of the danger and difficulty of the task ; and for two years the work has been in abeyance ; but only in abeyance, for it is the intention of the Archæological Department of the University of Pennsylvania, so soon as the times permit, to resume and ultimately complete the excavation of this most ancient city yet discovered.

It will be many years before the immense amount of inscribed material excavated by these expeditions, part of which is in the Imperial Museum in Constantinople, and part in the Museum of the University of Pennsylvania, has been published, or even rendered accessible to scholars. There are, it is estimated, between 30,000 and 40,000 inscribed objects, the inscriptions on which cover a period of over 5000 years These inscriptions are being published in fac-simile form under the editorship of Professor Hilprecht, and after the texts have been thus rendered accessible to Babylonian scholars it is proposed to publish a series of translations to make them accessible to the general public. Up to this date one volume in two parts has appeared, containing the more ancient texts

I may not close this preface without tendering my thanks to the liberal-minded patrons of research who have undertaken and carried out this great work of exploration, and under whose official sanction these volumes are published ; to the Professors of Robert College, who assisted us so materially ; to my colleagues in the expedition ; to Talcott Williams, LL. D., who by his wise counsel has been a mainstay of the expedition from first to last ; to M Pognon, Mr. Pinches, and Professor Sayce, Assyriologists, who assisted me with many helpful suggestions ; to Professor Gottheil ; to Professor Jastrow, who placed at my disposal the proofs of his Babylonian-Assyrian Religion ; to Dr. Ward, Director of the Wolfe Expedition, who has furnished me for publication a narrative of his explorations, and also permitted me to use as illustrations many valuable photographs taken by the Wolfe Expedition ; and last, but not least, to my dear wife, whose helpful courage kept me in the field when I was sorely tempted to resign.

JOHN P. PETERS.

St Michael's Church,
    New York,
        May 15th, 1897.

CONTENTS.

CHAPTER	PAGE
I.—Organizing the Expedition	1
II.—Obtaining an Iradé	19
III.—Impressions of Constantinople	44
IV.—The Discovery of Tiphsah	68
V.—The City of Zenobia	100
VI.—Deir to 'Anah	122
VII.—A City of Pitch	152
VIII.—Hit to Baghdad	165
IX.—Baghdad and Babylon	191
X—Nippur at Last	220
XI.—The First Campaign	242
XII.—The Catastrophe	279

APPENDICES.

A.—Subscription Paper of the Babylonian Exploration Fund	295
B.—First Application for Permission to Excavate	298
C.—Iradé Granting Permission to Excavate	301
D—Translation of Turkish Law on Archæological Excavations	303
E—The Geography of the Euphrates	310
F—Wolfe Expedition to Babylonia	318

ILLUSTRATIONS.

	PAGE
PORTRAIT OF E. W CLARK	*Frontispiece*
Originator of the University of Pennsylvania Expedition to Babylonia	
CLAY BARREL CYLINDER	14
Containing five hundred lines of inscription of Nebuchadrezzar the Great. Found in Babylon (The inscription contains an account of the buildings of Nebuchadrezzar, including canals)	
TURKISH HOUSES AT COUROUCHESME, ON THE BOSPHORUS	24
House of O. Hamdy Bey	
PORTRAIT OF O. HAMDY BEY	26
Director of the Imperial Ottoman Museum	
WHITE-TURBANED SOFTAS	29
SCENE IN THE ENVIRONS OF CONSTANTINOPLE	44
The Sweet Waters of Europe on a Friday afternoon	
MEVLEWEE DERVISH WITH INVERTED WATER-BUCKET HAT	59
ARMENIAN PORTERS CARRYING LARGE CASES OF GOODS	64
TURKISH DECK PASSENGERS	69
A TYPICAL CONE VILLAGE OF NORTHERN SYRIA	82
PLAN OF ZENOBIA	111
MAIN GATE OF SALAHIEH FROM THE DESERT	130
PLAN OF SALAHIEH	132

A Babylonian Water Wheel or Jird	136
Plan of Jabrieh	139
Ruins of City Wall of Unbaked Brick at Jabrieh	140
Water-Wheels of the Euphrates	141
Weaving Cloth among the Palms at 'Anah on the Euphrates	144
A Naoura Water-Wheel at 'Anah on the Euphrates	148
A Noachian Boatyard at Hit on the Euphrates	162
Plan of 'Anbar	177
The Ruined Tower of 'Akerkuf, near Baghdad	188
A Scene on the Tigris at Baghdad	190
Showing characteristic native boats, the long turadas, and the round, pitch-smeared kufas, with bridge of boats beyond	
The Tomb of Zobeide, the Favorite Wife of Harun-er-Rashid, at Baghdad	194
Tak-i-Khesra; the Ruins of the White Palace of Chosroes at Ctesiphon	198
Arab Khan on the Persian Pilgrim Route from Baghdad to Kerbela	206
Birs Nimrud, the Tower of Babel	214
Kal'at Amerika	234
The First Year's Camp, from the East, showing a great Trench in foreground.	
Affech Arab Building a Hut of Reeds and Mats	236
Nippur	242
Taken from a cast of the mounds, showing excavations of first year. The Temple Hill is to the right. Roman numerals indicate hills where excavations were made. Arabic numerals show the heights of the mounds in metres above apparent plain level.	
Arab Women	243

ILLUSTRATIONS

	PAGE
ARAB WORKMAN'S HUT	248
A DEEP TRENCH ON TABLET HILL (V)	250

    Showing constructions of Xerxes's time above, and remains of 2000 B.C. below.

THE MUTHIF OR GUEST HOUSE OF AN ARAB SHEIKH
    IN SOUTHERN BABYLONIA   252

FEMALE AVOCATIONS   256
    Arab women pounding grain to make bread.

MAP OF IRAK, OR BABYLONIA, FROM BAGHDAD TO UR
    In pocket at end of volume

MAP SHOWING ROUTES OF BABYLONIAN EXPEDITION
    ON THE EUPHRATES . . *In pocket at end of volume*

NIPPUR

OR EXPLORATIONS AND ADVENTURES ON THE EUPHRATES.

CHAPTER I.

ORGANIZING THE EXPEDITION.

American Oriental Society—An Expedition Proposed—The Wolfe Expedition—The Government and the Consulates—An Unexpected Friend—University of Pennsylvania—The Turkish Law—Application for Firman—Friction at Home—Organization—A More Extensive Plan—Personnel—A Consulate at Baghdad—Purchasing Supplies—Visit to London—International Co-operation Impossible—Purchasing Antiquities—Paris and Berlin—German Friendliness.

"ENGLAND and France have done a noble work of exploration in Assyria and Babylonia. It is time for America to do her part. Let us send out an American expedition."

At a meeting of the American Oriental Society in New Haven in October, 1884, those members of the Society interested in Semitic studies were called together by Professor Toy of Harvard, this proposition was laid before them, and a committee was formed forthwith to raise funds to send an American expedition to Babylonia. It was announced that the late Mr. Henry C. Bowen, editor of *The Independent*, would give five hundred dollars toward an expedition; and after some discussion it was agreed, that if $4500 could be provided, an expedition of exploration and reconnoissance only should be sent out, with Dr. Ward as director.

Among others to whom I applied as likely to be interested in work of this description, was the late Miss Catherine Lorillard Wolfe of New York. In reply, she invited me to breakfast with her. Bishop Potter was present at the breakfast, and his good offices were undoubtedly used in recommending the enterprise as one worthy of assistance. Miss Wolfe asked scarcely any questions about the particular enterprise, but showed interest in the general subject of Oriental exploration. After breakfast she gave me a paper signed by herself, promising to pay $5000 on demand for the purpose of sending an expedition to Babylonia. She alone was to send this out, and the $500 beyond the amount estimated by Dr. Ward as necessary for his expedition were to be used for purposes of photography. With her consent the money was turned over to the Archæological Institute of America, which assumed the responsibility for the expedition. Dr. Ward was appointed director, and to him was given as aide Dr. Sterrett. It was intended to attach to this expedition Dr. J. T. Clarke, director of the excavations at Assos, but the work on which he was then engaged rendered this impracticable. Some account of the Wolfe Expedition and its results will be found in an appendix to this volume.

With the collection of funds for this expedition, the original committee of the Oriental Society seems to have passed out of existence. Some of us, however, continued to labor individually to further the interests of exploration not only in Babylonia, but also in hither Asia in general. It seemed to me that much might be done if our Government would follow the policy of the French Government, and appoint as consuls, at places where archæological interests are important, men with some knowledge of and interest in archæology. At my suggestion, committees of the American Oriental Society and the American Institute of Archæology were appointed to urge this policy on the Government; and Mr. Cleveland was asked to consider the interests of science, as well as of commerce, in filling the consulships of Smyrna, Beirout, and Jerusalem, but in vain. Inspired by the achievements of the French consul-general at Baghdad, M. de Sarzec, I even corresponded with the authorities at Washington, and some of the merchants in New York who import wool from Baghdad, with regard to the establishment of a consulate at that city; but our commercial interests there proved to be small, and it was the policy of the Government to establish new consulates only where demanded in the interest of commerce: hence this effort also failed.

After the return of Dr. Ward, in 1886, I endeavored to collect funds to send out a second expedition for purposes of excavation. Mr. W. W. Frazier of Philadelphia became interested in the matter in the winter of 1886, and communicated with one or two gentlemen on the subject, and placed me in communication with others; but to no purpose apparently, for, excepting himself, no one seemed to care to take up such an enterprise.

In July of 1887, I was visiting at the house of a friend at Intervale, in the White Mountains, where I met Mr. E. W. Clark, the brother of my hostess. One Sunday morning, while walking up and down the verandah, waiting for the wagon to take us to church, Mr. Clark, knowing that I was much interested in Assyrian and Babylonian study, asked me some questions about explorations in those countries. In the course of our conversation I told him what had been done by the explorers of other countries. I also gave him an account of the Wolfe Expedition, and our failure to secure funds to follow it up by excavations, but without the slightest idea that he was likely to be interested in a matter of this description. To my great surprise, as the wagon came to the door and brought our conversation to a close, Mr. Clark said to me: " I think we can send out an expedition from Philadelphia. I should be glad to contribute, and I am sure that my brother will do the same. When we return to Philadelphia in the autumn, come and see me, and we will arrange the matter."

Convinced that what Mr. Clark undertook he would perform, and assured of the interest and co-operation of Mr. Frazier, I at once began to plan out an expedition to Babylonia, and to gather facts and figures, so that there might be no delay in the autumn. My original plan was a very modest one, involving for one year's work an outlay of $7500. Besides myself, I proposed to have one assyriologist, Mr. Pinches, of the British Museum, whose experience as curator would, I thought, render him peculiarly efficient in the field in determining rapidly the character of the objects found, cataloguing and reporting upon them, and preparing them for transport. I proposed further to secure the services, as photographer and business manager, of Mr. J. H. Haynes, who had accompanied the Wolfe Expedition in the same capacity, and who was at that time in Aintab in Turkey; and, as interpreter, of Mr. Daniel Z. Noorian, the interpreter of the Wolfe Expedition, who had followed Dr. Ward to this country. I corresponded with our minister in Constantinople, and with Dr. Long of Robert College, in regard to the method and chances of obtaining permission to excavate in Babylonia, and in general gathered all possible information during the summer, in order that I might have a definite plan to propose in the autumn.

True to his word, in the autumn of 1887, Mr. E. W. Clark took up with energy the matter of organizing a Babylonian expedition from Philadelphia, in company with his brother, Mr. Clarence H. Clark. After we had collected a few subscriptions, it was decided that it was desirable to connect the expedition with the University of Pennsylvania, and to ask the provost of that institution to act as president of the fund. The condition proposed to the University of Pennsylvania was that it should provide a fire-proof building with proper accommodation for receiving any such " finds " as might result from the excavations. The authorities of the university willingly agreed to accept the expedition on this condition, and a meeting was called at the house of Provost Pepper, November 30, 1887, at which some twenty-five to thirty persons were present, including Dr. Ward of New York, who gave a brief account of the work of the Wolfe Expedition, and described the results to be obtained by further work in Babylonia. I stated my plans, and gave such information as I could regarding the possibilities of conducting excavations in Babylonia, the available sites, the cost of the work, the results to be expected, and so forth. A subscription paper, intended to provide for several years' work, was presented for signatures, and some $7000 or $8000 were subscribed that evening.

Application for a firman to conduct excavations was at once made in the name of the University of Pennsylvania. The law concerning antiquities in the Turkish Empire, under which all such excavations must be conducted, provides that all objects found shall belong to the Ottoman Imperial Museum, foreign explorers not being permitted to take any antiquities from the country, but only photographs, squeezes, and the like. The application for permission to excavate must designate the spot at which the excavations are to be conducted, which must not cover an area of more than ten square kilometres, and a topographical map must accompany the application. The sum of twenty liras, or something less than $100, must be paid for the permission; and a deposit of one hundred liras, or $440, must be paid on the issuance of the permission as a guaranty of good faith, the same to be forfeited should the excavator not keep both the letter and the spirit of the law. A Turkish commissioner accompanies the excavator,—the salary of said commissioner to be paid, not by the Turkish Government, but by the excavator,—who shall at once take charge of all objects found, ultimately delivering the same to the Ottoman Imperial Museum at Constantinople. The permission runs for two years, with the option of extension for one year more. At the end of that time, if the work be not completed, a new firman must be applied for. This law is almost exactly the same as the Greek law, from which it was copied.

It was felt that it would be impossible to work under this law in the Turkish Empire. Advices from the Wolfe Expedition and from friends in Turkey were of such a nature, that we believed that everything in Constantinople was managed on the principle of corruption; that everything could be had for money; and that there was no real care for the antiquities, but only a desire through the law to find an opportunity of extracting money from foreigners. Acting on this belief, we determined to apply for a special permission. Our plan was to obtain a general permission to dig in Babylonia, accompanied with the permission to export some part, as large as might be, of the objects found. It was hoped, that, if the University of Pennsylvania could obtain such a permission, it might be possible to make arrangements by which other colleges, universities, and learned institutions could co-operate with it, undertaking excavations at various points.

Three of the professors at Robert College, Constantinople—President Washburn, Professor Long, and Professor van Millingen—were asked and kindly consented to act as an advisory committee to the expedition. Almost from the outset they advised us that it would be difficult, if not impossible, to obtain permission to excavate other than according to the terms of the law. The legation at Constantinople was of a different opinion; and accordingly letters were addressed to the Sultan, through the Turkish legation at Washington and our legation in Constantinople, asking for a special firman, not according to the terms of the law. President Cleveland showed much interest in the enterprise, and wrote a personal letter to Mr. Straus, our minister at Constantinople, expressing his warm approval of the proposition to conduct excavations in ancient Babylonia, and his hope that everything possible would be done to insure our success. Application was also made to the State Department to direct our minister to apply to the Sultan's Government for a firman, such as was desired, in the name of the University of Pennsylvania.

Some difficulty arose at this point. This had its origin in Philadelphia with one or two persons who felt that they should have been consulted before the scheme of an expedition was launched. They criticised the scheme proposed, claiming that the assyriologist of the expedition should be an American, and that the staff should include an architect and a surveyor, and perhaps also a botanist and a couple of officers of the Engineer Corps detailed by the United States Government for that purpose. This criticism was taken up outside of Philadelphia; and opposition was made to action by the State Department on our behalf, on the ground that, instead of a local expedition, an effort should be made to send out a national expedition on a larger scale, and representing all the Assyrian scholarship of the country. There was for a time a tempest in a teapot, which hampered us in our efforts to raise money, as well as in our efforts to secure assistance from the State Department in the matter of a firman. But as the presidents of Harvard, Yale, Williams,

Columbia, Cornell, Ann Arbor, etc., as well as representatives of the Metropolitan Museum of New York, the American Archæological Institute, and other similar institutions, hastened to forward letters to the State Department, indicating their desire that application for a firman should be made in behalf of the University of Pennsylvania, as requested by us, this latter difficulty was speedily removed, and instructions forwarded as requested.

In order to meet the difficulties which had arisen, and at the same time take advantage of the extended interest aroused by our proposed expedition, I endeavored to enlarge our sphere of operations by arranging a plan of co-operation with other institutions. Professor Haupt of Baltimore had worked out a plan of an expedition to excavate Mughair, and negotiations were entered into for the purpose of amalgamating the two enterprises. This proved impracticable; but, in view of the possibility of his organizing an expedition later, I regarded Mughair as in a manner pre-empted by him, and did not include it in the list of places applied for by me the first year.

In the meantime the organization of the Babylonian Exploration Fund was completed (March 17, 1888) by the election of William Pepper, M.D., LL.D., then provost of the University of Pennsylvania, as president; Mr. E. W. Clark, treasurer; and the Reverend Professor Hilprecht, Ph.D., secretary. I was chosen director. The Executive Committee consisted, besides the officers, of Messrs. C. H. Clark, W. W. Frazier, C. C. Harrison, Joseph D. Potts, Richard Wood, Stuart Wood, Maxwell Somerville, and Talcott Williams, of Philadelphia; Professor Langley of the Smithsonian Institute; and Professor Marquand of Princeton.

One unfortunate result of the controversy which had arisen was the publicity given to our plans, and the resulting exaggeration, both at home and abroad, of the

ORGANIZING THE EXPEDITION.

magnitude of our enterprise. This both interfered with our negotiations for a firman at Constantinople, and also resulted in the adoption of a far more costly scheme of work than the one originally proposed.

It was decided to take an assyriologist from America; and at the suggestion of President W. R. Harper, then a professor at Yale, his brother, Dr. Robert Francis Harper, a tutor in the same university, was appointed assyriologist without salary, but with all expenses paid. At the time it was understood that Professor Hilprecht's health was too delicate to permit him to serve in the field. Later the physicians decided that he could go; and, with the consent of Dr. Harper, he also was appointed assyriologist to the expedition, with the understanding that neither should outrank the other, but that Dr. Harper's name, as coming first alphabetically, should precede that of Dr. Hilprecht. Dr. Talcott Williams took Dr. Hilprecht's place as secretary, and from that time forward proved himself one of the wisest and best friends of the expedition. It was decided to add an engineer or architect to the expedition, and, if possible, a botanist, or a representative of the natural sciences in some form. All this increased expenses, and obliged me to revise my estimates, and ask for $13,500, instead of $7500, for the first year's work.

Owing to the publicity given to our expedition, applications for membership came in by the dozen from all parts of the country. Some of those who applied were laborers, who, filled with a spirit of adventure, wished to go out and dig holes in a strange land; some were teachers or scholars; some were physicians and scientists; quite a number were photographers; and some were adventurers merely. We finally gave up the scientist, as that would have increased our expenses to $15,000. As architect, surveyor, and engineer, the Committee decided to engage Mr. Perez Hastings Field of New York, then at the École des Beaux Arts, in Paris. As in the case of Drs. Harper and Hilprecht, Mr. Field's expenses were to be paid, but he was to receive no salary. Mr. John Dyneley Prince, then just graduating from Columbia, now a professor in the University of the City of New York, was accepted as an attaché of the expedition, paying his own way, and acting as secretary to the director. Mr. John Henry Haynes and Mr. Daniel Z. Noorian were engaged on salaries, as originally proposed, the former as photographer and business manager, the latter as interpreter, and, after excavations should commence, director of the workmen.

At the suggestion of Mr. John Cadwalader, Collector of the Port of Philadelphia, I renewed my formerly unsuccessful effort to induce the Government to appoint a consul at Baghdad. The import from Baghdad of coarse wools for carpet manufacture was at that time, before the McKinley tariff, largely on the increase. One firm in New York had even established an office at Busrah, and commenced the despatch of vessels to that port. In the judgment of Mr. Cadwalader, the appointment of a consul at Baghdad, or at the least a viceconsul, was really desirable from the commercial point of view. We asked for the appointment of Mr. J. H. Haynes as consul; and through the efforts of Mr. Cadwalader, assisted by Mr. McClure of the *Philadelphia Times*, the office was created by the President, and Mr. Haynes appointed. Through an unfortunate accident, however, no appropriation was made for any salary for the office. At the time when it was decided to create the office, the appropriation bill had already passed the House; but Mr. Belmont, chairman of the House Committee of Ways and Means, expressed himself ready to accept an amendment giving a salary to the consul at Baghdad, if such an amendment were introduced in the Senate. It was arranged that such an amendment should pass the Senate; but unfortunately the senator who was to introduce the amendment went to the Democratic Convention at St. Louis, and forgot all about it. Accordingly we had a consul without any salary, and the expedition was obliged to support the dignity of the office. On the whole, the disadvantages of this situation proved in the end to outweigh its advantages.

The duties of the organizer of an expedition are manifold, and his information should be very varied; if not, he must supplement it by much study, many interviews, and reams of correspondence. I was necessarily dependent upon others for my information. I received some help from Lieutenant Melville, the Arctic explorer; and other officers of both the Navy and the War Departments gave me advice regarding equipment. It was decided to purchase canned provisions, implements, tents, arms, saddles, bridles, etc., in New York. The provisions and implements were shipped direct to Baghdad; tents, saddles, and bridles were sent to Alexandretta; and the arms we took with us. Messrs. Oelrichs & Co. kindly gave me personal letters to their correspondents in Beirout, Aleppo, and Baghdad, the latter of whom, Mr. T. S. Blockey, became the trusted friend and counsellor of the expedition and all its members.

Although we had commenced negotiations at Constantinople in regard to a firman the preceding autumn, and made formal application in February, nevertheless at the time of our departure, in the month of June, it was still uncertain whether we could obtain permission to excavate. There was nothing for us to do but proceed on an uncertainty. Dr. Harper, Mr. Prince, and I sailed on the *Fulda*, June 23, 1888. Dr. Hilprecht and Mr. Noorian were to sail later, meeting me at Alexandretta at such time as I might direct. Mr. Field was in Paris. Mr. Haynes was presumably at Aintab in Turkey; but I had written him to meet me in London to help me in the purchase of outfit, and to procure the best and latest photographic equipment. It was July 1st when we landed at Southampton. A couple of bomb-like patent contrivances for the consumption of petroleum as fuel in camp, which I had discovered and purchased at the last moment, and brought over in my cabin (they did not ultimately prove serviceable), together with the large amount of arms and ammunition in my possession, caused me to be suspected of being an Irish-American dynamiter, and I had rather an amusing time at the custom-house.

Mr. Haynes had written me that he would come to London, as I desired, to procure photographic outfit, and assist me by his experience in the purchase of the thousand and one small objects necessary to any such expedition. Later he changed his mind; but the letter informing me of that fact miscarried, and I had no intelligence of his motions. I telegraphed to him, but in vain, as he had gone into the mountains; and it was not until August that I finally ascertained his whereabouts. Fortunately, Dr. Long of Constantinople arrived in London about this time, and rendered me much assistance. I also met all the assyriologists and Oriental travellers then in London, and catechized them one and all. I spent a day with Mr. Wilfred S. Blunt and Lady Anne Blunt at Crabbett Park, and another day with Professor Sayce at Oxford. Mr. Pinches, Mr. Budge, and others too numerous to mention, gave me valuable advice and assistance. Dr. J. Thacher Clarke was especially helpful. He most materially assisted Mr. Field, who joined me in London for a few days, and he also undertook the purchase of photographic material, being, from past experience with Haynes, in a position to judge approximately what the latter needed. Further, he placed in my hands a written promise to come to me, should I need him, without salary, in place of photographer or architect, should either fail me for any cause.

I also met in London the Hon. O. S. Straus, our minister to Constantinople, then on his way home on leave. He seemed thoroughly interested in our enterprise, and assured me that it had received from him as much attention as a matter of first-class diplomatic importance. He was hopeful of obtaining for us from the Turkish Government favorable terms, but did not wish to be quoted as making definite promises. It was his idea that we might be made agents of the Stamboul Museum, to conduct excavations in Babylonia, we furnishing the money, and receiving, perhaps, half of the objects found.

But my most memorable interview vas with the veteran explorer of Babylonia, the late Sir Henry Rawlinson. I had hoped that it might be possible to make some arrangements by which English, German, French, and American explorers should unite in endeavoring to secure from the Turkish Government a modification of the law governing excavations which would be more favorable to explorers; and one object which I had in view, in seeing Sir Henry Rawlinson, was to obtain his influence with the British Museum toward such co-operation. He and Mr. Bond, the chief librarian, seemed favorably disposed toward my plan, and at their suggestion I addressed a letter to the directors of the British Museum, formally proposing some sort of co-operation; but the directors did not look favorably upon a proposition which involved arrangements with other countries, believing that they could do better for themselves independently, and sent me a courteous note to that effect.

The British Museum is the place to which antiquities are ordinarily brought, and it is able to add to its stock of Babylonian antiquities year by year through purchase. This encourages the Arabs to dig here and there in Babylonia in a very destructive and unscientific way. Such antiquities as are brought have no pedigree, so that all that can be learned about them must be learned from themselves. But the most serious objection to this policy of encouraging dealers in Babylonia to secure and send out of the country large quantities of inscribed objects is, that, by the method of digging which the Arabs pursue, more is destroyed than is saved. Such a plan as I proposed in the most general way to the authorities of the British Museum would have tended to put a stop to this illicit excavation and export of antiquities from the Turkish Empire. The British Museum was at that time planning to send Mr. Budge to Babylonia to conduct excavations. I had received some intimation of this intention, and suggested, that, even if it were not possible to arrange for any general co-operation, it was desirable that we and the British Museum should not come into competition in any way, and therefore offered to submit to them our plans, with a view to securing co-operation between us; but this, also, they did not deem advisable.

To conclude the narrative of my attempts to secure some sort of co-operation between the countries and institutions interested in Babylonian exploration, I may add that an influential friend in Berlin, to whom I addressed myself for assistance at the German end, assured me that German feeling toward the English Liberal Government, then in power, was so bitter, that any proposition for co-operation which included England would not be considered for a moment. M. Heuzey, of the Louvre Museum, to whom I proposed my plan in Paris, asking for his assistance, if not in a general plan of international work, at least in a friendly co-operation between the French and ourselves, put me off with vague but polite phrases.

As it seemed impossible to make any arrangements in London which would tend to check illicit excavations in Babylonia and Syria, I determined to do what I could to divert antiquities to the United States, and if possible to secure something of value for the University of Pennsyl-

Clay Barrel Cylinder containing five hundred lines of inscription of Nebuchadrezzar the Great. Found in Babylon. (The inscription contains an account of the buildings of Nebuchadrezzar, including canals.)

vania Museum. I accordingly entered into negotiations with all the antiquity dealers in London. There was at this time an admirable collection in the hands of Joseph Shemtob. After long negotiations, conducted chiefly through Dr. Long and Dr. Harper, we succeeded in purchasing this collection for the sum of £350, less than we should have paid for excavating the same. This money was provided by the friends of the expedition and of the university, outside of the sum appropriated for use in the field. This is the collection known as the Shemtob Collection, now in the University of Pennsylvania Museum at Philadelphia. From the colophon of a Nabopolassar tablet in this collection, and from other information obtained later, I was led to surmise that the Arabs had discovered part of a royal library at Ibrahim Khalil, the ancient Borsippa. The bulk of the collection, however, came from ancient Babylon, as I learned later on the spot. Among the gems in it, which especially aroused the enthusiasm of Mr. Pinches and Professor Sayce, were a vase of Xerxes with a trilingual inscription; a barrel cylinder of Nebuchadrezzar II. with five hundred lines of inscription, the largest yet discovered; a curious, inscribed cone of Khammurabi of Babylon; and a stone mortar of Burnaburiash.

Later I purchased a small bronze Apis bull, regarding which Professor Sayce wrote to me: "It is wonderfully like one which I got at Sakkarah; the only difference being that mine is rather larger, and is of the Pharaonic period, whereas yours is of the Roman age. But the markings on each are the same, and I have looked in vain through the collection of bronze bulls at Boulaq for any with such perfect markings upon them." Curiously, this bull which I purchased came not from Egypt, but from the neighborhood of Cæsarea in Cappadocia; and in connection with this purchase I first made acquaintance with tablets in cuneiform script from the same region, of which I later purchased quite a collection in Constantinople. I had already, on the basis of a passage in the book of Jeremiah (xxxii., 10 *ff.*), reached the conclusion that the Jews wrote contracts and similar documents on clay tablets, like the Babylonians. The discovery of clay tablets in the cuneiform script in Cappadocia led me to suppose that we might ultimately find the use of clay tablets, and even of the cuneiform script, to have been adopted from the Babylonians through all hither Asia, as the discovery of the Tel-el-Amarna tablets later proved to be the case.

In order to make our purchase effective as speedily as possible, I detailed Dr. Harper to work on the Shemtob collection, report on it, catalogue it, prepare it for exhibition, and ship it to Philadelphia, which he did. After my departure from London, another collection, the so-called Khabaza Collection, was offered to Dr. Harper for sale. He reported it as such a favorable chance, that I commended it to Mr. E. W. Clark, who was then in London, and he purchased it for the sum of £200. These two collections together consisted of several hundred pieces, and constituted in themselves no despicable collection of Babylonian antiquities, far exceeding in value and amount all the Babylonian and Assyrian antiquities then in the United States.

July 25th, having received no word from Haynes, Prince and I went to Paris to study the collections of the Louvre, confer with French archæologists, and arrange with Field the details of his work and outfit. I met there, among others, Messrs. Perrot and Chipiez, the well-known authors of the histories of art in various ancient countries, and M. Leon Heuzey, director of the Department of Oriental Antiquities in the Louvre Museum. M. Heuzey showed us all the Babylonian objects in his charge, not merely those on exhibition, but also the objects not yet prepared for exhibition, forgeries, and so forth, and gave me some valuable information.

August 2d, having finally heard from Haynes to the effect that he would meet me in Constantinople, I returned to London, and completed the purchase of the thousand and one small objects needed on such an expedition. On the 5th, Prince and I left London for Berlin. Here I met my old fellow-student, Dr. Bernhard Moritz, and his comrades, Dr. Coldevey and Mr. Ludwig Meyer, who had returned the previous year from Babylonia, where they had conducted excavations at Hibbah and Zerghul. Their expedition was tentative, like our own Wolfe Expedition, having in view largely the determination of sites to be excavated, and the method of pursuing excavations in Babylonia. After its return a considerable sum was given to the museum for excavations in northern Syria, which led to the abandonment of the idea of conducting excavations in Babylonia. Under these circumstances, at the suggestion of my old teacher, Professor Eberhard Schrader, the father of assyriology, and on application of Dr. Steindorff, who was in charge of the Department of Oriental Antiquities in the absence of Dr. Erman, the authorities of the museum kindly directed the members of that expedition to place at my disposal any information which could assist me in my work. Accordingly, Dr. Moritz communicated to me the substance of the report of his expedition to the museum authorities, which included the recommendation of Nippur as the most promising site at which to conduct excavations. In company with Professor Schrader and Dr. Steindorff, I studied the Babylonian collections of the museum; and in company with Dr. Schrader, I had two delightful meetings with Professor Kiepert, the geographer, who gave me some unpublished map material.

A visit to Leipzig, where I had planned to meet

another of my old masters in assyriology, Professor Friedrich Delitzsch, was abandoned on account of sickness in the latter's family; and on the 8th of August I went to Dresden to join my family, and await news from Constantinople, on the advice of Mr. Pendleton King, Chargé d'Affaires *ad interim*, and Professor van Millingen, who were managing our negotiations there.

CHAPTER II.

OBTAINING AN IRADÉ.

Application Refused—Journey to Constantinople—Interview with Grand Vizier—Kiamil and Munif Pashas—Hamdy Bey—A Romantic Career—Artist Archæologist and Man of Affairs—Choice of Sites—A New Application—Ministry of Public Obstruction—Delay at the Palace—The Other Members of the Expedition—Wrecked on Samos—Work Assigned—Impatient at Delay—Unfortunate Happenings—Mr. Straus Dines with the Sultan—The Iradé Issued—A Change of Terms—A Wage Riot—Departure from Constantinople.

SEPTEMBER 1st, I received a letter from Mr. King, Chargé d'Affaires at Constantinople, to the effect that "the Council of State has decided that the Government cannot depart from the existing regulations about excavations on behalf of the Americans applying, as other countries would make the same request; but that they (the Americans) may be granted the privilege of buying from the Ottoman Government such antiquities as may be discovered, which are not needed for the Museum."

I left Dresden by the next train for Constantinople, the morning of September 3d, and was joined by Prince in Vienna the same evening. I had some difficulty with my rifles at the Austrian frontier, and the customs inspectors wished to make a careful examination of my effects; but after I had explained to them that I had been sent out from America to command an exploring expedition, and showed them with some ceremony my passport as evidence, they politely passed me and my effects free. From

Vienna we took the Oriental Express to Constantinople by way of Rustchuk and Varna, for the railroad through to Constantinople had not yet been built. It was in this train that we first became conscious that we were travelling toward Babel. Our fellow-travellers were two Greeks, two Italians, a half-dozen Frenchmen, one Russian, one Englishman, and a few nondescripts; and at Bucharest we took on two parties of Danes and Americans, not to speak of Roumanians, Turks, and other inhabitants of the Balkan Peninsula. It is curious to observe the gradual way in which you pass from civilization to semi-barbarism, and from Occident to Orient, between Vienna and Constantinople. Tuesday morning we were on the wide plains of Hungary. Shortly after lunch we entered the Carpathian Mountains, and the scenery became grand, and the people poor and picturesque. The section of Bulgaria from Rustchuk to Varna, which it took us almost the whole of the next day to cross, was very poor, very uninteresting, and very hot. There were no trees and few villages; but here and there they showed us battle-fields and graveyards, relics of the late war. A German restaurant in the middle of this day's journey was like an oasis in a desert. About evening we reached Varna, which seemed to consist of little but a bay. Here we were put in small boats and carried out to the Austrian Lloyd steamer *Aurora*. From Rustchuk on, our train had been uncomfortably crowded, but the conditions on the steamer were far worse. They put us in a room with two Greeks and a Frenchman, and it was only by dint of very vigorous protestations that I secured for Prince a bed in another room with one Russian and one Greek. On this steamer, for the first time, I saw the practice of deck passage, so universal in the East. With the exception of the small upper deck at the stern of the steamer, reserved for the first-cabin passengers, every available spot seemed to be occupied by campers-out, principally picturesque Turkish men and hideous Turkish women.

Very early the next morning we were in the most beautiful and fascinating of all straits, the Bosphorus, and about seven o'clock on Thursday morning, the 6th of September, we came to anchor in the Golden Horn. Before the steamer had ceased to move, we were surrounded by a host of small boats, and invaded by porters and hotel runners speaking every conceivable language horribly. These men kidnapped passengers and baggage in the most unscrupulous manner. We were rescued from their clutches by the appearance on the scene of the cawass of our legation, resplendent in gold embroidery, and armed with a sabre and some old-fashioned horse pistols. Prince, who could speak all sorts of out-of-the-way languages, like Turkish, Gypsy, Bohemian, and Danish, was able to enter into communication with him, and inform him that we were the persons he had been sent to bring on shore. Shortly after, Professor van Millingen arrived, and we disembarked. At the custom-house I observed, to my horror, that the porters in transporting our goods had driven the butt-end of one of my rifles through the ingenious wrappings which disguised its identity. Prince was carrying his in his arms, wrapped up in both our overcoats, much as one carries a baby. Now, rifles, revolvers, and cartridges are among the contraband articles which it is forbidden to import into Turkey, although they are openly exposed for sale in the most public streets of Constantinople. Nevertheless, in spite of the fact that one of the rifles had so unfortunately obtruded its presence on the observation of the officials, our three rifles, one shot-gun, and half a dozen revolvers, with their cartridges, and the like, passed the custom-house in safety after some disputation about the amount of baksheesh, which was at length fixed at one mejidie, or eighty cents.

President Washburn joined us at our hotel, the Hotel de Byzance in Pera, after breakfast; and at 11.30 we all went together to our legation to confer with Mr. Pendleton King, Chargé d'Affaires, and with Mr. A. A. Gargiulo, the wise and wily Dragoman. We certainly lost no time that day; for at two o'clock Mr. King, Mr. Gargiulo, Professor van Millingen, and I went to call on the Grand Vizier, Kiamil Pasha. He was cautious, but friendly, at least in manner. We conversed in English, drank Turkish coffee, and smoked cigarettes. The Grand Vizier said substantially what had been said in Mr. King's letter. I proposed to him the plan suggested by Mr. Straus, namely, that we might be made agents of the Imperial Ottoman Museum; to which he replied that it could not be done, because the same thing had been refused to others. In answer to my objection that it would not do, on account of the condition of the country, for us to be limited to one place, as the law required, he suggested that we might make as many applications as we pleased, under the names of the different members of the expedition. I tried to point out the necessity we were under to bring back with us some tangible results; and he said, that, when we had once found the antiquities, there would be no difficulty in buying them, as the museum did not really want them. He also said that there were objects in the museum which the authorities would be glad to sell.

This Grand Vizier, Kiamil Pasha, since deposed, was reputed to be a Jew by race, born in Cyprus. He was small and somewhat wizened, although apparently not over sixty years of age. His face was one of great shrewdness and deep cunning, as well as marked ability. He had a slight nervous affection of the facial muscles, which increased the almost morose solemnity of his appearance. He wore, like all the pashas I saw, a collarless black coat, with high-cut vest, and trousers of the same, thus presenting much the appearance of a clergyman, excepting for the fez. He spoke English excellently.

From the Sublime Porte, Mr. Gargiulo, Professor van Millingen, and I went, as the Grand Vizier had advised us to do, to see the Minister of Public Instruction, Munif Pasha. This man had been at an earlier date one of the leaders of the Liberal or Young Turkey movement. He had studied a little in Germany, and spoke French and German, both imperfectly, and a few words of English. In order to maintain his position under the present Sultan, he was forced to desert his old friends, become outwardly at least a pious Mussulman, and affect illiberalism. He did not receive us at first in a friendly manner. He denied that there were objects to be sold at the museum, and so interpreted the vote of the Council of State as to render exportation impossible. I explained to him how impracticable it would be to comply with that requirement of the law according to which would-be excavators must file a topographical plan of the place to be excavated with their application, since the only way to obtain such a plan of any place in Babylonia was to go out there and make one. I spoke to him also about the undesirability of being confined to one place in an almost unknown region like Mesopotamia, and mentioned what the Grand Vizier had said. As he did not take this kindly, I insisted upon our right, under the terms of the law, to excavate at several places, not simultaneously but successively. A long discussion ensued. Finally Gargiulo went over and whispered in his ear, after which he became somewhat more friendly, and said that he would talk with the director of the museum, and see me again the following Tuesday.

The next day, Friday, Mr. Prince, Professor van Millingen, and I went to call on Hamdy Bey, director of the Imperial Museum, at his house at Courouchesme, on the

Bosphorus. On account of our attempt to obtain special privileges, he had been hostile to us, and had not wished to see me; but when he was told that we were anxious to ascertain whether it were not possible to work under the law, he expressed himself as quite willing to meet me. I have already described part of our earlier negotiations for a firman, but have not referred to our direct negotiations with Hamdy Bey. Some time in the latter part of 1886, or the earlier part of 1887, he told one of the professors at Robert College that he had a most interesting site in northern Syria, presumably Hittite, which he would like to see explored. The cost of

TURKISH HOUSES AT COUROUCHESME ON THE BOSPHORUS.
HOUSE OF HAMDY BEY.

excavation he estimated at $4000. He proposed that the Americans should apply for a firman to excavate this site. This proposition was communicated to me in the summer or autumn of 1887. I sent word to him through Professor van Millingen that we would gladly furnish the funds, and excavate this site for him, if he would obtain for us the sort of permission to excavate in Babylonia which we wished. He replied that this site—it was Zenjirli—had been already taken by the Germans, but that he had another of the same character which we might have. Whether we excavated in Irak or Syria, however, we could have no permission outside of the terms of the law.

Our interview did not begin well. Hamdy told me, when I ventured to criticise some details of the law, that he had made the law, and that it was he who administered it. He denied that there was anything to be sold in the museum, when told what the Grand Vizier had said on that subject, and spoke rather disrespectfully of his Highness's knowledge of antiquities. He said, furthermore, that the museum would not sell to us part of the objects found, although it might give them; inscribed objects, however, they could not afford to let go. He agreed that we might excavate in three places successively, but not simultaneously, and that no topographical plans should be presented until we had reached the spot, and also that the caution money to be deposited should be made a nominal sum. He detained Professor van Millingen for a moment on the stairs, as we were leaving, to tell him that we need not fear about permission to export objects when found, or a part of them, and that he would deal liberally with us if we would proceed according to the law, and act fairly and honorably. It was arranged that we should visit the museum under the guidance of Hamdy Bey on Monday, the 10th, and that I should then submit for his approval the general plan of application, or a rough copy of the same. The conversation was conducted throughout in French. Hamdy Bey was affable and even charming in his manners. He showed us photographs of his famous Sidon "finds," and told us much about them over our coffee and cigarettes.

O. Hamdy Bey is one of the most interesting men in the Turkish Empire. He is by descent on his father's side a Greek. His grandparents were slain in the terrible massacre of Scio, in 1822; and his father, then a child, was sold as a slave at Constantinople. There he won the favor of a well-to-do Turk of liberal views, was adopted by him, and educated in the most advanced manner, chiefly in France. He was of course educated as a Mohammedan, and married a Turkish wife. In due course he rose to be Grand Vizier under the name of Edhem Pasha, and was still in his old age a member of the Council of State, and a man of great influence with the Sultan. Hamdy was designated by his father for the army. In those days French influence was dominant in the Orient, and French military prestige was at its height. Accordingly, Hamdy, after two years in a French boarding-school, was entered as a pupil at the Military Academy at St. Cyr. But, his father to the contrary notwithstanding, it soon became clear to himself that he was not intended for a soldier, and at the end of a year he begged to be permitted to abandon the military for a civil career. His request was granted, and he was sent to Paris to study law. Here he became infatuated with art, and privately enrolled himself at the École des Beaux Arts as a student of painting. As examinations in the Law School drew near, he devoted himself assiduously for a brief period to cramming law. Examinations successfully tided over, he returned to his art. In this way he contrived to devote three quarters of the year to art, and one quarter to law. So his four years of study in Paris passed by. He graduated from the Law School, and exhibited in the École des Beaux Arts. His father wished him to go in for a doctorate; but, this proving uncongenial, he was permitted to return to Constantinople to begin his career as a politician, for which he had almost as little taste as for military life. Before long he published an article on the inconsistencies of judicial procedure in the Turkish Empire, pointing out that in one set of courts Christians might act as judges, while in another they could not even be accepted as witnesses. This article did not please Ali Pasha, then Grand Vizier,

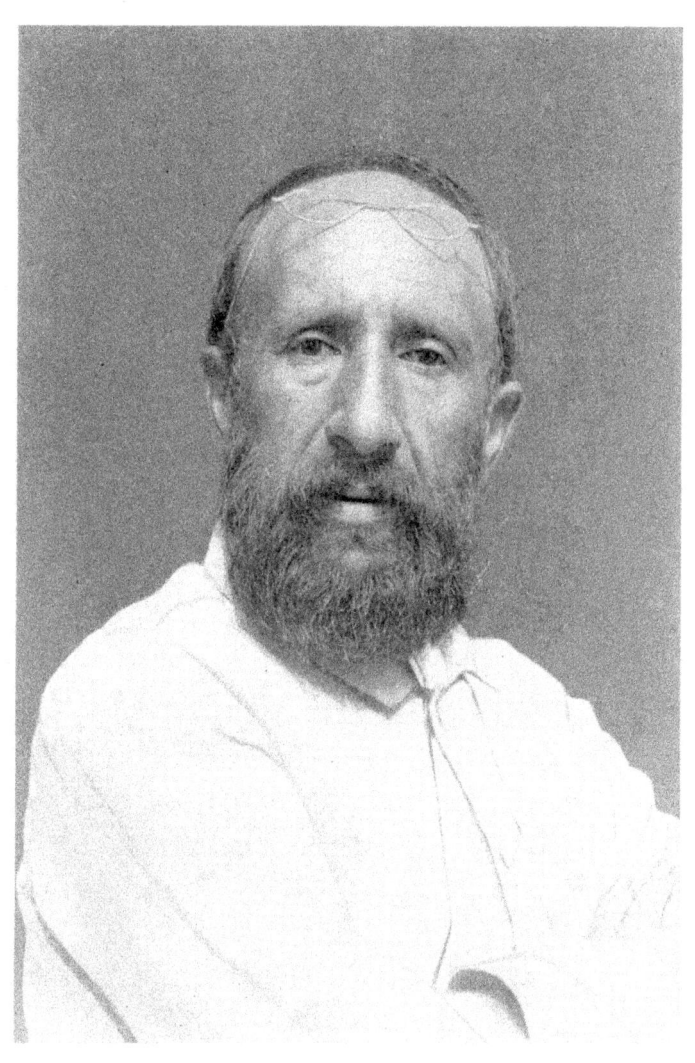

O. HAMDY BEY.
Director of the Imperial Ottoman Museum.

who was an enemy of his father; and Hamdy was forthwith appointed to a minor political post at Baghdad,—a polite method of banishment.

The Governor-General of the province of Baghdad was the famous and energetic Midhat Pasha. He was attempting to introduce all sorts of European reforms, running steamers on the Euphrates, digging canals, and waging wars to reduce the turbulent and savage Arab tribes to subjection. With him Hamdy at once found favor, and he was made director of the foreign affairs of the vilayet. In Midhat's suite, dressed and mounted as an Arab, in the corps of Arab irregulars created by him, he took part in the war with Hajji Tarfa and the Affech tribes in the Niffer marshes, which resulted from the attempt to levy taxes and to enforce military conscription in the dominion of that powerful chief. He had therefore served as a soldier in the very regions in which I was destined to excavate. Under Midhat Pasha, Hamdy found opportunity also for the more congenial labors of art and archæology, conducting excavations in the mound of Nebbi Yunus, on the site of ancient Nineveh, and sketching and painting the romantic and artistic scenes and peoples of the land of Haroun-er-Rashid. At the end of two years or thereabouts, Ali Pasha removed him from these too favorable environments by appointing him consul at Bombay. On the way thither, in the pestilential marshes of lower Irak, he fell ill with fever. This afforded him an opportunity, which he eagerly embraced, to return to the capital. He was at once appointed secretary of legation at St. Petersburg. He had been banished to a warm climate, and it had not killed him: now they offered him a cold climate as his exile. Tired of this species of honorable banishment, he begged leave to withdraw into private life. This being granted, he devoted himself wholly to his art, painting, among other things, a large battle-piece representing a scene in the picturesque war with the Affech Arabs, in which he had just taken part. One day, returning from a walk, he found his atelier in possession of emissaries from the palace, who had already impounded his great battle scene, and were waiting to carry him to the royal presence. No Turk receives such a summons without trepidation, for the ways of an Eastern potentate are still the ways of Ahasuerus. A summons to his presence may portend death or banishment, or it may mean glory and honor. He who is thus summoned to the royal presence may never reappear, or he may return a friend of the king. Hamdy's summons proved to be for honor. Abd-ul-Aziz was enchanted with the painting, presented him with a diamond snuff-box, and made him introducer of ambassadors.

Thus restored to official life, he was soon in danger of being lost to art forever; for offices and duties multiplied upon him, especially after the accession of Midhat Pasha to power. In consequence of the Bulgarian massacres and the appointment of the English commission of inquiry in 1876, he was sent out to prepare from the Turkish standpoint a counter-report of the Bulgarian revolt and the method of its suppression. At one time he was Prefect of Pera, the " Frank " quarter of Constantinople. During the Russian war he saw active service in the armies of his country; but his political career was unfavorably affected by the fall and disgrace of Midhat. He himself came under suspicion, and was obliged to retire into private life once more, where he lived for a period under police surveillance, devoting himself entirely to his art. In 1881 he was again restored to favor, and appointed director of the Imperial Museum at Stamboul, a position he has held ever since.

Being an artist rather than an archæologist, Hamdy at first wished to decline the appointment of director of the museum. But he was manifestly better equipped for the post than any man in the empire, and the Sultan laid his commands upon him, permitting him, however, to make the following conditions: that the law respecting excavations should be changed, and a small special budget assigned to the museum. These conditions granted, he promised at the end of ten years to give his Majesty a museum which, however small, should be deserving of the name. He further obtained permission to establish a school of fine arts. This was housed temporarily in a building belonging to the old palace, close to Chinili Kiosk. The first public exhibition of the pupils of this school took place in 1888. The school is modelled after the École des

WHITE-TURBANED SOFTAS

Beaux Arts of Paris, with its three departments of architecture, sculpture, and painting; and, corresponding to the Grand Prix de Rome, Hamdy proposed to establish a Grand Prix de l'Europe, to enable the successful competitors to continue their studies at the great art centres of the world. There is a staff of four professors, with Hamdy Bey as responsible director, the responsibilities of that post being financially similar to those of the presidents of some institutions of learning in this country. The students number somewhat over a hundred. Of these, the greater part are Greek and Armenian subjects of the Porte, but there are also Turks among them, even including white-turbaned softas from the mosques, so far has barbarian prejudice already yielded to civilization in the capital of the Ottoman Empire.

But Hamdy is even better known to the world by his archæological discoveries than by his artistic achievements, and some of these discoveries are of so remarkable a character that they are likely to exert a greater influence on artistic development than his more direct attempts in that direction. His first work as an excavator was, as already stated, at Nebbi Yunus, the site of Nineveh, while he was attached to Midhat Pasha's Government in Baghdad. In 1883, in company with Osgan Effendi, he explored the remarkable tumulus of Antiochus of Commagene, on the snowy summit of the Nemroud Dagh, or Nimrod Mountain, one of the peaks of the Taurus; but it was the discovery of the wonderful sarcophagi at Sidon in the spring of 1887 that achieved him fame as an explorer.

Hamdy is not only an artist and archæologist, he is also a man of affairs, and as such was appointed some years since a member of the mixed commission of the public debt, which has done so much to restore Turkish finances to approximate order and solvency. His is a career impossible in the modern West, but excellently illustrative of the possibilities and vicissitudes of the Orient.

I have described these men and their careers at some length, because they were the three officials with whom we were to conduct our negotiations, and on whom depended the success or failure of our work.

The unexpected turn which matters had now taken compelled me to make choice at once of three sites to be named in our application for permission to excavate. Ur (Mughair) I did not feel at liberty to take, for reasons already stated. Eridu (Abu Shahrein) was out of the question, because of the hostility of the Arabs in that region. Babylon, which Sir Henry Rawlinson had urged upon me, seemed too large and confusing. Moreover, it had served so long as a brick quarry, and also as a treasure mound for unauthorized diggers, that I did not know to what extent it had been looted already. I wanted a fresh site, and one which had played a *rôle* in the very earliest period of Babylonian history. Nippur (Niffer or Nufar) seemed to satisfy these conditions best. It was one of the sites recommended by the Wolfe Expedition, and was the site selected for excavation by the Germans. Haynes, who arrived at Constantinople on Saturday the 8th, confirmed the German recommendation, reporting it, according to his judgment, the most promising site for excavation of all those visited by the Wolfe Expedition, with water and workmen available, readily accessible for purposes of transport, and reasonably safe. For the second place I chose Borsippa (Birs Nimroud), on the ground of the discoveries recently made there by the Arabs, as related in the last chapter. For the third place, after some hesitation, I chose Anbar, out of loyalty to the Wolfe Expedition. I had already reached the conclusion that Dr. Ward's identification of this ruin with ancient Sippara was an error, but, in view of his account of the large size and promising appearance of the mound, I thought it well to hold in our hands the possibility of exploring it.

Monday, the 10th, accompanied by Professor van Millingen and Prince, I had my second interview with Hamdy Bey at the museum. He accepted the three sites named, and approved my form of application, which contained a clause dispensing with the topographical plan until the excavations had begun.

The following day Gargiulo visited Munif Pasha. He was very affable. He had seen Hamdy, and agreed that we might excavate at three places successively, but not simultaneously, also that the topographical plan should be dispensed with until we reached the site to be excavated, and that the cautionary deposit should be nominal. In the matter of the acquisition and exportation of the objects found, he was ready to make the same vague promises as Hamdy Bey, but would not consent that anything should be stated in the permission itself. I presented to him the formal application for permission to dig at Anbar, Birs Nimroud, and Niffer, and asked that matters might be expedited. He promised to do what he could, and said that the first step was to inquire of the local authorities whether there were any objections to conducting excavations on the sites named in the application. I protested against this as unnecessary, seeing that these sites were uninhabited, and in a region substantially a desert, and without roads, forts, houses, or canals, as mentioned in the law. He would not, however, remit these forms, and added that, should he do so, the Wali of Baghdad, feeling himself slighted, would be sure to throw every obstacle in our way. The most that I could obtain was an agreement to inquire by telegraph, and to send the telegram that same day. An answer might, he thought, be expected in from eight to ten days. Within that time no answer came. We visited Munif frequently, and also went often to Hamdy's. At the end of a little more than two weeks we induced Munif to telegraph again, but it was more than three weeks after the despatch of the first telegram before an answer was received. This answer objected to Anbar, but raised no objection to the other two places.

It did not seem to me desirable to contest the Wali's objection to Anbar, because of the great delay likely to be occasioned thereby. I saw Hamdy at once, and in order to expedite matters arranged to go with him to the Minister of Public Instruction the following day, and come to a final agreement. Accordingly, Thursday, October 4th, Gargiulo and I called for Hamdy Bey at the museum, and went with him to the Ministry of Public Instruction, or obstruction, as we called it among ourselves. After a private interview between Munif and Hamdy, they admitted us, and announced that they had been so much pleased by my course that they were ready to show me special favors, and that accordingly we would be permitted to retain and export such objects as were not required for the museum. These objects were to be given, not sold, to us,—a point of generosity on which much stress was laid,—but this was not to be put in writing. The minister had telegraphed to stop at Busrah the commissioner who had accompanied De Sarzec in his excavations the preceding winter, and who had also been with Humann at Zenjirli. He did this in order to save us travelling expenses, and to give us a man at a low salary. We were to pay him twenty Turkish liras a month, and were ourselves to be the paymasters. The deposit was to be merely a nominal one.

Now ensued a considerable period of delay. First the paper had to be drawn up by the Minister of Public Instruction and sent to the Porte; that is, the Grand Vizier. Then it had to pass the Council of State. After this it had to be reshaped and sent to the Council of Ministers, from which again it must pass up to the Sultan for his signature. In spite of close following, it was about October 22d before it passed the Council of Ministers. October 25th, Gargiulo and I had an interview with the Grand Vizier. The mazbata had not yet gone up for the Sultan's signature (I think his Highness had forgotten all about it): so he called in a secretary, and gave him in my presence the necessary instructions, which were favorable in allowing exportation of objects found. He promised that it should go up to the Palace on Sunday the 28th, and said that we might expect the iradé on Tuesday, October 30th, probably, or on Thursday, November 1st, at latest. So I went over to the Ministry of Public Instruction, and drank coffee and smoked a cigarette with Munif Pasha while we arranged the details of deposits and fees. At the same time he ordered the draft of the permit to be prepared, against the arrival of the expected order from the Palace.

I was never able to ascertain the inner history of the relations of the different persons concerned to this permit. Hamdy Bey from the outset insisted that the form of the application and permission must be strictly according to the law, and Munif maintained the same attitude. For any relaxation of the conditions, we must depend on their spoken word only. The Grand Vizier, on the other hand, encouraged and even urged us from the outset to make application not according to the terms of the law, and promised to secure special conditions. Whether he meant to do so and could not, I do not know. At all events, he did not do so, and his professedly friendly attitude toward us was actually the cause of long delay and considerable friction. It would have been better if we had from the outset adhered to Hamdy Bey, and to him only; and had I then had the experience of his honor which I made later, I should certainly have confided myself entirely to his hands.

These various delays had already kept me in Constantinople a month longer than I had expected to be there. When I reached Constantinople, at the beginning of September, there had seemed to be no reason why I could not conclude my business and obtain my firman in three weeks, or a month at the most. In any case, it was necessary to make some provision for the other members of the expedition. We expected the issuance of the firman any day, and it was desirable that they should be so situated that they could be gathered together to start for the field of work at a moment's notice. Moreover, to maintain them separately in Europe or America was far more expensive than to gather them together at some point in Turkey, where they could at least make a pretence of doing some work, and at the same time gain experience and become hardened for the campaign before them. Accordingly I arranged to bring them together at Alexandretta toward the end of September. Noorian reached there on the 20th of September. Haynes left Constantinople on the 27th of September to join, at Smyrna, Field, Harper and Hilprecht, who were to come together from Marseilles in a steamer of the *Messageries Maritimes*. Before leaving Constantinople, Haynes received notice of his appointment as consul at Baghdad; but his commission could not be issued until his bond had been filed, which occasioned delay, since the proposed bondsmen were in America.

Haynes, Field, Harper, and Hilprecht met at Smyrna Saturday, September 29th, and set out the same day in the steamer *Sindh* for Alexandretta. Sunday morning, at 1.10 A.M., the night being clear and the sea calm, they ran, head on, upon the island of Samos, which rises some 6000 feet out of the sea. They were kept on the ship for a day and a half, when they where taken off by a Turkish brigantine, without the loss of any of their effects, and landed at Vathy, the capital of Samos. There was at no time any danger, and the accident itself seems to have been due entirely to criminal carelessness. At Vathy the company of the *Messageries Maritimes* left them to shift for themselves for three days. They then took them to Smyrna in a small open steamer. The journey lasted all night, and there was only sitting room on the boat. At Smyrna they were again left to shift for themselves, with the information that their tickets would be good to Alexandretta by the Bell line of English steamers or by the Russian line. Haynes and Hilprecht went on by the Bell line the same day, and Field and Harper followed on the Russian steamer three days later, the two parties arriving at Alexandretta on the 12th and 13th of October respectively.

From Alexandretta, Hilprecht proceeded at once, in accordance with instructions from me, to Beirout. Mr. Rylands, secretary of the Society of Biblical Archæology, had urged me to make a new examination of the inscriptions of the Nahr-el-Kelb, near that place. This offered to one of our party employment promising possible valuable results, and Hilprecht seemed to me the best qualified to undertake the work. He was further to endeavor to secure through Dr. Post a graduate of the Syrian Protestant College at Beirout, who would be able to act as physician and at the same time make botanical and zoological collections for the expedition. Dr. Post had himself suggested this, thinking that he could furnish us with the right man at about five liras a month, and at his suggestion I had purchased while in London apparatus for the collections. He was, however, unable to obtain a man for us at less than ten liras a month, and we were obliged to abandon the idea of a botanical and zoological collector for that year. Hilprecht found one new Latin inscription, but otherwise his expedition was unproductive of results. He returned to Alexandretta overland on his own responsibility, searching for inscriptions by the way, and joined Noorian at that place toward the middle of November, remaining there until my arrival.

Field, Harper, and Haynes were, according to my directions, to spend their time as far as practicable in visiting sites in northern Syria, especially those in which excavations had already been conducted, like Zenjirli and Jerabus, the ancient Carchemish. Field was also to fill in a map given me by Kiepert. Harper was to look out for antiquities, and Haynes to photograph all places and objects of interest. They made their headquarters first at Aintab, and afterwards at Aleppo, at both of which places they were treated with much hospitality by the American missionaries there resident. They visited also the interesting ruins on Jebel Siman and in its neighborhood. Unfortunately Haynes's photographs of these ruins proved a complete failure, because, in his desire to save money, he used for his exposures old rolls which had been in his possession for a couple of years. The result of their two and a half months in northern Syria was nothing.

The difficulties of my situation in Constantinople were much increased by the restlessness of the men during this long period of waiting. Having no experience of Turkish procrastination and dilatoriness, they could not understand the long delay, and grew very restive under it, writing and telegraphing, both to me and to the Committee, expressions of their impatience,—an impatience which was certainly natural under the circumstances. One of them even proposed to return to the United States, supposing that we would be unable to obtain a firman.

At the time of my arrival at Constantinople in September, Dr. Humann was there negotiating with Hamdy Bey concerning the division of the objects found by the Germans in Zenjirli. They had excavated under the terms of the law, and afterwards packed the objects and brought them to Constantinople, with the understanding, it was said, that in return they should receive one half. I counted thirty-five large boxes in the custom-house, and was told that a number of smaller objects, including some Greek inscriptions, had been sent privately to Berlin. Ultimately the Germans succeeded in obtaining the lion's share of the objects found, including valuable Aramaic and cuneiform inscriptions, for German influence was very strong both at the Palace and the Porte.

Toward the end of October, Mr. Budge of the British Museum arrived in Constantinople to negotiate for permission to dig at Kouyunjik. The British Embassy made an earnest effort to secure for him special terms.

His object was to search for more remains of the royal library identified and partly discovered by George Smith. The proposed terms were that Budge should take all "finds" belonging to that library, and that everything else found by him should be the property of the museum in Stamboul. Our friends were of the opinion that these negotiations unfavorably affected ours, causing greater delay. But far more annoying and hurtful to us was an article published by Theodore Bent in the November number of the *Contemporary Review*. Bent had dug at Thasos the year before, under the supposition that that island belonged to Egypt. This the Turkish Government did not admit, and sent a gunboat to take possession of the objects found. Having tried in vain to secure their return from Hamdy Bey, Bent went with his wife to Syra, and engaged a small craft, with fifteen men to man it. With this he made piratical descents in the cause of archæology on the coast of Asia Minor. Not content with this revenge, he published in the *Contemporary Review* a most scurrilous personal attack on Hamdy Bey, in which the latter's wife and mother-in-law were not spared. Mr. Bent also alluded to us, stating that we were spending large sums to obtain a favorable firman, and that Mr. Straus was bribing Hamdy Bey in our behalf. All these things were against us. Moreover, just at this time there appeared in the New York *World* an infamous story about a disreputable American variety actress, who was said to have entered the Sultan's harem, and finally to have been poisoned there with a dozen other inmates. The whole thing was an invention from beginning to end. The woman had never had any connection with the Sultan, and was alive, and living with a petty Turkish official, at the time. This scandalous publication created prejudice and suspicion at the Palace against Americans and American affairs of all sorts.

Mr. Straus, our minister, returned to his post on the

5th of November, and at once took the negotiations into his own hands, showing the greatest interest in the matter. But now occurred the most exasperating delay of all. When a paper goes to the Palace for the Sultan's approval, the secretary makes a *résumé* of its contents. On the basis of this *résumé*, the Sultan ordinarily approves or rejects the application. He does not himself sign anything, it may be said, but merely expresses approval, which the secretary then indorses on the paper. It turned out in our case that the Sultan had taken it into his head not to be content with the *résumé*, but to demand the paper itself. The matter was therefore in his hands, and could not be pressed. On the 16th of November, nothing having been heard from this paper, Mr. Straus asked for an audience, but, as that was the birthday of Mohammed, the Sultan could not receive him. At last, on the 19th of November, Mr. Straus asked the Grand Vizier to make inquiry about the matter, and the Grand Vizier promised to do so. On the 22d I went to the Porte with Mr. Gargiulo to ascertain the result of his inquiries, and found that he had made none. Mr. Straus had, however, been invited to dine with the Sultan on Friday evening, the 23d, and the Grand Vizier said that it would be quite in accordance with etiquette to take that opportunity to ask the Sultan about the paper. As a last resource, Mr. Straus agreed to do so; and in a pause of the play after dinner, Friday, the 23d, he instructed Mr. Gargiulo to ask the Sultan whether he proposed to grant us permission to excavate or no. The Sultan appeared never to have heard of the matter before, and at once pronounced the magical words, "Let it be done accordingly," which constitute an iradé. He was then told that the papers were in his own possession, whereupon he repeated the words. The Grand Vizier and the second chamberlain were informed forthwith, and the thing was supposed to be done.

Saturday, the 24th, Mr. Gargiulo went up to the Palace to see if the iradé had been issued, but found that the secretary had received no instructions, and knew nothing about the matter. He then went to the second Chamberlain, who could not speak to his Majesty at that time because he was taking a nap, but promised to present the matter to him later in the day. Sunday, the 25th, Gargiulo went again. The mazbata could not be found; but the Sultan sent word to the Porte to go ahead with the matter, and he would send the necessary papers afterwards. Monday I went to the Ministry of Public Instruction with Mr. Gargiulo, and made the requisite deposit of 100 liras, and paid the permission fee of 20 liras, taking a receipt for the same. The necessary papers had not yet come over from the Porte, and therefore, although the permit was ready, it could not be issued. I asked Gargiulo to read the permission and see that it was all right. The word *sell* had been substituted for *give*, contrary to the promises made to us. Gargiulo said that the change had been made after the original draft had been shown to him. We asked to see the minister, and both of us expostulated with him, reminding him of his own words and those of Hamdy Bey. He insisted that this was just what he had promised, and that it could not be changed. We then went to the Porte to see why the Grand Vizier had not forwarded the papers, and were told that he had given the necessary orders, but that the papers had not yet been prepared, owing to the absence from his post of the man who should have written them.

Going out, we fell in with Hagop Pasha, privy purse and acting minister of finance. Near the entrance door within the large hall a number of poor, ragged women were squatting. We saw them spring up and rush at Hagop with menacing gestures and shrill scoldings, threatening to mob him. The soldiers on guard stood motionless, and for a few moments it looked as though serious injury might be done to the minister. He finally escaped into his carriage, and drove off as speedily as possible, leaving the women scolding and screaming after him. They were the wives of unpaid employees demanding their husbands' pay, asserting their needs, and threatening to mob the minister. The husbands had left their wives to collect their wages, because Mussulman women cannot be touched in public, and consequently may defy laws and occasionally enforce their just demands with impunity, where the men might forfeit their lives in attempting the same thing.

The more I thought of the form in which the permission to excavate was now being issued, the more anxious I became about it. Tuesday morning, the 27th, I had a conference on the subject with Mr. Straus. He also felt that he had been defrauded, and that what we had obtained was entirely out of proportion to what the Grand Vizier had promised, or even to what we were told had been granted. However, to reject this permission would insure another three-months' delay at the least, and it was therefore thought best for me to take it and go ahead. After I had gone, Mr. Straus was to resume his efforts to obtain the terms which we understood to have been originally promised. The committee of Robert College professors, with whom I had kept in the closest touch, were also of the opinion that this was the only thing to do.

On Wednesday the papers were not yet ready, and it was arranged that Mr. Gargiulo and I should go to the Porte the next day, Thanksgiving Day, Thursday the 29th, and I was to make every arrangement to start on Saturday by a steamer of the Russian line sailing on that day. Accordingly Thursday we went to the Porte, where we ascertained from the secretary that the papers had gone over to the Ministry of Public Instruction. We followed them up, arriving almost as soon as they did, to the surprise of the minister's secretary. As he was under some obligation to Gargiulo, we were enabled to find out through him that the change from *give* to *sell* had been made by order of the Grand Vizier; the latter had also ordered that the permission to excavate should not be given to me directly, but be placed in a sealed envelope addressed to the Governor-General of Baghdad, not to be handed over to me until my topographical plan had been presented. I saw the minister once more, and asked for a letter of recommendation to the Governor-General of Baghdad, and that a statement of our right to export should be put in the letter to him. This was promised, and at least in part executed.

In spite of the friendly exertions of the secretary, the permit was not obtained until almost four o'clock, three hours after our arrival. As a special favor, in order to avoid further delay, Gargiulo was permitted himself to take it to the Grand Vizier; but the latter declined to affix his seal on account of technical irregularities, and we were dismissed at last with the work not yet complete. This was the more unfortunate, as Friday was an official holiday on which no work could be done. That afternoon Professor van Millingen and I went to see Hamdy Bey, and bid him farewell. I complained of the change which had been made from *give* to *sell*, which he attributed to the Grand Vizier, expressing much indignation at the latter's interference.

Saturday morning, December 1st, Mr. Gargiulo and I went early to the Ministry of Public Instruction. By noon the technical error in the permission had been corrected, and we were permitted to carry it once more to the Porte, together with a letter of recommendation to the Governor-General of Haleb. The Grand Vizier was detained at the Palace, and did not arrive until about two o'clock. Thanks to Gargiulo, every one hurried, and the necessary papers were in our hands within a quarter of an hour after the Grand Vizier's arrival. In the latter's letter of recommendation to the officials on the route, it proved that he had left out the permission to carry arms which he had promised to give me. In fact, he had told me that we must not go through that country without being well armed. In answer to my remonstrances, he said that we would know how to get the arms through the custom-house, and that a written permission could not be given. While this letter of recommendation was being prepared, we returned to the Ministry of Public Instruction to obtain Munif's letter to the Governor-General of Baghdad. This was handed to us sealed; but we opened it and read the contents, to make sure that all was satisfactory, and then sealed it up again, according to the custom of the country, for no one dare take a note the contents of which he has not seen. My permission, however, I could not see, nor could I obtain a copy of it.

By much hurrying we were at the custom-house a little before three o'clock, where Prince, with the assistance of a clerk and a cawass from the legation, had everything in readiness for the embarkation; and at four o'clock, December 1st, we actually left Constantinople on the Russian steamer *Cesarewitch*.

CHAPTER III.

IMPRESSIONS OF CONSTANTINOPLE.

Negotiating a Loan—Friends and Antiquities—St. George and St Nicholas—Dangers and Dogs—Persian Passion Play—Bemoaning Husein—Self-Torture—Turkish Soldiers—Bektash Dervishes—Howling Dervishes—Description of a Service—Foot and Breath Cures—Dancing Dervishes—Entertained by Dervishes—The Doctrine of Love—Oddities—Porters and Firemen—The Climate

IT is impossible to pass over my three months' stay at Constantinople without a few words about my impressions and experiences. Constantinople is by all odds the most fascinating city I ever lived in,—fascinating by its strange mixture of squalor and magnificence, ugliness and glorious beauty, misery and merriment, by all the paradoxes and anachronisms and incongruities in which it abounds; fascinating also because of the romantic possibilities of each minute you live, each step you make. Who knows what may happen any moment, and what share you may have in it? One minute you speak of trivialities, the next moment you are discussing the fate of nations. Over your coffee and cigarettes you involve all Europe in war, and divide up the Turkish Empire. To march the Russians across the frontier, to give a province to Austria,—such things are a mere bagatelle. And you take part in all that is done, or think you do, which is the same thing. Never mind how insignificant you are, you cannot but feel yourself important in Constantinople.

Scene in the Environs of Constantinople. The Sweet Waters of Europe on a Friday afternoon.

One day I met the Bulgarian Minister of Finance, who wished to re-introduce the cultivation of rice at Sophia, and requested me to put him in communication with our American rice planters. Another day I was approached on behalf of the Turkish Government with a proposition to place a loan of $10,000,000 in America. As security for this, they were willing to pledge the revenues of Smyrna or Beirout, or in fact anything which was unpledged. It was becoming more and more difficult to obtain money in England or France, and the Porte was anxious to find new lenders. The American bankers to whom I referred the matter took counsel with their London correspondents, and refused to lend the money on any terms, because they would have no government protection behind them to secure payment. Later the loan was made by the Deutsche Bank, which secured a railroad concession as a bonus. This was the beginning of that new financial relation of Germany with Turkey which has so much to do with Emperor William's desire to maintain the integrity of the Ottoman Empire. Another day I was requested to procure a brace of the new hammerless Smith and Wesson revolvers for a Turkish official.

All the Americans and English in Constantinople were most hospitable. Mr. Pears, the author of *The Fall of Constantinople*, put us up at the Club de Pera, and there we took our meals for almost two months, meeting every one. We were frequent guests at Roumeli Hissar with the various professors of Robert College, at the Girls' College in Scutari, and at the houses of the missionaries residing in that quarter, as well as with the Azarians at the island of Prinkipo. We explored all the antiquities of Constantinople under the best guidance,—those admirably preserved walls, the best preserved walls in existence, I believe, the cisterns and mosques, the hippodrome, the seraglio, the palaces, and the various monuments of the Bosphorus. Almost all the antiquities in Constantinople outside of the museum are either Turkish or Byzantine; but there are here and there in out-of-the-way places a very few earlier inscriptions, which Dr. Long revealed to us. With his assistance, I endeavored also to come into contact with the dealers in antiquities, only to ascertain that very little from Irak finds its way to the capital. I secured, however, a good but small collection of inscribed clay tablets from the neighborhood of Cæsarea in Cappadocia. There was also offered me for sale a fine vase with a bilingual or trilingual inscription of Artaxerxes. This I identified as the vase stolen from the Tresorio di San Marco in Venice some years before. I sent word to Baron Blanc, the Italian ambassador, hoping that he might be induced to purchase it and restore it to Italy, but to no purpose. From one pasha who had been in Baghdad I bought a small barrel cylinder of Nebuchadrezzar, which I found on examination to be a forgery.

We spent much time in caiques, floating up and down the sapphire-blue waters of the Bosphorus, and exploring its romantic shores from the Marmora to Buyukdere. It was a lesson in comparative religion to observe the manner in which ancient sacred sites have changed hands and names, while preserving the primitive cult practically unchanged. So, on Giant Mountain, nearly opposite Therapia, there is a Moslem holy place said to be the tomb of the great toe of Joshua the son of Nun. In the days of the Byzantine Empire this was the tomb of St. Pantaleon, and in the heathen Greek and Roman times it was the bed of Heracles. There is a prehistoric tumulus there, which originally gave the place its sanctity; and with a changed name each new religion has retained the primitive cult. Moslems now place shreds of their garments and votives upon the ancient tomb, as Christians and heathen did before them. On the Princes' Islands one finds everywhere on the hills churches dedicated to

St. George, while close to the shore are the churches of St. Nicholas. St. George is the heir of Apollo, whose temples in heathen times stood on the hilltops, and St. Nicholas has inherited the seashore temples of Poseidon. To the church of St. George in the island of Prinkipo they used to send the insane to be healed, and the rings let into the stones to which they fastened them are still in the church floor. This, too, may be a relic of the earlier heathen past.

Our great recreation and refreshment was riding on horseback. Some of the Constantinople street horses are admirable mounts; and we scoured the country two or three times a week, frequently with Professor van Millingen as companion, from the Marmora to the Euxine on both sides of the Strait. The outskirts of Constantinople are said to be very dangerous, and we heard much of robberies, outrages, and murders. One day the papers announced the discovery in the Bosphorus, near Kadıkeui, of the body of an eighteen-year-old girl, with her hands tied behind her back. This was a harem execution, but the official inquest pronounced it suicide. We were advised always to ride armed, but never had any occasion to use our arms, although more than once after dark I rode alone by the lonely back road over the hills from Pera to Roumeli Hissar. Occasionally a surly Albanian shepherd would set on us his fierce dogs, to kill one of which causes a blood feud, like the killing of a man; but being mounted, our heavy long-lashed dog whips were sufficient protection against these. Once when I was riding alone at dusk through the filthy streets of the quarter called Kasim Pasha, a couple of soldiers made a feeble demonstration of doing me an injury; but a blow of the loaded butt-end of my whip, aimed at the head of the one who had grabbed my horse's bridle, was quite enough to secure me free passage, and my horse attended to the rest.

Actually my most serious adventure was with the common street dogs in the most frequented and civilized part of the whole city, the Grande Rue de Pera. I was returning from the legation to my hotel one rainy night, clothed from head to foot in white rubber. My unusual appearance aroused some of the dogs in the neighborhood of the legation, who were rendered cross and uncomfortable by the wet and cold, and they began to bark at me. This attracted others, until I was finally beset by a hundred or more barking, howling curs, whose noise was echoed by other dogs in the neighboring streets and alleys, until all Pera seemed to be a canine pandemonium. Rendered brave by numbers, they at last undertook to attack me; and I, being unarmed even with a stick, was much put to it to defend myself and my clothes. Fortunately they are great cowards, and I was able to scatter them for a moment at a time by charging them with screams and wild gestures. It took me a long time to fight my way home in this manner; but, long as the time was, I did not encounter a single one of those bekjees, or watchmen, who seem to be so numerous on pleasant nights, and who go about thumping their sticks on the pavement to show robbers that they are watching for them.

The dogs seemed to me, as to most travellers, one of the most curious features of Constantinople. Everywhere in the East, dogs are the most important part, if not the whole, of the sewage system. But the Constantinople dogs have had from time immemorial a fame different from that of the dogs of other places. They are curs, of a decidedly mixed race. One can trace several types; but the common dog is yellow in color, good-sized, with rather long hair. I think the original stock must have been the common shepherd dog of Turkey; and now and then one sees among them a large dog, black and yellow, almost exactly like the Turkish shepherd dogs of the present day. These true shepherd dogs are large and strong and fierce; but the Constantinople curs, their mongrel descendants, have certainly lost their ferocity. They have imbibed the traits of the human beings among whom they live. Men and dogs in Constantinople both have the same characteristics,—lazy, shiftless, good-natured, divided into various contending nationalities or cliques, living in the street, refusing to budge even when trodden upon, given more to barking than biting. On the tramcar streets, through which run the most preposterous tramcars in pairs, with a runner blowing a horn going ahead to warn people off the track, you often find maimed dogs, who have lost a leg because they were too lazy to get out of the way of the cars. By day the dogs lie sleeping in the streets, appropriating what of sidewalk there may be, and nestling in all the many hollows which have been formed in the neglected pavements. By night they prowl and howl. Sometimes a dog wanders into a strange street or district; then all the dogs in that district set upon him with much barking, and drive him out.

The people are very good to these street dogs, rarely maltreating or killing them. Foreign or half-foreign Christians sometimes poison the dogs in their neighborhood; but such conduct is resented by the people at large, and especially by the Moslems. In general the natives protect them, and in bad weather you will frequently observe benevolent householders furnishing food and shelter to mother dogs with litters of puppies. One pretty instance of this I remember in a side street through which I passed every day on my way to the Club. There was a mother dog with one puppy. Then some one gave them a piece of old matting to sleep on, placing it on the sidewalk where it was narrow, so that passers-by were obliged either to dislodge the dogs or step out into the street. Then they conveyed dogs and matting across the street to a more protected spot. When the rainy weather began, the same persons built the dogs a little house of matting and old bags, held up with sticks, occupying the whole of the walk at that point. Later they built a more durable house of stones and old pieces of tin, and all this time they furnished these dogs with food and drink. Nor is this an unusual case.

Not long after my arrival in Constantinople occurred the so-called " Persian Passion Play." This is celebrated on the tenth day of the first month, Moharrem, which fell that year, the year 1305 after the Hegira, on the 16th of September. It commemorates the death of Husein, son of Ali, killed in the battle of Kerbela. Professor van Millingen secured a special invitation from the Persian ambassador, under whose protection the play is given in the Valide Khan in Stamboul, and we went as his guests.

We crossed the bridge of boats from Pera to Stamboul shortly before sunset, and soon found ourselves part of a motley throng around the large khan occupied chiefly or altogether by Persian merchants. Passing through the gate, we entered a large court, surrounded by shops, and having a couple of small buildings and a fountain or two in the centre. The roofs, balconies, and windows were thronged with women and children, many of the former wearing black robes. Much of the front of the khan was draped in black, but a contrasting effect of brilliancy was produced by masses of lamps and huge chandeliers full of candles. We found our way through a large concourse of people, among whom were hundreds of Turkish soldiers, necessary to prevent serious disorder, to the spot beneath an awning roped off for the guests of the Persian Embassy. On the way we passed between two lines of men, one hundred and fifty or two hundred in number, armed with swords and knives, bare-headed, and with white smocks over their clothing. These men, whose business it was to gash themselves in sign of grief, are drawn chiefly, if not entirely, from the lower classes, and especially from the donkey-drivers, who are all Persians.

Soon after sunset the procession began to move. First came a couple of horses with little children on their backs, another horse carrying two unreal doves, and another with trappings stained in imitation of blood. With these were torch-bearers, and following them were mourners. Some of these beat on their breasts, some wore mourning, and one man bore in his arms a little child whose face and clothes were stained with blood, and which, with a pitiful look on its scared face because of the strange and terrible sights and sounds, clung with a nervous grip of its little hands to its father's collar. Then came the men with knives. Each brandished his knife or sword with his right hand, and with the left clutched his neighbor's girdle. Facing inward, they progressed sideways by a curious, violent step, somewhat like dancing, swinging their swords, and shouting, in time with the double movement of arms and legs, " Hasan, Husein!" After them came a motley crowd of men, some in Frankish or European dress (excepting the head); some in long Oriental robes; some wearing the red Turkish fez, some the black Persian fez, and some the turban. Many had bared their breasts; and almost all beat upon the breast in time to the cry of the knifemen, " Hasan, Husein!" In this order the procession passed twice slowly around the interior of the khan, and then went out by the gate to encompass the outside in the same way. When they returned at the end of about half an hour, many of the knifemen were stained with blood, which poured from gashes cut by themselves upon the shaven tops of their heads. Behind and between the ranks of the knifemen were Turks armed with sticks to protect the fanatics from their own swords. At this time, however, it did not seem to me likely that the men would do themselves real harm, and indeed I was sceptical about the genuineness of any of the blood.

After the procession had again passed twice around the interior of the khan, it went out by the gate as before; and we went by invitation into a room with a divan on three sides, where we were hospitably entertained with tea and cigarettes, and were enabled to sit down and rest. From the window of this room we witnessed the third scene, a complete novelty in the Persian Play, I was told. Persian school-children sang religious songs and hymns appropriate to the mournful occasion. Then, halting in front of us, an imam recited a number of short prayers, after each of which the children sang "Amen!" just as if they had been trained in an American or English church choir. Then they received some sherbet, or something of the sort, and went out by a side door through one of the houses.

For the fourth scene I obtained a place in the front rank of the spectators, and indeed I found myself almost among the actors, for the press was such that the barriers immediately about me were broken, and both rabble and mourners were pushed in upon us; but, being protected by a post, I was able to hold my own, though the knife-men were sometimes so close to me on both sides that we were almost in contact, and the sword-blades played uncomfortably close to my head. The interlude of the school-children had been tender and touching,—a great relief after the fierce demonstration of mourning in the two former scenes,—but it only served to render more terrible the two closing scenes. These were both alike, excepting that they increased in frenzy constantly, and that in the fifth scene the procession marched three times past us, instead of twice. The torches seemed more glaring, because the darkness had become deeper. Men heaped fuel into the iron braziers which the torch-bearers carried on the ends of poles, and others poured on kerosene-oil from cans to cause a blaze.

Among the horses, banners, and mournful musicians, there now appeared men with bared backs, violently scourging themselves with bunches of chains. The thud of the blows was sickening; and their poor backs were soon a revolting spectacle, bruised and bleeding. Other men beat their heads and faces with thorns. The knife-men were stained with blood from head to foot, and the men with sticks had the greatest difficulty in preventing the more frenzied among them from killing themselves outright,—a thing which happens not infrequently in Persia, I am told. The movements of these men, too, became more rapid and irregular, and their cries wilder and hoarser. Now they would rush, stagger, almost tumble, to our side; now crowd together and sway out toward the centre, until the two lines almost met. Several times I thought they would surely kill themselves, so violently they swung their swords. At one time they came to a lock about my post, and for a minute or more were stationary, close to me on both sides, one of them only an inch or two away. The blood was streaming in torrents down their faces and backs, they were blinded, and, in spite of the intoxication of excitement, strong men were staggering from loss of blood. I saw several carried away unable to stand; one fainted and fell to the ground. Several times I saw Turkish soldiers struggling with some man who was bent on killing himself, disarming him and carrying him off. Now and then friends would rush forward and wipe the blood from a man's eyes, or bind a handkerchief above them. The weirdness of the scene was beyond description,—the mournful, barbarous music; the muttering thud of a multitude beating the breast; the sobs of weeping mourners; the rapid strokes of the scourges; the wild cries of "Hasan, Husein!" the sudden flare of the torches, illuminating for a moment the outer darkness, and revealing the intent crowds around and on the housetops; the flashing swords; the streaming blood; the rapt, intense looks of all, even the European spectators. The excitement of the actors themselves had become such, that only through the greatest vigilance on the part of the Turks were the papers able to report on the following day that no deaths had occurred.

And yet they tell me that it is far less violent than it was even five years earlier. I inquired about the after results, thinking that men who had been marching, crying, swinging swords, and cutting and beating themselves, for almost three hours without intermission, must suffer horribly afterwards, but was assured that they would be all right in half an hour. I can only say that I saw a number of them twenty minutes or half an hour after the performance had ended, and they could not walk without assistance.

I have mentioned the soldiers who were on hand to police the Persian Passion Play. The garrison of Constantinople consists of 30,000 soldiers, and you meet them everywhere. Their barracks are on all the roads leading out of the city, and nothing is more familiar in the streets of all quarters of the city than military uniforms. In the immediate neighborhood of the Sultan's palace are stationed 7000 men, picked regiments, who act as his immediate guard. Every Friday there is a parade of a few thousand men in connection with the Selamlik. The Sultan is obliged to visit some mosque every Friday morning. The road on which he is to go is lined with soldiers on both sides, in order that no one may by any chance approach him; and after mosque he holds a review, which is followed by a reception. The Grand Vizier also never goes through the streets of the city without a guard. He drives in a close carriage; and behind him ride three mounted soldiers, each carrying his repeating rifle in his hand unslung, ready for immediate use.

Next to the Persian Passion Play, the most curious

and surprising sights in Constantinople, from a religious point of view, are the dervishes. I came in contact with four orders of dervishes,—the Bektashee, the Mevlewee, the Rufa'ee, and the Bedawee. These are all secret religious orders, having esoteric doctrines which are revealed only to the initiated. The Bektashee were founded by Hajji Bektash of Khorassan (died 1357), in connection with the Janissaries; and when Sultan Mahmoud put the latter to the sword in 1826, he proscribed the former also. They kept on increasing, however, and at the present day they are a strong and very influential order. They are suspected of being freethinkers, and are generally regarded as infected with pantheism. They sympathize to a considerable extent, certainly, with the heretical Shiites, or Persian sect of Mohammedans, in common with whom they reverence the memory of Ali, and bemoan on the 10th of Moharrem the death of Husein at Kerbela. The members of this order are drawn from the upper or educated classes, and represent in general the liberal and progressive elements. Some of them are even in favor of educating and emancipating women. The son of one of their sheikhs took me into what I may call the chapel of his tekke, or convent, which was a rude room with sheepskins around the walls for seats, and at one end a few candlesticks, censers, and the like. Here, he told me, they conducted services of prayer and preaching. According to him, they are mystics, believing in direct communion of the soul with God, and discarding all intermediaries, which is theoretically true of all Mohammedans.

Every one has heard of the howling dervishes (Rufa'ee), and knows something about their religious services or performances. They are one of the regular sights of Constantinople. Their most important tekke is on the Asiatic side of the Bosphorus, at Scutari. Here they hold a service every Thursday afternoon at the hour of prayer. First the dervishes sit on their sheepskins at the lower end of the railed enclosure, which occupies the larger part of the room, reciting their common prayer, a chapter of the Koran, the praises of Mohammed, of their founder (Rufa'ee, died 1182), and of former saints of the order. The old Sheikh squats alone at the other end of the room, facing them, with his back toward a small niche in the southwestern wall, which indicates the direction of Mecca. In and about this niche hang various weapons, axes, swords, and knives, relics of deceased members, and formerly used for purposes of religious self-torture. Not very many years since, the dervishes of this tekke were wont to burn themselves with hot irons, and cut and gash themselves with sharp weapons, as part of their religious ceremonial.

After the initial prayers were completed, two of the more experienced brethren were selected by the Sheikh as the ministers or servants of the occasion, and invested with black stoles in token thereof. A number of dervishes then stood up in line; the old Sheikh took his place at one end; one singer, who was joined later by three or four more, squatted on a sheepskin in front of them; and the dancing and howling began. The songs sung were love-songs, mystically interpreted of the love of the soul to God, exactly as the Synagogue, and, following it, part at least of the Christian Church, interpreted Solomon's Song. Similarly a mystic use is made of drinking-songs, intoxication being allegorically interpreted as spiritual ecstasy. The dervish idea is the idea of love of God, which is viewed in a one-sided, imperfect manner, and sought in ecstasy, rapture, passion, and abnormal excitement. As might be expected, the allegorical interpretation of love and intoxication has led in certain orders to abuses and abominations such as have stained the record of some sects of Christian mystics. So the Bektash dervishes are said to indulge in wild orgies in their zikr or ritual, and especially to employ intoxicants and hasheesh to bring on the ecstasy. They interpret actual intoxication mystically, while the Rufa'ee and others merely put an allegorical interpretation upon songs about intoxication.

While these love-songs were being sung, the line of dervishes was grunting and snorting, for so only can these peculiar sounds be described, the Mohammedan formula, "There is no God but God," accompanying the words by a double movement of the body, a swaying forward and backward, and a limping, stamping, side movement with the feet. Their motions and utterances kept increasing in rapidity. The ministers relieved them of their outer robes, and provided them also with linen skull-caps in place of the turban or fez. Outsiders joined the performers, and danced and howled as well and as long as they could, so that they might imbibe some of the spiritual afflatus. Two negroes took their places near the centre of the line, whom, from their dexterity and endurance, we judged to be regular members of the order. Little children danced and howled in the centre of the room in imitation of their elders. Now and then some of the outside performers dropped out exhausted, but more always came in to take their places, so that with the excitement the numbers increased also. The peculiar limping character of this portion of the dance, accompanying the vehement shouting of the name of God, may well be compared with the dance and prayer of the priests of Baal (1 Kings, xviii., 26, the literal rendering of the last clause of which seems to be, "And they limped about the altar which had been made").

After the dancers had become sufficiently excited, at a given signal the limping, swaying, movement stopped; and all began to bob very violently up and down without quite lifting their bare feet from the floor, flinging their heads wildly from side to side, often with hideous contortions of countenance and ecstatic grimaces. At the same time they uttered what seemed to be inarticulate sounds. This was ecstasy. The singers in front chanted even more wildly; a blind beggar who was bobbing up and down on the right of the line shouted, "The gates of heaven!" "Put love in him!" "Do it with love!" and other similar alleluias and fervid ejaculations; and the believers were greatly edified, but the unbelieving said that they were mad. In justice to the dervishes themselves, I ought to add that they tried hard to suppress the alleluia beggar.

But the most interesting and instructive part of the service was still before us. The old Sheikh now took his seat at the founder's place in front of the niche, and the healing of the sick began. First some clothing and a bottle of water for a sick person were brought to him, into which, after a brief prayer, he breathed, his breath being sanctified by the frequent repetition of the name of God. Then were brought a number of sick people, who were made to lie down, a few at a time, on their faces on the wooden floor, and he walked slowly backward and forward upon their bodies. Some of them were old and feeble, and some small children, but I could not see that any suffered the least pain from the operation. The children of the neighborhood regard it as great fun, and are always on hand to be walked over as many times as the ministers will permit. Occasionally the Sheikh sought to effect a cure by merely breathing upon the patient; and not a few were passed along the line of dervishes, still grunting and bobbing up and down, to be breathed upon by all. Indeed, mere presence in that atmosphere, saturated, so to speak, with the name of God, was supposed to be a tonic, physical as well as religious. It was an unusually successful and enthusiastic meeting; and a correspondingly large number of patients, some of them persons of position, presented themselves to be cured.

Some of these cases were pathetic, inasmuch as the patients were evidently grasping at this as a drowning man grasps at a straw,—as a last, desperate, almost hopeless chance.

Another order of dervishes well known to strangers is the Mevlewee, or dancing dervishes. They have a tekke in the very heart of Pera, the Frank or European quarter of Constantinople, where they dance every Friday afternoon. After prayers have been recited, a small band of flutes, tambourines, and Oriental drums, begins to

MEVLEWEE DERVISH WITH INVERTED WATER-BUCKET HAT.

play in the back gallery, and one or more singers in the same place chant hymns about Mohammed, the founder of the order (Jelal-ed-Deen Mevlana, died 1273), and the saints that have been. About the walls are framed scrolls containing the names of God, Mohammed, the first four caliphs, Hasan and Husein, and texts from the Koran. The dervishes are within a railed enclosure in the middle of the room, about which are places for spectators,—the men below, and the women in latticed galleries above. At the end toward Mecca the Sheikh squats alone, in the founder's place; and in front of him, in a semicircle, as though they were his pupils, sit the other dervishes, their backs against the railing. The head of each man is surmounted by a high, rimless hat of a coarse, light-brown felt, bearing some resemblance to an inverted water-bucket. When, in prayer, all at once, with much noise, they cast themselves on their faces on the floor, these singular caps add greatly to the effect. The floor within the railing is inlaid with hard, polished wood, well adapted to dancing.

The dance itself is really a very pretty sight. All solemnly and very slowly march three times around (dervish holy numbers seem to be 3, 12, and 1001) within the enclosure, headed by the Sheikh. As they reach the founder's place, each in turn makes a very low reverence with his arms folded on his breast, then skips across to the other side of the sheepskin, and repeats the reverence from that side, as his successor is doing the same from the other side, their high felt caps almost meeting in the centre. The Sheikh then takes his stand on his sheepskin at the founder's place; the rest throw off their mantles, appearing in long, full, white skirts and white jackets with long sleeves, and, again forming in line, move slowly around the enclosure until they reach the Sheikh. Each in turn kisses his hand, receives permission to dance, and twirls away from the Sheikh on one side as the next dervish approaches him on the other. Barefooted for the most part, they twirl on the left foot, moving themselves about with the right; the arms are extended, the right hand open upward and the left downward; the head is dropped on the right shoulder, and the eyes ordinarily closed. A few twirl slowly, and without much change of position, in the centre; the rest twirl more rapidly, their full skirts extended by the motion, moving in a circle about the central group. Each, therefore, turns upon his own axis, and also revolves about a common centre. The Sheikh remains motionless in his place; and one master of ceremonies, in a long mantle, moves slowly about among the dancers to see that all is done decently and in order.

After the dance has lasted some five minutes, at a given signal all stop instantly. Then they fall into line once more; each in turn seeks anew the Sheikh's permission, kisses his hand, and resumes his dance as before. This also is repeated three times. Before the end is reached, some of the novices become exhausted; they may then resume their mantles, and stand with the back against a pillar in a position of meditation until the dance is concluded. After the dance the music ceases, all resume their cloaks and their places, and prayers are again recited, this time especially for the Sultan. Then all arise, the Sheikh advances and utters in a loud tone what seems a blessing, all shout aloud a response, which sounds like the mystic syllable *hoo*, the gate is opened, the Sheikh departs with great solemnity, and the rest find their shoes and scatter irregularly as they will.

The following year my wife and I attended service in a less known tekke of this order, in a Turkish quarter of Constantinople, under the escort of Bedry Bey, who had danced there as a novice in his youth. After the service, although there was a lady with me, he introduced us to the private rooms of the dervishes, where we became the guests of one of them, who was also chaplain at a military hospital. Besides the dervishes, some officers were present. Cigarettes and coffee were served; and then our host took out of his pocket a box of hasheesh, and served out to those who wished it large balls, which they swallowed without ado.

Our host now proposed a visit to a tekke of Bedawee dervishes about half a mile away. Their ceremonial is almost identical with that of the Rufa'ee, but the color of their stoles and the Sheikh's robe was red instead of black. The shouting and dancing were, if anything, more excited and violent than those of the Rufa'ee, which I have already described. They also are supposed to possess the power of healing, both by treading and breathing; and the crowd which came to be trodden and breathed upon, or brought clothing and water-bottles to be breathed into, was even larger than that which I had seen at the Rufa'ee tekke. One of the dancing dervishes who had accompanied us went into the enclosure, and danced his peculiar silent, twirling dance, while the Bedawee were shouting and jumping. The other, our imam, or chaplain friend, told me afterward that he had called earnestly upon God for inspiration to do the same, but it had been denied him.

After the ceremonies were concluded, we were taken into the dervishes' parlor to drink coffee and smoke cigarettes. Here our Mevlewee friend insisted upon abasing himself, kissing, among other things, the dusty toes of my shoes, in order to show that he was a servant of every servant of God, by whatever name he called himself. He told me that the time would come when his religion and mine would be one, or rather when both would be lost in one all-true religion of the knowledge and love of God. Men should not quarrel and fight because of differences of belief, he said, but love one another. In that way the prevalence of truth would be hastened.

The object of the dervish is to attain to a mystical, spiritual communion with God,—an end which he often seeks by grossly mechanical and physical means. His watchwords are obedience and love. As a part of the discipline necessary to the higher life, he practises asceticism and even bodily torture; but in many particulars his asceticism is different from the monasticism of Buddhism, or the Roman and Greek churches. Celibacy is not necessary; indeed, all the sheikhs or abbots of whom I know are married, and in many orders the post of sheikh is hereditary. So, also, the other members of the order do not necessarily dwell together in the cloister, nor wear a distinctive dress; they are not obliged to forsake the ordinary avocations of life; and their connection with the order may be severed at will. As to their private life, one hears the same charges which were made so frequently against the monks of the Middle Ages, but it is especially the wandering beggar dervishes against whom these charges are made. Among the people at large the dervishes enjoy a very high reputation for sanctity. They correspond in many particulars to the prophets in Old Testament times.

Like all visitors to Constantinople, I felt upon my first arrival in that city as though everything were topsy-turvy. It seemed to me that people took pains to do things in a way just the opposite to that in which we are in the habit of doing them. If I wished to beckon some one, and beckoned to him with my finger with the hand upturned, I was doing what corresponds with us to putting your fingers to your nose and waving them. You must be careful in beckoning to turn the hand downward. If some one begged of me on the street, and I shook my head at him, it meant, not "no," but "I do not understand." To say "no," you throw your head backwards and cluck. If you wish to call a dog, you do not whistle, but chirrup. If you wish to stop a horse, you hiss at him. Of course, when you enter a mosque, you take off your shoes and keep on your hat, and, if you would follow Turkish use, the same should be done in entering a house. If you meet a friend, you do not bow, or touch your hat, or even shake hands with him, but make three motions with your hand,—one downward toward the ground, one toward the mouth, and one upward to the forehead. It is the pretense of taking up the hem of his robe, kissing it, and touching it to your forehead. If the person whom you salute be of high rank, then you bow low, almost to the ground, in making the salutation. If he be of inferior rank, you remain erect, and make a rapid pass with your hand, including the three motions in one. According to the rank of the person whom you meet, you make a salutation anywhere between the two extremes.

But these are only small things and among the least peculiar of those which the new-comer to Constantinople observes. Something more amazing is the way in which everything is carried on men's backs. The greater part

ARMENIAN PORTERS CARRYING LARGE CASES OF GOODS.

of the streets in Constantinople are not broad enough for the passage of carriages, and even one loaded horse or mule takes up almost the entire roadway. If you buy a piano in Constantinople, it is more likely than not to come home on a man's back. One day I met a porter carrying a good-sized marble column, and a few moments later another passed me carrying a coffin. When the cold weather set in suddenly, as it did by the middle of October, you could see processions of men carrying stoves through the streets on their backs. Once I met a man carrying an iron safe about three feet square. The men who perform these feats are Armenians, who come from various parts of Asia Minor and Roumelia, and labor at the trade of porter until they have saved enough money to go home and buy a house in their native town. They are organized in guilds. The heavy loads are supported upon an odd-shaped saddle which they wear on their backs, and here and there in the streets you will notice platforms meant for their convenience in resting their loads.

The fire department of Constantinople also arrests the attention of the traveller. The greater part of the city is built of wood, and terrible conflagrations are of frequent occurrence. In the European suburb of Pera the Government is said to set many of the fires itself, as the easiest way of clearing out old rubbish, with the intention of laying out broader and straighter streets. There is a constant watch kept on the summit of the old Genoese tower in Galata; a similar watch is kept on the tall tower of the Seraskierat in Stamboul, and another on a hill behind Candili, one of the Asiatic suburbs, a few miles up the Bosphorus. From this latter place a cannon is fired to give warning of a fire. The Government is trying to organize a fire department on European models, but I never saw anything in use excepting the old hand fire-engines. These are nothing but little hand-pumps, which are carried on the shoulders of four men. They are surrounded by a guard of about twenty almost naked wild fellows, who relieve the bearers from time to time. These run through the streets at top speed, without any regard for the unfortunates who may be in their road. Arrived at the place of the fire, I am told that they do more harm than the fire itself, like the old volunteer fire department which existed in New York when I was a boy. If the fire be at night, a bekjee comes under your window, strikes with his iron staff on the pavement, and cries out "Fire!" in such and such a quarter. It is rather aggravating to be waked up at two o'clock in the morning to learn that there is a fire in some Asiatic suburb of the city eight or ten miles away. But the bekjees are a nuisance altogether. They walk the streets all night long, rapping their staffs on the pavement to warn robbers that there is some one about, so that they may take good care to get out of the way. Until you are used to them, you are apt to be waked many times during the night; and each time they pass through your street all the dogs wake up and bark at them.

It should not be understood that the only sights in Constantinople are those which are curious. The natural beauties of its situation are almost unsurpassed, although the streets of the city itself are poor and squalid. Sancta Sophia is not inferior in grandeur and interest to any building in the world, and many of the mosques of Constantinople are wonderfully attractive. But the object of this chapter is to describe the impressions made upon me in my first visit, and not to write a guide-book to the beauties and antiquities of Constantinople.

During the first part of our stay in Constantinople the weather was often uncomfortably warm, both in and out of doors; but about the middle of October a sudden change occurred, and from that time on we suffered as much with the cold as we had before suffered with the heat. It was the temperature within doors, however, which caused the suffering, rather than that without. No provision is made for heating the houses, few of which have chimneys, excepting possibly for kitchen use. If you wish to put a stove in your house, you must run the stove-pipe out of the window, or cut a hole for it in your house wall. Coal is very bad and very expensive, and wood is the same. The ordinary means of heating rooms is the mangal, or charcoal brazier. The thermometer in our rooms often fell to 50°, and never rose above 57° or 58°. I noticed it the more, as I was engaged at the time on the translation for *Scriptures, Hebrew and Christian*, of the Book of Job (a most appropriate task, my friends assured me), and wished to be much at my desk. Prince found the climate very trying, and was under the doctor's hands most of the time; and we were both glad to leave Constantinople at last.

CHAPTER IV.

THE DISCOVERY OF TIPHSAH.

Smuggling by Order of the Grand Vizier—Pack-Mules to Beylan—A Filthy Khan—Unexplored Ruins—Simon Stylites—Stone Fields—Aleppo—Known to Assyrians and Hebrews—Turkish Currency—Our Caravan—A Cone Village—Ruins of Aleppo Plain—Conical Tels—Flogging a Muleteer—The Euphrates—A World Road—Euphrates Exploration—Meskene and Barbalissus—Pethor and Balaam—A Horse Fight—Kal-'at Dibse—Thapsacus, or Tiphsah—Story of Tiphsah.

IT was Saturday, December 1st, when we left Constantinople. On board we found a motley party: the cabin was Babel, but the deck was pandemonium. There the people camped out, spreading their bedding on the floor, and preparing their meals from material brought with them. There were a number of Turks and a few Jews, but the great mass of the deck passengers were Russian pilgrims on their way to Jerusalem. These people were vilely dirty, shock-headed, and forbidding-looking. They were packed so close that they actually touched one another, and movement seemed impossible. A number of them were in the hold, and, looking at them through the hatchway, it seemed as though they must have been pitchforked in, and fallen together in one tangled heap. How the ship was worked, it was difficult to understand; for it was almost impossible to pass from one portion of the deck to another, the crowd was so dense. The filth of these people and of the deck was something awful.

Monday morning, the 3d, we awoke in the process of coming to dock at Smyrna. The next afternoon about one o'clock we reached Chios. When I arose the following morning, we were off Rhodes; and at sunset we had just passed Kastelorhyzo or Meis, the ancient Megiste. The next morning when I went on deck, we were passing the little village of Kharadran in Cilicia, east of the Gulf of Addalia. All day long Cyprus was visible in the distance to our right. At 10.30 we rounded Cape Anamur quite closely. On the east side of the cape, at its ex-

TURKISH DECK PASSENGERS.

treme end, was the wall of an old acropolis; and below this, on the side of the hill, quite extensive ruins of the Roman city of Anamurion were to be seen. Early in the afternoon we were opposite ancient Celenderis, of which we saw little or nothing; and a little before sunset we passed the ruins of Seleucia Trachæa. About ten P.M. we reached Mersin. All the next day we were rolling about in the roads at that place, while it rained dismally.

It was seven o'clock in the morning of December 8, 1888, when our steamer cast anchor at Alexandretta, the modern Iskenderoon; and almost immediately afterwards Haynes was on board to meet us, accompanied by an agent who was to secure the passage of our goods through the custom-house. This precaution was especially necessary at Alexandretta. A discharged agent of the American missionaries, Jebra Hanna, had accused them of smuggling arms and other contraband articles into the country: consequently the custom-house authorities were suspicious of Americans. They had actually searched the persons of some of those members of the expedition who had arrived earlier, taking from Haynes a sealed letter of introduction, on the ground that he was defrauding the mails, and seizing various objects, including a number of cartridge-shells, bullet-molds, etc. It was only the shrewdness of Noorian that saved from seizure the better part of our rifles, which had been intrusted to Haynes for transport.

The Grand Vizier had urged upon me the necessity of carrying arms, had personally authorized me to carry them, and had promised me a written teskereh, or permission, to that effect; but when the permit was prepared and sent up for his signature, he changed his mind, as already narrated, and returned it unsigned, with a verbal statement that the Americans would have no trouble, and would know how to pass the rifles through the custom-house. But, thanks to the spite of this discharged missionary agent, the Americans did have trouble, and for a time the rifles were obliged to remain on shipboard. Then they were transferred to another steamer, whence Noorian took them in a rowboat late at night. As he was returning to the shore, a custom-house wherry, considering his motions suspicious, put out to examine his boat. He lowered the rifles, wrapped in rubber, into the water, on the shady side of the boat; and when the custom-house authorities arrived, they found nothing but a man taking a row in the moonlight. When the coast was again clear, he hauled up the guns, and carried them ashore; and that same night his brother

Jeremiah carried them up the mountain on his back to Beylan, where they were handed over to Haynes. So, obeying the directions of the Turkish Government, given through the Grand Vizier, we disobeyed and evaded the regulations of the Turkish custom-house.

In view of this experience, I had expected trouble for Prince and myself, but found none; the agent passing even our rifles through the custom-house without difficulty by means of a ridiculously small baksheesh, something which it seems to be the habit of the customs employees to levy quite indiscriminately on dutiable and undutiable objects alike. On the shore Noorian and Hilprecht were awaiting us; and by ten minutes of twelve we had repacked our effects, settled with the custom-house (from which I tried in vain, by means of an order from Constantinople, to obtain the release of the objects already seized), and were ready to start up the Amanus Mountains, each perched upon his pack on a pack-horse or mule.

There is a good carriage road, well engineered, and for the most part in good condition, built by French engineers, from Alexandretta to Aleppo, crossing the Amanus Mountains through the pass at Beylan, and utilizing in part the old Roman road; and you can hire a carriage and drive the distance in a day, or a day and a night. But a carriage costs money; and Haynes, to whom, as being on the spot and well acquainted with the country and its methods, such matters were intrusted, measured time and money by the Oriental standard: hence we, like thrifty Turkish travellers, chose the three-days' ride rather than the one-day drive; and perhaps it was as well that we should have made acquaintance with this mode of travel at the very outset. The road winds up the mountain side; but we went straight up on a rough horse-track, thus shortening the distance, and saving the toll for use of the road.

For three hours, perched high on our packs, our heels dangling about the heads of our beasts, we climbed up that mountain,—below us glorious views of the dazzling blue Mediterranean; above us towering, always more gigantic, the brown masses of the Amanus. At last we entered the Pass of Beylan, through which from time immemorial the armies of the East and West have marched to conquest or disaster. The Amanus Mountains reach at their highest point a height of 1843 metres, but the pass at Beylan is not quite 700 metres above sea-level. The village itself, chiefly inhabited by Christians, clambers picturesquely, house above house, the roof of one at the basement of another, up the northern slope of a great ravine; and through it runs the road by which you may cross these mountains.

Here in the stable of a dirty little khan we found four of our horses awaiting us, with a couple of servants. In less than half an hour we were under way once more, this time mounted on saddles, along the narrow road partly cut out of the mountain side, hanging over a ravine so deep that we shuddered to think what would be the rider's fate should one of our champing, plunging stallions, in his mad efforts to fight with all the other stallions, topple over the edge into the abyss beneath. Some distance above Beylan the modern road leaves the line of the ancient Roman military street; and some distance farther on, we, on our part, left the former to follow a short cut, supposed to be known to Haynes, down the eastern side of the mountains into the Antioch plain, leaving the pack-animals to follow more slowly. We lost the way, darkness settled down before we reached the plain, and it commenced to rain. However, there was nothing for it but to go ahead, although it was pretty rough work for both horses and men, climbing pathlessly down the side of those mighty mountains in the dark and rain,—fair symbol of the hardships and perplexities which, partly through our own fault, were destined to make our way difficult from first to last. Finally, about eight o'clock, we came upon a bad stretch of the carriage road leading across the marshes, and after floundering through the mud and rain for another hour, at nine o'clock we reached our intended halting-place at Murad Pasha Kyuprissi, or Murad Pasha's Bridge,—a stone bridge spanning the Kara Su, or Black Water, a few miles north of the point at which it enters the broad and marshy Lake of Antioch, the modern eb-Bahra.

The so-called khan at this point was a low hut, reeking wet, built of blocks of mud, by the side of a stagnant pool of water, with a similar hut for the stable. In the latter a couple of men were sleeping on the door, which they had taken off its hinges, if it ever had any, in order to keep dry. In the hut were two rooms, one of which we shared with three or four natives. Here there was a fire of camel's dung; and great sacks of the dried dung, which they call coals, were piled up on one side of the room. The smoke was stifling, the floor was mother earth, and over my head roosted a chicken. Haynes had left our beds here on his way to the coast, and the rest of the party quickly made use of theirs; but Haynes and I sat up until midnight, waiting for the pack-animals and servants to arrive.

Outside countless jackals howled incessantly, and as I listened for the first time to that which was to be my lullaby for so many months, I could scarcely believe that I heard the voices of four-footed beasts. It was as though hundreds of ill-fed, ill-housed, half-human babies were weeping and wailing in dismal misery. One could almost believe that the graves had opened, and the hapless infants of the past were bemoaning their sufferings once more. Is it because the jackal robs the graves of the dead that his note is so weird and ghoul-like?

By six we were up again, and by eight we were on our

march through mud and a dense fog, with occasional rain, over the plain southward. Prince's horse had broken down the night before, and he, poor fellow, had to remount a pack-horse. At 11.35 we reached el-Hammam, the hot-springs, on the edge of the eastern foothills. Here Haynes had left his own horse, Sargon, and our head man, Mustafa, on his way to the coast; and here we stopped an hour to lunch on black olives, bread, cheese and coffee, bait the horses, and make the readjustment required by this addition to our forces. By this time the fog had lifted, and we could see what sort of country we had traversed, and especially we could observe the great number of mounds covering the sites of ancient ruins. Hilprecht and I counted eighteen ruins within sight of el-Hammam, some of them of quite considerable size, not one of which, I believe, has ever been touched by the spade of the explorer. El-Hammam itself, with its sulphur hot-springs, was once a health resort, but no traces of ancient buildings are visible above the ground at present.

Resuming our journey, we left the carriage road, and took a track through the mountains to the southeast, passing around Jebel Siman. About the middle of the afternoon we entered the vast stone-fields which surround this imposing mass, 839 metres above sea-level, and 600 odd metres in apparent height. Jebel Siman, or Mt. Simon, is named after St. Simon Stylites, as being the great mountain of the region which Simon made famous by his crazy conduct, although not the actual point on which his column stood. Mohammedans have inherited his cult from the Christians, and converted him, I believe, into a saint of their own. At all events, a ziara, or Mussulman shrine, stands on the top of the mountain, and Simon's name and this locality are regarded with veneration. In the fourth, fifth, and sixth centuries this whole region was a favorite resort of ascetics and recluses, and the traveller is amazed at the number and extent of the ruins of monasteries and churches strewn about through these apparently impracticable stone-heaps. The whole country is one forbidding waste of desolate hills and heaps of limestone and basalt, broken up into rocks and blocks of all shapes and sizes, so thickly strewn over the ground that for miles you can scarcely see an inch of soil. And yet there are ruins everywhere. No civilized horse could travel over such paths as we traversed, oftentimes consisting apparently of nothing but great awkward bowlders, with deep holes between, the whole rendered doubly slippery by the drizzle which began toward nightfall.

Shortly after dark, having just crossed an unusually impossible hill, we found ourselves in a cultivated plain, by far the largest oasis we had yet seen in the wilderness, containing several villages, the most important of which was Dana. Leaving this to our right, and passing Hasra, or Hasrin, we finally halted at the little village of Turmanin, where a very respectable room in an apparently uninhabited house was placed at our disposal. As we were at prayers, for it was Sunday night, several villagers came in; and one old man, the head of the village, I believe, set a dish of curdled goat's-milk before us, which Noorian told me it was my duty to accept, eat with much relish, and pay for. This was the first of a long series of sacrifices of my palate and digestion to the demands of hospitality and politeness which I was destined to make.

The next morning we were up at 3.30; and at 5.30, in pitch darkness, we were following a guide over the same dreary, impracticable stone-heaps which we had traversed the day before. It was cold, and rain fell at intervals. Altogether we were very uncomfortable. Here and there in the road we found stone-cut cisterns, most if not all of which were manifestly ancient rock-cut tombs converted into cisterns in modern times. We also passed large heaps of stones raised by travellers. One of these heaps once started, for whatever unknown reason it may be, every passer-by religiously adds a stone, so that some of them are of great size. That they possess a religious significance, like the sacred trees, is shown by the rags of garments, and the like, by which those who pray there attach their prayers, as it were, to the sacred object.

As we neared Aleppo,—Haleb, the natives call it,—the stones with which the surface of the ground was covered grew smaller, and the earth more abundant, until at last we found ourselves on a stony plateau about 375 metres above sea-level. At precisely noon we reached our destination, having made the journey from Alexandretta in forty-eight hours and ten minutes.

Harper and Field were awaiting us at the Hotel Azizieh, a little Armenian hostelry, then a new experiment in Aleppo, where nothing of the kind had ever been seen before. Hilprecht, Prince, Noorian, and I took up our quarters in the same place; and Haynes was accommodated at the house of Dr. Graham, a medical missionary of the A.B.C.F.M., who, with his charming wife, rendered us many valuable services. For an Oriental city, Aleppo is, in comparison especially with Damascus and Baghdad, a progressive and enterprising place. There is an aspect of alertness and energy about the people, in refreshing contrast with the torpor and indolence of the southern Syrians and Mesopotamians. A common proverb says, *El-Halebi chelebi* ("The man of Aleppo is a gentleman").

The element of the mixed population most in evidence is the Armenian, presumably because it is the most aggressive and active element. The usual unsanitary conditions of Oriental cities prevail in Aleppo. The sewers, such as exist, are open gutters through the middle of the street. Close to Dr. Graham's house was an old Armenian cemetery, surrounded thickly by houses on all sides. The stones all lie flat; the Mussulmans not allowing Christians to be buried with upright head-stones, an honor reserved for the faithful. With a thrift and economy somewhat inconsistent with our ideas of reverence, this old cemetery was utilized by the principal industry in the neighborhood, and dye-stuffs and blue and purple yarn were spread out on the tombstones to dry. There is a thriving trade in forged antiquities at Aleppo, including cuneiform inscriptions and Assyrian and Babylonian cylinders, as we soon learned to our cost. Harper had a small collection of these antiquities awaiting our arrival, which we purchased at a low price, after Hilprecht and I had also looked at them. They turned out to be, almost if not quite without exception, forgeries. Later they were handed over to the Government, in the person of the Kaimakam of Alexandretta, and ought to be in the museum at Constantinople, where I have been unable to find them.

Aleppo itself is an ancient city; and presumably there are real antiquities somewhere under the surface, if one could only dig for them. The city is mentioned in Egyptian records of the second pre-Christian millennium. It is also mentioned in the Assyrian annals. Shalmaneser II. (860–824 B.C.) tells us that the city of Khalman surrendered to him without a siege, whereupon he " offered sacrifices to Dadda (Hadad Rimmon), the god of Khalman." Aleppo seems to be the Khelam (Helam) by which David and his Israelites defeated the Syrians (2 Sam. x., 15 *ff.*); and the country between Aleppo and the Euphrates was known to the Jews as Aram Zobah, in distinction from Aram Naharaim, east of the Euphrates. In the Greek period the place was called Berœa, but it regained its old name with the Arabic conquest. It resisted the crusaders under King Baldwin, and fell twice before the Mongols. Its vicissitudes have been many, and its history long. I had no time to explore for local antiquities, as my business was to leave the place as quickly as possible; but, with the exception of one Hittite and a few Greek and Arabic inscriptions, no traces of the ancient city have been found, excepting the citadel. This rests on an artificial or partly artificial mound, faced with stone, which must have been used for the same purpose for three or four thousand years.

I had a special letter from the Grand Vizier to the Wali Pasha, or Governor-General, but the latter was sick. Mr. Poche, our consular agent, took our affairs in charge, and speedily procured a buyurultu, or special road order, for our party, commending us to all officials in the vilayet of Aleppo (Haleb), as also a letter to the semi-independent Mutessarif of Deir on the Euphrates. The Wali also sent four mounted zaptiehs, or gensdarmes, to be our escort; namely, a captain (or head of a hundred), a sergeant, a corporal (or head of ten), and a private. As we should be obliged to pay all of these men for their services according to their rank, and feed them besides, we objected to the honor of such an escort, and asked for one private only, merely as an evidence that we were under government protection. Finally the sergeant was omitted; but our honorable rank, and the fact that we had brought a special letter of commendation from the Grand Vizier, prevented any further reduction.

It was also necessary to provide ourselves with money of the proper description to circulate on our journey. The standard coin in the Turkish Empire is the gold lira, worth \$4.40. The coin of reckoning is the piastre, one hundred of which nominally make a lira. But as all silver money in the Turkish Empire is at a discount, and the methods of counting differ greatly, you will not find the same estimation at any two important cities. In Baghdad the lira was counted at $102\frac{1}{2}$ piastres, in Constantinople at about 108, in Aleppo it was about 125. But not only does this bewildering difference of estimation exist, the coins in circulation in one place will not pass in another. In Constantinople the common coins were the mejidie, a larger silver coin worth nominally 25 piastres, or quarter of a lira (*i. e.*, $1.10 of our money), but in reality, while I was in Turkey, worth about 80 cents; the quarter mejidie, or beshlik; the piastre and double piastre, all of these modern silver coins; and the para and double para, ancient-looking copper objects, having the general appearance of stamped tin tokens, and worth respectively $\frac{1}{4}$ and $\frac{1}{2}$ piastre. Of all these coins, only the lira, the mejidie, the para, and the double para pass current in all the provinces. In most parts of the empire the smaller silver coins are not to be had, an insufficient number having been coined; and in Baghdad, for some reason, the people will not accept them.

In Aleppo and its neighborhood there are in circulation the most curious and unhandy silver and copper coins of large surface dimensions, but thin, and very often made so concave as to be bowl-shaped, for greater inconvenience. These are all old, some of them dating back to the sixteenth century, or even earlier. They have there, also, a more modern looking coinage, of some copper composite, for fractions of a para. Few of these coins circulate in Baghdad or Constantinople. In other parts of the empire the lack of small currency is supplied by the use of foreign coins. In Baghdad the silver coins in common use are the Indian rupee and the Turkish keran, and their denominations. In Palestine you meet Egyptian copper. Here and there in the interior you meet the Austrian thaler of Maria Theresa. Along the coast you meet francs of every nation in the Latin union, but especially France; and everywhere you are apt to be served with foreign gold coins, French Napoleons, English pounds or Russian imperials, the Turkish gold coinage being almost as insufficient as its silver. Checks do not exist; paper money of the Imperial Ottoman Bank is available only where said bank has a branch; and you are compelled to carry what you need in hard cash, and in denominations suited to your wants, as well as to the idiosyncrasies of the community. Change being so scarce, and so difficult to obtain, it follows as a consequence that you never can obtain it without paying for it. Even in the shops where you are a purchaser you must make the change, and often go out on the street and pay one of the numerous money-changers having stands there a high commission for changing your coin for you. The item of exchange amounts to a great deal in a short time under such circumstances, not to speak of the annoyance of the constant change of currency, and the actual burden of copper and silver which you are obliged to carry, in our case amounting sometimes to a mule-load or more.

Haynes had contracted with a muleteer from Baghdad to furnish us with the proper number of animals, and to be in readiness to start Tuesday morning, December 11th; but there were the usual Oriental delays, and it was Thursday afternoon before we actually got under way. Perhaps it was as well for our comfort that we were delayed; for during the whole intervening time it rained incessantly, and often violently, and in fact it was raining when we finally left Aleppo. Our caravan consisted of twenty-four mules and pack-horses, for which we paid at the rate of about seven dollars an animal for the month's journey to Baghdad. With these were nine Arab muleteers, seven donkeys, a mare, and a dog, who were included in the contract, feeding themselves. This large number of animals was necessitated, first, by the fact that some of the expedition effects had been purchased too late to be sent by the circuitous and very long water journey to Baghdad, and must be carried with us; and, secondly, by the fact that the country through which we were going was so poor, and its poverty so emphasized at that particular time by the failure of crops, that we were compelled to carry with us considerable supplies of food and fodder. Deir, Anah, and Hit were the only places at which we could rely on procuring anything.

We had with us five servants mounted among the packs, of whom Mustafa, our head man, was a Turk and a Mussulman, the rest being Armenians. Nordık, the cook, was a small man of distinctly Indo-European type. Artin or Harootoun and Kework (George) were of the more common heavy Semitic type, which furnishes Constantinople alike with its bankers and its porters; the former fairer, the latter dark, and both large, powerful men. Hajji Kework, or Pilgrim George, our last man, was a Gregorian or orthodox Armenian, while the rest were Protestants, and had made the pilgrimage to Jerusalem, whence his title of Pılgrim. He was distinctly Mongolian or Tartar in type, of somewhat short and squat but powerful frame, broad face and high cheek-bones, with small, narrow, very bright black eyes, swarthy dark complexion, and coarse black hair. He was a remarkably intelligent man, and very active and industrious. He followed us at first on foot, not having been engaged, but seeking employment, and soon made himself so useful that he was not only engaged, but ultimately became my most trusted servant. Our guard consisted of three handsome, manly, well-mounted Kurdish zaptiehs. We ourselves were seven in number, all well mounted and well armed. We were consequently a large and formidable caravan, such as individuals and small parties seek to attach themselves to for the sake of protection in those insecure regions.

It was twenty minutes past two o'clock on Thursday, the 13th of December, 1888, when we finally made our start from Aleppo; and it was scarcely more than two hours later when we halted at the village of Jebrin. This was a cone village, containing, I suppose, about sixty or eighty families. Some of these lived in a single cone hut. The more prosperous a family becomes, the more huts it builds. The house which we occupied consisted of thirteen cones, built around a courtyard, the cones contiguous to one another. These cones, with the upper portions joined by a wall, formed the enclosure on three sides; on the fourth was a wall of field-stones and mud. The bases of these cone huts are built of stones; the upper portions, of mud mixed with chopped straw. The village was full of dogs, which ran from cone to cone along the walls between, barking at all strangers as they passed.

The guest-room assigned to us consisted of two cones, between which there was an arch of stone. The walls within were white-washed, and decorated with painted devices, and ornaments made of painted reeds, feathers, and paper. On both sides of the door outside, in front of the cones, were raised places where the occupants slept in summer. Our cones were further distinguished by possessing a small stone pavement in front of them, raised about two feet above the courtyard. The other huts were flush with the mud of the court, which was abundant and very nasty.

To the south of Jebrin a few columns were visible above the ground; those on the inner side of an inferior sort of marble, those on the cuter of basalt. There were large numbers of basalt troughs about the village, and worked blocks of basalt had been utilized by the natives in building their cones and the walls of their courtyards. I observed three or four interesting pieces, including an old door, made entirely of basalt,—keyhole, bolt holder, and all. This region is full of remains scattered about everywhere; those which are visible on the surface, so far as I observed, all belonging to the late Greek or Byzantine period. Tels were to be seen on all sides.

About half an hour west of Jebrin, and six miles southeast of Aleppo, is the similar cone village of Nirab. At this place there were discovered, in the spring of 1895, two steles with Aramaic inscriptions. Both are tombstone

A Typical Cone Village of Northern Syria.

inscriptions of priests of Sahar-en-Nirab, or the moon god of Nirab, and both are archaic. This town is mentioned by Thothmes III. in the list of conquests made by him in Syria. Not only, therefore, is it an extremely ancient place, but it has also retained its present name unchanged from the earliest times. Presumably many of the other villages and tels which abound in that neighborhood cover equally early remains, although the visible antiquities are all of a later period.

The next morning we were up at half-past four; but it was hard work to start our large caravan promptly, and we did not leave Jebrin until eight o'clock. The first village which we passed was a very small one, Umm-el-Asaine by name. Shortly after passing this, Field, Noorian, and I made a détour southward to the village and tel of Aleb. Evidently this tel represented a ruin of some place which had existed during a number of centuries. From its summit we could still see Aleppo a little to the northwest, while to the north of that again towered the distant Jebel Siman. To the south of us, not very far away, lay the salt lake of Sabghah, and beyond this rose quite abruptly the range of hills called Jebel Has. The people of Aleb said that on the top of Jebel Has there was a plateau with farms and cultivated lands. To the southeast, farther away, lay Jebel Shbeit. There were innumerable villages visible; and the whole plain, as far as the eye could reach, was sowed land. Only one or two villages possessed a few stunted olive-trees. With this exception, there was not a tree in sight. The villages were partly cone villages, and partly they consisted of black, long, low tents, built about with brushwood. These latter represented the transitional state, where the bedouin were beginning to pass over into the condition of house-dwellers. The land in this section belonged, we were told, to wealthy Armenians living in Aleppo. The villagers were all their tenants.

The plain was dotted with tels, evidences of a much larger and more civilized population by which this country had once been occupied. The most important of these ruined mounds seemed to be Tel 'Aran, to the southwest, and Dhamne to the east, with Jebul to the southeast. Near Umm-el-Asaine we saw some indications of an insignificant ruin columns and blocks of basalt and marble, but nothing which would indicate the character or the date. About mid-day we passed Tel Dhamne, and about two o'clock we forded the Nahr-edh-Dhahab, or Golden River, quite a large stream. This is the Daradax of Xenophon, and on this river stood the palace and "paradise" of Satrap Belesis. One would judge from Xenophon's description that in those days the country was by no means destitute of wood, whereas at the present moment there are no trees whatsoever, with the exception of the few stunted olives to which reference has been made. The same process of denudation probably took place here which took place in other parts of what is now the Turkish Empire even before the coming of the Turks. War and invasion resulted in the destruction of forests; and, moreover, the people cut down the trees for their own use, without replanting. But the final catastrophe which made this particular section utterly barren occurred toward the end of the thirteenth century, when Sultan Bibars of Egypt (1260–80), being engaged in war with the Ilkhans of Persia, "caused all the women and children to be removed from northern Syria, while the country was laid waste from Aleppo as far as Mesopotamia and Asia Minor, and the brush and trees were burned, so that the Mongols should find no food for themselves or shelter for their cattle." *

At the point where we crossed the Nahr-edh-Dhahab there was a small tel, Qeris, representing some ancient city or fortress. About three o'clock we came to Tel

---

* Howorth, *History of the Mongols from Ninth to Twelfth Century*, Part III.

Hamaimeh, at the foot of which was a fine spring. We ascended this tel to take observations, and an Arab of the neighborhood, seeing what we were about, ran to assist us. He supposed, as we soon ascertained, that we were making observations with the view of coming in force to dispossess the Turks and take possession of the country. He was a Moslem Arab, but, like all the Arabs, hated the Turks right heartily, and would prefer the rule of some Christian power to their rule.

We had scarcely passed Tel Hamaimeh when it was ascertained that Haynes had left the legs of his camera behind, and a zaptieh was sent back to Aleppo to fetch them. About 4.40 we reached the village of Deir-el-Hafr, Cloister of the Hoof, where there was at the time of the Arab conquest a monastery dedicated to St. John. What ancient city may have stood here I do not know. The present Deir-el-Hafr is a small and very dirty cone village, near a tel of considerable extent but no great height. These tels, generally of a conical shape, are a characteristic feature of the Aleppo plain, and in some parts of the plain almost every village has such a tel in its immediate vicinity. Possibly the curious tel still used as a citadel at Aleppo may furnish an explanation of their meaning and origin. Chesney describes this as having an oval base about 450 by 250 yards. Its height is nearly two hundred feet, and it is chiefly artificial, having its lower slopes faced with stone. The citadel on this cone dates in the main from the times of the crusaders, but it appears certain that the tel itself is far more ancient, and that it was originally built as an artificial hill to contain the acropolis of the city. According to the Arabic historians, it stood outside of the city at the time of the conquest. From the same source we learn that at that time the tel now included in the small town of A'zaz, about twenty miles north of west from Aleppo, was the citadel of that place.

Several caravans which had followed us from Aleppo

with the purpose of securing the protection of our presence on the road to Baghdad—among them an official with the rank of kaimakam on his way to his post at or near Busrah, and a wealthy Baghdad murderer who travelled in a litter—were already there before us; and although our Yuz-Bashi, or captain, went ahead and exercised his authority among the inhabitants, we could secure no good place to spend the night. The Baghdad murderer, as we learned his history a little later, had caused a certain gay young English Lothario in Baghdad, who had done his honor an injury, to be assassinated by night in the suburbs of that city. For this he had been tried and acquitted; but the English Government had prosecuted the case relentlessly, taking it from court to court, until the poor murderer's funds, or rather those of his mother, were almost entirely exhausted. He had just been acquitted at the court of last resort in Constantinople, and was on his way back in triumph, impoverished but vindicated.

We spent the night in two very small and very dirty cone huts,—four of us in one, and three in another. The fleas were countless. During the night an attempt was made by the villagers to steal from both our huts, but without success, thanks to the fleas, which kept us wakeful. We were up before half-past four, glad of the prospect of continuing our journey. It was raining hard. Our huts were flush with the mud outside; and as the rain fell faster and faster, the mud began to flow inside. The muleteers did not wish to start. The Kaimakam and the Baghdad murderer were also opposed to starting, and used their moral influence with our guards to induce them to take the same view of the situation. As the next day was Sunday, we had intended to spend it at rest. They thought that we might just as well stay where we were, and rest the Saturday, instead of travelling in the rain. I gave imperative orders to start, and to start at once, but no progress was made. A portion of the mules had disappeared. It turned out finally that there was a large cave under the village, which was sometimes used as a stable by the inhabitants; and into this a portion of our mules had been driven among the mules of the natives. At length Noorian and the Yuz-Bashi took the muleteer whose mules were missing, and flogged him until he was glad to bring them forth. It was our first conflict with muleteers, and the method in which we won the victory seemed to me shocking. I was afraid that there would be bad blood between us and the muleteers from that time on. In reality, the muleteer who got the flogging seemed to appreciate it thoroughly, and was a good and serviceable and willing servant the rest of the way to Baghdad.

It was not until ten minutes before ten that we made our final start that morning. About mid-day we passed into the real desert. Before this we had travelled between ploughed fields. Now civilization ceased altogether. There were no more villages, and such evidences of habitation as we saw were in the shape of black camel's-hair tents; for the Anazeh Arabs roam through this region, going north and south. About one o'clock we stopped for lunch at Tel Gamgum, about which there were evidences in the shape of smaller mounds of former settlements, but not of any importance. An hour later we reached the Mehdub, where were the remains of large barracks, built in the time of Abdul Aziz, we were told, to hold the Anazeh Arabs in check. About three o'clock we began to pass down a little valley leading from the plateau on which we had been travelling to the Euphrates. At 3.30 Field and I, who were riding in advance of the rest, caught sight of the Euphrates.

Our excitement at the first view of the river was great. We felt as though our work in Babylonia had at last begun. We were on the shores of the great historic river,—The River of the Hebrews, which, in conjunction with the Tigris, had in the course of many centuries made Babylonia, and which was intimately associated with the entire history of the region which we were to explore. We had entered the sphere of Babylonian influence. This river had been the road by which the Babylonians had marched westward, and along which, at a later date, western armies had in their turn marched into Babylonia.

The valley of the Euphrates is to-day an avenue of ruins from Samosat, where it breaks through the Taurus Mountains and enters the Syrian plain, to Ur of the Chaldees and beyond. Along this ancient highway, connecting the East and West, lie the carcasses of the nations that have traversed it,—Babylonian, Assyrian, Hebrew, Persian, Greek, Parthian, Sassanian, Syrian, Palmyrene, Roman, Arab, and Turk,—carcasses of stone and brick and clay, lying along its course, broken and dismembered oftentimes, and heaped together in inextricable confusion, though ever and anon the lifeless body of some ancient city embalmed in desolation still preserves its shape, defiant of the hand of time.

Below Hit, in the alluvial delta of the two rivers, Tigris and Euphrates, existed one of the primeval seats of civilization,—one of Dame Nature's kindergartens to teach her children the rudiments of the higher life. Out of this valley westward, toward the fertile uplands of northern Syria, downward to the rich coast lands of the Mediterranean, outward to Cyprus and the Isles, southward to the rival valley of the Nile, the road of commerce and conquest had been the Euphrates; and for a large part of the way the Euphrates is no more than a road,—a narrow pathway sunk one hundred or two hundred feet beneath the plateau of a sterile wilderness swarming with wild Arabs. In the earliest ages this was the road that led the conquerors out, and over which conquest and civilization travelled westward hand in hand. Later it became the road by which conquerors entered into the very heart of Babylonia. So it was that Babylonian and Egyptian, Syrian and Assyrian, Persian and Greek, Parthian and Roman, Sassanian and Byzantine, Moslem and Christian, surged back and forth along the highway between the Eastern and the Western worlds, battling for possession; while savage Arabs from the surrounding desert watched their opportunity to rob, murder, and plunder the weak and weary contestants, and themselves take possession. It is the records of these struggles that are written in brick and stone and mortar along the shores of the great river.

The Euphrates now flows through a dismal desert,—a stream of muddy water, with tamarisk and poplar jungles, wild licorice and durra fields, and a few small towns and villages, occupying a narrow deep depression in a sterile treeless plateau inhabited only by nomads. But this has not always been the case. In ancient times Mesopotamia, from the river Khabor northward and westward, seems to have been fairly well wooded, well inhabited, and prosperous, while the Syrian side of the river, from the bend by Barbalissus and upward, was rich and densely settled; and even to the south and east of this the ruins of important cities may still be found; and the Assyrian annals tell of forests in the same direction, remnants of which have been but lately rediscovered. In times of prosperity and progress, and when a strong power controlled part or the whole of the Euphrates valley, civilization invaded the desert and established posts and roads, which checked and drove back the Arabs and extended the area of cultivable lands, like the roads and stations between Palmyra and the Euphrates. But war and plunder, unbounded and lawless self-seeking, have done their work; and the rich valley of the Euphrates is now almost uninhabited, while the few small settlements which still exist are compelled for the most part to pay tribute, or brotherhood (kubbe), as it is called, to the Arabs of the desert.

Modern exploration of the Euphrates begins with the year 1835. In that and the two following years, and again in 1841, the English Government undertook a survey and the navigation of the river with a view to securing a shorter route to India. British steamers navigated the stream from Birejik downward to its mouth, and back again to Meskene. "Iron swam on the Euphrates," as the natives expressed it, which some ancient prophet had predicted as one of the portents that should precede the overthrow of the Ottoman dominion. But here the English let the matter rest; for in course of time the Suez Canal made a Euphrates valley railroad or a Euphrates line of steamboats unnecessary from the strategical point of view of safe and speedy communication with India, and even deprived the Euphrates of such commercial importance to the outside world as it had until then possessed. Some thirty years later the famous and enterprising Midhat Pasha, while Governor-General of Baghdad, perceiving the great importance of the river commercially and strategically as a means of communication between the eastern and western portions of the Turkish Empire, endeavored to establish a regular steamboat service upon its waters, and also to hold the Arabs in check by a strong line of military stations. For a couple of years steamboats ascended the river annually as far as Meskene, and it seemed as though the Euphrates were about to regain some part of its ancient importance. But these hopes proved short-lived: the Russian-Turkish war intervened, and the reactionary party gained the ascendancy. Midhat "died" in exile in Arabia, and the rest of the Europeanizing party apostatized or disappeared: so the Euphrates fell asleep once more. To be sure, the Sultan as Sultan has granted to the Sultan as private concessionnaire the monopoly of steam navigation on the Euphrates River, and a very inaccurate map has been prepared under Turkish auspices for the guidance of said august concessionnaire. There is also a line of zaptieh stations along the river sufficient to collect taxes from the fellaheen and give escort to Turkish officials, but not enough to subdue the Arabs and afford real protection to the country.

Meskene, the station at which we had planned to spend the night, lies at the point where the Euphrates most closely approaches the Mediterranean (about 101 miles). A little below this the river bends quite sharply toward the east. Either Meskene, or the ancient Barbalissus (two miles lower down), or Thapsacus (six miles below that), forms the natural port of Syria on the Euphrates; and on account of this there has probably always been a town near this point. Some of the most famous ruins on the Euphrates lie above Meskene,—such as Jerabus, the ancient Carchemish, the Hittite capital, where Nebuchadrezzar defeated Pharaoh Necho (Jer., xlvi., 2); Bir or Birtha, the modern Birejik, a zeugma or point of passage of the river from the earliest times to the present day; and Samosat or Samosata, the capital of Comagene, the Kumukh of the Assyrian inscriptions, situated near the point at which the Euphrates breaks a passage through the Taurus Mountains. The cities of this region are mentioned over and over again in the Egyptian and Assyrian records. Had it been practicable, I should have liked to march from Aleppo to Samosat, and thence follow the Euphrates downwards. This was of course impossible, and we had taken the shortest road from Aleppo to the Euphrates, without regard to ruins.

It was our intention, as already stated, to spend our first night on the Euphrates at the zaptieh station of Meskene. This proved to be a long and hard ride of an hour and a half down the Euphrates valley, through very sticky mud. One of our zaptiehs, who had been sent on in advance, had arranged for our accommodation in quite comfortable quarters, which were very acceptable; for it had rained all day, part of the time hard, and we were wet and cold. One of our men, Artin, had fever during the night. We occupied a long, low room, in which there was a rough, dirty platform raised above the ground on either side for seats and sleeping-places, and in the walls of which there were holes for windows. Our men cooked and slept at one end of the room; we were in the middle; and some stone-cutters and shepherds occupied the other end.

A military surgeon stationed at Meskene, a Cypriote by origin, paid us two or three visits, bringing with him a musical album, which was evidently a rarity and a great treasure in that wilderness, and which he, poor fellow, supposed would please us as much as it pleased him and his fellow-members of the garrison. On Sunday morning he set it going while we were holding prayers, rather disconcerting by his well-meaning entertainment the seriousness of our devotions. It was quite pathetic to observe the loneliness of this half-educated man, acting as surgeon in a garrison of Turkish soldiers. He was a graduate of the Imperial Medical School at Constantinople. He was the first military surgeon whom I had met, but from later experience I should suppose that almost all of them are either Christians or Jews. I cannot speak highly of the medical training which they receive in the Medical School at Constantinople. Besides the surgeon, the only other disturbing element which we encountered at Meskene was cats, which walked over our faces in the night as we slept, and induced much disturbance and some slight profanity in the camp, men hurling their boots at the cats, and hitting, not the cats, but unoffending comrades.

Sunday morning dawned cold and clear. We observed the day as one of rest and recuperation, and killed a sheep to make a feast for our muleteers as well as for ourselves. In the evening the zaptieh whom we had despatched to Aleppo arrived, bringing the legs of the camera. The following morning, Monday the 17th, our advanced guard, Field, Noorian, a zaptieh, and I, were on the march by half-past seven. Three quarters of an hour's riding brought us to the ruins of ancient Barbalissus, now known as Kal'at Balis; at least that is the name given to the ruins on Kiepert's map, but the only name which we heard among the natives was Old Meskene. The ruins are extensive. Most conspicuous is a minaret of brick, with several lines of Arabic inscription in Kufic characters. This inscription was so far above the ground that it was impossible to obtain an accurate transcript. Noorian copied three lines, which seem to read: "In the name of God, the merciful and gracious, Bekr Mohammed ibn Eyub Khalil, prince of believers, has gone up." As I am unable to identify this Bekr Mohammed ibn Eyub, the inscription does not help to date the minaret. Chesney describes this as " a remarkably fine octagonal tower, rising from a square base to the height of 75 feet, and having an interior staircase."[*] Ainsworth adds that there were, in connection with the minaret, "several sepulchral chapels, Saracenic arches, and fragments of other edifices and structures."[†] With both of these statements my observations agreed, excepting that I should scarcely call the large vaults beneath and about the minaret " sepulchral chapels."

Part of the ruins of Balis are Arabic, and part Roman. To the latter category belong a badly ruined square tower with a wall of enormous thickness, and the remains of a large building in which lay some good capitals of the Græco-Roman period. It may have been this tower which was pointed out to Benjamin of Tudela, in 1163 A.D., as the

[*] *Expedition to the Euphrates and Tigris*, vol. i , p. 416.
[†] *A Personal Narrative of the Euphrates Expedition*, vol. 1., p 260.

remains of "the tower of Balaam the son of Beor. (May the name of the wicked rot!)," which he built for magical purposes. Benjamin accordingly identified the site with Pethor on the Euphrates of the Book of Numbers, the home of Balaam the soothsayer. In this he is mistaken, for "Pethor by the River" of the Hebrews is manifestly identical with Ana-Ashur-utir-azbat, "To Ashur I have taken and restored the city, which the Hittites call Pitru," mentioned several times in the inscriptions of Shalmaneser II., King of Assyria (860–824 B.C.), as situated "on the river Sagura on the farther side of the Euphrates." The Sagura is the modern Sajur, which empties into the Euphrates two or three days' journey above Balis, not far south of the ancient Carchemish. More precisely Pethor has not yet been located. While it is probable that the site of Balis was occupied from the earliest times, yet our knowledge of the place dates only from the Roman period, when it appears as Barbalissus, or, according to Ptolemy, Barbarissus. In the Talmud it is called Barbarith. The place played a part in the crusades, and was taken by Tancred in the year 1111. In the first part of the next century it was captured by Zenghis Khan and his Tartars. In the latter part of the same century Abu'lfeda, prince and geographer, describes it as "a port of the Syrians"; that is, a place from which they took ship for Irak. It was finally destroyed by the Sultan Suleiman in the sixteenth century, we are told, in consequence of a religious quarrel.

An hour beyond Barbalissus, on a point of the plateau jutting well into the Euphrates valley, were the ruins of an old fort called Sheikh Hasan. Chesney and Ainsworth incorrectly describe this as a tomb. A moat had been cut to separate this point or promontory from the plateau behind. Owing to the frost, which had glazed the surface of the cliff with a thin coating of ice, we found the greatest difficulty in ascending to the neighborhood of this fort. The rock of the fort we could not scale at all, but did ultimately succeed in reaching the plateau behind the moat. On the southeastern slope of this was a round building, which from appearances we judged to belong to the mediæval Arabic period, in which case the fort should probably be assigned to the same date. But what the original name of the place was, or by whom it was built, I do not know. While Field was making observations here, my horse, Niffer, which I had staked safely, as I thought, broke loose, jumped a deep gulley, found his way to Field's horse, Munger, which had been staked at a considerable distance from him, and made a fierce attack upon him. The latter broke loose also, and the two together went in search of the horse of the zaptieh, and a tripartite battle was joined. We were all afraid, knowing the fury with which stallions fight, that one or more of our animals would be killed or maimed, or that all of them might stampede into the desert, and leave us alone on a promontory overlooking the desolate Euphrates valley. It had taken from a half hour to an hour to ascend the slippery, icy surface of the cliff; and we were compelled to make the ascent two by two, one helping the other; but in my excitement I descended on the run, jumping from ledge to ledge, which, if I had slipped, would have insured an accident of the most serious character. I arrived in the nick of time, and, by dint of attacking the three fighting horses with shouts and stones, I succeeded in getting hold of the end of Niffer's rope, and pulling him out of the *melée*. By the time I had dragged him off and staked him, and had returned to secure another combatant, the zaptieh, who had slid down most of the way on his hands and seat, arrived, and we separated the other horses. This was a sample of the conflicts between our horses, which we were obliged to guard against constantly.

From Sheikh Hasan on for about an hour the Euphrates ran so close to the cliffs, that the path was very narrow, and at times almost dangerous. The white cliffs rose from two to three hundred feet above us on our right. The rock is very soft, and immense fragments are constantly falling. At the end of an hour we reached the small ruin of Kal'at Dibse. At this point the bluffs cease, and are succeeded by low hills like those which border the Euphrates on the other side; and these hills, receding, form a great bay, on the edge of which Kal'at Dibse is situated. The ruins now visible are of brick, and rather insignificant in appearance; but the name and site at once suggested to me that they were the remains of a place of great importance, namely, Thapsacus,—the famous zeugma, or place of passage of the Euphrates. Thapsacus is the Græco-Latin transliteration of the Semitic name Tiphsah,—that is, place of passage, or ford,—which we find in the Hebrew Scriptures as the name of the city at the northeastern boundary of Solomon's kingdom on the Euphrates: "For he had dominion over everything beyond the river, from Tiphsah even to Gaza" (1 Kings iv., 24). Now, the name Dibse, allowance being made for the change of the mutes from surds to sonants, is identical with Tiphsah. The place was, I knew, approximately in the position assigned to Thapsacus by the Greek and Latin writers. The situation, in itself considered, was an admirable one, commanding a fertile plain formed by a deep bay setting into the plateau, and backed by a narrow defile along the river to the northeast. Moreover, the situation permitted that ready communication with the southwest which the historical references to Tiphsah or Thapsacus require. When I reached camp that evening, I consulted everything which our small portable library contained. The only reference to Tiphsah that I found was in Sachau's *Reise durch Syrien und Mesopotamien;* but he identified el-Hammam, a site one day and a half farther down the stream, with

Tiphsah. As I learned later, he did so on the authority of Chesney's Euphrates and Tigris Expedition. Chesney's ground of identification was the discovery in the river near el-Hammam of some masonry with lead clamps, on account of which the natives call the place Hadjar-Ressass (stone and lead). But el-Hammam does not correspond with the position ascribed to Thapsacus in Xenophon's Anabasis; namely, three days' journey, of five parasangs each, beyond the Daradax. Moreover, el-Hammam does not control the southwestward road toward Hamath and Emesa, as Thapsacus should, but the road south toward Palmyra. In point of fact, as Ainsworth, who was with Chesney, shows in his description of the site, without understanding the bearings of his evidence, el-Hammam was the ancient Sura, a border fortress of the Roman Empire toward the east until the time of Diocletian. It manifestly, therefore, could not have been Thapsacus. Dibse, on the other hand, which was already sufficiently identified by its name as ancient Tiphsah, was at precisely the proper distance from the edh-Dhahab River, the Daradax of Xenophon. There is also at this point a "camel ford," which corresponds with the account of the passage of the river given by Xenophon.

This was the great zeugma, or place of passage, of the river Euphrates for the caravans of commerce, and also for invading armies moving both eastward and westward. It is at the bend of the stream where it changes from a southerly to an easterly course, eight miles below Meskene, and six below the ancient Barbalissus. Situated as it was on a large fertile bay in the valley of the stream, with a depression in the plateau behind it, down which descended the roads from Hamath, Emesa, and Damascus, it was well adapted to become a great commercial emporium, and to command the road between East and West. At this point was the extreme limit of the Hebrew

Empire in the days of the glory of King David, when Judah aimed at the dominion of southwestern Asia. To accomplish his designs it was necessary to control the passage of the Euphrates, and for that purpose he held Tiphsah. For the same reason it was occupied by the Assyrians and Babylonians. Here it was that at a later date Cyrus the Younger informed his Grecian troops that they were marching against the Great King; and when they hesitated whether to follow him or to turn back, Menon, anxious to show his allegiance, plunged into the stream, and led his Thessalians across through water that did not quite reach to the neck, for the Persians had destroyed the bridge of boats which formerly spanned the river at this point. Thapsacus was a large city in those days, so Xenophon tells us. Alexander crossed the river at the same point, carrying the victorious arms of the West into the very heart of the East. Here he launched in the river the vessels which he caused to be built by Phœnicians in the Mediterranean, and carried overland to this point, imitating wittingly or unwittingly the example of Sennacherib, who, finding it impossible to conquer Merodach-Baladan and his Chaldean followers in any other manner, built ships on the Mediterranean coast, transported them overland to Til Barsip, the modern Birejik, launched them in the Euphrates, manned them with Phœnician sailors, and so navigated the Persian Gulf and conquered the Chaldeans in their last stronghold on the Elamite coast (694 B.C.).

Some time after the Christian era, Thapsacus began to lose importance; and finally, in the fourth century A.D., it passed altogether out of knowledge. By a happy chance we had rediscovered this ancient biblical and classical site, so important in history, because it controlled one of the main passages of the great river, and was a point of transfer on the direct road of commerce between the lands to the northeast and the lands to the southwest of the Euphrates. I announced the discovery in *The Nation*, May 23, 1889. On the 25th of July, in the same year, Dr. Bernhard Moritz read a paper before the Royal Prussian Academy on "The Ancient Palmyrene Country," in which he announced a similar identification. It is to be hoped that some future explorer may be able to delay at this point at least long enough to determine the precise direction of the road or roads leading inland from Dibse, and to ascertain whether any Roman milestones are yet to be found there. Some day, moreover, the site must be excavated.

CHAPTER V.

THE CITY OF ZENOBIA.

Mules and Pedometers—Battle of Siffin—Castle Ja'ber—Lions and Wild Pigs—Ruins of Sura—The Roman Frontier—Resafa a Desert City—Nikephorium—Rakka—Alexander and Harun-er-Rashid—Unknown Ruins—Turkish Administration—The el-Hamme Gorge—Palmyrene Tombs—A Skeleton City—A Twin Fortress—Story of Zenobia—Castle Dabausa—Deir ez-Zor—A Wily Priest—Forged Antiquities—Population of Deir—Civilizing the Arabs—Incidents of Travel.

OUR second night on the Euphrates was spent at the zaptieh station of Abu Hareire, which was so small and mean that we encamped outside of it. Abu Hareire lies on the same large bay in the plateau in which Dibse is situated, and is seven hours and a half from Meskene. One caravan hour is usually estimated as three miles. In my experience caravan rates differ considerably, according to the roads, the mules, and the muleteers, and even from day to day according to the moods of the two last; but I should set the average at nearer two and three quarters than three miles an hour. Field and I tried to ascertain the actual average rate of our caravan by placing a pedometer on the head mule; but the superstitious muleteer broke the instrument in pieces the first day, and then reported that the mule had done it. Unfortunately we had no more pedometers.

It rained during the night, and the next day was disagreeable, although but little rain fell. Our course lay eastward across the plain to the ruins of a town which the zaptiehs called Abu Hareire. It is situated on a nose of rock running down to the very edge of the river. There is an old minaret here, not unlike the one at Barbalissus, and about this are ruins of a mosque and perhaps of some other buildings. Higher up on the hill are more extensive remains. In the soft limestone of the bluff near the river shore caves have been hollowed out, which are used partly as sheepfolds, partly as troglodytic dwellings. I presume that these are the ruins of Siffin, or Sikkin of the Arabs, Sephe of the Romans. It was in this neighborhood that Ali and Moawia fought the great battle, so important for the future of Islam, with the caliphate as the prize, in the year 657 A.D. Ali had almost won the victory, when Moawia's troops put the Koran on their lances, and demanded the cessation of hostilities and an appeal to the sacred book. Ali's own followers compelled him to yield to this demand, with the result that Moawia became caliph, and Ali saint and martyr.

Opposite Siffin, on the other side of the Euphrates, was a ruin of fine appearance called Kal'at Ja'ber. This first appears, perhaps as early as the third century A.D., as Dauser or Dausara. In the account of the fatal Persian campaign of Julian the Apostate, it is called the Castle of Dauana; and Procopius, the historian of Justinian, calls it Dabanas. Near it Chesney and Ainsworth reported a small ruin called Deir Mahariz. Benjamin of Tudela calls this Sela Mid Bara, and says that a large colony of Jews lived there in his day. Later Ja'ber and Mahariz played quite a part in the conquest of this country by the Seljukian Turks. Suleiman the grandson of Seljuk was drowned in the Euphrates near here, and buried at Mahariz. Afterwards Sultan Selim the Grim (1512-20) built a mausoleum and founded a convent of dervishes in his honor. The present ruins of Castle Ja'ber are said to date from the time of Selim. Both Ja'ber and Mahariz are now uninhabited.

For almost an hour after leaving Siffin our road lay close to the cliffs, with a tamarisk jungle on our left, where the zaptiehs said that there were lions. The caravan was therefore brought carefully together, no animals being allowed to straggle. It is a fact that there are lions in the jungles of the upper Euphrates; and we found many persons who related stories of meeting them, or gave us authentic information of encounters on the part of others. There are abundant traces of wild pigs all over the Euphrates plain, and the amount of surface rooted up by these animals is almost incredible. I have seen, as we rode along in the early morning, acres of land which looked as though freshly ploughed, but which had in reality been rooted up by wild pigs in the course of one night. Nevertheless, although these creatures were so abundant, in my four trips up and down the Euphrates I never actually saw one. Looking down upon the tamarisk jungle from the bluffs above, we could often see hundreds of jackals busily running hither and thither, but we never saw either a lion or a pig.

At 4.20 P.M. we reached the site of the zaptieh station of el-Hammam, but were told that the station itself had been swept away in the inundations of the previous year, 1888. We were therefore compelled to pitch our tents by the side of the tamarisk jungle near a solitary Arab hut. While hunting in the jungle for partridges or waterfowl, I found several other huts, and met a number of armed Arabs. When I asked some of these Arabs of the Euphrates valley what they called themselves, they responded, "Fellaheen"; and on further inquiry I found that the river valley is divided into innumerable districts or tribes, each of which has a different name. These fellaheen, or tillers of the soil, are, I presume, the almost unchanged descendants of the men who tilled the soil here in the times of Sargon, Abraham, David, Sardanapallus, Nebuchadrezzar, and Alexander. They are very miserable, and very low in the scale of civilization. They are oppressed by the bedouin, who levy kubbe (the so-called brotherhood money) upon them at will; while the Turkish authorities, although affording them no protection, plunder them even more ruthlessly, under the name of taxation. A number of very dirty and half-naked specimens brought us milk, and stood about our camp-fire begging for tobacco. The muleteers and zaptiehs told dreadful stories of lions, and an immense bonfire was kept burning all night, while armed watchmen guarded the animals. However, we heard nothing but the wail of countless jackals, like the lamentations of disembodied babies.

The next morning we started at a quarter before six. The night had been cold with quite a severe frost, and we could get no water to wash in before starting. Our breakfast consisted of hot milk and hardtack. The day was beautiful but very cold. We rode at first with the full moon behind us and the flush of dawn in front. While it was still dark we passed the ruins of Hammam. The name " Hot Baths " suggests some ancient watering-place, but there are very many ruins and towns of this name in Turkey at the present time which could not originally have been watering-places. Later generations have often imagined that the ruins which they saw must represent great bathing establishments, and have named them Hammam accordingly. These ruins represented in reality the ancient Sura, which was for three centuries a border fortress of the Romans against the Parthians, until Diocletian (286-306) pushed forward the border to the river Khabor. The frontier on the Euphrates was guarded in the earlier days of the Roman Empire by Kallinikus, now Rakka, on the Mesopotamian side of the river, and Sura on the Syrian side. Below the latter there was a chain of fortresses—Resafa, Oriza, Cholle, Aracha, and Palmyra—guarding the eastern frontier. Sura was captured by Chosroes in 540 A.D. Procopius says that it was a town lying on the Euphrates River next to Zenobia, and that it had such despicable fortifications that when Chosroes besieged it, it could not hold out even for half an hour, but was forthwith taken by the Persians. At that time it had a population of 12,000. It was recaptured by Justinian's famous general, Belisarius; and Procopius gives the following account of the rebuilding and fortification of the place by Justinian: "But King Justinian, having rebuilt this also, like Kallinikus, and surrounded the small town entirely with a very strong wall, and fortified it with an outwork, it was prepared no longer to yield to attacking enemies." It is mentioned in the next century, in the history of the Moslem conquest, as an important fortress. It fell into the hands of the Arabs almost immediately after the conquest of the fortress Zenobia. After that time the place has no history. Chesney found the name "Sooreah," or "Suria," still attached to the ruins, but I heard only the name "Hammam." The ruins here, like those at Dibse and Barbalissus, are of brick.

The passage of the Euphrates connecting Sura with Kallinikus did not lie directly opposite Sura, but some distance farther down the Euphrates, much nearer to Kallinikus than to Sura. It is the remains of the bridge connecting these two places which Chesney found, and which he supposed to be the remains of the bridge of Thapsacus. This bridge was almost directly opposite the very picturesque ruins of Harakla, on the Mesopotamian side of the river. Harakla is evidently some ancient Heraklea, but further information about its history we do not possess. Sachau visited it in 1879, and reported the ruins to be those of a castle of the Roman-Greek period. He supposes it to have been erected to protect the passage of the river. It is built of great blocks of white gypsum, like the Roman fortresses farther down the river on the Syrian side.

About a day's journey (twenty-two Roman miles) almost due south in the desert stand the ruins of Resafa, the Reseph of the Bible (2 Kings, xix., 12), one of the oldest cities of this region. It is mentioned in the Assyrian annals, between the years 818 and 737 B.C., and its governor was one of the eponyms of the famous Eponym Lists, which shows that at that time it was an Assyrian city, and not merely a subject kingdom. It appears in the lists always either just before or just after Nisibis. Later, as already mentioned, it became a Roman frontier fortress against the Parthians and Persians, and a station on the route from Palmyra to the Euphrates. Jaubert, in 1840, described Resafa thus: "It is entirely deserted, but cannot be called ruinous; the walls and many of the interior buildings being in an excellent state of preservation. The town displays a mixture of ancient, with Saracenic, Mohammedan, and Christian architecture; the last being of a comparatively late period, since there is a well-built modern Greek church within the walls." I was unable to visit the town on any of my trips past it, and Sachau had the same experience. Either there were hostile Arabs in the neighborhood, or no guide could be found, or there was no water to be had at the ruins, and no way of carrying any. A native who professed to be well acquainted with the ruins of Resafa, and who seemed to be a man of intelligence rather above the common, assured me that it can be visited only in the spring, on account of the lack of water. There are no inscriptions above the ground, according to him, but by digging many can be found. At my urgent request, Haynes made a successful attempt to visit Resafa on his way to Nippur in 1893, and reported substantially what Jaubert had reported half a century earlier. The ruins which both these travellers saw probably date chiefly from Justinian's restoration of the place in the sixth century A.D.

At eleven o'clock we were opposite the extensive ruins of Nikephorium, or Kallinikus, now known as Rakka. This lies near the mouth of the river Belikh. It was erected by Alexander the Great after his successful passage of the river Euphrates. Later it took the name of Kallinikus from Seleucus Kallinikus. Nikephorium, or Kallinikus was, as already stated, a frontier fortress against the Parthians and Persians until the time of Diocletian. Julian, on his Persian expedition in 363 A.D., found it to be both a strongly fortified city, and also a place of considerable commercial importance; and such it continued throughout the Roman period. A century after the Arab conquest the Abbasside caliphs rebuilt the place, and changed the name to Rakka (exalted). Here Harun-er-Rashid established his residence after he had aroused disaffection in Baghdad by the murder of the Barmecides. It offered a stout resistance to Tamerlane and his Tartars in the fourteenth century, and was still an important city when the Ottoman Turks annexed this region in the first half of the sixteenth century. Since then it has fallen into ruins. Chesney found it quite uninhabited; but when Sachau visited it, a force of from thirty to forty wild Turkish zaptiehs were stationed there. Both Ainsworth and Sachau report the ruins as very extensive. Ainsworth says that almost everything above ground is Arabic. The remains of Harun-er-Rashid's palace he pronounces very fine. The city lay on the edge of the plateau, overlooking the Euphrates valley. It was decagonal in shape, and the walls were built of brick.

On our side of the river there were two small mounds called el-Habash. On one of these were Arab graves, one of which had been dug up by jackals or hyenas the night before. There were several coarse, red marble columns lying about. Half an hour eastward lay another mound called Kubba (dome).

At one o'clock we came to cliffs rising abruptly out of the river. A path had once existed at the base of these cliffs; but this had been swept away in the inundations of the previous summer, and we were compelled to make a détour over the gypsum hills and the plateau above. We returned to the valley again at the earliest possible moment by a very precipitous route, which the caravan avoided. We lost the latter, accordingly, and did not rejoin it until it had almost reached the station of Sabghat. On a bluff of the plateau, a quarter of an hour before reaching the latter place, we saw a ruinous fort called el-Heil, apparently the same as the Nechele of Moritz's map, but not given on any other map, so far as I know. Almost every one who journeys over this route finds some new ruins, and a glance at the map of Ptolemæus shows that there must be still many places awaiting discovery. Unfortunately his map of the region is so incorrect in regard to what we do know, that it does not materially help us to identify what we do not know.

Sabghat is the residence of a mudir, the official next in rank below a kaimakam. In the Turkish administration there are first provinces, under the government of a wali, or governor-general. These provinces are divided into sanjaks, each sanjak administered by a mutessarif, or governor; the sanjaks are divided into kaimakamliks, governed by a kaimakam; each kaimakamlik in its turn is divided into mudirliks, administered by a mudir. There was no village at Sabghat, but only a station for a half dozen zaptiehs, with a khan for the Mudir. Here we exchanged the three Kurdish zaptiehs whom we had brought from Aleppo for two Circassians. Regularly, zaptiehs should be exchanged at each station, but by a special arrangement the three who came with us from Aleppo were to conduct us to the border of the vilayet of Haleb. Of course they expected and received a baksheesh for their services.

We rode all the next day through a flat plain, absolutely without a point of interest, arriving at Ma'dan, a station with five zaptiehs, at 2.45 P.M. The next morning, sending one of our zaptiehs, a Turk, with the caravan, with which went also Hilprecht and Prince, the rest of us with the other zaptieh, who was a Kurd, started to visit the ruins of Halebieh. The caravan went by the regular road, back over the plateau, while we followed a rougher road along the valley. The hills, which were of gypsum mixed with sand, were at first low and even rolling. We rode very fast, and the Kurd's mare made our animals almost unmanageable. About ten o'clock we reached the ruined fort of Kassabe, on a small hill a little distance from the river, by which there was also a deserted and dilapidated mud village. On the plain were two or three tent villages. The plain was all of it cultivated in durra, which rendered riding difficult, for wherever the land is cultivated it is cut up into small plots by little dikes containing irrigating canals. The water to supply these is raised from the river either by water-wheels (naouras), or by ox-buckets. At about this point a ridge of trachyte, called el-Hamme, begins to approach the Euphrates. It has been forced up through the gypsum and limestone to a height, close to the river, of three hundred or four hundred feet. Through this the Euphrates breaks its way in a narrow gorge, having a minimum width, according to Chesney, of two hundred and fifty yards, and a depth of seven fathoms. The greater part of the el-Hamme range is on the south side of the Euphrates, and extends, we were told, two or three days' journey back into the desert in the direction of Palmyra. Just at the commencement of this gorge, on the Mesopotamian side of the river, Sachau found on a height the ruins of a town built of gypsum and basalt, and along the river in the valley below the remains of a dam or dike. These ruins were called Jabr Abu 'Atish.

About eleven o'clock we reached the ruins which our guide called Halebieh, situated in a valley in the el-Hamme. The river at this point runs due north and south. The valley in which the ruins lie is peculiarly barren and wild looking, and is strewn everywhere with large blocks of trachyte. To the north of the city there is the bed of a mountain torrent. Here there are a number of tower tombs of the Palmyrene type, besides a considerable number of rock-cut tombs. One of the tower tombs, the most northerly, which appeared to be better preserved than the rest, I visited. Outside the walls were of gypsum, much crumbled; but within they were of small pieces of trachyte set in much mortar and plastered over. A flight of steps wound around within, and in the heart of the tower was a chamber about nine feet square and fifteen feet high. On each of the four sides of this was a broad niche some five feet above the floor, and below these niches smaller niches with pointed arches. At one end of each of the large niches, raised about three feet above its floor, was a hole four feet long and two and a half feet high. These niches were the receptacles for the dead, but all were empty.

Ainsworth found in one of the tombs in this neighborhood an unintelligible Greek inscription; while in another Lynch unearthed a female mummy, its face covered with a thin mask of gold-leaf. No later traveller has ever found anything, and very few have even visited the place.

Chesney, in describing these ruins, says that "the necropolis occupies a prominent situation in the valley, and along the declivity of the hill westward of the town, and it is remarkable for a number of square towers of precisely the same construction as those near Palmyra. These monuments of mortality usually consist of three stories, the lowest and middle appear to have been tenements of the dead, whilst the upper story served as a place of defence, and terminated either with a flat or a pyramidal roof surrounded by battlements." The ruins of the city itself, which according to his measurement is twenty-six miles from the town of Deir, he thus describes, after saying that the walls are built of fine gypsum: "In the town are the ruins of a temple, and an extensive palace containing many ornamented apartments; and also numerous well-constructed private dwellings, supported by arches; and in general the buildings are so well preserved that the mind can scarcely be brought to feel that all have so long been unoccupied."

Either this description was inaccurate, or the ruins have changed much in the last sixty years. The tombs in the necropolis are, as stated, distinctly of the Palmyrene type, but much less pretentious and imposing than those of Palmyra. The city, as one sees it from without, is admirably preserved; and indeed it is a surprise, the effect of which I can hardly describe, to find directly across one's path in a gorge of these barren trachyte hills, where the Euphrates is at its wildest, what seems to be a walled city in perfect preservation. It is built in the form of a triangle, its base along the Euphrates, and its apex on an isolated hill 315 feet in height. The walls are strengthened by towers 150 to 250 feet apart; and so well are they preserved, that as you stand without, they look almost as though built yesterday. But you enter by the gate, to which the valley road conducts you, not a living city, but the skeleton of a city, disembowelled and fleshless. Within the walls all is blank; only on the northern side, half-way up the hill, partly within and partly without the wall line, stands a palace fortress of early Byzantine style, fairly well preserved (F in the cut). This building has fine domes of brickwork and arches. It was once three stories in height, and two of the three stories are still well preserved. At A and A' on the cut are the principal gateways with large tower buildings, and a paved street runs through the city from one gate to the other. These towers and also the other smaller towers along the walls all had vaulted rooms within, and all are evidently of Byzantine construction. At B″, and apparently also at B and B′, there were smaller gates. I say apparently at B and B′, for the walls along the Euphrates were not so well preserved as those on the other two sides. The river at the present time is about one hundred feet from the walls, and must always have been about the same distance away, but in flood it washes against them.

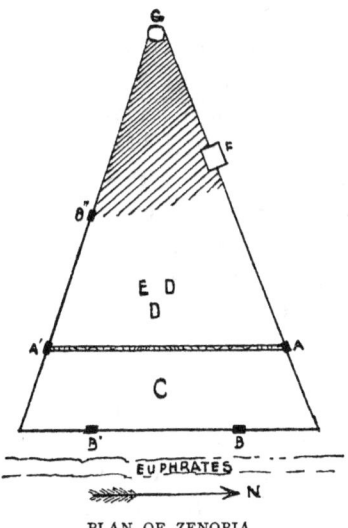

PLAN OF ZENOBIA.

At C we found a couple of capitals of the late Corinthian transition period. Perhaps there had been a colonnade at this point. At E there seemed to have been a market-place or forum. Several columns and troughs were visible; but no plan could be traced without excavation, as everything was too much buried. At D and D′ were the remains of two buildings with apses, exactly orientated, which, as far as I could judge without excavation, were once churches. At B″ the hill begins to be very steep. The acropolis at its apex, and a small part of the south wall adjoining the acropolis, are of different work from the rest of the city. The walls elsewhere are built of large blocks of gypsum cut in rectangles; but here the stones are smaller and of irregular shape, trachyte also being used. This part of the wall and the tower, or acropolis, on the hill, seem to have been destroyed, and rebuilt with fragments of trachyte found ready to hand. The acropolis must have been a place of great strength, owing to its situation. Even on the city side the wall is difficult to scale, on account of the steepness of the hill. It is too much ruined to determine the plan; but there are vaults built of brick masonry underneath the structure, which reminded me somewhat of those at Mount Pagos in Smyrna, excepting that they are smaller, and only one of them is threefold. At the time of my visit there were no other ruins in the city; but stones from the houses which once lined the streets have been used by the Arabs to build rude shelters for themselves and their sheep, and a cave in the hill (near B″) has served a similar purpose. South of the city there are a few more tombs, and also the foundations of two rough basalt walls running from the hills to the river, which seem to have been an outer line of fortification. On the other side of the river, from one to two miles lower down, on a bluff with a valley behind, stand the ruins of Zelebi, or Chelebi, which were visited by Sachau, and are described by him, in his *Reise durch Syrien und Mesopotamien*, as a castle or fortress rather than a city. Moritz identifies this latter place satisfactorily with Chanuga, mentioned by Procopius. Just below Zelebi, according to Chesney and Ainsworth, are the remains of a canal which ran to the Khabor, and which is ascribed by Isidorus of Charax to Semiramis. The el-Hamme dike of trachyte continues for about an hour beyond Halebieh, and the road between the hills and the river is at places very narrow. At the narrowest point I observed remains of what looked like a barrier or gateway of gypsum blocks. There were quantities of katta, or pin-tailed grouse, among the ruins; but these birds are exceedingly shy, and difficult to shoot. I succeeded in obtaining only one.

Haynes made some nine photographic exposures at Halebieh; but all of his photographs, up to and including Deir, turned out failures, for a reason already mentioned. This is the more to be regretted in the case of Halebieh, as we had placed considerable reliance upon the success of our photographs, and made our sketches and descriptions in connection with them, and also because no other photographs of this interesting ruin had ever been taken.

At the time of my first visit I could learn no other name for these ruins than Halebieh. Later I found that the place is still known in Damascus and at Palmyra by its ancient name of Zenobia. It was an outpost of Palmyra in the time of its splendor to control the commerce of the Euphrates. Fortunately for our knowledge of the history of this place, Procopius devotes much space to an account of its fortification by Justinian. It was the middle one of three castles which Justinian built in the desert along the Euphrates; Sura being above it, and Mambri below it. Zenobia had built a small town here, which she had named after herself. In Justinian's time the walls of this town had become so ruinous that they were absolutely no protection against the Persians, who entered it at will. Justinian resolved to rebuild it entirely, to colonize it with a sufficient number of fighting men, and to make it a bulwark and an outpost against the Persians. Inasmuch as it was far removed from assistance, it was necessary to make it very strong, which the original Zenobia had not been, for it had been overlooked by an overhanging hill. In short, Justinian enlarged the original Zenobia considerably, and changed its shape, giving it its present triangular form, with the citadel occupying the overhanging hill. This latter he surrounded with a wall on all sides, both within and without the city. On the river side, since in time of flood the river sometimes rose to the top of the battlements, doing the walls much injury, he built as a protection an outside wall of trachyte. But not only did he provide for the defence of the place, he also built there churches and a government house, and added to this public baths and markets. It is substantially the city of Justinian, described by Procopius, the ruins of which the traveller sees at Zenobia to-day.

It was near the town named after herself that Aurelian is supposed to have captured the famous Queen of the East in 272 A.D., after her five days' flight from Palmyra on a she-camel. A woman of a different sort played a part in the surrender of the city to the Arabs almost four hundred years later, if we may believe the romantic story of the Arabic historian of the conquest, al-Wakedi.[1] According to his somewhat apocryphal narrative, Halebi and Zelebi, or Riba and Zilba as he calls them, were connected by a tunnel beneath the Euphrates, and the double fortress was regarded as impregnable. But Zelebi was the dower of a Christian widow whose father, the infamous Yukina, formerly Governor of Aleppo, had turned renegade. He persuaded her to treachery; the Governor of Halebi was invited to a feast and murdered; and by means of the tunnel under the Euphrates and the assistance of the Vizier, formerly a resident of the cloister of Deir-Hafr, Halebi was handed over to the Moslems. After the conquest the town of Zenobia seems to drop out of history.

As already stated, the el-Hamme dike continues for about an hour beyond Halebi. Beyond this there was a large plain fairly well cultivated, and about the middle

[1] Ainsworth, *The Euphrates Expedition*, 1, 331 *ff.*

of it a ruined mud village called Tubne, uninhabited, where Chesney and Ainsworth report brick ruins. Opposite this, on the other side of the river, Chesney and Ainsworth report important remains of an ancient city, now called Sur-al-Humor. We spent the night at the zaptieh barracks of Terif on this plain. The general course of the day had been southeast by east. By passing over the plateau the caravan had made the trip in seven hours. Our road, following the bends of the river, was two hours longer.

The next morning we rose at three o'clock, and left Terif at four. I despatched Noorian and the zaptieh in advance to secure rooms in the khan at Deir; and Harper, Hilprecht, and Prince accompanied them. Haynes, Field, and I turned aside to visit the ruins called Tabus, which were some three and a half hours beyond Terif. These ruins are magnificently situated on a very high bluff overlooking a rich plain. At the western end of the plain is the fountain of 'Ain Tabus, from which a small stream flows into the Euphrates. We went up to the plateau on the west side of the bluff, as Sachau had done before us. On the plain there was no frost, but it was quite heavy a little way up, and the ascent was slippery and difficult. There is nothing of any importance at Tabus. One ruin to the west was merely a tomb. To the east was a sorry fragment of what may have been a tower, the substructures of some houses, and perhaps a little piece of wall. All seemed late, although the site itself is ancient, the Roman Dabausa. It was a castle rather than a town, as the size of the site shows. Toward the side of the desert it was protected by a deep cut in the rock. We found a path down the east side, and the remains of a bridge over a ravine. The old road to Dabausa from the valley seems to have ascended this ravine, but the fall of fragments of the cliff rendered it impossible for us to trace it with certainty.

Shortly after passing Tabus, we left the rich alluvial plain, our road leading over a stony barren plateau. At ten o'clock we passed a miserable little ruined tower; and about eleven we passed a little hill called Tel-el-Hejef, presumably the Shef-el-Aiaash of Chesney, below which was a spring of naphtha and bitumen, called 'Ain Abu Juma, and a brick ruin. Ainsworth says that "there are other springs of the same description in the neighborhood, and they occur where the volcanic rocks have broken through the marls and gypsum, which are superimposed by breccias and selenitic sandstones." Here trachyte again crops up through the gypsum, and at some places in this neighborhood there are also banks of mud and sand conglomerate of considerable height.

It was 12.40 P.M. when we reached the town of Deir. The name, which means "monastery," would imply that in pre-Mohammedan times it was the site of a religious foundation; but I have been unable to obtain any information that would identify it with such a site. Moritz says that the earliest mention of the place which he can find is from the year 1331 A.D. Abu-'lfeda, in his *Chronicle*, records an overflow of the Euphrates which covered the plain up to the heights of Rehaba, and broke "the dam in Deir Basir." Ainsworth identifies Deir with Deir Abuna, and gives Idrisi as authority for the statement that there stood on this spot before the conquest a monastery famous for its great antiquity. But whenever it was founded, it is at the present time the most important town on the Euphrates between Birejik and Busrah. It is the seat of a mutessarif, and is at present an independent sanjak. It is a town of about 10,000 population. In the thirties, according to Ainsworth, it was a town of only about 2500 population, and governed by an Arab sheikh, who paid tribute to the Turks. Excepting the soldiers of the garrison and the officials, there are no Turks resident there. To distinguish it from other Deirs, it is known officially as Deir ez-Zor, that is, Deir of Syria, or the Syrian side of the Euphrates. It lies close to the desolate plateau which stretches back from the Euphrates valley, but immediately below it that valley broadens into a large and fertile plain. The river branches just above Deir, and the town lies on the branch known as the Jafr canal, which is fordable. There is also a rude bridge across this canal, fit only for foot passengers. The Euphrates proper is neither fordable nor bridged.

A Syrian Catholic priest met us outside of Deir, and invited us to be his guests,—an invitation which we politely declined. We saw a good deal of him later, and he and his brother tried to sell us forged antiquities. At the outset we were all taken in; and Harper and Hilprecht had quite a contest as to priority of right, and which should have the honor of buying the antiquities. Fortunately the man did not accept our first offer. Later, Hilprecht found some frauds in the possession of the priest's brother. This, and something I learned through Noorian, awakened my suspicions, and I sent for the first lot again. On closer examination, it proved that they were all forgeries. Among them was a curious plaque with a Buddhistic figure upon it, and underneath, written in cuneiform characters, the word *Buddha*. Later, in Baghdad, we saw several pieces of the same manufacture, of Indian type, with inscriptions in cuneiform characters, evidently composed by one who knew something of the cuneiform script.

According to the Syrian Catholic priest, there are 1600 families at Deir. Of these, four or five are Greek, eighty Syrian Catholics, and the rest Moslems, with the exception of four or five Jews. How much reliance can be placed on this religious census I do not know. Later I ascertained that the Armenian Catholics have a station at this point. Syrian Catholics and Armenian Catholics, be it said, are Syrians and Armenians who have left their ancient national churches and acknowledged the supremacy of the Pope of Rome. In general these Roman-Catholic sects of the ancient Oriental churches are allowed to retain their own ritual and language. The priests marry and are bearded. These schisms started in the sixteenth century A.D.

The population of Deir was, on the whole, the lowest that I had ever seen in any town. Numbers of both sexes and all ages had lost an eye; and most of them seemed to be scarred by "the Aleppo button," or by small-pox. All of the women were tattooed, and most of the men. One peculiarly ugly form of the tattoo which the women of the Euphrates valley favor is the blueing of the lower lip. They generally also have dots of blue on the cheeks and forehead, and frequently on the tip of the nose. I once reached Deir after the whole female population had been tattooed afresh, and while the colors on their lips, cheeks, noses, foreheads, breasts, wrists, and ankles, were still a staring bright blue. The effect was indescribable. In addition to the tattoo, by way of further ornament, the women wear nose-rings. A few of them wore the untidy-looking large rings, fastened in the central cartilage of the nose, and falling down over the mouth. More common are the rings fastened in one of the nostrils, and falling only as far as the upper lip. Least untidy, but also least common, are the very small rings in one nostril, so arranged that the jewel fits closely into the curve of the nostril on the side. These latter rings are sometimes, when properly contrived, quite as ornamental as ear-rings.

The town of Deir seems to be thriving, as towns in that country go, and I was told that property was increasing in value. There were two large khans in the place, and our rooms in the older khan actually had glass windows. We found the markets fairly good, and it was even possible to buy Syrian wine and Norwegian beer.

There were some covered bazaars, of rude construction to be sure, and more were in process of erection. One or two of the houses which I visited were fairly well furnished in semi-European style, although the exteriors presented a mean appearance, which they do also in Damascus, for that matter. The streets were very dirty, and were used freely for filthy purposes. The mud, moreover, was peculiarly sticky, owing to the lime in it.

There were 800 soldiers stationed at Deir,—400 infantry, and 400 mule-riders. The latter are the successors of the camel corps employed by the Romans to keep the Arabs in check. I called on the Mutessarif, and presented to him my letter from the Wali of Aleppo. He was very affable, and answered me many questions about the Arabs. He spoke highly of Sheikh Faris of the Shammar, the friend of Mr. Wilfred and Lady Anne Blunt, of whom the latter speaks so favorably in *The Bedouin of the Euphrates*, and said that he was in good relations with the government. He laughed at the pretence of civilizing the Shammar at Kalah Sherghat, under their Sheikh, Ferhan Pasha, and said that Turki Bey, one of the head sheikhs of the Anazeh, had done much better, having already built several villages near Aleppo, and promising in fifteen years to have all the Anazeh in villages. On my expressing a wish to have some photographs of Deir, he ordered the captain of the zaptiehs to send an escort to protect us against the children of the town, a precaution which proved necessary. He also asked for photographs, which he never received, as they all proved failures. The Mutessarif's " palace " is a miserable one-story structure of field-stones and mud. Deir used to be a part of the vilayet of Aleppo, but the Mutessarif now reports directly to the Sultan. Only the revenues are paid at Aleppo, and cases of great importance are appealed to the Wali there.

Sunday, the 23d of December, we spent resting. Some

extracts from a letter written on that day may supplement the account which I have given of our journeyings, and furnish a more vivid picture of the delights of travel along the Euphrates:—

"My chief difficulty is the cold. It freezes every night, and you can get no fuel half of the time; and the other half, when you do get some wood, you are suffocated with the smoke and cannot stay in the same place with your fire. However, we rise anywhere from three to half-past four in the morning, and get under way a couple of hours before sunrise, just when it is coldest. The sun, which has shone all the time since we left Meskene, is very warm when there does not happen to be a cold wind blowing, and toward the afternoon we generally become too warm. . . . We breakfast standing, on coffee, native bread, or hardtack, and canned tunny fish. At noon we halt, provided we have not been so unlucky as to become separated, and lunch on cheese, dried black olives, and figs, or helvar, a sort of candy which Nordik, our cook, carries for us. We dine off bulgur (cooked wheat) and canned corned beef, unless we have been fortunate enough to get a bird or two; but we have no time for systematic hunting, and the game, though abundant, is very shy. We have heard many desperate lion stories, but so far the lions have remained in the jungle. The whole plain is rooted up by wild boars, but we have not seen one yet. Jackals howl close to us each night, and we often find graves which they have dug up. The Arabs have occasioned us no trouble. Hilprecht and Prince say that when I came suddenly on some in the jungle, they raised their guns at me, and then, seeing others behind, desisted. I saw nothing of this. I made a salaam and they returned my salute. . . . I do not see how these poor Arabs live. They are not half-clothed. They would come and stand about our fire to warm their bare legs, and I have seen them wading in the river, clothes and all, without any place to warm themselves at afterward. Their clothing is of the thinnest. They live in black tents, open in front, or closed only with a little brush. They are very low and degraded. These are all the people we have seen since Saturday the 15th at noon, until we reached Deir yesterday. Deir is a town of 10,000 people, planted out in the desert on the Euphrates. The houses are built of small stones set in immense amounts of plaster. The people are hideous. The little girls frequently have their hair stained with henna, and feather tufts are placed on the heads of some of the children, like red Indian ornaments. The men have the fore part of the head shaved like the Persians. The facial type is heavy and low. Two days of last week we could not get water to wash in, although we were so near the Euphrates, and even when we can get water, washing arrangements are poor and dirt is rich."

CHAPTER VI.

DEIR TO 'ANAH.

A Fall in the River—The Captive Israelites—The Roman Frontier—An Arab Fortress—Rehoboth of the River—Abundant Ruins—Salahieh—An Unknown Palmyrene Ruin—A Fortress of Saladdin—Fauna of the Euphrates—Ruin Mounds—Water-Wheels—Wild Asses—Xenophon—Storms on the Euphrates—Another Unknown City—Zaptiehs and Barracks—Approaching 'Anah—Palm-Trees—A Romantic Situation—The Town of 'Anah—The Palace—The Governor—History of 'Anah—Half a Century Ago—'Anah of To-day—The People of 'Anah—Arab Cruelty—Mode of Travel.

OUR farewell to Deir was a dispute with the landlord of the khan over the amount of money to be paid for our entertainment. There was no real question; and when we refused to be imposed upon, and took our departure without paying his exorbitant demands, he seemed to conclude that we were in the right. From Deir we took with us but one zaptieh. As soon as our road brought us to the river-bank, we went down to the river, as usual, to water our horses. Hilprecht's horse, Marduk, which was very short-necked, undertook to step a little into the water in order to drink with greater ease, the result of which was that he and Hilprecht both fell in. The water was only about three or four feet deep; but when a man who cannot swim falls into a river, especially if the river is icy cold and he is on the top of a plunging horse, he is very apt to feel sure that he is drowning, and do everything but put his feet on the bottom. For everybody excepting Hilprecht, who thought that his last moment had come, and the horse, which seemed to share the same conviction, it was a very ludicrous five minutes before horse and rider could be pulled out of the shallow water and set on *terra firma* again. Unfortunately our luggage had gone on in advance, so that it was impossible to procure a change of raiment; but some of our servants half-stripped themselves to furnish dry clothing, and the final result was that Hilprecht and our head man, Mustafa, were both sick for the next few days.

Not far below Deir, on the opposite side of the river, Chesney notes a " mud wall." Moritz visited this, and found it to be a ruin of some importance, which he proposes to identify with the ancient Phaliga. On our side of the river Moritz marked a ruin mound a little below Deir, Tel Gofra, which we failed to see. At quarter before eleven we reached the tel of Abu-Nahud. This is quite a small mound; but the surface all about it and in fact the surface of the whole plain, on from this point, until we reached the end of our journey for the day, was strewn with fragments of pottery. Abu-Nahud itself is almost a mound of pottery; and the same was true of the mound of Nahtum, which we passed at 2.20. Moritz heard this called Zubari. It is almost opposite eb-Buseira, which is at the junction of the Khabor and the Euphrates. The latter presents a most imposing appearance in the distance, looking like an effective fortress; but we were told that it was almost in ruins, and that only fifteen zaptiehs were stationed there.

It will be remembered, that, according to the account in the 17th chapter of the Second Book of Kings, the 6th verse, " the king of Assyria took Samaria, and carried Israel away into Assyria, and placed them in Halah, and by the Habor, the river of Gozan." It seems to be pretty well established that the " Habor " here mentioned is the Khabor of Mesopotamia. It is possible, therefore, that some of the large population which at an earlier date occupied the broad plain of the Euphrates opposite the mouth of the Khabor may have been of Israelitic origin; and some of the numerous small nameless mounds, of which there are many scattered over the plain, may cover the site of Israelite towns and villages. At all events, the plain was once very thickly settled. It is unusually broad—the largest plain which I noticed along the middle Euphrates—and very rich. The bluffs on the Arabian side trend away from the river a great distance, and are so low that they scarcely deserve the name of bluffs; but rather the valley of the Euphrates and the desert plateau seem to run into one another. On the northern or Mesopotamian side of the river also the country is perfectly flat, the only hills visible being the Hejef tels to the northwest of Deir.

The Khabor was from the time of Diocletian the frontier line of the Roman Empire, and the modern eb-Buseira represents the ancient Circesium. Ptolemy gives this place as Khaboras. Earlier it was called Charax, a name which Xenophon transferred by mistake to the river. He found here a large and important settlement. When the Romans fortified the town, and made it a frontier fortress against the Persians, they gave it the name of Circesium, their transliteration or adaptation of Charax. Ammianus mentions it as a large and well-fortified city in the latter half of the fourth century A.D. It was captured by the Arabs in 639 A.D. through a treacherous device of the same Yukina who captured Zenobia; and after the Arabic conquest, under the name of Kirkasiyah or Karkisha, it still continued to be an important city. It is situated on the edge of the plateau overlooking the junction of the Khabor with the Euphrates, and was a place of considerable extent. Sachau, who visited the ruins, describes some of the walls as of enormous thickness, and built of bricks with a great deal of mortar. The Talmud and, following that, Benjamin of Tudela, confuse Karkisha with the ancient Hittite capital of Carchemish, and not a few modern writers have followed their error. Since the Turkish conquest the place has fallen into utter ruins. Chesney and Ainsworth heard it called Abu-serai ("father of palaces"), a name derived from its abundant ruins; and I fancy that the unmeaning eb-Buseira is a corruption of this most appropriate title. There are also some ruins on the opposite side of the Khabor, which represent an ancient suburb of Circesium.

Diocletian has been criticised for extending the Roman frontier from Nikephorium on the Belikh, to Circesium on the Khabor; but it must be said that the Khabor, and not the Belikh, was the natural frontier of the Roman Empire against the Persians. As far as the Khabor, Mesopotamia is habitable, and to a considerable extent a fertile country; whereas beyond the Khabor all is desert until one reaches Babylonia. Xenophon, in his *Anabasis*, points out clearly the difference of the two regions. From the passage of the Euphrates at Thapsacus, to the Khabor, which he calls Araxes, there were many towns and villages full of corn and wine; but beyond the Khabor the country was a plain, level as the sea, without trees, but full of wormwood and aromatic plants. There were no inhabitants, but only ostriches, wild asses, bustards, and gazelles. On the Arabian side of the river the Palmyrene territory extended to about the same point; but from this downward, as far. as Babylonia, the country is habitable only along the shore of the Euphrates, and all behind is a desert fit only for the wanderings of bedouin savages.

The caravan went directly to Meyadin, the goal of the day's journey; but Haynes, Harper, Field, and I turned aside to visit the ruins of Rehabah, on the brow of the plateau directly back of Meyadin. On the edge of the plateau, twenty minutes to the west of Rehabah, we came to a ruin which I supposed to be the Sheikh Hannes of Sachau. It was Arabic, and seemed to be a tomb. Rehabah itself is a fortress built on an island of gypsum, in part artificially severed from the plateau, and scarped all around to make it steeper. This mound was paved with blocks of stone, like the artificial mounds on the Aleppo plain already described. It is about two hundred and fifty feet in height, and steep on all sides. On the southeastern side are the remains of an old road or stairway which once gave admission to the castle. This is irregularly circular, and forms a castle within a castle, having an outer wall of stone strengthened by towers, and an inner circle of walls of brick and mortar. The hard red, or flesh-colored breccia, which frequently overlies the gypsum and marl on the Arabian plateau, was freely used in the construction of the outer walls, giving the castle a color effect very different from that of other ruins along the Euphrates; so that Arab writers describe it as Rehabah el-Hamra, or "Rehabah the red." On entering the ruin, one observes that by far the greater part of the fortress was built of bricks; and the casemated inner walls and the vaulted substructures of the interior, all of brick, are much better preserved than the outer walls of stone. Abundance of ornamental Arabic tiles and pottery, as well as glass fragments, occur in the heaps of rubbish in the interior of the castle. Sachau found on a high inner wall on the western side of the castle an illegible inscription in Kufic characters on black and white tiles; but, although we searched for this inscription, we could not find it. Below Rehabah, on the plain, are the remains of other buildings, showing that at some time there was a town close beneath the walls. The whole surface of the plain from Rehabah to the Euphrates at Meyadin is so covered with fragments of pottery and glass, that Sachau supposed that the town must have covered all the intervening space, but the entire plain northward and southward is similarly strewn with sherds and bits of glass, and the whole broad plain can scarcely have been one city. Rather the plain was densely settled, and covered with numerous unwalled towns and villages, of which these are the remains. Rehabah was built to protect this broad and fertile plain, and received the name Rehabah ("broad") because of the breadth of the plain. In front of it there is a deep, broad trench, the bed of a canal, which Idrisi tells us was derived from the river at this point. At Rehabah the caravan road, still often used by caravans from Damascus by way of Palmyra, reached the Euphrates. Its position, therefore, was one of considerable strategic importance.

On account of the name, it has frequently been identified with "Rehoboth of the River," mentioned in Genesis xxxvi., 37, and 1 Chronicles i., 48, as the city of Shaul, King of Edom. Ainsworth, who identifies the two, says that he found here " a great number of bricks, the surface of which was covered with vitrified bitumen converted into green slag, similar to what are met with in many other Assyrian ruins." I did not observe any such signs of antiquity. According to Moritz, an Arabian writer of authority distinctly states that it was built in the first half of the ninth century A.D., in the time of Caliph Mamun, son and successor of Harun-er-Rashid, by his general, Malik-ibn-Tauk, on a new spot, where no castle had stood before; but Ainsworth quotes al-Wakedi as naming Rehabah among the places conquered by the Arabs from the Christians before Rakka, and as being the site of a Christian bishopric. It is mentioned in Arab annals at various times as a place of considerable importance, and especially as offering a successful resistance on more than one occasion to the attacks of the Mongols. Indeed, it was an almost impregnable outpost of the Mameluke Sultans against those invaders at the close of the thirteenth and the beginning of the fourteenth century A.D. Half a century after the Turkish conquest, in the latter half of the sixteenth century, it is described by a contemporary traveller as in ruins, with but a few poor inhabitants. Now it is entirely deserted, but is still one of the best-preserved and most picturesque ruins along the Euphrates.

Between Rehabah and Meyadin, as already stated, we found quantities of sherds, a canal bed, and the remains of a few houses. Meyadin lies in front of Rehabah, on the banks of the Euphrates. It stands on a mound of débris of considerable height, evidently the accumulation of a long period of occupation. On the riverside Sachau observed the remains of a massive brick wall. Excavations conducted for the practical purpose of obtaining stones for building new houses have unearthed coins of the time of Abu-Bekr, but nothing earlier, so far as I could ascertain, although there must be older remains beneath. The surface-remains, here and over the whole plain, may be referred to the Arabic period, from the time of the conquest onward. The period of the Abbasside Caliphate at Baghdad was evidently a period of peculiar prosperity to this region.

We reached Meyadin after dark, and found the rest of the party installed in the so-called palace of the Kaimakam,—a one-story structure, built of small stones and mud. Meyadin seemed to be a thriving town of eighty families. I noticed a couple of palm-trees there; but the real palm country commences a week's journey farther down the river, and palm-culture at Deir or Meyadin is rather a luxury than a matter of profit. Between Meyadin and Deir, along the course of the Euphrates, are several small villages which we did not visit, as our course was in a straight line southeast over the plain from one point to the other. Villages are still more numerous on the shores of the Euphrates below Meyadin; and some of these latter, like Ishara, which is situated on a tel higher even than that of Meyadin, are evidently heirs of ancient sites.

The next morning, Christmas Day, we were up at four o'clock, and the caravan was under way at a few minutes past five. We were still crossing the broad plain in a direction south of southeast, moving toward the point at which the river and the bluffs again come together. As we rode along the plain, we could see on the bluff beyond Rehabah, first the small ruin of esh-Shibli, then es-Sereij, and finally, where the bluff bends well in and is low, Imam 'Ali. All these are ruins of Arabic towns occupied when Rehabah was a fortress, and when a canal carried the waters of the river close to the bluffs. The last of the three, which I visited, consisted of a ruined mosque and minaret, and a number of modern-looking houses, just such as one sees in the present towns along the river, together with a graveyard. Hilprecht and Prince visited es-Sereij, and reported it to be of the same character; and the zaptieh made a similar report concerning Shibli. The towns on the banks of the Euphrates, of which we passed three in rapid succession, Ishara being first and most important, are larger than those on the bluff, and are still inhabited, while the latter are deserted. There is no longer any channel for the river near the bluffs, as there formerly was; and there is no strong power which holds the Arabs in check by means of a fortress like Rehabah. The consequence is, that the towns and villages, such as there are, are confined to the valley of the stream, standing on the very banks of the river. It would not be considered safe, even if the water for house use and for irrigation could readily be obtained, to place a village or town at the present time upon the plateau. It would be too much exposed to the raids of the bedouin; and the latter would surely look upon the choice of such a position as a sort of challenge to them, and an invasion of their territory. The towns and villages along the river, even those as large and important as Meyadin, are compelled to pay the bedouin the so-called kubbe, or brotherhood money,—a blackmail of variable amount, levied in the same manner in which the Highlanders of former centuries were wont to levy on the Lowlanders in Scotland, or in which David, when he was a freebooter, levied upon the churlish Nabal. If the kubbe is paid, the Arabs are supposed to protect those who have shown themselves so brotherly and kind; but if the kubbe is not paid, they not only do not protect them, but may even themselves raid them, precisely as David proposed to raid Nabal for refusing to pay blackmail because none of the latter's flock had been stolen. Sachau, in his *Reise in Syrien und Mesopotamien,* describing his journey of the winter of 1879–80, states that Ishara was deserted. I found it a large and flourishing village under the Kaimakam of Meyadin.

Somewhere about this point, but on the opposite side of the river, stood that Zeitha where, after conquering the Persians, the Emperor Gordian was murdered, and his coadjutor, Philip the Arabian, made sole Emperor in 244 A.D. After murdering Gordian, the troops erected a tumulus in his honor, which is often mentioned by later writers.

At about 11.30, shortly after passing the large village of Abd-ul-Hamid, we came to the village of Shueit. Just beyond Shueit, the river runs up to the bluffs of the plateau, which have again become pronounced and high, and the road leads back over the plateau. Here the canal which ran by Rehabah formerly rejoined the Euphrates. Around Shueit the plain was better cultivated than before, and the durra fields were very extensive. It will be evident from the account which I have given, that this part of the Euphrates Val-

Main Gate of Salahieh from the Desert.

ley, about the junction of the Euphrates and the Khabor, was once very populous; and even yet it is the most thickly settled portion of the stream between Birejik and Hillah.

A ride of three hours and a quarter across the plateau brought us to the noble ruins of Salahieh. The effect as one approaches Salahieh from the plateau is very striking. The traveller sees rising before him out of the desert a fortified city, which seems at first sight to be still inhabited. A wall, some fifteen feet in height at the present day, built of gypsum, stretches along the plateau almost north and south from one ravine to another, a distance of about half a mile. In the centre of this wall gate-towers still stand, well preserved, to the height of thirty or forty feet. The more northern of the two gate-towers of this central gate is so well preserved, that one can go into the rooms of the second story. There is another smaller gate northward of this. The thickness of the walls is about ten feet. The city was built on a rectangular plan, so far as the conformation of the cliffs allowed. As already stated, two ravines running down into the valley were taken advantage of to strengthen the situation of the town on the north and south. On the east, its strongest fortification was the edge of the plateau, the bluffs being at this point some two hundred feet above the level of the valley of the river. The streets all run at right angles, and can be readily traced by the lines of the house foundations in gypsum. The main streets are about fifty feet in breadth from house line to house line, the others narrower. At the northeastern corner, at the point marked H, on a small point or promontory jutting out at an angle, was a citadel. The inner wall of this toward the city still stands to a great height; but the larger part of the outer wall, if there ever was one, on the edge of the precipice, must be buried in the vast masses of rock which have

132   NIPPUR.

broken off and fallen into the plain. The rock of the cliffs is so stratified that the softer strata are beneath. As air and water wear away these softer strata, great blocks break off from above, and are precipitated into the plain below. There are some heaps of ruins within the city, but nothing which looks like a building of importance, and no inscription, no columns or decorations.

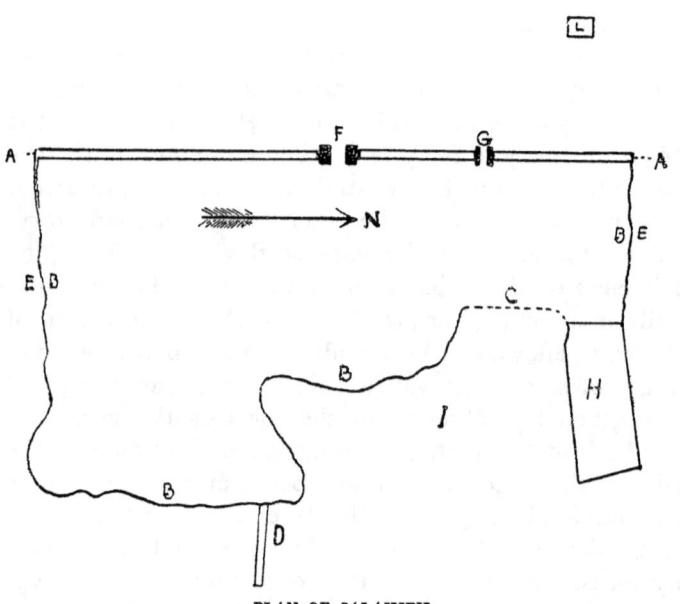

PLAN OF SALAHIEH.

A—Great wall across plateau from ravine to ravine, B—Small wall on edge of bluffs; C—Place where no wall can be surely traced, D—Wall guarding pass up face of bluff from Euphrates Valley, E E—Ravines, F—Main gate, G—Small gate; H—Citadel; I—Space within walls occupied by houses, accessible only by path through D, K—Ruined tower tomb, L—Mass of ruins

Everything is rectangular and massive. F is the main gate; G, a smaller gate north of this; H, the citadel; K, the ruin of a massive tower, apparently a tomb, on the plateau, and a little more than a quarter of a mile to the northwest of the city; L, a small shapeless heap of ruins between that and the city, perhaps the ruins of another and smaller tomb. There is a ruin on a promontory to the northeast, separated from the city by a deep ravine. I did not visit this, but suppose it to have been the remains of still another tomb. I have been unable to ascertain the ancient name of this place, or to find any reference to it in ancient writers. Its modern name, Salahieh (belonging to Salah; that is, Salah-ud-Din), gives evidence that it played some *rôle* in the wars of the famous Saladdin; but its architecture and its tombs show that it was originally built by the Palmyrenes. It holds a strong position on the plateau, with a broad plain below it southward, while immediately beneath it the Euphrates flows close to the bluffs, so that this fortress controls the passage absolutely. It seems to have been the southern fortress of the Palmyrene territory on the Euphrates, as Zenobia was the northern. Kiepert's map marks roads from this point back to Sukhne, near Palmyra; and I am inclined to think that there was a direct route from here over the desert, shortening the distance to Palmyra, although I could not obtain any reliable information with regard to the existence of old wells or stations indicating such a road.

I have already, in the previous chapter, called attention to Procopius' account of the three fortresses in the desert toward the Persian frontier fortified by Justinian. The most southerly of these, named Mambri, he describes as five milestones from Zenobia. Now, five milestones below Zenobia there is nothing. If we could substitute for five milestones ($\sigma\eta\mu\varepsilon\hat{\iota}\alpha$) five stages ($\sigma\tau\acute{\alpha}\delta\iota\alpha$), we might suppose Salahieh to be Mambri. It is, at all events, safe to say that whoever built Zenobia, built Salahieh also. Another name which some travellers have heard for this ruin is the Turkish name of Kan Kalessi ("bloody castle ").

The zaptieh whom we had on this day was very ignorant of the country, and unable to give us so much as the name of the ruins, much less to tell anything about the roads desertward from Salahieh. He had not been long on the station, and the government had not paid him for four months, which was nothing unusual. A shepherd showed us a road down the bluff to the plain. It was a narrow and difficult path, but had evidently been used in ancient times as well as at present, since there were traces of fortifications to guard it. In the face of the bluffs below the old town we noticed a number of very pretty birds, which we mistook for some new species of doves, and which we saw at no other place along the river. I find that the English expedition sixty years before had observed a colony of these birds at this same place, and nowhere else. Ainsworth says (vol. i., p. 377):

"Most rivers of the extent and magnitude of the Euphrates have some forms of animal life peculiar to themselves,—some their hippopotami, their crocodiles, or alligators; others, as in South America, their river porpoises and manati or sea-cows. As yet the Euphrates had only presented us with two remarkable typical representatives,—the large and fierce trionyx or turtle, and the gigantic lizards or monitors; but we were destined to be charmed at this spot (and at this spot only) by the presence of a beautiful and elegant little bird, a tern or sea-swallow, which, building in the cliffs above, now congregated in numbers at the bows of the steamer, or flitted about, imparting life and animation to scenery which, it must be admitted, was, from the general absence of animal life, dull and dreary enough.

"This pretty bird was six inches in length from bill to tail, and twenty-three inches in extent of wings. The head, neck, back, and belly feathers were jet black; the inner and upper wing coverts, black; upper and outer scapular and humeral portions of the wings, pure white;

the lower wing coverts and lower dorsal regions, ashy blue; the bill, flesh-colored; the legs, orange-red. In the young birds the belly was spotted, and the wing coverts were gray."

About an hour beyond the ruins of Salahieh on the plain stand the modern zaptieh barracks, where we spent the night. It was Christmas evening, and we held a brief service in memory of the great event of that day. The next day's ride was a short one over a broad plain, through sparse tamarisk jungle. At nine o'clock we passed the small mud village of Mujawada, on the Euphrates, partly in ruins. At twelve o'clock we passed a ruin mound called tel Medkuk, sixty feet in height, with graves on the top, small and very conical. Half a mile farther on we saw another smaller, unnamed mound. There was no pottery on either mound, but quite a considerable amount between them. To what date the ancient site or sites represented by these mounds belonged, we could not conjecture from anything on the surface. At twenty minutes before two we reached the little town of Abu-Kemal, on the banks of the Euphrates, built partly of mud huts, partly of tents and reed huts. This is the residence of a kaimakam; but he has no mudirs under him, and his "palace" is a miserable little mud hovel. He very hospitably vacated for our benefit two rooms on the roof of this "palace," and another small room was assigned to our servants. We did not exchange visits with him, because he did not seem to care for this courtesy; but instead he sent for Noorian, and questioned him about America.

There was a rude ferry here, and here for the first time we saw ox water-wheels working. These, which are the characteristic water-wheels of the Babylonian plain (jird is their native name), consist first of an excavation in the river-bank, down which the water-skins can be lowered perpendicularly to the water. Above this there is a framework sustaining two block wheels, about which the ropes run. From this a decline is cut landward, which the oxen (ordinarily there are two wheels together) descend to drag up the skins, and ascend to lower them. To the bottom of each skin is attached a long rope, and to the neck a shorter one; so that the neck is held up and the water held in until the wicker platform is reached, on which, by the action of the ropes themselves, it is poured out. From this platform it is distributed, sometimes to a great distance, by little mud-built channels. These wheels are in operation from before sunrise until after sunset.

On another trip I noticed at Abu-Kemal a mule with the shape and markings of a wild ass. On the bas-reliefs of Ashurbanipal's palace at Nineveh there are several representations of wild-ass hunts. Xenophon found these animals still very numerous in the Mesopotamian desert in his day. Chesney sought for them without success, but succeeded in obtaining the skin of one from a native; and Layard says that he heard one bray in the Sinjar hills on the other edge of the desert. Evidently they are now reduced to a dodo remnant. The same is true of the lions, once so common over all western Asia. The elephant and ostrich, formerly inhabitants of these regions, have vanished altogether.

From Abu-Kemal we could see, a few miles to the southwest, low hills with three low peaks, called Thelatha, ("the three"), which are quite a landmark. A little to the east of south in the distance was visible el-Kaim, where are Arabic ruins. On the other side of the river was an approaching line of bluffs, on the point of which, between Abu-Kemal and el-Kaim, were the ruins of el-'Irsi, extremely picturesque to look at. Kiepert's map, following the map of the English expedition under Chesney, has a number of errors at this point. Several towns given by him do not now exist, and probably never did.

A Babylonian Water-wheel or Jird.

They are the names of tent villages, which appear and disappear with great rapidity. Even the mud villages are by no means permanent, and the names of localities change frequently: so, where Chesney found the name Querdi opposite Abu-Kemal, we found the name Suwe.

The British explorers observed a river or canal entering the Euphrates a little above the hills on which the ruins of 'Irsi stand. For this they heard the name Musah. Xenophon, in his account of Cyrus's march against his brother Artaxerxes, says, that, after leaving the river Khabor, they marched through a desert five days' journey (thirty-five parasangs), and came " to the river Maska, a plethron broad; where was a large deserted city, named Korsote, which is surrounded by the Maska." Ainsworth identifies the Musah with the Maska; and, as there is no other river reported as entering the Euphrates on the Mesopotamian side within possible limits, the identification is presumably correct. In that case, Korsote would have been a little west of 'Irsi on the plain. If Xenophon's parasangs were of the proper length, this situation would be impossible, and we should have to look for Korsote and the Maska much farther down stream. But a study of the map in comparison with Xenophon's text will show that his parasangs vary somewhat according to the country traversed. According to him, Cyrus marched from Thapsacus to the Khabor in nine days, fifty parasangs. From the Khabor to Pylæ, the gates of Babylonia, he marched in eighteen days, one hundred and twenty-five parasangs. There were two and a half times as many parasangs from the Khabor to Pylæ as from Thapsacus to the Khabor, but by actual measurement the distance is less than twice as great. Accordingly the parasangs below the Khabor must be counted as shorter than those above. Properly speaking, the parasang is an hour's journey; that is, about two and three quarters miles, varying to two and a half or three miles.

It was off the mouth of the Musah that one of the steamboats of Chesney's expedition, the *Tigris*, was sunk in a hurricane, and twenty men lost. Ainsworth gives a detailed account of this incident, and a vivid description of the extreme violence of wind storms on the Euphrates, one of which in a similar manner overwhelmed part of Julian's fleet of 1100 boats at 'Anah, causing great loss of life.

Somewhere between 'Irsi and Zeitha stood, I should judge, the city of Dura or Europus, built by the Macedonians in the fourth century B.C. Julian found the place deserted in the fourth century A.D., and no modern traveller has found any trace of the site.

The following morning we started from Abu-Kemal at 6.25, reaching el-Kaim, our destination, at 12.20. It was a day of wadis, several of which, of large size, come down from the plateau between Abu-Kemal and el-Kaim. Chief of these are Wadi Ali and Wadi Jaber. We passed the latter of these two wadis some four hours and twenty minutes after leaving Abu-Kemal, and ten minutes later reached the large ruins of Jabrieh, incorrectly given by Kiepert as a village on the other side of the river. The wall on the south side of this ruin, running east and west, is twelve hundred paces long. The west wall, running at right angles with the south wall for nine hundred paces, ends in a great mound or series of mounds, which represent, probably, the citadel, including the palace and temple of the town. The east wall starts out at right angles to the south wall, but after two hundred paces it seems to have come to the bed of the river, and so bends gradually around until it reaches the mound in the northwest. The river now lies some distance away from the town. Its bed is constantly shifting, and it is broken into more than one channel by islands. These walls were built of unbaked brick; and the south wall at the present time is a succession of conical tels, the large bricks of which it was built showing at only a few places. Inside of the outer walls of unbaked brick was an inner wall of baked brick. The interior of the ruins was very thickly strewn with fragments of bricks and stone and

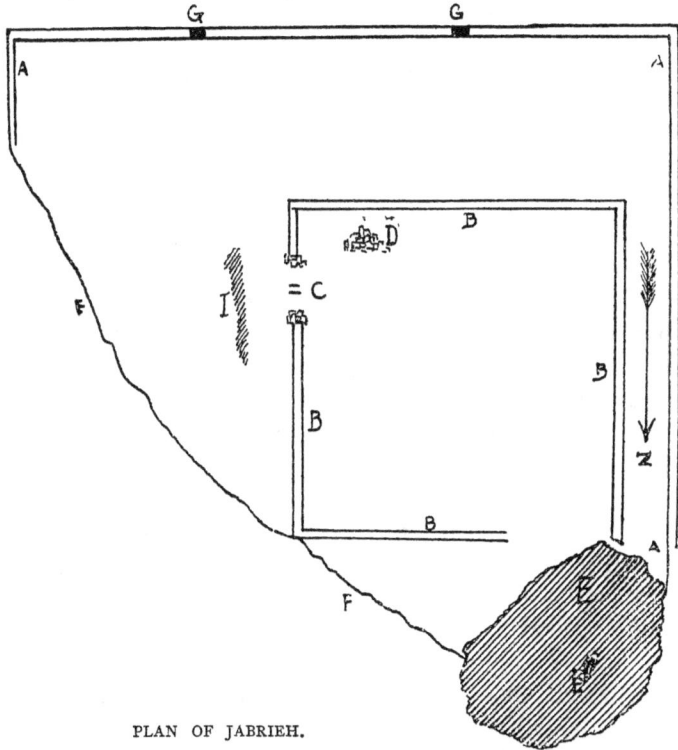

PLAN OF JABRIEH.

A—Outer wall of unbaked brick, B—Inner line of walls, C—Gateway with remains of stone structures, D—Remains of brick buildings, E—Large high mound of citadel covered with shapeless masses of stone, É—Foundation walls of buildings; F—Probable ancient course of river, G G—City Gates, I—Wall like mound.

potsherds, mostly of a green color, very few of which were glazed or in any way ornamented. The zaptieh said that sometimes coins were found here, but we could not procure any specimens in the neighborhood; nor could he give us such a description as to enable us to ascertain what was the character of the coins, or even to make it certain that any had been found. Rude as was the pottery found here, it should be said that it is superior to that now in use among the few miserable natives in this region.

The plan of the city was somewhat thus: A A represents the south wall, twelve hundred paces in length. At the eastern end the wall is so well preserved that the individual bricks are clearly distinguishable. E is a large mound or mounds, much cut up by gulleys, where stood originally, I suppose, the temple and palace, which constituted the citadel of the place. On this mound there is a modern graveyard; and at one point, E', there are the remains of a structure of stone, which seems to have been built at a date more recent than the date of the original buildings which occupied this mound, as the materials of those buildings were used in its construction. At B are the remains of what appears to be an inner line of walls of baked brick. D is the ruins of some building of no very great size. G and G are gates in the southern wall. C is a gate to the inner town. This was more elaborate and substantial than the gates in the outer wall, and was provided with stone threshold and door-posts. One traveller who observed these ruins supposed them to belong to the Assyrian-Babylonian period, on account of the sun-dried brick walls; but such walls were in use everywhere in early times, and are found in Palestine as well as in Babylonia. The earth walls are, however, an evidence that the city was not built by the Romans or the Palmyrenes. What ancient site we have here, and to what period the ruins really belong, I do not know. Chesney in his map gives these ruins as 'Anka, and identifies the site with Phœnix.

I noticed that the baked bricks scattered over the surface of the mound are somewhat greenish in color, the same thing which we observed later at 'Anbar and various other points in Babylonia; but this is due to lack of iron

Ruins of City Wall of unbaked Brick at Jabrieh.

in the clay, and can scarcely be taken as an indication of date. So, also, the potsherds, which were strewn over the surface of the city within the walls in large quantities, were of a character too general to allow dating, at least on the basis of our present knowledge. The building-stones which had been used were generally gypsum from the bluffs on the plateau near by, but we also found pieces of a volcanic stone.

At el-Kaim, where we spent the night in the zaptieh barracks, there are the remains of some structure, apparently of Arabic origin. There are also four or five ruined water-wheels, or naouras, at this point, and, from el-Kaim, downward to Hit, these are the characteristic ruins. At the present day not one in ten of these naouras still serves to raise water; but Chesney's expedi-

WATER-WHEELS ON THE EUPHRATES.

tion, in 1837, reported two thirds of them to be in use. This is only one of the evidences of progressive retrogression within this century in the valley of the Euphrates.

El-Kaim lies on a low point of the plateau which runs almost to the banks of the river. The existence of the ruins of 'Irsi on the Mesopotamian side of the river, with Jabrieh and el-Kaim close together on the Arabic side, would seem to show that at one time this was a populous and important section. Ainsworth says that sixty years ago this was the point at which caravans from southern

Syria and Palestine to Baghdad and Persia first touched the Euphrates. I did not hear of any such route existing now; but I met natives later who had made the journey from Aleppo to Baghdad by a route south of the Euphrates, only touching that river at one or two points. Ainsworth identifies el-Kaim with the Agamna of Ptolemy.

We had very poor quarters in the barracks; and I, with Field and Harper, occupied one of the small rooms over the gate. The floor of this room consisted chiefly of large holes; and the stairway, by which access was had to the court, was almost entirely broken away, so that we had to reach our quarters by scrambling. The zaptieh stations along the river are all in a miserable condition. Almost all of them are dilapidated, some of them to such an extent that it is difficult to see how they can continue to be inhabited; while at not a few places they have fallen to pieces altogether, or have been swept away by the river. The road is no longer used as a post road; but the government continues to maintain zaptieh stations for the purpose of holding the line of the Euphrates, collecting taxes from the few unfortunate inhabitants of the valley, and keeping watch on the bedouin. At el-Kaim there was a mudir, who was compelled to hold his court of justice in the open air. In spite of a cold, raw wind, I enjoyed a bath in the river after the hot ride of the day.

Friday, December 28th, we arose at four o'clock, and were under way by 5.16, reaching Nahia at 1.55. The river makes a bend at this point; and our course turned from the southeast, which it had been since leaving Deir, to north of east. It would have been a great saving in distance could we have gone in a direct line from el-Kaim to 'Anah, but this seemed to be impracticable on account of the Arabs. We found the map incorrect in the names of places, and, in general, the relative distances of the towns between Deir and 'Anah were wrongly given. There were numerous wadis coming down from the desert, as on the previous day; and the bluffs of the plateau were more broken, forming hills and ranges of hills. The stony ground of the plateau comes down to the river in many places, and islands begin to appear here and there. The coloring of the bluffs at various points was very picturesque. In the neighborhood of Nahia, instead of a creamy white, which is the color at most points along the stream, the color was bright yellow. There was no Nahia on Kiepert's map, but I think that it is the place intended by his Hadaoua.

December 29th, with a view of reaching 'Anah early, we arose at 1.30, and started on our days' march at 3.10. Our course was still somewhat more northerly than on the preceding day. At first it led over a low, broken plateau, with a range of hills not far away to our right, running northeast and southwest. At eight o'clock we found ourselves again in the narrow valley of the river, which was here under cultivation. The plateau on our right was worn and cut into separate, rounded summits, the strata of which dipped toward the Euphrates. Some of these rocks had a pinkish-brick hue, and the various colors added to the picturesqueness and strangeness of the scene. We passed some old cotton-fields and numbers of ruined water-wheels, which are legion in this part of the river. At 8.10 we passed a mosque and the ruins of a village called Imam Beshed, or Meshed. The houses of this village had been built of small stones set in mud. In not a few cases the mud had been washed away, and the small stones continued to retain their position. Portions of houses in this state showed not only the lower floor, but stairways and a second story, and in some cases even a third story. The mosque itself was fairly well preserved, and was decorated in the interior with frescoes on the ceilings and walls, while an inscription ran about the frieze. The work dates from the time of Caliph Mamun, son of Harun-er-Rashid. This mosque is much more elaborate than anything now existing in that region; and the remains not only of the mosque, but also of roads and bridges, all dating from the Arabic period, indicate conditions of prosperity in the time of the Abbasside Caliphate which have not been reached since.

At 8.35, at a sharp bend of the river, we came upon the island and village of Azarieh, where we first saw, not single palm-trees, but palm-groves, and where the climatic conditions of Babylonia began to take the place of those of Syria. As Deir is the last town in Syria, so 'Anah may be said to be the first town in Babylonia. Just beyond Azarieh the river enters a narrow gorge, and we were obliged to turn back over the hills. These consist at this point of naked lime rock, cut up into wild and picturesque shapes by deep wadis. At nine o'clock we descended into the deep gorge called Wadi Rawa, and followed this down almost to the river-shore, coming out opposite the extremely picturesque town of Rawa, which consists of a fringe of palm-trees and mud walls, extending for about a mile along the narrow strip of land between the cliffs and the river on the Mesopotamian side. On a bold promontory to the right of the town stands out an immense, barren-looking building,—the barracks erected by Midhat Pasha to hold the Shammar Arabs in check, where stood in Ainsworth's day a castle and a tower. Around this promontory the river almost doubles on its own course. It is narrow and rapid, and there are rocks in the channel. Beyond the promontory was another ribbon of palm-trees; while on our side of the river, stretching for six or seven miles in one narrow strip, between high barren hills on the one side, and the river on the other, and covering half a dozen islands in the channel of the stream, were visible the innumerable palm-trees among which stands the town of 'Anah. It

Weaving Cloth among the Palms at 'Anah on the Euphrates.

was by far the most beautiful and picturesque site which we had seen on our journey along the Euphrates.

It was twenty minutes past nine o'clock when we began to enter the town; and we rode for fifty minutes along its single street, between palm-trees and mud walls on either side of us, before we reached the palace of the Kaimakam, said to be in the centre of the place. The day had been cloudy, and for fear of rain we accepted the Kaimakam's offer of rooms, but they were so small that we had to pitch two tents in the courtyard in addition. As soon as we were settled, I sent word that I would like to call on the Kaimakam, to which he replied, that, as he had given me the only rooms fit to receive guests, he would call on me, which he accordingly did. He informed me that a flood the spring before had destroyed the greater part of the palace, and that they had not yet begun to rebuild. He had only been in 'Anah two or three weeks; but it was three and a half years since he had left Scutari to take office in the provinces, and he would much like to get back to the Bosphorus once more. He was an old man, Abbas Effendi by name. He said that thirty years before, Omar Pasha had made the country safe against the Anazeh and the lions. Before that time the people of 'Anah had been compelled to live entirely on the islands, because the mainland was so unsafe. Twenty years before, Midhat Pasha had killed Abd-ul-Kerim, the famous Shammar chief, and scattered the Shammar Arabs on the other side of the river; and now this road, that is, this country, was very safe. He had asked, he said, for a post-office at 'Anah, but his petition had not yet been granted. There are, in fact, post-offices only at Deir, Hit, and Ramadieh; but at no other point along the Euphrates, from Aleppo to Baghdad, can one either send or receive letters through the mail.

The chief industries of the town are the domestic manufacture of woollen and cotton goods (principally abbayehs or Arab cloaks, and the like) and the cultivation of dates, durra, cotton, and fruits. The fruits are cucumbers, apricots, figs, pomegranates, sour oranges, and sweet lemons. Abbas Effendi assured me that we needed no zaptiehs to accompany us in our rambles about the place, even when we wished to photograph, as the people were much more civilized and less turbulent than those at Deir. While he was with us, the Turkish official who had been travelling in our company arrived, and asked for rooms, to which request Abbas replied that he had given all that he had to us. I protested that I did not wish to cause him or these others such inconvenience, and that we would pitch our tents and restore to him his rooms. But he would not listen to this proposition, replying that we, as foreigners, were the guests of honor, and that the others should go outside and pitch their tents, which they did.

The Kaimakam's knowledge of the history of 'Anah was limited, and not at all accurate. As the name shows, the place must once have been sacred to Anu, the ancient Babylonian god of heaven, or his female half, Anath. We find in Palestine towns of the same name. Anathoth, a Levitical city, near Jerusalem, the home of the Prophet Jeremiah, was such a place, Anathoth being merely the plural of Anath. Cities with this name were manifestly sites sacred to Anu or Anath, where shrines of that divinity existed. There is, to the best of my knowledge, no mention of this particular city in any Babylonian or Assyrian inscriptions which have yet been found. The first mention of the city which I have found is in Xenophon, who calls it Charmande. The next is in the "Parthian stations" of Isidorus Charax, about the beginning of our era. In the account of the ill-fated expedition of the Emperor Julian, in the fourth century after Christ, Anath or Anatho appears as a town of importance, situated both on the islands of the stream, and also on the Arabic shore of the river, the citadel or castle lying on one of the islands. The people were independent and self-reliant, and undertook to oppose the passage of the Romans. In this they were assisted by the elements, a violent storm destroying many of the Roman ships. Julian finally succeeded in reducing the town to submission, partly by force, partly by diplomacy. Some of the inhabitants he deported; others, with a certain Dusæus at their head, he admitted to an honorable alliance. After the dissolution of the Abbasside Caliphate the place seems to have enjoyed a semi-independence; and various travellers describe 'Anah as governed by an Emir, and the people as proud and self-reliant. These conditions continued even after the Turkish conquest of the country; and Tavernier tells us that two hundred years ago the town was still self-governing, and ruled by its own Emir. When the old independence was finally destroyed I cannot tell; but at least it has long since vanished, and 'Anah is now governed like any other town on the Euphrates.

The statement of our good Kaimakam about the security of the country was, as we learned afterwards, very much exaggerated. Since the time of Midhat Pasha the Arabs have been allowed to get the upper hand. The old barracks at Rawa are deserted, and there is only a small force of zaptiehs and soldiers at 'Anah. Benjamin of Tudela tells us that in his day, in the twelfth century after Christ, Rawa as well as 'Anah was a fortified town. The abandoned remains of buildings on the islands, including the remains of bridges which once connected the islands with the shore, as also remains of roads and bridges on the mainland in this neighborhood, already referred to, prove that this region once enjoyed a period of great prosperity and importance. The natives refer the ruins on the islands to the Persian period; and while such statements are generally the merest idle and unscientific guesswork, I fancy that they are, in this case at least, correct.

Ainsworth describes the ruins on the islands sixty years ago as follows: " The islands in the centre of the stream rise very little above the level of the waters, and none of them have rock terraces, but they are embellished by a dense and luxuriant vegetation, chiefly of palm-trees and pomegranates, out of which peer the ruins of former habitations, and here and there the white-washed dome of a sepulchral chapel.

" In the largest of all, to the southeastwards, were the ruins of a once extensive castle. This old island castle was connected by a bridge, now in ruins, to the Arabian side, and by an irregular ridge of rocks and masonry, called Nizan, to the Mesopotamian. These, as may be imagined, constitute at the low season serious impediments to navigation. At that time the waters tumble over the ledge on the east side, with a fall of about two feet, in a broken foam. On the west side, one of the arches of the bridge being broken, a steamer can be steered through with due care. A wall extending across from the upper part of the island to the western shore also crosses the passage, but, being broken down near the island, it has a narrow pass from thirty to forty feet wide. This gate is surmounted by a parapet which advances from the island just above it, and turns the water at an angle into the main stream. On the hills beyond the town were two small Arabian castles, called Abd Allah and Zahun; and another of a similar character, called Abû-n-diyah, defended the further extremity of the cliffs on the Mesopotamian side."

There has been a considerable change in the appearance of these ruins since that description was written. The bridge and the wall have both vanished almost entirely. The forts mentioned by Ainsworth seem to have vanished also. There are, in fact, few visible remains of

A Naoura Water-wheel at 'Anah on the Euphrates.

the past in 'Anah, in spite of its great antiquity. The houses are built of field-stones set in mud. When a house becomes ruinous, it is deserted; the inhabitants building a new house, and leaving the old one to fall into ruins. The consequence is that at least half of the houses which one sees are unoccupied and in various stages of decay. Each house has about it a garden of palms, pomegranates, figs, and the like, and underneath the palm-trees they cultivate wheat or some other grain. The gardens are surrounded by walls of mud and field-stones. Water-wheels for irrigation are very numerous; and while many of these are ancient ruins, there are sufficient in use at the present time to water every garden. The water is carried from the wheels by raised aqueducts; and these, crossing the single street at an elevation of three or four or five feet, and at very frequent intervals, render that a somewhat difficult thoroughfare for loaded animals. It is altogether too narrow for any wagons; and indeed there are no wagons, or any sort of vehicles, in that country.

'Anah is the most charming town on the whole river. It is indescribably picturesque, with its rude fortress-like houses embowered in gardens of palms and rosy pomegranates, surrounded by high walls, and watered by huge water-wheels with arched aqueducts, their dripping sides covered with moss and ferns and flowers. In front of it the cool, brown river surges and eddies over rocks and among palm islands covered with ruins of Persian forts and bridges, Arab mosques and water-wheels, and aqueducts of all nations and ages. Behind, close at hand, rise abruptly the steep, barren, unclothed hills of a yellow-whitish marl full of fossils; while across the river, as far as the eye can reach, there is a level, monotonous waste of grayish-brown desert. Below the town the river is full of palm islands; above, the vista of the stream is closed by a beetling cliff crowned with massive masonry, with a soft green fringe of palm-trees far beneath.

The people of 'Anah are singularly fine-looking, quite unlike the wretched population which we saw at Deir. From their features, I should say that they were pure-blooded Semites of the Arab stock, not mixed with other elements. They are more polite, suaver, and more courtly, than the denizens of the other river towns. The women are very shy, which, from the Arabic standpoint, is an evidence, I presume, of culture, refinement, and blood. On sight of us in the street, unveiled beauties would dodge into passage-ways or turn their backs. Those of whose features I caught a glimpse were fair to look upon, except for the unfortunate habit of tattooing in blue the under lip, the nose, forehead, cheeks, and chin. Of course, they wear nose-rings. Ainsworth says that their noses were " generally adorned with a large turquoise." He found a considerable Christian and Jewish population occupying separate quarters of the town. There is still a considerable population of Jews here, but unfortunately I did not learn this until later, and therefore did not visit them.

Sunday was a rainy day, so that it was impossible to secure a good photograph of 'Anah. Most of us spent the day in writing letters, which could not be mailed for a week, and resting. Since leaving Aleppo we had been one hundred and twenty hours in the saddle, or, to use Xenophon's language, we had travelled fifteen stages, one hundred and twenty-four parasangs; and the opportunity of spending the day lying down, or sitting in some other position than astraddle, was not to be despised. As at Meskene and Deir, we had a sheep killed, and treated our muleteers to fresh meat.

The jurisdiction of the Kaimakam of 'Anah is very extensive, extending in a narrow strip along the river about a six-days' journey, three on either side of 'Anah; but there is nothing back of the river. The Kaimakam has twenty foot-soldiers and fifty-two zaptiehs at his disposal, the former of whom, during the time that we were there, loafed about by day, and sang songs and shouted all night long. The Kaimakam was probably used to this, and did not mind it; but, in spite of their fatigue, it interfered with the sleep of some of our party. There are said to be three or four hundred occupied houses in 'Anah, which would mean a population of about two thousand souls. We were able to secure barley for our horses at this point, and laid in a supply for several days, inasmuch as at the smaller places nothing could be obtained. Our horses had had a rather hard time of it, and some of them had developed sores; but they were happy in comparison with the pack-animals. The backs of some of these poor creatures were a dreadful sight to behold, and it was sickening to see the way in which they were dressed. At Abu-Kemal they burned a hole in the back of one donkey with a red-hot iron in order to drain a wound. From our point of view, the Turks and Arabs, but more especially the latter, are exceedingly cruel in their treatment of animals. They will not kill a creature to put it out of pain, leaving it to die a lingering death of itself. On their side, they consider our idea of killing a creature to prevent it from suffering as barbarous and inhuman. At 'Anah our muleteers took a worn-out donkey to the water's edge, contriving that he should fall in and be swept away and drowned, but they would not themselves kill him.

CHAPTER VII.

A CITY OF PITCH.

Fortress of Thilutha—A Swamp—An Island Town—Naouras—Modern Arab Life—Persian Ruins—Arab Industries—People of the Town—A Hot Cave—Troglodytes—More Island Towns—Bitter Streams—Bitumen Springs—The Town of Hit—A Shipyard—Antiquity of Hit—Herodotus—The Mouth of Hell—History of Hit.

WE left 'Anah at half-past six o'clock on the morning of Monday, December 31st. As we went along, I observed on the houses a decoration which I had also seen in Deir; namely, colored plates set in the outer walls of the houses. Many of the houses were deserted, and our zaptieh said that the people had grown poor and many had left; but why they were poor, he did not know. He himself was a Kurd, and had been stationed at 'Anah for ten years. As we were behind the caravan and some of the loads fell off shortly after starting, and as it was impossible, owing to the narrowness of the street, to pass the loaded animals in front of us, it took us seventy minutes to reach the southern limits of the town. Five minutes beyond 'Anah, and connected with it by gardens, is the village of Jemeyle, with a different town government, but really constituting a part of 'Anah. It took fifteen minutes more to pass this.

After passing the town, the hills on both sides of the river become lower. The valley between the river and the hills, on the Arabian side, is not more than two hundred yards wide, and on the Mesopotamian side even narrower. There are a number of small wadis cutting their way through the hills, the rock of which everywhere is a soft limestone carbonate, full of fossils. About half an hour below 'Anah, around a bend of the river, is the small rocky island of Telbeis, the ancient Thilutha. This was a strong fortress in the days of the Emperor Julian, so strong that he could not take it. Now it is a tiny islet, almost, if not quite, uninhabited, but the ruins of old fortifications are still visible.

Our destination for the night was the barracks of Fehemi. Just in front of these barracks lies the Wadi Fehemi, which forms at its junction with the Euphrates a swamp difficult to cross. Harper was riding in front, when his horse, Burnaburiash, began to sink, and continued sinking until he found himself standing astride of the animal, with his two feet in the mud on either side of him, whereupon he picked off his saddle-bags and rifle, and returned to rejoin me on the edge of the swamp. The horse, relieved of his rider's weight, succeeded in some manner in extricating himself. A caravan of donkeys was crossing at the same time, and several of them almost disappeared in the mud, so that the Arabs who were driving them had to pull them out by the tails and ears. It took us almost an hour to find a safe way across this swamp to the barracks beyond.

The first day of the new year, 1889, we reached Haditha, or New Town, situated partly on an island in the river, and partly on the mainland on both sides. Here we were quartered in a farmhouse used as barracks, because the former barracks were destroyed by the flood of 1888. There were five zaptiehs and one foot-soldier at this post. The farmhouse was a good specimen of the sort of farmhouses which occur isolated or in groups on the Euphrates from Haditha to Hit. A high wall of small stones set in much mud surrounds the court, on three sides of which are buildings of the same material. These farmhouses look like forts, especially as they often have a small round watch-tower attached for watching the water-wheels. Nor does their fort-like appearance belie their character; for they were intended to afford protection against the bedouin, as well as shelter. Here, for the first time, I observed closely one of the native ovens for baking bread. It was built of small stones and mud, with one opening at the top, and another at the side. A fire is kindled in this oven; and when the fire has reduced itself to ashes, wet meal, kneaded in the form of cakes, is plastered on the inside walls, where it remains until it dries, and the cakes fall into the ashes and are regarded as cooked.

Ali Effendi of Baghdad, Mudir of Haditha, came to call on us, dressed in coat and trousers. He told me that there were three hundred houses in Haditha, and that there were twice as many before the flood of last spring. No steamer had been up the river for nine years, he said. Midhat Pasha had caused the naoura dams, which are built out into the stream so as to direct a current upon the water-wheels, to be broken, and a steamboat to run up to Meskene; but the people did not like it, because they could not obtain a strong enough current for their naouras. These are built in this manner: three or four piers, or sometimes long bridges of stone resting upon arches, are run out into the river. At the end of the piers or bridges are built from one to five wheels. These wheels, which have a diameter of fifteen to twenty feet, are made of crooked mulberry or tamarisk boughs, the only wood available. Generally they have paddles of palm-leaves, and collect the water in rude clay jars tied to the wheel. I have observed pieces of old bottles and all sorts of broken pottery used where jars failed. The wheel is hung at an angle, so that the upper part overhangs a small trough, into which, with much waste, the jars are emptied as the wheel revolves; and, by the way, the same clay jars, with an end knocked out, often serve for water-spouts on houses. The Mudir caused a wheel near our camp to be set in motion for my benefit.

Later we crossed to the island, and the Mudir escorted us over the town. The flood of the spring before had covered almost the entire island, and a large portion of the town was still in ruins in consequence. No lives had been lost, however, as the people had escaped in boats to the mainland. At the upper end of the island we were shown a ruin, which we were told was an old palace of the Persian kings, built by Yizdeshur. It was originally a finer building than any now to be seen in that country. In the time of Julian, Haditha, then called Baia-Malcha, was, in fact, a residence of the Persian kings. The Yizdeshur of the Arabs is evidently a corruption of Ardeshir, or Artaxerxes, the name of the founder of the Sassanian Empire. The foundations of the buildings at this end of the island, and the retaining wall are quite massive, and may well have belonged to the Persian period; but, from some plaster mouldings which I saw, I should suppose that the upper portion of the present ruins is Arabic. Moreover, near these ruins are the ruins of an old mosque. Haditha is mentioned by that name by the Arabic historians, and was a place of some importance during the Abbasside Caliphate.

After we had inspected the ruins, the Mudir took us to see the native method of weaving, where the weaver sits in a hole in the ground. We visited also the mill where durra and barley were ground, with a fine mixture of straw and dirt of all kinds, to form the flour out of which the coarse bread of the country is made. A wheel, with paddles of palm-leaves, revolves in the water. Attached to the shaft of this is a second wheel, with cogs on the inner rim. This turns another small wheel with cogs, the axis of which is perpendicular to the axis of the other two. Attached to the upper end of the axis of this latter wheel is the upper millstone, the lower millstone being stationary. Above the upper millstone hangs a bag of matting; and a stick attached to the bag by a string, and laid on the millstone, shakes the bag, causing the grain to fall out into a hole in the stone, whence it finds its way between the upper and the nether millstones. The millstones are both very soft, and the flour falls from the stone directly on the ground, so that much dirt and earth are mixed with it.

The Mudir then took us to his own house, where, in a rude room with mud walls and dirt floor, we sat on rugs before a smoking fire and drank coffee. Only two cups were provided for the whole company, and these were passed two or three times around. The coffee was made in three pots, being first cooked in the largest, then drained into the second, and then into the third. The Mudir also took us into some of the houses of the town to show us the rude wheels on which the women spin cotton thread. Everywhere we saw both men and women making woollen thread on bobbins, which they carry about with them wherever they go, spinning the thread in the intervals of their conversation. The island is less than half a mile long, and about six hundred feet in width. The people have six boats in all, by means of which communication is kept up between the main portion of the town on the island and the smaller portion on the mainland. These boats are small, flat-bottomed scows. The oars are crooked sticks, with small pieces of wood nailed to the end for blades. The women of Haditha are neither so bashful nor so well favored as those of 'Anah, and in general the facial type at Haditha is not pleasing. The nose is inclined to be broad at the end, and even to turn up slightly. The faces are broadish, and I saw a very few bluish eyes. I should judge that there is some mixture of population here and at most of the river towns. The people are pious, and there are numbers of ziarets on the mainland.

The bluffs in this neighborhood are of gypsum and marl, and are full of caves, many of which are used as houses by the poorer parts of the population. The cultivable area between the river and the bluffs is from two to six hundred feet in breadth, and is all utilized. Beyond Haditha, on both sides of the river, are villages, called Beni Dahir and Birwana respectively, which are really a continuation of Haditha itself. There are also several smaller islands in the stream below Haditha which are inhabited.

The next morning, an hour after starting, we reached a point where the bluffs came down to the river with no intervening plain, so that we were compelled to turn back over the plateau. We soon found ourselves in a ravine called Wadi Hajlan, near the mouth of which are hot sulphurous springs of considerable volume. Beyond this wadi lie several other gorges and gullies, which make the road extremely difficult. These passed, our course lay over a high plateau some distance back of the river, so that we did not see the island city of 'Alus, given as el-Ouzz on Kiepert's map. About nine o'clock we observed smoke rising from the ground close to our left. Supposing that it came from an Arab camp, we rode up, and found a depression of two hundred feet in diameter, looking as though the surface rock were falling at that point. From a small hole in this depression steam issued intermittently, carrying with it a strong odor of bitumen. Close to this small hole was a larger hole, down which we scrambled into a cave. This we explored for three quarters of an hour, without, however, exploring the entire cave. The rock was gypsum. In one room the heat was intense, elsewhere there was an ordinary cave temperature.

At half-past twelve we were opposite the island town of Jibba, a place of the same general character as 'Alus and Haditha. From a point near the road we could see the palm-trees on the island. An hour later we reached the narrow valley of the river, almost opposite the village of Joaniya. The bluffs along the river from Haditha to this point, and beyond, were full of caves, many of which were inhabited. Seeing no houses, one is apt to suppose that there are no inhabitants; but every little ravine which seams the bluffs contains one or more caves, which are the homes of the fellaheen of the district. The place at which we stopped for the night was called Baghdadieh, but there was no village of any sort, the entire population of the neighborhood dwelling in caves. We pitched our tents in a large valley setting back into the plateau, with almost precipitous sides, two hundred feet or more in height. The night was a very cold one, with a sharp frost.

The river from 'Anah to Hit is full of islands, the sites of ancient cities; and the rocky shores are full of caves, the dwellings of modern troglodytes. Haditha, 'Alus, and Jibba are all strikingly similar. Each is a picturesque island, covered with graceful palms which reflect beauty and romance on the miserable mud huts of the present inhabitants. Each possesses a few insignificant remains of ancient fortifications, which the natives invariably refer to Yizdeshur (Ardeshir). In the great flood of the summer of 1888 these islands were all more or less submerged. At Haditha, as stated above, the people escaped to the hills of the mainland without loss of life, but their houses were ruined. At Jibba much injury was done, and ancient ruins, including an inscription, so the natives told me, were carried away. Some of these islands, and especially Telbeis, have been reduced in size, in the course of centuries, by the action of the water; and it is probably owing to such inundations as that of 1888 that the ancient remains are so insignificant and unsatisfactory, for all of these island towns seem to have been at some time places of importance. Haditha, as already stated, was a royal residence of the Persian kings in the time of the Emperor Julian. 'Alus is the Uzanesopolis of Ammianus, the Auzara of Ptolemy. It was named after the old Arabian Ishtar goddess, Alus or Alusa. As 'Anah, or Anatho, was a city dedicated to the Babylonian goddess Anath, so 'Alus was dedicated to the old Arabian goddess Alusa. What the ancient name of Jibba was, I cannot determine.

The next morning we started at ten minutes past three, in order to reach the interesting and important town of Hit as early in the day as possible. We climbed the bluffs by a very steep mule-path, and then travelled for four hours across the plateau, finally descending by a gentle slope to the river-bed. At half-past seven we passed a water-course, the water of which our animals refused to drink, although they were very thirsty. On tasting it, we found it to be bitter, with the flavor of bitumen. Ten minutes later we crossed another stream, called Wadi Sihali, with water of the same character. Here there is quite a plain, where stood formerly the village of Sihalieh, which was destroyed by the floods of 1888. We were told that the people migrated to Koubeitha. In the river were two small islands, called Flewieh, containing a hamlet. Three quarters of an hour later, after crossing some low, sandy hills, we came to Wadi Merrej, another bitter stream, said to rise near Koubeitha, a town some three or four hours inland from Hit. This town, we were told, contains some three to four hundred houses, and is occupied by merchants, who buy wool from the Arabs, and sell it at Aleppo. A quarter of an hour later Hit was sighted, due ahead. It is on a hill, or rather a line of hills running along the Euphrates, perhaps partly natural, but certainly, in part at least, artificial, from thirty to a hundred feet in height. Behind it and around it is quite a large plain, partly sandy, partly rocky, and partly muddy. Down this plain flow several streams of bitter water from various bitumen springs. Directly behind the town are two springs within thirty feet of one another, from one of which flows hot water, black with bitumen, while the other discharges intermittently bitumen, or, after a rainstorm, bitumen and cold water. This latter is the source of the bitumen of commerce of a great part of Babylonia. It belongs to the Government, and is rented to any one who wishes it, at the rate of one mejidieh a day. Where rocks crop out in the plain about Hit, they are full of seams of bitumen, and one observes the same seams on the face of the bluffs on the edge of the plateau. The rock in which these veins occur is gypsum. The water in all the streams behind the town, and especially in the stream from the hot spring, is so full of bitumen, that, while the water itself looks clear, anything that is placed in it becomes quickly clogged, and here and there, where obstacles have obstructed the flow of the water, the streams are bridged over with bitumen.

Hit has been inhabited since the natives of the Babylonian plain learned to use pitch or bitumen as mortar, and from that time to this it has been the principal source of supply of that product. As already stated, the chief bitumen springs lie close behind the modern town. Beyond and around these stretches a dismal black plain, fetid with the smell of sulphuretted hydrogen, and out of this plain a black valley leads to Koubeitha. Bitter streams trickle downward to the Euphrates. The rock which crops out here and there beneath your feet, and the cliffs that border the plain, are seamed with pitchy deposits. Above the town hangs a cloud of smoke from the burning bitumen in the furnaces of the shipwrights and the ovens of the housewives. Strings of women pass by on their way to and from the river, and the vessels balanced on their heads are made of wicker-work or porous earthenware smeared over with bitumen. In their belts the men carry short clubs with round balls of bitumen for heads. You enter the town and meet a man in the narrow streets hastening homeward with a vessel full of hot bitumen to make or mend some household utensils. The roofs of the houses above your head are smeared with bitumen; but on the streets beneath your feet, the place for which we consider it especially adapted, it is rarely used. They are mud and vile ordure. The private conveniences, such as there are, are on the roofs of the houses, projecting over the streets, and often the streets themselves are used; but the all pervading smell of bitumen protects the nose, and the health also, so that in the recent cholera epidemic, Hit, despite its filth, escaped infection.

The houses of Hit are built of field-stones plastered with mud, which, when they go to ruin from the washing of the rain-storms, collapse in heaps of stones. In the course of some thousands of years during which the place has been inhabited, these piles of stones, with other débris, have grown into a line of hills along the river-bank behind the fringe of palms. On the highest of these, almost precipitous toward the plain, sloping less steeply toward the river, stands the little modern town. In spite of the rudeness of its construction and its filth and poverty, this is very picturesque. A striking feature of the place is a lofty and well-proportioned minaret, which leans quite perceptibly. On the northern and southern sides of the town along the river are luxuriant palm plantations; on the east is the river; and on the west extends the flat, barren plain described above, which, with its desolation, its black-seamed, burned-looking rocks, and the overhanging smoke from the furnaces of the shipyards, gives a general impression of a used-up section of the traditional hell.

The shipyard is south of the town, on the shore of the river. Here from the most remote antiquity they have manufactured clumsy boats of crooked tamarisk and mulberry branches covered with mats and wattled twigs, the whole thickly besmeared with bitumen, like Noah's Ark. One meets with these bitumen boats of Hit all over Babylonia, and boats of the same description have been manufactured there forever. We had a bitumen furnace fired for our benefit. An arched passage is built of bricks, with a door at one end, and an opening for the chimney at the other end. On top of this are two tanks, in which is placed bitumen from the spring behind the town. A little furze and thistle, the wood of the region, are used as kindling beneath the tanks, and on the top of this some bitumen is thrown for fuel. As the bitumen in the tanks becomes soft, it is constantly stirred with a plough-shaped stick by two men, one on either side.

There is a ferry at Hit, which I had occasion to cross the following year. The Jezireh, or Mesopotamia, at this point is perfectly flat. A little lower down on that side of the stream there are naphtha wells, and still farther down occur salt lakes. At Hit for the first time we met, beside the lighter-colored dates, the sweeter black ones so familiar below Baghdad. Here also we found pomegranates in abundance, and sweet lemons,—an insipid, watery fruit.

I have already said that Hit is a very ancient city. On the uninhabited portions of the ancient mounds on which the modern city stands, the inhabitants occasionally dig holes to obtain stones for building purposes. At the surface they find colored tiles and bits of Arabic work of various sorts, then Kufic and Byzantine coins, then Parthian money. All these I have seen myself in a depth of five to eight feet. Below this, so they told me, they found "idols," which I take to mean the small clay figures so common in old Babylonian sites. Herodotus calls the town Is, and says, speaking of the building of Nebuchadrezzar's great quays at Babylon (Book 1, Chap. 179): "The bitumen used in the work was brought to

A Noachian Boatyard at Hit on the Euphrates.

A CITY OF PITCH. 163

Babylon from Is, a small stream which flows into the Euphrates at the point where the city of the same name stands, eight days' journey from Babylon. Lumps of bitumen are found in great abundance in this river."

In a note to this passage, Rawlinson says: "This place seems to be mentioned in the tribute paid to Thothmes III. at Karnak, from Nineveh, Shinar, Mesopotamia, Babel, etc., under the name of *Ist*, the chief of which brought 2040 minæ of bitumen, which is called sift, answering to zifte, its modern name in those parts, Rich says. In Egyptian Arabic, zifte (like the Hebrew zift, Exod. iii., 2) means pitch, bitumen (sift), and incense also.

"Is is undoubtedly the modern Hit, where the bitumen is still abundant. The following quaint description is given by an old traveller: 'Having spent three days and better, from the ruins of old Babylon we came unto a town called Ait, inhabited only by Arabians, but very ruinous. Near unto which town is a valley of pitch, very marvellous to behold, and a thing almost incredible, wherein are many springs throwing out abundantly a kind of black substance, like unto tar and pitch, which serveth all the countries thereabouts to make staunch their barks and boats, every one of which springs maketh a noise like a smith's forge in puffing and blowing out the matter, which never ceases night or day, and the noise is heard a mile off, swallowing up all weighty things that come upon it. The Moors call it "the mouth of hell."''

"The name of this place was originally Ihi, or, with a distinctive epithet attached, Ihidakira, meaning "the bitumen spring." In the Is of Herodotus we have Ihi with a Greek nominatival ending. The same place is probably indicated in Ezra viii., 15, 21, 31, where we have Ahava. Isidore of Charax writes the name as ἀείπολις in his Parthian stations (p. 5). Ptolemy has Ιδικάρα (v. 20), and the Talmud Ihidakira, as the most northerly town of Babylonia. Zosimus also writes Δακίρα (iii., p. 165; and Ammianus, Diacira (xxvi., 2). Hit is probably the same name with a feminine ending."

Ammianus relates that Julian, in his expedition against the Persians, having crossed to this side of the river, found that the men of Diacira had fled, whereupon he massacred the women and children and sacked the town.

CHAPTER VIII.

HIT TO BAGHDAD.

Lost—Nebuchadrezzar's Canal — Ramadieh — Official Annoyance — Charmande—Lowlands—Nahr Malcha—Telegraph Poles and Buffaloes—An Ancient Cemetery—Bridges—Kal'at Feluja—Exploring 'Anbar—'Anbar not Sepharvaim—Description of Ruins—History of 'Anbar—Sir Henry Rawlinson — Robbing Graves — Jewish Settlements—Sport on the Euphrates—Agricultural Conditions—Volume of the River—An Arab Ruin—Farm of the Sultan—Zaptieh's Pay—Canals—'Akerkuf a Canal Centre—Ancient Name—Reach Baghdad—Triumphal Entrance

FRIDAY, January 4th, we rose soon after one o'clock, and by 2.15 the whole caravan was under way. The sky was cloudy, and we could see nothing. Our course was apparently south-southeast, over a plain partly sandy, partly composed of mud and loam. We passed a bitter stream from the bitumen springs called Ma'e Mireh, the minaret of which place we had seen the day before, and shortly after found ourselves on low, sandy hills. Here the zaptieh's horse fell down, and he found that he had lost his way. I was compelled to officiate as guide, and by means of map and compass steered the caravan back to the road. It was so dark that we were obliged to keep close together, and constantly to call from one end of the caravan to the other, to make sure that none had strayed away.

Our zaptieh was a Le'beid Arab. He said that his tribe musters five to six thousand tents, probably a gross exaggeration. He had been in the service thirty-five years, and had a wife and seven children, the oldest fourteen. He received five mejidieh a month, or about four dollars, with one loaf of bread daily for himself, and three okes of barley and a ration of straw for his horse. The money part of the pay was six months in arrears. He said that when zaptiehs go as escort with Europeans, they always receive a good backsheesh; with Persians, a smaller backsheesh; and with Turks, nothing. It was our habit to give the zaptieh about half a mejidieh a day, or three days' pay.

At five minutes past six we reached the gypsum hills of A'kuba, stretching across the plain to the banks of the Euphrates. The sun rose as we crossed these hills, the most glorious sunrise I ever saw. Just below A'kuba, running south seventy degrees east, we observed the well-marked, fairly high banks of the old canal of Sa'adi. We followed this for an hour and a quarter, as far as a ruin mound called Tel el-Adar. At this point the canal turned sharply back to the left, and then disappeared. From the name, which I met again near Nejef, and the traditions connecting themselves with this canal, I presume that it is identical with the canal which is known to have been built by Nebuchadrezzar along the edge of the Arabian plateau, from a point just below Hit to the Persian Gulf.

At nine o'clock we found ourselves passing over fields strewn with considerable remains of pottery, but with no visible tel. At 9.20 we passed the little ziaret of Aweis el-Karrani, just beyond which were some low foot-hills of another gypsum range, called el-Tuweiref, cutting the plain almost in two. At 11.55 we were passing a group of about a dozen small conical hills, composed of mud and gypsum, of most peculiar appearance, known as el-Beradhin. In the neighborhood of Ramadieh there are numbers of farms and palm-groves, and the region seemed more prosperous than almost any that we had seen. The plain is very broad at this point, and the plateau of the

Arabian desert low. The Jezireh, across the Euphrates, is quite flat. The land is so low on both sides of the river, that inundations are frequent, and many more or less permanent ponds are formed. A little below Ramadieh, on the other side of the river, are the ruins of an ancient mud-walled town.

At half-past twelve we passed the bed of a deep canal, called Wara, from which a number of branches ran in every direction, apparently meant for purposes of irrigation. There was no water in the canal at that time; but a quarter of an hour later we crossed on a new brick bridge, a remarkable sign of progress, the still used canal of el-Tash. At one o'clock we reached Ramadieh. This proved to be a comparatively bustling, new-looking town of four or five hundred houses. Whereas, in all other places excepting Deir we had been lodged in zaptieh barracks, we found here a khan, newly built of burned bricks made at Ramadieh, and adjoining a new government building of the same material. I saw also one private house of the same sort. It must be understood that buildings of brick are a rarity in that country; and it is still more rare to find buildings of new bricks, for, if the natives use brick at all, they generally use old bricks from some ruin site. But if our accommodations were more extensive and better than elsewhere, as though to make amends for this, the people were extremely annoying and rude, encouraged to be so by the officials. The Kaimakam, Emin Bey, was absent, sick, at Saklawieh. In his absence, the under officials seemed to wish to show their authority. They came to the khan, demanding not only to see, but also to carry away with them, our passports, and to search our luggage, both of which we refused to permit. It was with great difficulty that we finally got rid of them, and the large mob that accompanied them, which seemed to be on the lookout for an opportunity to pilfer us.

Ainsworth identifies Ramadieh with the town of Charmande mentioned by Xenophon, but without any real grounds. Xenophon's description of the march down the Euphrates is meagre in the extreme. All that he says of Charmande is contained in his brief notice of the desert stations from Korsote to Pylæ. They marched thirteen desert stages, ninety parasangs, having the Euphrates River on the right, and arrived at Pylæ. In this march many of the beasts of burden died; for there was no grass nor any trees, but the entire country was barren. The few inhabitants along the river supported themselves by making millstones and taking them to Babylon, where they sold them for food. "And across the Euphrates River during these desert stages there was a large and wealthy city, named Charmande. From this the soldiers purchased supplies, crossing over thither on skins." Ramadieh is too close to Pylæ to be thus described. If this were Charmande, Xenophon would have described it as at the end of the desert stages. The Charmande of Xenophon was 'Anah. If Ramadieh is an ancient site, which is very probable, it has not yet been identified.

The next morning the officials of the town took their revenge for our refusal to gratify their curiosity by neglecting to provide us with a zaptieh escort. We had arisen about one o'clock with the intention of making an early start. After waiting for some time for the zaptieh, we finally started without him at 4 A.M., leaving Noorian behind to find and bring him. By waking up all of the officials, pounding upon their doors, and allowing them no rest, he succeeded in obtaining one some two hours later. The zaptieh himself was a pleasant fellow, and more than willing to accompany us. He was a Kurd. He said that his salary was four months in arrears. Nominally he received ninety piastres in gold ($3.60) a month, one oke of wheat a day, three okes of barley for his horse, and fifteen piastres (sixty cents) a month for straw for his horse. A backsheesh in hard cash, worth several days' pay, was important to him.

Our route lay over an alluvial plain a little south of east by the stars. I observed several small canals, which I at first supposed were for purposes of irrigation; but they turned out to have been dug to intercept the locusts, which are a terrible pest along the whole Euphrates Valley. About an hour and a half after starting, we came to some low hills,—foot-hills of a larger range,—which we skirted in an almost easterly direction. They looked in most places as though composed of clay mud, but did in reality consist of various colored marls, with gypsum, alabaster, and selenite intermixed, broken into fantastic shapes. Under various names they continued to a point as far beyond Kal'at Feluja as I could see. They are nowhere of any size, and consist of a succession of small ranges, running approximately east and west as far as Saklawieh, where they turn to the south. They are the border land of the great Arabian Desert. At about nine o'clock, after passing through some foot-spurs of the hills running down to the Euphrates, we found ourselves in a large irrigated plain, cultivated in barley, with a few Arab tents on the river-bank and on the edge of the hills on the other side of the plain. On our right was a pond or lake called el-Tara. It is at this point that one begins to meet the very low land so near the level of the stream that constant inundations occur, forming lakes and marshes. From here to Kal'at Feluja and beyond, the river, when its waters are in the least swollen, must be restrained by low dikes from overflowing the country on the Arabian side.

At half-past ten we rounded the last low foot-hills jutting forward toward the river, and found ourselves in a plain stretching to the southeast as far as the eye could see. Here the telegraph wires, which had followed the hills most of the way from Ramadi, crossed the river to Saklawieh, just beyond which is the canal of the same name, identified by the best geographers with Isa of the Arabs. A little below was the ancient Nahr Malcha, or royal canal. From an early date there has been a great ship-canal connecting the Tigris and Euphrates at about this point. In the time of Trajan this canal was the Nahr Malcha, which left the Euphrates near here, and entered the Tigris just above Seleucia. At the close of the twelfth century A.D., the connecting canal was the Nahr Isa, leaving the Euphrates at nearly the same place, but entering the Tigris above Baghdad. This canal was still navigable for boats of considerable size as late as sixty years ago, when one of the steamboats of the British expedition steamed through it from the Euphrates to the Tigris, a distance by the canal of forty-five miles. Now it is a huge muddy ditch.

There are a post-office and telegraph station at Ramadi; and we had hurried into that town with a view to using both, especially the latter, in order to telegraph to Mr. Blockey at Baghdad to secure us a house, but found that no mail left Ramadi before Friday of the following week, and that the telegraph wires were down somewhere between Saklawieh and Baghdad. The telegraph poles in this country are all of iron, as there is no wood with which to make wooden poles. The buffaloes and camels use these poles as rubbing-posts, on account of which deep trenches are dug about them to keep the creatures off. Nevertheless, so valuable is the privilege of using a rubbing-post, that both buffaloes and camels climb down the trench and up again on the other side, as we often observed. The contented look on the faces of the beasts, as they rubbed their itching backs, could almost make one fancy that they were ejaculating "God bless the Duke of Argyle!" The practice is not, however, good for the telegraph poles, which have to be straightened up at frequent intervals. We were told that wild Arabs also occasionally contrive to break the wires; but whether it was buffaloes or Arabs that had done the damage, we were unable to telegraph to Baghdad.

At half-past eleven we were opposite the long, low mound of 'Anbar, close to the river on the other side. At twelve o'clock, to the right of our road, we observed a small mound, called, as we were informed, Juha, used as a cemetery at the present time, and apparently having served the same purpose from all antiquity. Its surface was no more than six feet above the level of the plain about it. All around lay fragments of pottery, and the modern graves on the top of the mound were decorated with ancient bricks and pieces of bricks. A number of jar-coffins were exposed on the edges of the mound, or above the ground about the mound. We found some five in all. They consisted of two large jars put together mouth to mouth. One of these jars was a little smaller than the other, so that its mouth could be inserted within the mouth of the other. Sometimes the lips just joined one another, and sometimes they overlapped considerably. The most complete coffin of this description, which we found, measured 188 centimetres from end to end. Another, which we measured on the following day, had a head-piece 56 centimetres in length, and a foot-piece 66 centimetres in length. Pieces of many other coffins of the same sort lay scattered about; and some Arabs, who were digging a grave on the mound, told us that they often found bones there, but never antiquities, by which I suppose they meant beads, seal cylinders, and the like. There were quantities of small stones of all sorts, along with a number of fragments of millstones, but nothing which necessarily indicated anything other than a graveyard. As head and foot-stones, on a new Arabic grave, we found two pieces of marble with an inscription in Hebrew letters. There are no Jews living at the present time nearer than Baghdad; but in ancient times 'Anbar was the seat of an important Jewish school of learning, and the centre of an enormous population. These gravestones are the only relics which we noticed of the occupation of that region by the Jews. To the southward of Juha, not very far away, two small groups of mounds were visible, apparently of the same character.

We spent half an hour exploring Juha, and then galloped on to overtake the caravan, which had passed us in the meantime. It took about an hour's fast going to reach Kal'at Feluja, which lies at the end of the rude bridge of boats which now spans the river. Presumably this bridge is of much the same type as the bridges which once connected Mesopotamia and Syria, at Tiphsah, 'Anah, and elsewhere. The bridges on the middle Euphrates have all disappeared, but from Feluja downward there are still a few. The next bridge below is at Musseyib, on the pilgrim route from Baghdad to Kerbela. There is also a bridge at Hillah, there is sometimes one at Diwanieh, there is one at Samawa, and possibly there may be one or two farther down, with which I am not familiar.

Kal'at Feluja was once upon a time, as the name indicates, a fortress or castle; and the remains of a large Turkish or Arabic building of burned brick are still to be seen. The present natives use the old ruins as a quarry from which to obtain material to build their miserable huts, when they are not too shiftless to do even that. There are not much more than a dozen houses in the place, of which several are so-called cafés for the refreshment and entertainment of the travellers who of necessity make the bridge a stage on the journey to or from Baghdad. On the Arabic side of the river there is some cultivation of the ground, and a few gardens of trees. In the Jezireh there appeared to be no cultivation of the soil. Pebble hills some twenty to thirty feet in height come down quite close to the Euphrates, leaving, however, an alluvial strip between them and the river, on which lie the towns of Feluja, Saklawieh, and ancient 'Anbar. These pebble hills are spurs of the rocky plateau of Mesopotamia to the north.

We found shelter for our whole caravan in one of the cafés at Feluja; and, excepting that we shared our accommodations with a few fleas, we were more comfortable, and warmer, than at any other place. The following day being Sunday, the caravan rested, and after service we set out on foot to visit and explore the mound of el-'Anbar. After a walk of three quarters of an hour, we reached a low hill, which I should have supposed to be natural had it not been covered with fragments of brick, glass, and pottery. This was only one of a series of outlying mounds, all of which were strewn with fragments of masonry. I had brought with me a rudimentary spade, and we dug a little. The bricks which we found were each 20 by 20 inches. One, which I broke open, had a fragment of pottery burned in it. We had no experience to guide us in the determination of Babylonian remains, and it is rather interesting to me to read now the notes which I made at that time. These large bricks were of a pale color, and gave one in some way an impression of antiquity. Besides these, there were smaller bricks of a reddish color, and in shape and size more closely resembling those in use among ourselves. We had already seen bricks of both sorts at Jabrieh on the Euphrates. As a consequence of the examination of various ruins which we had seen up to that time, I noted, that, "The bricks of the region seem to me to be at the present day very much what the ordinary bricks were in the most remote period. There are certain special sorts of bricks which one may identify as belonging to a certain period, but the ordinary bricks cannot be identified.

The same is true of the pottery, so it seems to me. You find all along the Euphrates Valley the same pottery, sometimes with a blue or green glaze, and sometimes with simple line ornaments. The sites are sometimes early, sometimes late, but the pottery seems always the same." I have seen no occasion to alter these very general conclusions, which were reached at that time. But we were not all so conservative. One of our assyriologists thought that by the pottery he could detect three periods at 'Anbar,—one Babylonian, one Greek, and one Turkish. We found here also a number of fragments of what he pronounced to be Babylonian bricks " like those of Ur," but which another of our party declared to be porous volcanic stones, which in reality they were. Here and everywhere over the mounds of 'Anbar we found vitrifactions due to a great conflagration, some in glass, some in brick, and some on the volcanic stones.

Twelve minutes from the first small hills, which were due north-northwest from Kal'at Feluja, we came to the main mound of 'Anbar. Almost isolated at the eastern end of the mound is the high point known as el-'Aker. This name is given on Kiepert's *Ruinen Felder*, but, curiously enough, the name 'Anbar does not appear there. We found at several places portions of house walls, but all late, and built of older material. In a depression toward the northern part of the tel a piece of rough, reddish marble column was lying on the ground. Not far from this was a large ruined ziaret, in which we found a marble capital with late Oriental decoration, but badly broken. Near this was an isolated hill where there seemed to have been a tower. We found here part of a wall standing, but it was late, composed of older fragments. We dug a little at this point, tracing a heavy foundation of masonry.

Dr. Ward proposed the identification of the site of 'Anbar with the ancient Sippara, the Sepharvaim of the

Bible. He thought that he found a double city, divided in two by a great canal, or by the main channel of the Euphrates. He supposed also that he traced in the ruins the lines of an ancient temple or two of the Babylonian period.

The following year I visited 'Anbar quite alone. The description from my note-book of that date will supplement what I have said above:

"In the afternoon I rode out entirely alone to revisit 'Anbar. First I rode up to a hill with tombs on it, from the top of which I had a good view of the country. At Kal'at Feluja the pebble hills reach to the water's edge; to the north they leave a considerable extent of fertile and well-cultivated plain between themselves and the river; and in this, nearer the river than the hills, lies 'Anbar. I approached it this time by the bed of a good-sized old canal, higher than the plain, which brought me almost to 'Aker, the eastern extremity of the mound. This is no tower or acropolis, but only part of a wall of mud brick. The wall, which is easily traceable on the south, east, and north, makes at this point a curve; and there being a hollow with no mound within, the effect produced, particularly by the mass A, which is higher than the rest, was that of a tower. From 'Aker I followed the line of wall until it disappeared on the northwest. Between it and the city mound was a well-marked depression, but on the northwestern and western side no wall was visible. I should say that on the inner or city side of A, the unburned bricks of the wall were visible in position. They were of small size and inferior appearance. On the northwestern side the mound was highest. Here it rose abruptly from the plain, and had evidently been much washed against by the Euphrates; for the plain is very low, and only protected by a small mud dike along the river-bank. I examined this face carefully with a view to its construction. It seemed to consist of a clay terrace, in which were occasional small layers of unburned or burned brick. There was a broad, deep depression running in some distance, and to the west of this (west-northwest point of the mound) was the highest part of this face and of the mounds. Here, on top of the terrace, was brickwork, apparently of walls, and in one place a part of a small tower. The material of the construction was burned brick, the bricks small and badly burned. This place I judged to have been the old acropolis or palace, the more especially as it projected slightly beyond the mound to the west of it, and was marked off from that by a slight depression, while, as already said, it was cut off from the mound to the east by a deep, broad bay. The surface of this portion of the mound was very thickly covered with fragments of brick, so thickly that for forty or fifty feet from the edge the ground was not visible beneath them. That part of the mounds which lay to the east of the large depression, which extended somewhat more than half-way through, is small, low, and insignificant, and is largely covered with tamarisk scrub. The appearances of a conflagration, which impressed me so strongly on my first visit, seem to be confined to the western and southern parts of the mounds, which are, however, much the largest part of the whole. The mound is nowhere more than thirty (or perhaps forty from lowest plain level) feet high; and, after the mounds which I have seen in the interim, it did not appear so large as before."

The Euphrates, or a canal from the Euphrates, washed the northern shores of the city in the days of Julian; and it is evident, from the present appearance of the ruins, that a canal was conducted from the Euphrates into the very heart of the city. It was the partial division made by this canal which led Dr. Ward to suppose 'Anbar to have been a double city, lying upon both banks either of the Euphrates or of a great canal from the Euphrates.

On the basis of his account of the ruins, we had applied for permission to dig at this spot as one of three sites, but the permission was refused. I learned later from Bedry Bey, the commissioner assigned to us by the Government, that this was because 'Anbar lies in a Sennieh, or private domain of the Sultan. The ruins are of great extent, and it certainly would be interesting to explore them.

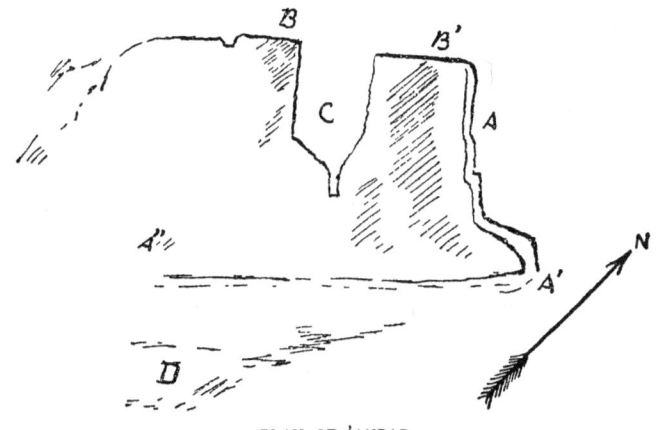

PLAN OF 'ANBAR.

A A' A"—Wall Line, A'—'Aker; B B'—Steep front on W and N.W, B—Supposed Acropolis, C—Deep Depression, D—Mound without the walls.

Abu'lfeda, in his history, narrates that Nebuchadrezzar built the city of Persabora, where 'Anbar later stood. In the days of the Emperor Julian it was an important city; and he captured it in his Persian expedition, after a desperate resistance. The period of 'Anbar's greatest prosperity was during the Arabic era. It was then a place of great wealth, and the seat of an advanced culture. It was also a favorite residence of the Jews, who inhabited several important towns in this immediate vicinity. Even in Julian's day there was, not far beyond 'Anbar, a city inhabited entirely by Jews. The remains to be observed on the surface at the present time are presumably altogether remains of the Arabic period, although some individual bricks and fragments of pottery, as well as Sassanian coins which have been found there, belong to an earlier time.

In answer to some inquiries about 'Anbar, which I addressed to Sir Henry Rawlinson, the veteran assyriologist and explorer of Babylonia, he wrote, under date of March 13, 1889, a most interesting note, which I quote in part:

"I think I told you, when you spoke to me on the subject in London, that the site had not been recognized in old Assyrian and Babylonian history; and that the Arab story of Nebuchadrezzar's colony was considered apocryphal, not being confirmed by any competent authority, but, on the contrary, discredited by the negative evidence of nearly contemporary geography. There may have been a Parthian city (Pacoria or Tiridata) in the vicinity, if not on the same site; but the true historical foundation of 'Anbar, or, as it was originally called, Firuz Shapur, took place at the hands of Shapur Dholahtaf, King of Persia, in about A.D. 350. A few years later (in A.D. 363) the new city was completely destroyed by Julian, as described by Ammianus and Zosimus, and the vitrified pottery observed by you may have been due to the conflagration of this period. The city rapidly recovered after the Roman invasion, and became the refuge of all the Christian and Jewish colonies of the neighborhood. The first Christian bishop was appointed in A.D. 540, and the Jews must have flocked in soon after in large numbers (especially from Pombeditha, which became deserted, the Academy being suppressed), as at the time of the conquest of 'Anbar by Ali (in A.D. 657) there are said to have been 90,000 Jewish inhabitants. Saffah, the founder of the Abbasside Caliphate, made 'Anbar his capital, and so it remained until the founding of Baghdad by Mansur (in A.D. 762).

There is nothing more to be said about 'Anbar until the time of Benjamin of Tudela, who, strangely enough, confounded it with the old academical city of Pombeditha, owing, probably, to the Jewish doctors of this latter city having all taken up their abode in the new settlement on the Euphrates, when the ancient Academy was deserted. Possibly, indeed, 'Anbar may have been known as the second Pombeditha in the time of Benjamin. The original city of that name was, however, at Thishobar, or in the immediate neighborhood."

We remained at 'Anbar until half-past two o'clock in the afternoon, when Harper and I set out to revisit the mound of Juha, which we had seen the day before. We were accompanied by Mustafa and Kework, the strongest man in our employ. Two enormous vultures were sitting on two recent graves. They seemed half-gorged, and allowed us to approach them very closely before they heavily flapped away. The two fragments of old Hebrew gravestones, which had been set up as head and footstones over a modern Arabic grave, we appropriated, and handed them to Mustafa, who put them in the pannier over the back of his animal, and started for camp at once, accompanied by Kework, while we stayed to dig up some graves with a pick. None of the coffins of the two-jar type which we found were large enough to allow a body to be placed in them at full length. They seem rather to have been receptacles for the dead, after those dead had already been buried for a sufficient time to allow the flesh to waste away. All of the coffins, however, were full of fine, light, packed dirt or dust, which had sifted in, completely filling them, so that it was difficult to ascertain precisely the condition in which the bodies had been interred. Owing to the fact that the coffins were, as described, filled with dust, and because we had nothing but a pick to work with, little time at our disposal, and two fighting stallions to hold while we worked, we could not even determine approximately the original position of the skeletons in the jars. We found in no parts of the coffins which we dug out, or which had previously been dug out, anything but bones, dust, and in one place a couple of feathers. The uniformity of the method of burial in jars fitted one within the other was interesting and curious. Later I found at Nippur burials of this same sort.

From the first captivity onward, the Jews played a great *rôle* in Babylonia. Only a small part of them, descendants of those deported by Nebuchadrezzar, returned to Judæa. The greater portion preferred to remain in Babylonia. These continued to call themselves Galutha, the captives (literally, the " captivity "). The study of the law was pursued among them; ancient traditions and literature were collected and preserved; laws, rites, and the like were reduced to writing, codified, developed, and commented upon. The captives, as they called themselves, made pilgrimages to Jerusalem, contributed to the support of their brethren, and pathetically bewailed their own exile, very much as is done by Jewish pilgrims to Jerusalem at the present day. The beautiful Pilgrim Psalter, or Songs of Degrees (Psalms cxx–cxxxiv) is a collection of hymns sung by the pilgrims of this Babylonian " captivity " on their pilgrimages to the temple at Jerusalem. After the destruction of the temple by Titus, and the further dispersion of the Jews by Hadrian, following the suppression of the revolt under Bar-Cochab, the Jews of the Babylonian " captivity " received a considerable accession of numbers, and a far greater accession of influence. From that time onward, for some centuries, Babylonia was the true home of the Jewish nation and religion.

There were two great centres of the Jews in Babylonia, —one, in which was Sura, near Babylon itself; and the other, and more famous centre, at Nehardea, or Nearda, which was either at or near the junction of the Euphrates and the Nahr Malcha, not far below 'Anbar. This was for a long time the religious centre of the Jews. Here was their greatest school, and here resided the Resh Galutha, or Head of the Captivity. During the Parthian period, in the first century A.D., two brothers, Asinai and Anilai, made Nehardea for a brief period a practically independent Jewish state. For a long time Nehardea continued to be a Jewish city; and no Christians were found there, we are told, until the close of the third century A.D. In the fifth century, however, the place became the seat of a Christian bishop. Nehardea was followed by Pombeditha as the seat of the great Jewish university, and the centre of religious and national life to the Jews of Babylonia. This was situated on the Euphrates somewhere, I should judge, in the same general region, and not far above Nehardea, but its precise location is not known. The name is explained as meaning " mouth of a canal called Beditha." The place is also sometimes called Golah, or " Captivity." It was destroyed in 588 A.D., whereupon the Jews took refuge, as already stated, in Perisabor or 'Anbar. That part of the Euphrates Valley, in the low marshy land, much cut up by canals and ponds, was the centre of a large, wealthy and important Jewish population under Parthians, Persians, and Arabs, from the beginning of the Christian era, or earlier, until the foundation of Baghdad and the decay of 'Anbar,—a period of eight hundred years or more. It is to be expected that some day we shall find much more serious remains of this important period of Jewish occupation than a couple of fragments of late Jewish gravestones on an insignificant burial-mound.

It was some time after sunset before we left Juha; and, although we galloped fast, it was already pitch dark when we reached Kal'at Feluja. In order to secure a house to receive us on our arrival at Baghdad, I sent Noorian forward in the night with our one zaptieh. We had asked for two zaptiehs from Saklawieh, for there is no station at Kal'at Feluja; but they sent us only one, saying that they had no more.

At Feluja our journey down the Euphrates came to an end, for here the road to Baghdad leaves that river. For precisely three weeks we had journeyed along the banks of the great river. In describing that journey I have dwelt mainly on the antiquities which mark the course of the stream,—dumb relics of ruined towns and castles, which yet narrate most eloquent stories of that which has been. But although the Euphrates is far more important for its past than for its present, yet even this is not devoid of interest. To the sportsman it is a region possessing some attractions, with its jungles full of wild pigs, with lions, lynxes, and the like at rare intervals. Foxes, wolves, jackals, and hyenas are abundant, if one might condescend to shoot them. The elephant and ostrich have vanished, but a lucky hunter might chance to find a wild ass; and gazelles, at least, are plentiful. Francolins, pigeons, rock partridges, and numerous water-fowl invite the shot-gun. Crocodiles, if they ever existed in the Euphrates, as old writers aver, have given place to the great monitor lizard, and the huge turtles of the river are reported to be dangerous adversaries. The river is full of enormous fish, which are an important source of food-supply to the natives. At Haditha, and probably also elsewhere, they dry them, and then pound them into a sort of flour, in which state they are stored for later use.

The agricultural possibilities of the Euphrates must also attract the attention of the traveller. The alluvial bed of the river, generally two or three miles in breadth, between steep banks of marl or gypsum from a hundred to three hundred feet in height, is amazingly fertile when irrigated, and the only fertilizer which it requires is the water of the river. Such cultivation as now exists above

'Anah is chiefly of durra (a coarse, maize-like grain), with a little wheat, sesame, and barley. Immense tracts of waste land are overgrown with licorice. Tamarisk, poplars, mulberries, and a species of osier willow, with a few olives, are the only trees I observed in the upper reaches of the river; but from 'Anah downward, palms fringe the stream, and cover the islands at every settlement; and with these one finds, in addition to the tamarisk and the mulberry, fig-trees, pomegranates, lemons, and oranges. Below 'Anah, cotton is added to the other crops. The actuality is small, but the potentiality with a civilized government and means of transportation is great. The Euphrates is a natural channel of communication between the eastern and western portions of the Turkish Empire, and the day must come when railroads and steamboats will ply on and along its shores. Then the old sites will revive, and become wealthier and more prosperous than in times of old; for the Euphrates has a future as surely as it has had a past.

From Meskene to Feluja along the river, according to the measurements of the British expedition, is $585\frac{1}{2}$ miles. From Feluja to the Persian Gulf the length of the stream is $445\frac{1}{4}$ miles. Above Hit it occupies a bed which it has worn in the rock. Below Saklawieh it flows through an alluvial country formed by its own deposits, where there is no rock, nor even a stone as large as a pigeon's egg, with the exception of a few so-called pebble hills, which are spurs of the rock plateau above, and formed originally islands in the great sea at the mouth of the river. The fall of the Euphrates in the territory described is about six inches to the mile. Between the mouth of the Khabor and Abu Kemal the average width of the river is 400 yards, its depth 18 feet, and the velocity of its current at flood 4 miles an hour. From this point downward there is a progressive diminution. At 'Anah the figures are 350 yards, 18 feet, and

4 miles; at Haditha, 300 yards, 18 feet, and 4 miles; from Haditha to Hit, 350 yards, 16 feet, and 3 miles; from Hit to Feluja, 250 yards, 20 feet, and less than 2½ miles. Below Feluja the stream is dissipated in canals and marshes, but returns to approximately the same dimensions at Samawa. While a much longer river than the Tigris, its current is less rapid, and the volume of water discharged less than half as great. The mean velocity of the current of the Euphrates at Hit is 4.46 feet per second, and of that of the Tigris at Baghdad, 7.33. The quantity of water discharged by the Euphrates is 72,804 cubic feet per second; and by the Tigris, 164,103 cubic feet.

It was our intention to visit 'Akerkuf on the road to Baghdad. One of our muleteers professed to know the road, and, in default of a zaptieh, we took him as guide. We had purposed going north to 'Anbar to photograph the walls, and from there to 'Akerkuf; but there was a dense fog, which rendered photographing impossible, and we accordingly chose the more direct road. Following the guidance of our muleteer, we journeyed first south of east over alluvial soil, passing, half an hour from Kal'at Feluja, some ruins known as Kullat-el-Ahrab. There were mud-brick walls in the form of a square, while fragments of baked bricks and pottery lay about. Twenty minutes later we reached the edge of the pebble hills. The soil was first gravelly, developing later into hills of pebbles, with patches of loam in the little valleys between, and layers of gypsum cropping out at intervals. From time to time there loomed silently out of the fog great caravans of camels on their way to the bridge. Little by little the fog lifted, and at 9.30 we could see a large building, which our muleteers called a serai, somewhat south of east. They told us that there was there a Sennieh of the Sultan; and that this serai was the place of residence of the official in charge, and contained the offices, storehouses, etc. Beyond this in the distance was a ruin mound, which we were told was 'Akr-el-Ajedat. Half an hour later we found ourselves on the southeastern edge of the pebble hills, with stubble-fields of durra on our right; and ten minutes later we turned to the southeast to go to a ruin, visible in the distance, which our muleteers pronounced to be the ruins of 'Akerkuf, but which actually turned out to be the ancient site known as Sennadieh. We passed on our right, at a distance of a quarter of a mile, a small low tel crowned with a large ziaret, which seemed to be an unusually holy place, and consequently also a favorite place of burial. Our muleteers called this Hahr-Mahmud. Here we began to cross the beds of old canals. The first of these which we crossed, and which we were told was called Muradieh, serves at the present time as a road. The beds of these canals are all above the level of the plain, and the banks are often very high. In less than an hour we crossed four or five such canals running in different directions, and in the bed of one of them we travelled for about a quarter of an hour.

It was a little after eleven when we reached the ruins of Sennadieh. In a plain shut in on all sides by tels and canal-banks was a field of ruins,—bricks, pottery, tiles, and fragments of walls. Toward the northern end of this field a section of a domed building was still standing. This building was in the form of a square below, each side measuring 8.25 metres over all. On this was set an octagon, and on the octagon a dome, the latter broken through at the top. This form of construction is not unlike that adopted by the Byzantine Greeks from Justinian's time onward, and which after the conquest of Constantinople, under the influence of Sancta Sophia, became the regular form for mosques throughout the Turkish Empire. The sides of the octagon were highly decorated with a pattern in fine glazed blue tiles and light-colored decorated unglazed brick tiles. The pattern was in arabesque lines. This was the best-preserved portion of an extensive ruin with very massive walls. It was Arabic and of a good period. The ancient name of the place was Sındea. Close at hand, south twenty degrees west, was another ruın, called Musbugh.

From Sennadieh our course to the serai on the Sennieh was about due west. This serai was larger, newer, and in better condition than the ordinary zaptieh barracks which we had found along the road, but of a similar pattern. We were assigned a room on the roof, from which we obtained a fine view of the various ruin mounds and points of interest in the neighborhood. 'Akerkuf was visible in the distance over the pebble hills seventy degrees east of north. Tel Kenise, which is supposed to represent the ancient Cunaxa, where Cyrus was killed in battle with his brother Artaxerxes, lay not far away from us almost due south. Other ruin mounds were visible in different directions. The official in charge of the serai called on us shortly after our arrival. He was a pleasant, elderly gentleman, and said that he had accompanied de Sarzec in his first diggings six or seven years before. The serai had only been built one year, and he had only been in charge of it four days. He had under hım six zaptiehs. The private domains of the Sultan in this region are large, and constantly on the increase. These lands are exempt from taxation, and the acquisition by his Majesty of so much of the cultivable land of the province has seriously curtailed the revenues of Baghdad. The old gentleman was uneasy about our rifles, and uncertain whether he ought not to command their seizure on the ground that they were forbidden. We therefore had them packed away; and, after they were thus removed from sight, his trouble in regard to them seemed to vanish also. Two or three members of our party, among them myself, were taken sick that night, whether as a consequence of something eaten, general fatigue, exposure to cold, or the water of the place. In the case of the rest of us, it amounted to little more than a temporary annoyance; but with Prince it developed into a real illness.

The next morning, January 8th, we were under way by half-past five. The Governor of the Sennieh gave us a zaptieh, who turned out to be a better guide than our muleteer of the day before. He received, so he told us, a lira a month as salary, with an allowance of half an oke (less than a pound and a half) of bread daily, and three okes (or less than nine pounds) of barley and a sufficient supply of straw for his horse (an oke is 2.83 lbs.). His salary was about four months in arrears, but the total debt of the Government to him amounted to some sixty liras. He receives each year a salary of only about seven months.

We merely touched the edge of the pebble hills, our course, with that exception, being over alluvial soil. Some distance to our left were two small hills, apparently sand-hills, with ziarets upon them. Ten minutes after passing these, we found ourselves in the bed of the old Muradieh Canal, travelling eastward. The canal was very crooked, and a quarter of an hour later it bent so much to the northward that we were compelled to leave it. Our course now lay over a plain covered by a network of old canals, whose banks rose like hills on every side of us. Wild gourds grow in abundance on the surface of the plain. At 6.40 we crossed a canal running at about right angles. At 6.45 we crossed a canal running north thirty degrees east. At 6.48 we crossed another canal at right angles. At 6.55 we crossed a canal running north twenty degrees west, and at 6.57 another running parallel to this. I need not mention all the other canals we crossed, as these will suffice to show how numerous they are in that section. The Arabs told us that all of these canals ran to 'Akerkuf; and if this is not literally and exactly correct, at least it seems to be the fact that 'Akerkuf is the centre of the canal system covering all this section. About seven o'clock we joined the caravan track leading from Kal'at Feluja to Baghdad, which we should have followed on the preceding day, had not our muleteers lost their way in the fog. Along this we journeyed for a while, passing half a dozen huge canals running in various directions, and then turned off northward into a perfect maze of canals, in the centre of which, on the edge of a great marsh, stands 'Akerkuf.

This prominent ruin consists of an immense mass of solid sun-dried brick, on the summit of a rather low mound, which latter is littered with fragments of burned brick, pottery of all sorts, and glass in small quantities. The portion of the tower still standing measures, according to Hilprecht's count of the layers of brick, ninety-six feet. Its corners are approximately toward the cardinal points. The unbaked bricks of which it is built average twenty-eight and a half centimetres in length and breadth, and eleven centimetres in thickness. They are all laid flat, and not, as at Nippur, some on the edge, and some on the side. After each seven courses, or thereabouts, there is a layer of palm matting, while through the bricks at irregular intervals run ropes of palm strands. There is a slight depression to the south and southwest of the tel, and small mounds to the south, east, and west. To the west, northwest, and north, stretches the marshy lake called Khor-el-Hasai. Various tels can be seen in different directions, while almost innumerable canals intersect the country, having 'Akerkuf or its neighborhood as the special centre from which they radiate. Baghdad was visible a little to the south of east, and the golden domes and minarets of Imam Musa shone out a little to the north of east. Without excavation, it is perhaps impossible to say certainly what sort of place 'Akerkuf

The Ruined Tower of 'Akerkuf, near Baghdad.

was, and to what period it belonged. Inscribed bricks have been found there bearing the name of Kurigalzu, presumably Kurigalzu the Second, a king of the Cossæan dynasty, who ruled in Babylon from 1306 to 1284 B.C.; and the place has been designated by some Dur-Kurigalzu.

'Akerkuf has ordinarily been supposed to be the remains of an ancient ziggurat. It does not seem to me, from the examination of the ruins which I made in my two or three visits, that this can have been the case. I am inclined to think that it is the ruin of an ancient tower or fortress which guarded a great canal centre. In the time of the Abbasside Caliphs it is metioned, under the name of Akakuba, as an important point on the canal system between 'Anbar and Baghdad. Somewhere in this neighborhood, or a little farther to the south, stood, in Julian's time, the city of Maogamalcha, which opposed his progress toward Ctesiphon after the capture of 'Anbar, and which he took and destroyed after a desperate resistance.

We left 'Akerkuf at quarter-past ten, taking a course nearly southeast. We soon found ourselves in another network of canals, crossing in seven minutes as many large canals. Half an hour after starting, we reached an Arab encampment, about which were a number of camels feeding. We had seen a similar encampment to the north of 'Akerkuf. This whole country, up to the very walls of the great city of Baghdad, is a "no man's land," wandered over by Arab tribes, and unsafe for the unprotected traveller or solitary horseman.

Shortly before noon we crossed the stream of Washash, flowing almost east to the Tigris. Our guide told us that during the winter season the water flows from the marsh to the north of 'Akerkuf toward the Tigris, but in the summer it flows from the Tigris toward the marsh. The litter containing the Baghdad murderer came to a halt in this stream, the mules refusing to budge. They even undertook to roll in the water; and it was with some difficulty that the murderer was extricated, and carried to the shore on the backs of men.

Outside of Baghdad, Noorian, and the zaptieh who had been sent forward with him, were awaiting us. Bedry Bey, the commissioner appointed by the Government to attend us in our excavations, was also there on horseback, attended by his servant on foot; and two cawasses from the English Consul-General were on hand to add ceremony to our entrance. It was quite a pompous procession. First came the two zaptiehs; then the two cawasses; then I, escorted by Bedry Bey, who rode his horse a neck behind mine; then the several members of the expedition; and finally the caravan with its attachés, numbering some fifty beasts or more. The streets were so narrow that it was almost impossible much of the time for two of us to ride abreast. On the way, another cawass from the British Consul-General met us with a note from the latter, inviting us to dine with him that evening, and announcing that he would call upon us as soon as we had had time fairly to settle ourselves in our house. The whole town seemed to have heard of our coming; and, thanks to the British Resident, our entrance resembled a triumphal procession.

A Scene on the Tigris at Baghdad, showing characteristic native boats, the long turadas, and the round, pitch-smeared kufas, with bridge of boats beyond.

CHAPTER IX.

BAGHDAD AND BABYLON.

The British Resident—A Turkish Toothache — Antiquity Dealers—Our Commissioner—Ancient Baghdadu—Modern Baghdad—The Date Mark—A Trip to Ctesiphon—The Palace of Chosroes—Purchase of Antiquities—A Holy Shrine—Audience of the Wali Pasha—Leave to Depart—The Start—A Khan—Excavations at Abu Habba—The Garden of Eden—Babil—Nebuchadrezzar's Tree — Antiquity Ferrets — The Hanging Gardens—Hillah—Birs Nimrud—The Tower of Babel.

OUR house in Baghdad was on the eastern side of the Tigris, where all the consuls and foreign residents reside. The rent which we paid for this residence, unfurnished, was eighteen piastres (seventy-two cents) a day. It was a large and commodious building, containing accommodations for the whole party, our luggage, our servants, and our horses. We had scarcely alighted on the day of our arrival, before Major Talbot, acting Indian Resident and British Consul-General in the absence of Colonel Tweedy, and Mr. Blockey, our financial correspondent in Baghdad, called upon us. That evening Harper, Field, and I, together with Mr. Blockey, dined with Major and Mrs. Talbot at the British Residency, and the following evening the other members of the party were entertained in a similar manner. The Talbots were charming in every way, and Major Talbot took as much pains with us as though we had been an expedition sent out by his own government. He proposed to go with me to see the Wali Pasha, and offered to send the next day and inquire when the latter would receive me. He informed me that Mustafa Assim Pasha, the then Governor-General, was, on the whole, a good official, and one who would be likely to do what he could to be obliging, more especially to any one presented by the British Resident. The English Government maintains a large establishment at this point, and the British Resident is a man of much importance. The expenses of this establishment are borne by India, the British Consul-General being Resident in behalf of the Indian administration. He has a force of Sepoys at his disposal, and a gunboat on the river; and there is in the Residency a post-office, which is a station of the Indian postal system. Owing largely to this display, the British Resident takes a high position in the estimation both of government and people. He is reckoned as second in importance only to the Governor-General. It was accordingly of the greatest value to us to have Mr. Talbot so ostentatiously and immediately acknowledge us as his countrymen. His conduct was all the more graceful, because he had not received any official notification in regard to the mission in advance of our arrival.

The next morning Major Talbot sent to the Governor-General to inquire when he would see me, and ascertained that he was sick with a toothache, and could see no one. I went with Bedry Bey to see Mr. Blockey, our correspondent, and M. Henri Pognon, the distinguished assyriologist, who was then acting as French and Russian Consul at Baghdad. I soon ascertained that there was a great deal of work to be done to put matters in shape before leaving Baghdad. The boxes, which had been sent directly from England and America, had all been opened, and a good deal of small pilfering had taken place at the custom-house. It was necessary to have everything repacked, re-adjusted, and divided into suitable weights for mule-loads. Then there were a great many small things to be bought, both for the excavations and also for our own personal comfort. Among other things, it was necessary to have tools and baskets made for the use of the workmen in excavating at Nippur.

It was also desirable to ascertain what antiquities, if any, were in Baghdad, and where they came from. This was not an easy task, as Bedry watched us with the eyes of a lynx, and when he was not himself in our house, so arranged that his man-servant, Elias, should be there. We were therefore under constant espionage. Bedry was said to be in league with the Daoud Thoma ring of antiquity dealers, and to confiscate antiquities found in the possession of others. Consequently the dealers fought very shy, and we found the greatest difficulty in opening communications with them. Daoud Thoma was Hormuzd Rassam's head man in his excavations, and it is publicly claimed by the British Museum officials that tablets belonging to those excavations have been making their appearance piecemeal ever since. Certainly, Daoud Thoma and his brothers have conducted a considerable business in antiquities ever since Rassam left Babylonia, purchasing from the Arabs of Jimjimeh and other towns, who make their living chiefly by digging in the ruin mounds; and also, it is said, employing their own paid agents to dig at various points. In addition to this, Daoud has a large general business in Manchester goods of all sorts, which he imports and sells in Baghdad. Bedry was very intimate with him, and lived in one of his houses.

The stories regarding Bedry current in Baghdad were many and curious. He had been sent out as commissioner to accompany M. de Sarzec and M. Sevelinges in the excavations at Tello. After the close of those excavations he had been retained in Irak, and employed in various capacities by the museum; and now he was to be our commissioner. Munif Pasha had informed me that

Bedry was his appointee and a friend of his, and told me that I could make arrangements with him to my own satisfaction. This I understood to mean that Bedry was there for the purpose of being bribed to let us have what we wanted, and, in case we did not bribe him, to put every possible obstacle in the way of the expedition. We had information from others whom Bedry had accompanied as commissioner, which led us to suppose that we were dealing with a very hard customer, who was there exclusively for the purpose of getting money, and would sell us our own antiquities if we would buy them; and otherwise would sell them to Daoud Thoma or his brothers. It became necessary, therefore, to take every precaution to render it impossible for him to carry off without our knowledge the antiquities found by us. Bedry began by recommending to us as workmen persons whom we knew to be connected in one way or another with Daoud Thoma, and we naturally concluded that he was attempting to impose upon our ignorance, bringing us into a connection which would allow Daoud to rob our trenches. Those were days of intrigue, treachery, and suspicion. Bedry suspected us of trying to outwit him and purchase contraband antiquities, and we suspected him of undertaking to victimize us by making us dig antiquities for the benefit of his friends.

One day M. Pognon took us all to see the remains of old Baghdad, or Baghdadu. On the Mesopotamian side of the river are the remains of a terrace or platform of an old temple or palace. Two great fragments of masonry jut out into the river near the upper bridge. Beneath, for nine or ten feet above the water, these consist of large, hard-burned bricks laid in bitumen, and stamped with the stamp of Nebuchadrezzar. Above is later work of the Arabic period, the bricks of which are different in shape, smaller in size, and not laid in bitumen. We went to the ruin of this old quay or terrace in a very

The Tomb of Zobeide, the Favorite Wife of Harun-er-Rashid, at Baghdad.

large kufa, a round-bottomed boat, or coracle, made of wicker-work covered with bitumen. These boats are still a characteristic feature in Babylonia, and they have been in use from the earliest times, as is attested by the ancient Assyrian bas-reliefs. We examined a number of bricks with the Nebuchadrezzar stamp upon them. I am not aware that any other ruins of the Babylonian period have been discovered in Baghdad, but this quay is quite enough to show that it was built long before the time of the Arabic conquest.

Baghdad is mentioned in old inscriptions as early as the year 2000 B.C. It bore at that time the name of Baghdadu. It was rebuilt by Nebuchadrezzar, as the bricks in the quay prove. Later, it seems to have fallen into ruins, and the Arab historians speak as though the city built by Mansur in the year 762 A.D. was an entirely new foundation. According to their account, there was at that time nothing at the place, about fifteen miles north of Ctesiphon, but an old monastery. Mansur planned to make of it a stronghold to control an unfriendly region, and robbed both Wasit and Madain to strengthen and beautify his new fortress. Under Mansur's successors, and especially under Harun-er-Rashid, it became the greatest and most wealthy city of the day, a centre of art and literature.

Outside of the ruins above mentioned, there is little in the way of antiquities to be seen at Baghdad. There are a few minarets containing tiles of beautiful workmanship of the time of the Abbasside Caliphs. The tomb of Zobeide, the favorite wife of Harun-er-Rashid, is shown just outside the city walls. This, with its pineapple dome, is rather curious than beautiful. As for the old walls of the city, they are entirely ruined. But if there is little to be seen in the way of antiquities, the town and the people are certainly sufficiently curious and interesting. It is the unadulterated Orient. Among the other curiosities of the place, at the time of my first stay in Baghdad, was a vile and brutal-looking man who insisted on walking through the bazaars stark naked. He was regarded as a holy man, inspired of God, on account of his insanity or eccentricity, and the authorities did not venture to stop his exhibition of himself.

The oddest sight among the people is the Arab women. The lower classes are like those we had seen along the Euphrates Valley, with tattooed lips and disfiguring nose-rings; but the better class of the Arab women in Baghdad cover their faces carefully with heavy, black horse-hair visors, which project like enormous beaks a foot in front of them. Their nether extremities are incased in great, loose, yellow boots, reaching to their knees, and fully displayed by their method of draping the garments in front. The men, even in midwinter, generally have the breast exposed, and the women are not so particular about the covering of the breast as of the head. The children of the commoner classes, even in January, ordinarily wear but one garment, open almost to the waist, and not reaching below the knee.

Baghdad is a trying place in which to reside during midwinter. It was built for the six months of intense heat, and in the damp cold of December and January it is too much like a great gloomy vault. The streets where business is transacted are roofed over, so that no sun can penetrate.

One of the unpleasant features of life in Baghdad is the so-called Baghdad date mark, the same which is known elsewhere as the Aleppo button. This is a boil which attacks the face or the extremities. It appears in two forms, known to the natives as male and female respectively. The former is a dry, scaly sore; the latter, a running, open boil. It is not painful, but leaves ugly scars. The natives all carry somewhere on the face, neck, hands, arms, or feet the scars of these boils, which they have had as children. European children born in the country are apt to be dreadfully disfigured, as in their case the boils invariably appear on the face; and whereas native children have, as a rule, but one boil, those born of European parents are sure to have several. Adult foreigners visiting the country are also liable to be attacked; and women rarely escape disfigurement, if they stay in the country for any length of time. The boil or boils last for about a year, after which there is no more likelihood of a recurrence of the trouble than in the case of small-pox. The disease exists along the rivers Tigris and Euphrates and in the country adjacent, including some places as far from the rivers as Aleppo; but there are individual towns and regions which seem to be exempt. The cause of the disease has never been ascertained, nor a cure found. Only one of our party was ever afflicted with this trouble, Haynes, who stayed in Baghdad continuously for a much longer time than the rest of us. Noorian had had the boil in infancy.

We made but one trip of exploration while at Baghdad. Friday, the 19th, Haynes, Field, Noorian, and I, with two servants, Hajji Kework and Artin, went to Ctesiphon. We rose at three o'clock, and started at five. When I came to put on my belt, I found that my revolver had been stolen. We never recovered it, although we were quite convinced that a young man who had attended us on several occasions, and had been very free in offers to help about the house, was the one who had appropriated it. American and European firearms are contraband in Turkey, and their rarity enhances their value enormously. The zaptieh detailed to accompany us did not arrive at the time agreed upon, and we started without him. He overtook us shortly after we had crossed the river Diyala, two hours south of Baghdad. Just before crossing that river, we passed a ruin mound called Tel Blegha, consisting chiefly of tombs and fragments of pottery; and shortly afterwards we passed two more ruin mounds, Reshad and Hırsum. Just afterward we crossed an old canal, and passed a ruin mound known as Bed'a. We reached Ctesiphon at half-past nine.

The ruins of Ctesiphon are of considerable extent, but it was raining hard, and we could see but a few feet in front of us; so that we examined carefully only the ruins of Chosroes' palace, and the mound to the south of it, a hundred paces or so away. The arch of the ancient reception hall of the palace is open toward the east. It is one hundred and six feet in height, according to Layard, and about the same by my count of the layers of brick. There are forty-seven paces, or almost one hundred and fifty feet, from the opening to the rear wall of this hall. The supporting walls of the arch are seven metres in thickness. There is a door in the middle of the west end of the hall, and the eastern side is entirely open, as already stated. Near the opening, on both the north and south sides, are doors. The one on the south leads through a vaulted passage behind the façade, which is still standing. This façade is six stories in height, and the walls at the bottom are six metres thick. The front of it was originally stuccoed, as was the interior of the great reception hall. The building back of the façade originally ran as far westward as did the reception hall, as is shown by the remains of the foundation walls and some remains of superstructures on the south side. The façade itself is in the nature of a false front, not indicating truly the character of the building behind it. Most representations of this palace of Chosroes restore a building on the other side of the reception hall, representing the south side to be the same as the north; but, although I examined the mound carefully, I found no present evidence of the former existence of a building on the south side similar to the one on the north. In front of the great reception room, eastward, was a mass of rubble, which led

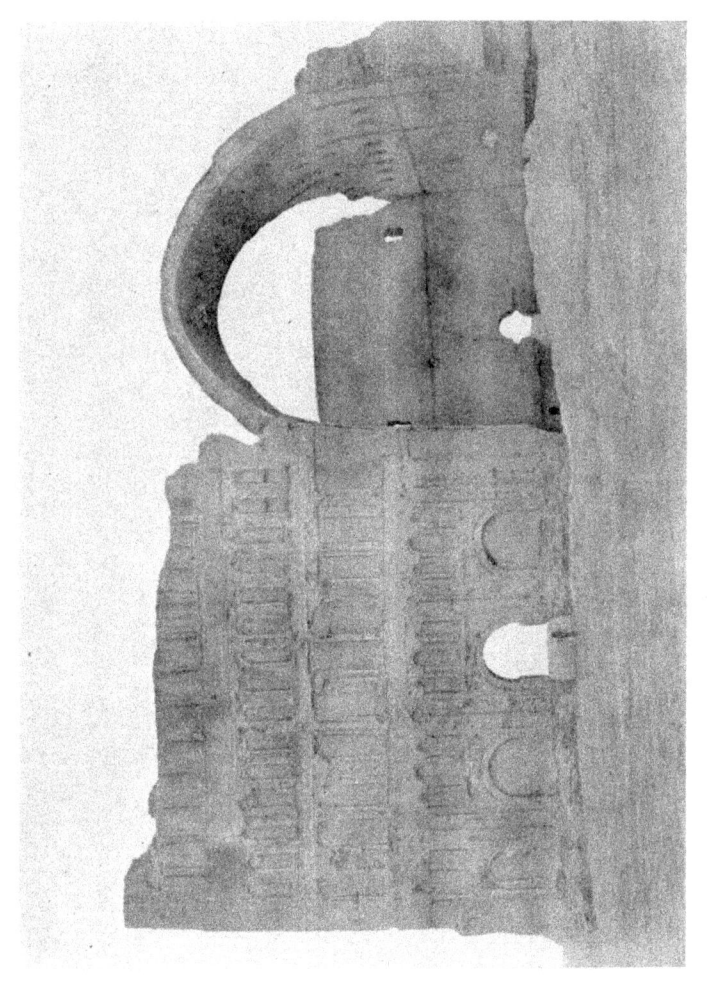

Tak-i-Khesra; the Ruins of the White Palace of Chosroes at Ctesiphon.

me to suppose that the hall may once have extended eastward beyond its present point; but, as I found no foundation walls, it is quite possible that the rubble had fallen from parts of the builidmg which are still standing. Noorian climbed to the top of the arch, and found a brick with a piece of green pottery baked in it. He also found a Babylonian brick with an inscription of Nebuchadrezzar: for as at the present day, so also in the past, it was the custom of all races in Babylonia to use older material along with the new in their constructions; and Babylon especially was the great quarry from which, after Nebuchadrezzar's time, new builders derived their material.

Ctesiphon became the capital of the Parthian Empire about the beginning of our era. After the fall of the Parthian power, it became the winter residence of the Sassanian-Persian monarchs. The present visible ruins are mainly those of the " white palace " of the famous Chosroes. The open-arched hall was his throne-room. It was presumably in this hall that Saad, the Arab general, found the wonderful silk carpet, one hundred and twenty ells long and sixty broad, representing a paradise or garden; the flowers, fruits, and shrubs done in gold embroidery and precious stones. The city was so wealthy at that time, that, out of the spoil, Saad is said to have distributed $1500 to each of his 60,000 soldiers. Layard, in his *Nineveh and Babylon*, says that the plan of the palace is that of modern Persian houses, a great iwan or open chamber for summer residence, flanked by sleeping and other rooms, forming separate stories to the height of the centre hall. Architecturally, the building is a curious combination of Oriental and Occidental motives. The six-story façade, while clumsy and barbarous in execution, is unmistakably Greek by descent, while the great arched throne-room is equally unmistakably Asiatic. And this combination is generally characteristic of all the Parthian and Sassanian remains which one finds in Babylonia.

Ctesiphon, or Madain, as the Arab writers call it, was captured and plundered by the Arabs in 636 or 637 A.D. When el-Mansur built Baghdad in 762 A.D., he used Ctesiphon, and particularly the "white palace," as a quarry for his new city, precisely as the builders of Ctesiphon had used Babylon and the great structures of Nebuchadrezzar; but so colossal was Chosroes' iwan, and so strongly built, that, after all his attempts to demolish it, what still remains is to-day the most picturesque and effective ruin in all Babylonia. It is known either as Takht-i-Khesra ("throne of Chosroes") or Tak-i-Khesra ("arch of Chosroes").

Close to the arch on the northeast is a Persian ziaret dedicated to Imam Musa, and a khan built out of the fragments of the ruins. To the southeast a large piece of the city wall is still standing. Close to the palace to the south is a large, low mound, which doubtless covers some of the buildings of the ancient city. Owing to the rain, our photographs of Ctesiphon were almost entirely failures.

Across the Tigris from Ctesiphon stood the city of Seleucia, built by Seleucus Nicator at the close of the fourth century B.C., as the capital of the new Greek empire. The mounds which mark the site of this city stand out quite prominently, but did not seem to be as extensive as those of Ctesiphon. The city itself, even after the Parthian conquest, is said to have been larger and wealthier than its rival across the river. Pliny reports it as having a population of 600,000 in his time. The Parthian monarchs allowed it to exist side by side with their capital, Ctesiphon, and to retain its independence and its own republican form of government; and, though having a large Syrian and Jewish population (the latter until the Greeks and Syrians united in falling upon the unfortunate Jews and driving them out), it maintained its Greek character until taken and sacked in a Roman invasion in the time of Marcus Aurelius Antoninus. On its ruins, Ardeshir, or Artaxerxes, the founder of the Sassanian dynasty, erected the town of Veh Ardeshir as a suburb of Ctesiphon across the river.

One afternoon Bedry and I undertook a ride about the walls of the city, but Bedry's horse ran away just outside the gate and threw him. I found him sitting on a tomb badly shaken up. His horse was recaptured, and he mounted, only to be thrown again, this time on his head. That ended my explorations under his guidance. The next day he sold his horse.

The old walls, as I have already stated, are now almost entirely destroyed. They had been allowed to go to ruin, and were crumbling away long since. One pasha sold them as bricks, in a time of distress. Midhat Pasha caused a great part of the remainder to be torn down with the view of extending the town and turning the ancient wall into a park, as has been done in so many German cities. As is usual in Turkey, the work was begun and never finished. On the northern side of the city an old gate is still standing. Near this is the oldest minaret, dating from the time of the Caliphs. It is in the form of a cone.

Above and below Baghdad, on both sides of the Tigris, are gardens of palm-trees, pomegranates, oranges, lemons, and the like. Underneath the palm-trees they grow wheat. The gardens and cultivated land extend but a very short distance back of the river on both sides. A few miles up the river is el-Kathim, or Kathemain, where there is a sacred mosque of Imam Musa, an object of pilgrimage to pious Shiites. This mosque is very gorgeous. The two domes, four minarets, and a part of the façade of the mosque, are overlaid with gold. It is the most resplendent thing I ever saw; and from whatever direction the traveller approaches Baghdad, the glittering domes and minarets of Kathim are the first objects which meet the eye. The people of the place are very fanatical, and will not allow Christians even to approach closely the door of the outer court of the mosque. Not knowing this, I rode up to the gate in order to look in. Forthwith every one dropped his wares and his bartering, and rushed at me with cries and threats to drive me from the sacred precincts. To obtain a good view of the mosque, it is necessary to secure admittance through friends to some of the houses in the neighborhood, from the roof of which one can unmolested study the shrine of Imam Musa.

It was Monday, the 21st, two weeks after our arrival at Baghdad, that Mustafa Assim Pasha's toothache vanished, and he was finally able to receive us and attend to our business. We were presented by Major Talbot, the British Resident. The hour of audience was between nine and ten A.M. By Major Talbot's directions, I mounted five members of the expedition on horseback, with a servant at each man's bridle-rein. Major Talbot came with quite an escort to take us to the palace, and our procession through the streets formed a pageant as interesting to the natives of Baghdad as Barnum's circus is to the citizens of our towns. On the whole, it was more exciting, for the streets are extremely narrow, and the soldiers at the head of our column had actually to beat the people out of our way, while our wild stallions occasionally made frantic plunges, which endangered the goods of the merchants in the bazaars. Our advance guard consisted of two mounted cawasses on caracoling horses. Their duty was to clear a passage, driving foot-passengers to one side, and obliging mules and camels to dive down by-ways and alleys. Next followed Major Talbot on horseback with a Sepoy at his bridle-rein; then five of us, each mounted, and each with a servant at his bridle-rein. Last came the dragoman of the British Residency, mounted and attended in the same manner. As we entered the gate of the serai, a squadron of soldiers presented arms, and the same was done at every turn. Outside the door of the reception-room the Wali Pasha, Mustafa Assim (a fine-looking man in military uniform), met us, and ushered us into the divan. Major Talbot had told me beforehand to do without question whatever he indicated, whether it seemed to me proper or not, and I had agreed to do so. The Wali received Major Talbot as a person of high distinction, led him to the head of the divan, and offered him the seat of honor by his side. But Major Talbot drew back, and motioned to me to take that place. It was the most graceful act of diplomatic courtesy that could have been imagined. It was intended to make the Wali treat me as a person of great importance, and technically placed me above the British Resident himself, if that were possible. The effect of it was that from that time forward the Wali treated me with a respect that could have been obtained in no other way. I am glad to say that the valuable assistance rendered to the expedition by Major Talbot on this and other occasions, was later recognized by our Government, which addressed a communication to the British authorities, thanking them for the courtesies extended to us by their representative in Baghdad.

Our interview with the Wali lasted half an hour. We drank coffee, smoked cigarettes, and transacted our business in French. The Governor-General told us that we were going to the most dangerous part of his vilayet, but that he would use every possible means to protect us, and that a battalion of soldiers stationed at Diwanieh should be at our disposal. I asked him to waive the question of a topographical plan, required by our permit, allowing us to commence excavations at Nippur without one, and make one at our earliest convenience afterward.

To this he declined to consent. He did not speak in favorable terms of our commissioner, Bedry Bey, whom he distrusted, as every one else seemed to do. Indeed, he told us frankly that Bedry drank too much. We had already been told the same by a German expedition which Bedry had accompanied as commissioner, and informed further that the only way to handle him was to keep him drunk, feed him well, and, having thus conciliated him, secure what was wanted by bribery. Otherwise, we were assured, he would make us trouble, and the objects discovered would not reach the Imperial Museum, after all. Poor Bedry was painted much blacker than he was, as I found out later by experience. The Wali gave us permission to start for Nippur on Wednesday morning, the 23d; then Bedry was sent for, and we were officially put in communication with him; being left, however, to settle between ourselves our financial relations,—a very unfortunate and unbusiness-like arrangement.

On our return from this interview, our house became instantly a scene of bustle and confusion. Mule-loads were made up for fifty odd mules, muleteers were contracted with to take us to Nippur, and every one was busied getting things into working order. That same evening I called on Bedry to arrange money matters with him, but found him sick in bed. My own comrades were not in much better condition. After the hard month's march from the coast to Baghdad, they were naturally worn out, and the life of relaxation and irregularity in Baghdad did not tend to improve their condition. Prince broke down altogether, and by the advice of Dr. Bowman, the military physician connected with the British Residency, resigned from the expedition. Major and Mrs. Talbot kindly took him into their own house, and nursed him there until he was able to return home.

We were to have started at a very early hour on Wednesday morning, January 23d. At five o'clock our muleteers came to say that it was raining, and asked us whether we proposed to start in the rain. We told them that we did, and that the rain would make no difference with us. At half-past six they returned to give us the same information, and ask the same question, and it was nine o'clock before they were ready to start, and ten o'clock before we finally got in motion. Our caravan consisted of sixty-one horses and mules, with men and donkeys besides, and we were escorted by six zaptiehs on mules, and by Bedry Bey and his servant, so that altogether we made a very formidable party. It rained hard most of the day, and there was a bitter wind from the south. I have rarely suffered more from the cold; and, owing both to the cold and the rain, it was utterly impossible to write notes, or even to make careful observations of our course. We travelled almost due south, reaching Khan Mahmudieh at four o'clock. On the way we passed many low mounds and old canal beds, but little of interest. The khan in which we stayed at Mahmudieh was by far the largest and best appointed I had yet seen, lying on the line of travel of the Persian pilgrims to Kerbela. These khans are rectangular structures, with blank walls on the outside, pierced by a large gate on one side only. Over this gate there is frequently an upper room with window openings. In the interior of the khan is a large space open to the sky, in which there are sometimes one or two raised platforms. In the khans on the pilgrim routes, these platforms are provided with praying-places properly orientated toward Mecca. Around the great open court are booth-like places for guests, raised three or four feet above the ground; and if the khan is a large one, there is a second, and sometimes a third, row of these booths opening on a covered corridor within. Guests, as they arrive, take possession of any of the booths which they find empty, string rugs across the opening, and encamp for the night. Their animals stand below in the corridor or court. Below the booths are mangers and tethering-places. There is no rent, but one gives the khanjee at the door a backsheesh in the morning. Many of the khans are pious foundations.

The next morning all of us, excepting Haynes and Bedry, started to visit Abu Habba, guided by the chief man of the village, and escorted by two of our own zaptiehs, together with a zaptieh named Abbas, who had been about a month with the Wolfe Expedition on its trip south of Hillah. He had married a wife out of the proceeds of that journey, and now prayed for his benefactors each time he saw her, so he told us. The day was rainy, and the guide professed to lose his way; but, as one of Daoud Thoma's brothers was in charge of Abu Habba at that time, we suspected that by his instructions the man was trying to prevent us from reaching the place. We finally found our way by means of a map and compass. We examined the excavations at Abu Habba with some care, but saw no evidence of the private digging which we had suspected was being conducted there.

Abu Habba represents the ruins of ancient Sippara, supposed to be the Sepharvaim of the Bible (2 Kings, xvii., 31). Hormuzd Rassam's excavations at this point produced most remarkable results, the inscriptions found exceeding in number and antiquity those found up to that time at any other site in Babylonia. His excavations, as we saw, were conducted in a very unscientific manner, without much regard to buildings or strata; but certainly he was successful in the one thing at which he aimed,—the discovery of inscriptions. At the time of our visit the mounds were the private property of the Sultan. Since our visit two campaigns of excavation have been conducted there by the Turks, but without the success which attended Rassam's work for the British Museum. There are several mounds in the neighborhood of Abu

Arab Khan on the Persian Pilgrim Route from Baghdad to Kerbela.

Habba, the most important of which is Deir, and many large dry canals, including one triple one called Yusuffieh.

It was almost half-past eleven when we left Abu Habba, and, after watering our horses at the neighboring ziaret of Seid Abdullah, we directed our course toward the conspicuous mound of Hushm-edh-Dhib. This appeared to be at the intersection of a network of canals, and I presume that it represents the remains of the fortress and station for the control and protection of those canals. It was one o'clock when we reached the Hillah road, close to the ruined khan of Bir. Some distance away we could see the castle-like ruins of Sheyshubar. Three quarters of an hour later we crossed a large, dry, triple canal, which from that point on to the end of our day's journey ran parallel to our road; and throughout the whole day we were constantly passing smaller canals and ruin mounds covered with pottery. Just beyond the triple canal the pilgrim road to Kerbela and Nejef branched off from ours. An hour later we passed Khan Haswa, by which there is a very small village of the same name, both located on the edge of pebble hills like those in the neighborhood of Kal'at Feluja. These pebble hills are a spur of the Mesopotamian plateau projecting into the alluvium, but I believe that they are not continuous from Kal'at Feluja to Haswa. Beyond Haswa, for a long distance, the ground was covered with fragments of pottery. Then came a sort of dry marsh. At about quarter-past three we came in sight of a fringe of palms, indicating the position of the river Euphrates a few miles away to our right. A little later we passed a low mound covered with pottery; and a few minutes afterwards we noticed on both sides of us fields of pottery and bricks, with small heaps of what looked like iron slag. Everything indicated the former existence of phenomenal wealth and prosperity where now there is an utterly barren and uninhabited desert. This region was once known as Gan

Eden, or Garden of Delight; and it was its amazing fertility in ancient times which gave the local color to the Hebrew legend of Gan Eden, the Garden of Eden.

About four o'clock we passed another great canal centre, and the remains of something that looked like an ancient reservoir. At quarter-past four, at the deserted Khan Nasrieh, we passed another great canal ganglion. At about quarter-past five, on a rude bridge of modern construction, we crossed a canal full of water, hollowed out in one of the channels of a large ancient triple canal; and five minutes later we reached Khan Mahawil, where Haynes and the caravan had been awaiting us some hours.

The next morning we were up at six o'clock, and started ahead of the caravan with the intention of visiting Babylon. Our course was almost due south on the Hillah road. Shortly after starting, we crossed the largest triple canal I had yet seen, now called Nahr Mahawil. Five minutes later we passed a small mound covered with pottery, and five minutes after that another. Twenty minutes later we were passing over the low mounds of Tel Kreni, which are quite extensive. A few minutes after ten, after crossing the deep bed of the Shatt-en-Nil, which, in connection with the Euphrates, once formed a moat for Babylon, we crossed the line of the old wall about Babil. Like the mound itself, this wall has been used as a brick mine for all the surrounding country. An excavation of thirty feet in depth showed that it was built of bricks laid in bitumen. This particular excavation was made, I believe, with a view of obtaining material for a dam on the Hindieh Canal. Bedry informed us that excavation in the mounds of Babylon for such purposes is now forbidden; but either Bedry was mistaken as to the fact, or else the prohibition is utterly disregarded.

The mound of Babil itself is thoroughly honeycombed with excavations. So far as those excavations reveal the character of the structure, it is one huge mass of burned brick. It was not, however, built entirely at one time. In one place I observed well-made columns of bricks, the spaces between which had been built up later, thus turning a construction resting upon piers into a solid mass. In another place I noticed a doorway which had been filled with rubble brick, after which a solid structure of brick had been erected in front of it. The removal of a part of the structure by brick-miners had revealed the walled-up door within. Bitumen was used as mortar in a portion, at least, of these brick structures; and the impressions in the bitumen showed that sometimes mats had been placed between the layers of brick. On top of the masses of baked brick was a mass of unbaked brick, about thirty feet of which I found in place. Between the layers of the unbaked bricks were thin mats, such as are now in use in that country, quite unlike the heavy mats I had observed at 'Akerkuf. There were also ropes or cords of reeds running through the bricks, as at 'Akerkuf, excepting only that those used at Babil were smaller. There were also occasionally palm beams thrust in among the unbaked bricks to strengthen the construction. Near the doorway, which I have described above, Hilprecht picked up a brick of Nabopolassar. All of the other bricks which we found here, and all that I have found elsewhere, brought from Babil, bear the name of Nebuchadrezzar. The mound is orientated approximately northeast and southwest, so that its corners point toward the cardinal points of the compass. It is much longer from the northeast to the southwest than from the southeast to the northwest. In the diggings on the mound, as well as on the surface, I found fragments of green glazed pottery, sometimes imbedded in bricks. Toward the northern end of the mound, on its summit, was a wall of the same sort of gypsum composite rock which underlies the pebble hills at Haswa and Feluja, surrounded again by bricks. There were everywhere fragments of enamelled bricks, and these looked as though they had been exposed to the action of fire in a great conflagration. It is said that little or nothing in the way of antiquities has been found at Babil. While we were there, a lad brought us the trunk of a small alabaster statuette of late Greek work, which he claimed to have found on the spot. Bedry beat him, and confiscated the statuette, which he later presented to me.

South ten degrees east of Babil is the mound of Homeira, constituting a portion of the ancient ruins of Babylon. Near this, and around a bend in the river from Babil, lies a complex of mounds, known in its several parts as Kasra, Amram, and Jimjimeh. Between Babil and this complex of mounds lie the low but quite extensive mounds of Mujellibeh. All these are parts of Babylon. In the mound of Kasra, in a deep hole, lies a rude lion carved in black basalt. The lion is struggling with a serpent. This hole was dug and the lion unearthed by Rich in 1811. The Arabs have since bored a hole partly through the lion in their search for treasure. Not very far away, growing on the mound itself, is a very large old sidra-tree, known by the name of Athele. Local tradition says that this is the tree under which Nebuchadrezzar took shelter when he ate grass like an ox; and the same tradition attached itself to the same tree, even then fabulously old, in Rich's day.

It is the mound of Amram, or Jimjimeh, which is the most fruitful in antiquities; and it is here that almost all of the clay tablets and cylinders have been found which have reached Europe and America. We had heard in Baghdad that a library had been found in place at Jimjimeh by the Arabs, and afterwards broken up by them in their endeavor to escape arrest by the authorities. We were shown the place where this remarkable find was made. It was merely a hole in the mound, and nothing showed in what sort of a building, if any, it had been found. Afterwards Hilprecht was shown by the officials such of the "finds" seized by the Turks as still remained. On investigation, it turned out that the so-called library was a cache, or deposit of contract tablets; and that the breaking-up of the tablets was due to the Turkish authorities, who seized them, and threw them into bags to carry them to Hillah. What remained was absolutely valueless. In our presence the Arabs of Jimjimeh burrowed with their hands among the graves which now cover the mound, and brought out a few fragments of tablets, one or two of which contained written characters. The mounds near Jimjimeh are almost entirely covered with graves, but the natives make nothing of disturbing these in digging for tablets. The principal mound at this point is known as Amram, from the tomb and ziaret of Amram, son of Ali, which stand there. At the present moment these mounds look almost like a rabbit warren, they are so full of holes made by the Arabs in their diggings. North of Jimjimeh, some deep excavations had been made for the purpose of obtaining bricks for the Hindieh dam. These excavations revealed enormous walls or masses of very large bricks laid in bitumen. The village of Jimjimeh lies at the foot of the mounds toward the Euphrates, and I believe that almost every native of that place is an antiquity ferret. On a later visit to Babylon I was shown, by the man who discovered it, the place where the famous cylinder of Cyrus was found. This was on the mound of Amram, but not in the corner of a building. It was in a sort of niche in the face of a long wall. Bedry assured us that through his activity antiquity digging had been entirely stopped, both at Babylon and elsewhere. This was somewhat amusing, in view of the collections we had just been purchasing in Baghdad and London, which had come principally from Jimjimeh, but partly from Birs Nimrud.

Much has been written about the ruins of Babylon. They have been thoroughly mapped, and not a few scholars have tried their hands at a restoration of the ancient city on the basis of their understanding of the indications of the mounds. I do not think that any representation of the ancient city can be of much value until systematic and scientific excavations have been conducted there.

The mound of Babil is now generally supposed to represent the hanging gardens of Nebuchadrezzar. The description which I have given of the appearance of that ruin, as revealed by excavations conducted there, may suggest that it was originally a lofty structure resting on piers and columns, at least in part. This would accord with the ordinary idea regarding these hanging gardens. It was afterwards, for some reason, built into a solid mass. Some suppose, however, that Babil represents the ziggurat of the temple of Bel-Merodach. If so, that ziggurat must have been of a construction entirely unlike any other ziggurat which has yet been unearthed.

It was about three o'clock in the afternoon when we reached Hillah. The caravan remained on the east side of the river to avoid the bridge tolls; but we crossed the bridge of boats, as our khan, a miserable place (said to be the best in Hillah, however) was on the western side of the river. There was no accommodation for our horses, which had to be sent elsewhere. Reshid Bey, colonel of the regiment which is stationed partly at Hillah and partly at Diwanieh, and a friend of Bedry, came to see us at once, and invited us to stay with him. This I declined to do, but accepted an invitation to dine on the following evening. I had left Noorian at Jimjimeh to see about engaging workmen to accompany us to Nippur. He reached the khan about seven in the evening, rather down in the mouth, and afraid that he could find no workmen who were not under the thumb of Daoud

Thoma and Bedry Bey. He had, however, arranged with some men to come and see him the next day, and talk the question of employment over further.

The next morning, leaving Haynes, who was feeling very miserable, to rest, and Noorian to hunt up antiquities and information, the rest of us, with Elias, Bedry's servant, an Arab guide, and two zaptiehs, started for Birs Nimrud at half-past eight, reaching there about ten. The country between Birs Nimrud on the one side, and Hillah and Mahmudieh, or rather Baghdad, on the other, is capable of almost boundless productivity, but is now a complete desert. In the neighborhood of Hillah, and down the course of the Euphrates, land which was cultivated a few years earlier was at the time of my visit lying waste; and the very palm-trees, which line the river for miles at this point, were dying on account of the failing of the waters. The Euphrates had been for some years flowing more and more into the Hindieh Canal, and thence into the Abu Nejm and other great swamps. They told me that five years before, the revenues of the Mutessariflik, or province of Hillah, were eighty-five thousand Turkish liras, but in 1889 they were only ten thousand. This difficulty with the Hindieh Canal is an almost periodical one. From the remotest antiquity the Euphrates has broken down all dams and dispersed itself through the Hindieh into the great swamps, at uncertain intervals, depending upon the strength of the dam and the watchfulness of the government. But in addition to the diminution of the revenues of the Mutessariflik of Hillah owing to the diversion of the Euphrates, there was also a diminution caused by the fact that each year more of the cultivable and cultivated land becomes the property of the Sultan, and is hence removed from taxation.

The appearance of the mound of Birs Nimrud is well known, for it has been often described and depicted. It is orientated so that the corners point approximately towards the cardinal points of the compass. The remains of the tower proper are toward the southwestern edge of the ruins, and not, as at Nippur, the northwestern. To the northeast of the ziggurat are the remains of rooms and chambers which formed, apparently, part of the great temple of Nebuchadrezzar, of which the tower was the ziggurat, or high place. A good many of these rooms were dug out by Rassam, but nothing of any importance was found in them. The walls of the rooms which were excavated, and which still remain as left by the explorers, were built entirely of sun-dried brick. Rawlinson and the French both excavated here at an earlier date. Both dug in the tower of the ziggurat itself, and in the corners of that building Rawlinson found inscribed cylinders of Nebuchadrezzar. On the east side of the tower we were shown the excavations said to have been made by the French, where they had laid bare vast masses of baked red bricks. The lowest stage of the tower, as shown by these excavations, consisted of a very high terrace of sun-dried bricks, on which were smaller terraces faced with baked brick. On the summit of the whole structure there is now a curious mass of baked bricks, looking like a tower split in two. This is somewhat more than forty feet in height, as measured by the layers of bricks, of which there are one hundred and thirty still in place. It is pierced by holes in which there were originally cords or beams to strengthen the masonry. About this tower lie huge masses of bricks fused together. Apparently this fusion was the result of a conflagration, the heat of which was sufficiently great to melt the enamel on the bricks. The bricks themselves were twisted, curled, and broken by the heat. Enamelled bricks ruined by fire were found all around the mound, a few of them of a dark-red color, but most of them yellow, and some of them almost black. Some of these, as well as some of the unenamelled bricks, bore the inscription of the great Nebuchadrezzar.

Birs Nimrud, the Tower of Babel.

The view from the top of the mound was very beautiful. To the north was a great swamp full of water, from which ran a stream, looking like a silver thread, connecting it with the Hindieh Canal. Beyond were villages. To the east we saw the palm-trees of Hillah; while to the northwest lay a very small village shaded by palm-trees, where Rassam used to live while conducting his excavations. All else was flat and barren, or bearing nothing but camel-thorn and rushes.

A few minutes to the northeast of Birs Nimrud lies the mound of Ibrahim Khalil, or Ibrahim the Friend, with a ziaret in the centre. This mound represents ancient Borsippa, the sister-city of Babylon, while Birs Nimrud represents the temple of Nebo and the ziggurat. On the eastern and southern edges of the mound of Ibrahim Khalil are the trenches which yielded results to Rassam in the way of inscribed objects. He seems to have found no constructions of any importance, and to have made no efforts to trace buildings as such. I knew beforehand, from our London collections, that diggings were still conducted at Ibrahim Khalil, and obtained further information to that effect while at Hillah. I had the good fortune to meet the individual to whom had belonged the objects from Borsippa sold to me in London by Shemtob. I ascertained from him that they were all found in the mound of Ibrahim Khalil, but was told that there was little dug out there in comparison with the amount brought from the mounds of Babylon. A colophon on a tablet of Nabopolassar, in the London purchase, suggested the existence of a library at Borsippa. It was on that account that I had desired to obtain permission to excavate there. My intention was to try Nippur first, and, if that should prove impracticable, to remove to Borsippa, at which point we were comparatively close to civilization, and could be readily protected. I supposed, moreover, that it would be possible to conduct excavations at Borsippa for a longer time than at Nippur. The information derived from Layard's account of his excavations at Nippur, as well as the information brought home by the Wolfe Expedition, had led me to suppose that that place would be practicable but for a brief part of the year. In laying out my plans, therefore, for this first year's work, I had expected, when we should be obliged to leave Nippur, to come to Borsippa and work there.

In the eleventh chapter of Genesis there is a legend to the effect that when all the people of the earth were of one language, as they journeyed hither and thither from the east, or in the eastern country, they found a plain in the land of Shinar, and took up their abode there; and having become settled residents of the soil, they undertook to make bricks and burn them very thoroughly; for bricks constituted the stone of the land, and bitumen the mortar. "And they said, Come, let us build us a city and a tower whose summit shall be in the sky; and let us make us a name, lest we be scattered over all the earth. And Yahweh looked down to see the city and the tower which the children of men built. And Yahweh said, Lo, these are one people, they have all one language, and this is the beginning of their doings, and now nothing is impossible with them of all which they have planned to do. Come, let us go down and confuse their language, so that they may not understand one another's speech. And Yahweh scattered them thence upon the face of the whole earth, and they ceased to build the city. Therefore its name was called Babel, because there Yahweh confounded the language of the whole earth." The story, as we have it here, comes from the Yahwistic narrative, and was written down probably somewhere in the eighth century before Christ, two hundred years or so before Nebuchadrezzar. How much older the story itself may be, it is difficult to say. It suggests to us an unfinished building of great size, constructed of baked brick.

Now, in the clay cylinders of Nebuchadrezzar found by Sir Henry Rawlinson in the corners of the ziggurat of Birs Nimrud, we read:

"Nebuchadrezzar, king of Babylon, the rightful ruler, the expression of the righteous heart of Marduk, the exalted high priest, the beloved of Nebo, the wise prince, who devotes his care to the affairs of the great gods, the unwearying ruler, the restorer of Esagila and Ezida, the son and heir of Nabopolassar, king of Babylon, am I.

"Marduk the great god formed me aright and commissioned me to perform his restoration; Nebo, guider of the universe of heaven and earth, placed in my hand the right sceptre; Esagila, the house of heaven and earth, the abode of Marduk, lord of the gods, Ekua, the sanctuary of his lordship, I adorned gloriously with shining gold. Ezida I built anew, and completed its construction with silver, gold, precious stones, bronze, *musukkani* wood, and cedar wood. *Timinanki*, the ziggurat of Babylon, I built and completed; of bricks glazed with lapis-lazuli (blue) I erected its summit.

"At that time the house of the seven divisions of heaven and earth, the ziggurat of Borsippa, which a former king had built and carried up to the height of forty-two ells, but the summit of which he had not erected, was long since fallen into decay, and its water conduits had become useless; rain storms and tempests had penetrated its unbaked brick-work; the bricks which cased it were bulged out, the unbaked bricks of its terraces were converted into rubbish heaps. The great lord Marduk moved my heart to rebuild it. Its place I changed not and its foundation I altered not. In a lucky month, on an auspicious day I rebuilt the unbaked bricks of its terraces and its encasing bricks, which were broken away, and I raised up that which was fallen down. My inscriptions I put upon the *kiliri* of its buildings. To build it and to erect its summit I set my hand. I built it anew as in former times; as in days of yore I erected its summit.

"Nebo, rightful son, lordly messenger, majestic friend of Marduk, look kindly on my pious works; long life, enjoyment of health, a firm throne, a long reign, the overthrow of foes, and conquest of the land of the enemy give me as a gift. On thy righteous tablet which determines the course of heaven and earth, record for me length of days, write for me wealth. Before Marduk, lord of heaven and earth, the father who bore thee, make pleasant my days, speak favorably for me. Let this be in thy mouth, ' Nebuchadrezzar, the restorer king.'"

Nebuchadrezzar describes the condition in which the ziggurat was when he found it. It was built long before his day, and built with very ambitious ideas. It was forty-two ells in height, but the summit had never been completed. The consequence of this failure to erect the summit was that the water struck into the unprotected mud bricks forming the mass of the interior of the ziggurat, dissolved them, and broke and bulged out the casing walls of baked bricks by which the different terraces were held in, reducing the whole to a huge mass of ruins. The water conduits referred to are such as Haynes found on the sides of the ziggurat at Nippur, designed to carry off the water from the surfaces of the upper terraces, and save the whole structure from decay. These conduits are useful only in case proper arrangements are made to carry into them the water falling on the surfaces of the upper terraces. The failure in this case to " erect the summit," and the consequent soaking of the water into the clay bricks of the interior, soon rendered these conduits useless.

The striking similarities of this story to that of the Tower of Babel are, outside of the site, the extremely ambitious nature of this ziggurat of Borsippa which

Nebuchadrezzar found in ruins, and the fact that after it had been raised to a great height the work was abandoned, leaving the building in such an incomplete condition that its ruin was inevitable.

As Nebuchadrezzar found it, the tower was little more than an enormous mass of ruins. He built it over entirely, and made it a seven-staged ziggurat. It is the ruins of Nebuchadrezzar's ziggurat which constitute the present Birs Nimrud, and the explorations which have been conducted there revealed the seven stages still existing.

Now, Nebuchadrezzar gives no similar description of the ruined and incomplete condition of any other ziggurat which he rebuilt. He rebuilt, among other places, the ziggurat of Esagil in Babylon, but he says nothing of its ruined condition. Evidently the ruined condition of the ziggurat at Borsippa, in connection with its great size and ambitious design, made a strong impression upon his mind, or the mind of the writer of his inscription. This is not a positive proof that it made a similar impression on the world at large, yet the natural induction is that the ruined condition of this ziggurat was notorious, and impressed all beholders. How long before the time of Nebuchadrezzar it had fallen into such a condition, it is impossible from our present information to say. Nebuchadrezzar says "long since," and does not mention the name of the original builder, calling him merely "a former king," as though its original construction were a thing of the remote past, the details of which were long since forgotten. But whatever the date, Nebuchadrezzar's account of the ruins of this ziggurat corresponds so well with the story of the eleventh chapter of Genesis, that one is inclined to attach that story, at least tentatively, to this ruin. The proximity of the site to Babylon led to its connection with that well-known name, Babel, in the Hebrew story.

CHAPTER X.

NIPPUR AT LAST.

A Turkish Dinner—Antiquity Dealers—Strained Relations—Diwanieh—Provincial Officials—Turkish Hospitality—First Sight of Nippur—Sukh-el-Affech—The Arrival—Affech Land—A Great Chief—An Unruly Country—Kal'at Amerika—Mistakes—Begging Arabs—Making a Map—Arab Dances—Camp Building—War Averted—Digging up Graves.

ON the evening of our trip to Birs Nimrud, Hilprecht, Field, and I dined with the Turkish Colonel. The dinner was quite a novelty to me. It was a splendid but decidedly miscellaneous meal. Before dinner we had date arrack, almonds, and cigarettes to whet our appetites. The first course consisted of chicken and potatoes. Each man was provided with a knife, fork and spoon, which he retained during the entire dinner, the dishes being changed at each course. We all plunged into one central dish, and it was polite for each person to eat faster than every other. At each end of the table were bowls of pickles, in which we went fishing with our forks or spoons as we saw fit. Once, as a mark of distinction, the host presented me with a tidbit on his fork. As a concession to Frank usage, we had beer to drink with our dinner. After the chicken came spinach cooked in the most delightful way imaginable, for the Turks certainly know how to cook. With this was served a very peculiar sort of sour oranges, which are better than lemons for squeezing over anything. Then came some excellent meat pills, for I scarcely know what else to call them. After this we were served with delicious sweet cakes floating in a luscious sauce; then cabbage with meat chopped in it; then rice pilau with chicken tidbits mixed in; then a dish which I have forgotten; then more sweet cakes of another kind; then oranges. We then washed our hands with soap and water, and rinsed out our mouths, after the Turkish fashion, and went into another room, where coffee and cigarettes were served, and where several guests, including a Jewish millionaire, Menahem Effendi, were awaiting our arrival.

During my absence, Noorian had contracted with twenty workmen from Jimjimeh and a dozen from Birs Nimrud, whom he thought he could control in spite of Bedry's intrigues, for five piastres a day for pick-men, and four each for shovellers and scrapers, wages to commence four days later, and in the meantime the men to receive two piastres a day. As these men were all, or almost all, notorious antiquity thieves, he selected them from two rival villages, in the hope of preventing fraud or collusion, by means of rivalry and mutual distrust. But this bi-partisan plan did not work altogether satisfactorily, as will be seen later. He had also found some antiquity dealers in the place, and that evening I had interviews with two Jews, brothers, one of them under the ban, and sought after by Bedry as an offender against the antiquity laws. It was these two brothers, it seems, from whom came some of the most valuable pieces of the Shemtob collection purchased in London, notably the Nebuchadrezzar cylinder found in Babylon, the Nabopolassar tablet found in Borsippa, the Artaxerxes vase, and the Burnaburiash cone. It was not possible to obtain from them precise information of the place where each object was found. I believe that the Artaxerxes vase and the Burnaburiash cone were both found in Babylon.

Most of the other antiquities had been dug out by Jimjimeh men, presumably in Babylon, but some came from Borsippa, and some from other unknown mounds.

Sunday morning, January 27th, we went with Bedry to call upon the representative of the Mutessarif, the latter official being absent in the swamps of the Abu Nejm region, looking after the taxes on the rice crops. We found the Serai, or government building, to be built for the most part of bricks bearing the Nebuchadrezzar stamp, and evidently taken from the ruins of Babylon. We were pleasantly and hospitably received; much was said of the danger of the country, and we were given a large escort of zaptiehs. It turned out that those sent with us from Baghdad were to be quartered on us, and we were to be wholly responsible for their support. The poor fellows, according to Bedry's statement, were seven months in arrears in their salaries, and he succeeded in obtaining for them about one month's pay. We arranged to leave Hillah for Nippur the next day, the caravan taking the direct route, while Bedry, Harper, and I went by way of Diwanieh, the residence of the Kaimakam under whose jurisdiction we were to be.

After lunch, Menahem Effendi and Dr. Azriyahu, the military physician of the place, also a Jew, called to take us to the synagogue to show us the Pentateuch rolls, of which they had several besides the one in use. None of these was old or of any value. They told us that the population of Hillah was about twelve thousand, of whom one third or one quarter were Jews; and the population of Baghdad about ninety thousand, of whom one third were Jews.

While Harper and I were visiting the synagogue, Noorian and Hilprecht were investigating antiquities. They made an appointment to go and see one of the Jews whom I had met the day before, who was to take them to a place where there were antiquities. An unfortunate word from Haynes aroused the suspicions of Bedry, and he had them shadowed by Elias, his servant, who reported that they returned with their pockets stuffed out. This was true, for they had brought a quantity of the things to show me before concluding the purchase, which was made with money Prince had placed in Hilprecht's hands for this purpose. The antiquities were with some difficulty returned to the Jew for safe keeping the following morning. Bedry asked me point blank if I had bought antiquities in Hillah, and it was fortunate that I was able to say no. He demanded from the Mutessarif the arrest of one of the two Jews who had sold the antiquities to Hilprecht. The Mutessarif ordered his arrest, but he could nowhere be found, although I saw him drinking coffee in a public café. It was quite plain that he and the officials of the Serai understood one another. Bedry naturally became more suspicious after this incident. He endeavored to make me employ the Sheikh of Jimjimeh as chief of our workmen, and actually had the impudence to engage men for us on his own responsibility, whom I refused to accept.

Matters between Bedry and me were strained when we left Hillah on the morning of the 28th of January. He was anxious to wait until he had seen the caravan depart from Hillah, and I had made up my mind to start before the caravan, in order that Noorian might have free hand in the matter of workmen, and that Hilprecht might have fair opportunity to confer with the antiquity dealers. In consequence, Bedry was in a frightful humor, and beat first his horse and then the muleteer. We were attended by Elias and two zaptiehs, and only took one mule- or rather horse-load of baggage, but some soldiers accompanied us with a load of cartridges for the garrison at Diwanieh. We passed a great number of canals, old and new, but all were dry, and the country was manifestly suffering from drought, caused by the low water in the River Euphrates. It was two o'clock in the afternoon when we reached Imam Kasım, or Jasim, a ziaret surrounded by a small mud village of Jebur Arabs, where we stopped for the night. This is a sacred burying-place for the Arabs of the neighborhood. Who the Imam was who is buried there, I do not know, nor how far his fame extends, but the number of graves which surround the place is quite considerable.

We slept in our clothes in the little coffee-house, and started the next morning at about half-past seven. At twenty minutes before ten we passed the small tel of el-Zune, which covers some unknown town. Other tels were visible in various directions, from time to time,— Abu Kazal, Abu Jellin, Wennet, Si'dum, Mahani, and Zaghul. All of these we passed at some little distance on the right or left before our noon-day meal, which we ate by the Euphrates. So narrow and so shallow was the river here that a man crossed it without wetting himself above the middle of the leg. The country was very barren. Here and there we saw the black tents of the Jebur Arabs, and the country on either side of the river was dotted with mud forts, in which live the sheikhs of the country. There are quantities of fairly modern canals, but all were dry. No trees were to be seen except a few stray palms here and there, perishing with thirst by the side of some dry canal. Sa'adik, one of our zaptiehs, was anxious to inform himself regarding America. He asked me whether we had a sultan, and when I told him no, he assumed that America must be a dependency of Turkey, and asked me whether we had a wali. With much difficulty, in my poor Turkish, and with the aid of my fingers, I explained to him that we were all equal, and that every four years we made one man head of all the rest, and each four years a different man. This impressed him greatly, and I found him later imparting his information about America to an admiring party of Arabs.

It was twenty minutes before four when we reached the Serai at Diwanieh, after fording the river Euphrates, which scarcely reached at the deepest point to my horse's belly. Diwanieh lies on both sides of the river, but the important part, where are the Serai and the military barracks, is situated on the eastern side. It is said to be a place of about three thousand inhabitants. There was no bridge. There were a few boats in the river, but there was not sufficient water to float them. About a quarter or a half of an hour above Diwanieh, on the east side of the river, is the ziaret and little village of Abu Fadhil.

Diwanieh is the seat of a kaimakam, and a battalion of infantry is stationed there. We were the guests of the Kaimakam, Khalil Bey, of Trebizond, who showed us every possible hospitality. The poor fellow had received no salary for seven months, so he told me. I brought a letter from Reshid Bey, the colonel of the regiment, to Ibrahim Bey, major in command of the troops at Diwanieh; and he, with his second in command, Mustafa Bey, showed us much hospitality. We were installed in the Kaimakam's reception room in the Serai, where we were members of the council by day, and slept by night. The Turkish method of transacting business in a provinical serai is very amusing. Everything seems to be done in a sort of public talkee talkee, in which anyone feels at liberty to take part. Documents are passed about to each stray comer, and all express their opinions. However, the Kaimakam acted quite promptly in sending off our letters to the Mutessarif, Yaya Bey, and the head Sheikh of the Affech, Hajji Tarfa, who were said to be in the Shamieh, or region west of the river. We were almost murdered with hospitality. As soon as we came in we were presented with cigarettes and coffee, which were renewed, from time to time, during the period of three quarters of an hour, while we were transacting the business of the letters, and discussing them with the whole divan. Then we changed to tea and narghilehs. Then came a miscellaneous but very solid dinner, at which we all ate out of one dish, every one waiting for me to start, stopping when I stopped, drinking when I drank, and eating when I ate. It was a dinner of only about four courses, but they were solid. Then came coffee and the narghilehs, and all the notables with them to pay their respects and enjoy a sociable evening. Here, as everywhere, Bedry told incredible lies about me, for the purpose of making my position great, and thereby also aggrandizing himself. I was treated as a man of most marked distinction, but as it cost nothing, it was not a disadvantage, and, indeed, Bedry always knew how to secure entertainment and dignity at the least possible expense. At Imam Jasim, for instance, we had a whole house and a large courtyard, and portions of several other houses; we fed our three selves, our servants, two soldiers, two muleteers, together with all the horses, seven in all, three meals for each man and each beast, and we hired a man to watch the horses all night—all for the magnificent sum of one dollar.

It was quite late when at last the company asked leave to retire, and we went to bed in the judgment hall, or reception room, or whatever else you may choose to call it, where the entire business of the kaimakamlik is transacted. Before we were dressed the next morning, the Kaimakam and the notables were on hand, and it was with much difficulty that I obtained permission to eat a breakfast of bread and coffee before being compelled to commence drinking and smoking Turkish things once more. I was seated by the side of the Kaimakam and courteously invited to assist my host in the ceremonies. When any one arrived we arose and moved our hands toward the lips and head, he doing the same. Then we sat and he sat; we repeated the ceremony and he did the same, first to us and then to each person present. Within a minute a servant brought him a cup of coffee and a lighted coal. With the latter he lighted the cigarette which had already been given to him. Every now and then the servant brought in coffee all around.

After a while we were invited to go and see the barracks. Everywhere the soldiers presented arms to me as though I were a high official. In the barracks the commanding officer treated us to coffee and narghilehs, and the Armenian military doctor, who ought to have known better from a medical point of view, made us smoke cigarettes and drink lemonade. At twelve o'clock we sat down to a very solid breakfast of six or eight heavy courses, which was followed by three cups of coffee and narghilehs. In the evening we dined at the barracks with Ibrahim and Mustafa. This dinner was very elaborate and very Turkish, but the hospitality was unbounded, and indeed I have never seen any hospitality equal to that of the Turks. We stayed a long time after dinner, and they told us much of the danger from the Arabs in the region to which we were going, over whom, they said, the government had no authority. Some of the officers had been prisoners in Russia, and spoke a few words of Russian. They had also imbibed ideas with regard to the greatness of domains outside of Turkey and of the advances made by Western civilization. Their imprisonment had had in so far a civilizing influence. In answer to their questions we told them about the greatness of America, and especially about the wonders of electricity, but here it was not always possible to obtain their credence. They would have believed any tale I told them about witchcraft, or bogies and magic, but it was difficult for them to believe the actual truth in regard to the achievements of modern science.

The town of Diwanieh is a miserable little collection of mud hovels, more than half of them deserted, surrounded by a mud wall which a man could kick down at most points, if so disposed. There was a telegraph station, as well as a post-office, there, however, and I was able to make arrangements for the weekly despatch of mail to us, and also for the forwarding of telegraphic despatches, should any arrive. During the whole course of our work at Nippur we were thus in comparatively close connection, through mail and telegraph, with the rest of the world.

We left Diwanieh about half-past eight on the morning of Thursday, January 31st. Our course lay east through a perfectly flat plain, on the verge of which, north twenty degrees east, were just visible the palms of Daghara, on the canal of the same name. At about half-past ten we entered a region covered with brush and camel thorn, quite a contrast to the absolutely uncovered clay one generally sees. In this tract we found large numbers of camels feeding under the care of Arabs, who said that they were not their owners, but only bedu, or herdsmen. They called themselves Araksi Arabs, a name which I never heard before or afterward. Shortly after noon we reached the Daghara Canal, and forded it at the little village of Sheikh Halhal, of the Dheleyha Arabs, formerly a sub-tribe of the Affech. The Daghara was narrow, but deeper and swifter than the Euphrates at Diwanieh, and far more water passes through it. We halted on the other side for lunch, and scarcely had we started again at quarter before two, when we caught sight of the mounds of Nippur to the northeast, and the tents of our party shining white upon the summit. I had become so familiar with the appearance of Nippur from cuts and drawings, that it did not seem to me like an unknown mound, at least as soon as I came sufficiently close to recognize the contour.

Our road led through a swamp region on a course a little north of east, toward Sukh-el-Affech (market of the Affech), the palms of which were visible in front of us.

We met a corpse wrapped in reeds, carried on the back of a mule. Asking the cause of his death, we were told that he had been murdered. They were on their way to bury him in a sacred spot.

I wished to go directly to Nippur, but Bedry insisted that this was neither practicable nor desirable, since we ought to see the Mudir of Affech and the acting chief of the Affech tribe at once, and establish friendly relations with both of them. In point of fact there is no direct road across the swamps to Nippur, and one must make a detour, although it is not necessary to go as far around as Sukh-el-Affech. We had with us a guard of five mounted zaptiehs, besides an unmounted one who was returning to his post at Affech; nevertheless, Bedry seemed much alarmed for fear of an attack, for that country has a bad reputation. It was only an hour's march from Hajji Halhal's village to the Sukh, but we were obliged to ford a deep and swift stream before reaching the latter. Sukh-el-Affech seemed to be practically a series of islands, and consisted of a long string of villages built among palm trees. Wherever there is cultivation, there must be irrigation, and a village such as Sukh-el-Affech means a system of canals. The place was as amphibious as Venice. The water comes from the Euphrates by means of the Daghara canal, which also forms the marshes to the west and southwest of Nippur.

We had a brief interview in the open air with the Mudir, and also with Hajji Tarfa's eldest son, Mekota, who was acting chief in his father's absence. Both the Mudir and Bedry begged me to stay at Affech for the night, on account of the danger and difficulty of the journey across the marshes to Nippur. But I had told Haynes that I would reach Nippur that evening, and I meant to keep my word; moreover, now that I had caught sight of the mounds, I could not bear to make any further delay, feeling that I must reach my work as speedily as possible. Bedry decided to remain at the village, and Harper and I went on, accompanied by Mekota and his younger brother, Mohammed, and a number of armed Arabs on horse and foot, eleven in all, besides three or four of the zaptiehs. It was a three hours' hard ride, and there was much and deep fording. The horsemen brandished long bamboo lances, and the footmen carried old-fashioned, gaudily decorated flint-locks of inordinate length, or discarded, double-barrelled, muzzle-loading shotguns from India, and all wore in their girdles impossible ancient pistols, knives, and bitumen-headed clubs. The chiefs rode bareback on mares which they guided with halters only, dashing off every instant in a wild gallop, shaking their lances at imaginary foes, while the footmen fired their pieces in the air, sang, screamed, and danced war-dances. Our stallions reared and plunged in wild excitement; the fun waxed fast and furious, and it was impossible to resist the mad contagion. We dashed through canebrakes, floundered in marshes, splashed across innumerable canals, stumbled and tumbled up and down the intricate ravines of the old ruin mounds, lost ourselves in their mazes, howled, yelled, fired shots in the air, and at last came upon our comrades encamped on top of the mounds, and fearing that the whole Affech nation had risen to attack them.

The guard of Arabs who had accompanied us demanded to be fed and housed, and as the camp was in an entirely disorganized state, and there was not sufficient accommodation for ourselves, we were obliged to send them to the nearest Arab camp, the chief of which, Berdi (Marsh Grass), had already befriended our party on the mound. They had arrived at Nippur, and pitched their tents on the preceding day. They reported the country much disturbed, and full of wars and rumors of wars. Ferhan, the great Shammar chief, was said to be about a day's journey from Nippur, and not far from the line of their march from Kheygan down. Once they were surrounded in a menacing manner by apparently hostile Arabs, and another time the inhabitants of the village in which they were lodged ran out on a false alarm of an attack. Several times they saw the signal of alarm waved from mounds near their line of march and, when they appeared on the mounds of Nippur, the neighboring Arabs ran their flocks into shelter, supposing them to be a hostile foray. It was said that a fight had taken place at Nippur, or near it, a few days before, in which one Shammar was killed. The Shammar had carried off a number of Affech sheep, we were told, whereupon the Affech had seized a number of Shammar camels. The Shammar gave five horses as a pledge that they would return the sheep, whereupon the camels were returned, and war was averted. Such were the stories which we heard on our arrival at Nippur.

Niffer, as it is ordinarily written; Nufar, as I heard it from the Arabs; ancient Nippur, lies on the northeastern edge of the territory of the Affek or Affech Arabs, between the Tigris and the Euphrates, about one hundred miles east of south from Baghdad. Originally a portion of the great Shammar bedouin tribe, one of those hordes which ever and anon pour out of the interior of Arabia to overrun the neighboring lands, the Affech became, a few generations since, ma'dan, that is, settled Arabs, dwelling in huts and tilling the soil, an advance in civilization which is, of course, regarded as a sad degradation by their bedouin kinsfolk and neighbors. Their country is marshy, and intersected with numerous canals, among and along which lie their villages. Each village consists of a few huts of marsh reeds and palm mats, with a guest house, or muthif, of the same, grouped about a mud castle. The latter is the residence of the chief, with his wives and children, and one or two trusty kinsmen. More than this he dare not admit, for fear of murder, for no chief feels himself secure, even among his own people. The land is the property of the chiefs, and is tilled for them by their tribesmen, whom they, on their part, are bound to defend and provide for. The fertility of the soil depends entirely upon irrigation by canals, and water is therefore one of the most common causes of the frequent wars. A tribe up the canal dams the water for the purpose of irrigating its own soil, and a tribe below seeks to cut the dam by force, whereupon a war ensues. The headquarters of the Affech nation is the Sukh-el-Affech, which lies about six miles southeast of the Nippur mounds. The village of the chief, which lies close to this, was known as Shatt-el-Hosein.

The chief of the Affech, Hajji Tarfa, which is, being interpreted, Pilgrim Tamarisk, is the most powerful and independent chief of southern Mesopotamia. A little more than twenty years before the Turks attempted to levy taxes and enforce conscription among the ma'dan Arabs of that region. The Governor of Hillah and a battalion of soldiers came to Sukh-el-Affech for this purpose. But the Arabs from all the country around collected, surrounded them, and massacred the governor, the colonel, and every soldier not of Arab origin. It is claimed that Hajji Tarfa took no part in the massacre; nevertheless, he at once put himself at the head of the tribes, and maintained for some time a successful rebellion against the government. Finally Midhat Pasha, then governor-general of Baghdad, built a dam across the Daghara canal, by which the water of the Euphrates is brought into the Affech marshes, thus drying up those marshes and rendering the country accessible to his troops in front. At the same time he engaged a large force of Montefich Arabs to fall upon the Affech from the desert in their rear. Taken thus in front and rear, they were severely punished, and compelled to recognize a nominal allegiance to the Turkish Government; nevertheless, the Turks were unable to establish any actual authority over them, the conscription has never been enforced, and no taxes have been levied; so that, although defeated, they were yet practically victorious. Partly, doubtless, this is due to Hajji Tarfa's diplomatic ability in placing money, horses, and the like where they will do the most good. He has even made himself *persona grata* with the authorities, and, in addition to his position as sheikh of the unruly and turbulent Affech, he is also the Sultan's tenant on some of the latter's private estates on the other side of the Euphrates. During the first year of our excavations he actually took up his residence on those estates among the rice marshes, relegating the government of the Affech to his son Mekota, a turbulent and treacherous youth, with the apparent intention of avoiding responsibility for the complications which he foresaw in consequence of our expedition.

But Hajji Tarfa, although a great and powerful chief, does not possess absolute sway even over the few tribes constituting the so-called Affech nation. The authority of a sheikh is largely moral, depending upon his ability, wealth, and the like, or upon the need of a leader to resist some outside adversary. In times of peace and security the various petty chiefs, who loosely recognize his leadership, are apt to fight with one another. So at the time of our arrival the el-Behahtha Affech to the west, and the el-Hamza Affech to the south were in hostile relations to one another, and each laid claim to the mounds of Nippur. It was with the el-Behahtha that Layard stayed in 1851 during his two week's work at Nippur, when he was brought to the mounds by boat each morning and carried back the same way each evening. In those days the el-Behahtha were the leading members of the Affech nation, and their chief, Agab, the head chief. Now the el-Hamza have the chieftaincy.

To the north and east of Nippur stretches a desert,

roaming ground of various tribes, the most settled of which are the es-Sa'id, a small tribe of bad repute, half-bedouin and half-ma'dan. These also lay claim to the mounds of Nippur, as forming a part of their lands. Such were the conditions of the country, as we learned them later by experience. But of all these things we had no previous information, and when Mustafa Assim Pasha told me in Baghdad that I had chosen the most difficult and unruly portion of his province for our excavations, I received his statement with many grains of salt, suspecting him of some ulterior motive.

Friday, February 1st, we commenced the erection of a permanent camp. We had thirty-two workmen with us from Jimjimeh and Birs Nimrud, six of whom had brought their wives and families. All of these had to be provided for, as well as our own people. Haynes had pitched the tents on the highest point on the southwestern side of the great canal, said to be the Shatt-en-Nil, which divides the mounds of Nippur into two approximately even halves. He supposed at the time that this situation on the summit of the mounds would be the safest, the most healthy, and the most comfortable. From there we could look over the country and observe any purpose of attack upon us better than if we had been upon the level. We were also less liable to malaria when thus removed from the marshes, and we should be likely to have during the warm weather cool breezes. I named the camp Kal'at Amerika (Castle America). But our site, as we learned later from sad experience, was a great mistake. We were compelled to carry water a long distance up hill, which was expensive even when the marshes were full. We were very much annoyed by sand storms. There was always a high wind, and the loose soil of the mound raised by this wind enveloped us with clouds of dust, which was sometimes quite intolerable, while on the plain below there was no dust whatever. The mound itself was a no man's land,

Kal'at Amerika, the First Year's Camp, from the East, showing a great Trench in foreground.

and we were under the protection of no tribe, but exposed to the invasions of all. We were very conspicuous, perched on the top of a ruin mound, and by our position invited plundering by the neighboring natives.

We made a contract with Berdi to build us huts like those of the country, made of bunches of reeds arched together, the whole covered with palm-leaf mats. Berdi had been the first to welcome us, and he occupied the camp nearest to us on the south, hence he secured the contract. He was a bright, cheery fellow, short, and rather stout, and overflowing with energy and animal spirits. Our camp was so mapped out as to form an almost square enclosure, with our tents in the centre. There was a hut for our commissioner, Bedry Bey; a hut for our guards; a stable for our horses; a kitchen and dining-room, with storeroom attached for food and equipments, as well as for antiquities; a hut for Haynes, who preferred that to a tent, and in connection therewith a stable for his horse, from which he could not endure to be separated, and a photographic workroom. Field, Noorian, Harper, Hilprecht, and I occupied tents in the centre of the enclosure. Later, another tent was pitched near the large opening on the south side, to accommodate an additional force of zaptiehs, and a small open tent was placed there to act as a guest room. One of the mistakes of our first year was that we provided no muthif, or guest house, in which to receive the guests who might visit us. The small tent which we placed at the opening of the camp was not satisfactory, and no self-respecting sheikh would consent to be received there. The consequence was that they overran our private tents, sat on our beds, explored our goods, fingered our firearms, and filled our clothes with fleas.

While we were building the camp, Field was hard at work making a topographical plan of the mounds, so that we might commence excavations immediately. I was for the most part engaged in receiving visitors and arranging our diplomatic relations. Toward the middle of the first morning Bedry arrived with the Mudir of Affech. Mekota also appeared. He turned out to be a thorough beggar, asking for everything that he saw. In the matter of dealing with the Arabs, I was compelled to trust entirely to the experience of Noorian and Haynes, who had themselves had very little. We had not brought much with us in the way of presents. What we had was in the form of abbayehs and red Arab boots. I gave Mekota, by Noorian's advice, an abbayeh and a gold lira. When I think of it, I am surprised that this great man should have consented to accept so small a gift. (He did, in fact, afterwards feel that he had demeaned himself by taking the lira, and endeavored to return it.) His acceptance of the gift was supposed to place us under his protection, and as he was the representative of his father, Hajji Tarfa, in the latter's absence, we were constructively under the protection of that great chief. Bedry wished me to have Mekota and some of his men live with us on the mounds to protect us, but, with the advice of Haynes and Noorian, I refused this guard on the ground that they would be a great burden and expense, and would want everything we owned. The camp was fairly overrun with Arabs, curious to see the foreigners and their strange things, all that day. That night Field completed by hard work a hasty and incorrect plan of the mounds, which was accepted by Bedry as fulfilling the requirements of the law regarding the topographical plan.

Saturday, the 2d, we were again overrun with armed Arabs, including the all-asking Mekota. It was impossible to keep them out of any place, and so numerous were they that, had they so wished, they could easily have wiped out all our little party. Bedry was seriously alarmed at their appearance and their numbers, and had an attack of fever, due in part to fright. He did not re-

Affech Arab building a Hut of Reeds and Mats.

quite Berdi's Arabs liberally enough for their work for him, in consequence of which they danced a war-dance in front of his cabin, singing threatening and uncomplimentary songs, which added greatly to his terror. He begged hard that we would arrange with Mekota to accept from him Arab guards, but this we all believed it unwise to do.

Mustafa, our head man, and a zaptieh were sent off to Diwanieh early in the morning, carrying Field's map and a telegram from Bedry to the Governor-General accepting the same. They were also to buy straw for the horses and mules, for none was to be had at Affech. The kitchen, dining-room, storeroom, and stable were completed by evening of that day. Both that day and the preceding we had a high, cold wind and quantities of dust, but the sun was very hot. That night there set in a violent storm of wind and rain, which lasted until Monday morning. The weather became very cold, and the whole camp was completely demoralized. It was impossible to get a pleasant word or a pleasant look from anyone. The stable was about blown down in the storm, so that it had to be rebuilt. The dining-room fell to leaking badly. The kitchen was in such a state that the cook could scarcely cook, and the only comfortable place was bed. Monday began cold and unpleasant, but cleared up beautifully, so that before the end of it the damages done by the storm were repaired, and much additional work completed.

Mustafa and the zaptieh returned from Diwanieh on Tuesday, reporting the country through which they had come as much disturbed. They brought the mail, and also a despatch authorizing us to commence excavations. That day saw almost the entire work of camp-building completed. We were again visited by the Mudir and Mekota, with a number of the notables of the neighborhood, and the more distinguished of Mekota's tribesmen, all of whom we were compelled to feed. We were overrun with armed Arabs all day, and in the afternoon occurred an incident which might have closed the expedition with disaster before it had well begun.

Some of the el-Behahtha Arabs came to visit us. They claimed that Nippur was within their territory. They had taken care of Layard at the time of his excavations, and consequently regarded themselves as having a prescriptive right to take care of us, and resented deeply our pre-emption by the el-Hamza. Sharp words were exchanged between them and Berdi's men, who were building our camp. Suddenly both parties flew to arms and began to dance war-dances, the el-Behahtha just to the west of our camp, and the el-Hamza to the south. Between the two was a deep ravine, the way around which was through the camp. The method of the Arab wardance is very curious and interesting, when you have no personal stake in the matter. The sheikh, or some prominent member of the tribe, brandishing a spear or gun in his right hand, springs violently into the centre of the crowd, first rushing forward and then leaping up and down, and chants some sentence appropriate to the occasion, which he composes for the purpose. All his followers take up this sentence, chanting it over and over, leaping up and down violently, turning round and round, and brandishing their spears or guns in the air. Now and then some one fires a pistol or gun to increase the noise and excitement. After a while the sheikh, or some one else, having thought out a new sentence, rushes into the midst of the crowd and chants that in the same way as before, whereupon it is taken up in the same manner. A great sheikh, like Mekota, will seldom dance himself, but, after having set his followers going, stands to one side and watches them until he is ready to give them a new song. Berdi acted more like a common tribesman, and one could perceive no difference between him and his men, either in conduct or appearance.

Realizing that if the war-dances were not checked, the

matter might become very serious, I summoned Berdı and bade him make his men stop that singing. I told him that he was our friend, and that we had contracted with him to build our huts. We proposed to continue under his protection, but in order to do so, we must see that he did not provoke difficulties which would render our stay at Nippur impossible. He agreed to check his men, and went off professedly for that purpose, but as soon as he had joined them he commenced dancing as violently as the best, and leading them in songs in defiance of the el-Behahtha. I sent for him once more, and remonstrated with him for his failure to do what he had undertaken to do. He was pleasant and merry, and went back smiling and promising to quiet his men. But as soon as he reached them he fell a-dancing and singing as before. To a third message he returned a fierce and indignant reply that he could not and would not stop his men so long as the el-Behahtha were dancing there and hurling defiance at him, and that I should make them stop and drive them from the mound if I wished his men to be quiet. The el-Behahtha had perpetrated a taunt which enraged him beyond control. It was: "Matches in his beard who contradicts us," *i.e.*, may the beard of him who opposes us be burned,—a most insulting song, in view of the sacredness of the beard.

It was evident that something must be done at once; therefore, taking Berdi at his word, I started to go to the el-Behahtha, and called Noorian to go with me and interpret. He realized the danger of such a course much more than I did, as he understood all that the tribesmen were saying to one another. I realized only the danger in which we were in case the dancing developed into fighting, as it seemed likely to do. At the same time, the whole situation appeared to me intensely ridiculous. The Arabs were like so many little children, and I felt very much as I should were I to find two bands of street lads calling names at one another. I was distinctly their master by virtue of the fact that I was a grown-up man and they children, and I felt no hesitancy therefore in going to the el-Behahtha, and a little irritation at Noorian's refusal. I told him that if he wished he might stay behind, in which case I should go alone. As I started out of the camp, one of our workmen threw himself in front of me, blocking my way, and drawing his hand across his throat, a pantomime meant to tell me that the el-Behahtha would certainly kill me if I went. I burst out laughing, and pushed him to one side, telling him that they would do nothing of the sort. Noorian, who was anything but a coward, seeing that I was determined to go, joined me, and entered into my mood of regarding it all as a joke. I called upon the el-Behahtha to stop that dancing, and go down off the mound. I told them that I did not want them to make a muss and litter about the camp, and that if they wanted to fight, and would go down on the plain, I would send the whole el-Hamza tribe after them. I caught hold of one or two of them and actually began to shove them along in front of me. Some made threatening gestures with their weapons, but I took their threats as jokes, and treated them accordingly. Noorian entered into the spirit of the matter admirably, and interpreted my little jokes far better than I made them, so that soon the whole party of us were roaring with laughter, and we were successfully driving the Arabs down the hill. It was fortunate that I in my ignorance treated the matter in the way I did, and that we succeeded in making the Arabs see the joke. The next day the Behahtha returned in force, accompanied by an imam,—sure sign of mischief,—for the purpose of attacking the Hamza, but fortunately the latter did not appear. A day or two later war broke out between them, and several men were killed. During the whole time of our stay at Nippur the bringing together of the Behahtha and the Hamza was extremely dangerous, and war was constantly breaking out between the two tribes.

Digging trenches for draining, and the like, in connection with our camp, brought us on Monday and Tuesday a few remains of antiquity, such as inscribed bricks, a medical or magic bowl with a Jewish inscription, a couple of fragments of inscribed stones, two large earthen vases, and an earthen coffin. One of the vases was found in my tent. There was a slight inequality in the floor of the tent, and when the men undertook to level it, they discovered that it was caused by a large earthen vase, some three feet in height. This lay upon its side, and had been used as a coffin, but there was nothing inside except earth and some fragments of bones. It was removed intact. In front of Field's tent an earthen coffin of urn shape was dug out. This was begged from us by the husband of the woman who baked our bread, and became our bread-oven. A three-handled funerary vase, found in front of Harper's tent, was emptied of its contents, and made a receptacle to hold water for the men in the trenches.

It was observed that the men who had been sent out to collect bricks were bringing all of the bricks from one place, and that a number of these were inscribed, some bearing an inscription of Ur-Gur. On investigating the place where they were digging, I found that they had discovered a brick tomb within which was a clay coffin of the Parthian period. Not wishing to have the tomb disturbed in this manner, and not being prepared as yet to commence digging systematically, I stopped the work and had the hole refilled, which had one unfortunate result. Word got about that we had found treasure, and we were disturbed by Arabs prowling about after gold. But I can best describe the life and work of the first year by extracts from my personal diary, and from letters written at the time.

CHAPTER XI.

THE FIRST CAMPAIGN.

The Arabs—Acting as Physician—Engaging Workmen—First Trenches—A Jealous Chief—Layard—An Arab War—A Race—Sick Flocking to be Healed—Heat and Vermin—Inscribed Tablets—Hebrew Bowls—War Indemnity—Unwelcome Reinforcements—An Arab Muthif—The Mudir resigns—A Threat—Sickness—My Disciples—Heat—The Kaimakam—An Accident—A Hurricane—More Workmen—Flies—Bedry and the Arabs—A Wild Boar—Through the Marshes—Delehem—Supposed Corruption—Immorality—Thieves—Shatt-el-Hai—De Sarzec—Tello—War and Love—A Bedouin Camp—Yokha—The Wool Tax—Bismya—Back at Nippur—Kurigalzu—A Tablet Kiln—Stolen Antiquities—Increasing Turbulence—Our Iradé—Suspected — Thieves Arrested.

ON Sunday, February 10th, I wrote to Mr. E. W. Clark as follows:

"These Arabs are not unlike our Indians, savage, treacherous, picturesque, and the worst thieves and beggars I ever met. Day before yesterday, at the door of our camp, one man broke another's head with his club, and was stabbed in return. . . . All these Arabs go armed, and we often have a hundred or more, armed with old flintlocks, fowling pieces, spears, swords, clubs, and knives, sitting about the trenches, wandering around the camp, or visiting us in our tents. Each man suspects his neighbor's intentions. . . . Our sudden appearance on horseback anywhere causes the shepherds to run their flocks away, a feat to which the latter seem well trained. Yesterday morning, when Field was out riding, two shepherds got hold of him and made signs of cutting his throat. He was cool headed, and treated it as a joke. After work was over, I rode out to inspect the more distant diggings. As I was approaching the little hill where they were, some shepherds behind began to shout at me, and two men on the hill commenced to gesture me away. [Presumably they were searching for the treasure for which they supposed us to be digging, and did not wish to be interfered with.] I paid no heed, and rode closer, whereupon one of them levelled his gun at me. I was entirely unarmed, and almost involuntarily checked my horse, but then instantly started on again, concluding that it would never do to show fear under any circumstances, and surmising also that the man was more likely to shoot if I turned back than if I kept on. When I was

ARAB WOMEN

pretty close I saluted him [salaam 'aleikum], whereupon he lowered his gun and returned the salute [we 'aleikum salaam]. I think it probable that in both cases the men were only trying to frighten us, though if we had showed any fear they might have done something. . . . One part of my duties will amuse you, my duties as physician. The people come to me from all around, and I have had cases of bowel troubles, liver troubles, palsy, sore eyes, deafness, etc., brought to me. I feel their pulses, look at their tongues, inquire about their symptoms, prescribe for them rationally if I can, and, if I cannot, concoct a vile mess that cannot hurt them, and order a diet. But this medicine business is becoming embarrassing. Yesterday a chief brought me his wife and sister to prescribe for. I pretended to feel their pulses as usual, but really I have never succeeded in finding an Arab pulse yet, for their skin, even that of the women and children, is like the hide of oxen. There is no danger of my falling in love with my female patients, for while the men and boys are often fine looking, the women are hopelessly disfigured by nose rings and tattooing.

"We are slowly increasing the number of our workmen. We began with thirty-two, working at three, four, and five piastres a day [piastre equals four cents]. We took on eleven more from the natives who are coming in asking for work, but the chiefs came and reclaimed them, carrying off one man by force. The reason for this is that the chiefs want to be paid in addition to their men. After prayers this morning, as we do not work on Sunday, Noorian and I started for the village of Berdi, the sub-chief of our region, to demand an explanation of his conduct, and, if he would not come to terms, to go to Sukh-el-Affech, send for Hajji Tarfa to return, and arrange with him and complain of Berdi. We met Berdi on his way to our camp, and he turned back with us to his village. There he received us in a well made reed and mat hut, his muthif, or guest house, which was entered by a door not above three feet square. When I got in I could see nothing, and he had to guide me to a cushion. When I became accustomed to the light, I saw that the place was absolutely packed with men, armed as usual. Later, he took me into his castle, a mud fortress, in which were his reed huts for himself and his family. He arranged to give us all the men we want, we to pay them three piastres a day and him five. We asked for thirty men for to-morrow, which is as many as we can digest at once. Later, he arrived at our camp to say that there are five ' brothers,' chiefs of five sub-divisions of his tribe, and not to offend them we must take fifty men, so as to divide equally among them. He could not see that thirty could be divided among five as equally as fifty."

The first entry in my personal diary referring to the excavations is under date of—

"February 13th, Wednesday, 1889. Excavations were commenced February 6th, with the thirty-two men we brought from Jimjimeh. The tomb found a few days before close to the camp suggested a place to work (I.) until we got some idea of what we could do, and how to do it. We found ourselves in a graveyard, in which the coffins, urns, and ashes were in all possible positions at every depth. It was interesting to find, between one and two metres beneath the surface, in the immediate neighborhood of slipper-shaped coffins, inscribed Hebrew bowls. After a few days the work was concentrated about a columnar brick structure in the middle of a small gully, in and around which we were digging. To-day this was brought into a regular plan of a trench through the mound. The second or third day, our force being augmented by a few of the neighboring Arabs, we commenced three trenches in a small oval mound at the northern end of the canal-like depression (II.), but here we found nothing. At the beginning of this week we commenced excavating the portion of the mounds known as Bınt-el-Amir, or Prince's Daughter, the Temple Hill (III.). At the same time a small trench was begun across a very large, deep gully from where we first began to dig, because three fragments of inscribed stone had been found at this point (IV.) Nothing of importance was found here, and this morning this spot was abandoned. At the same time we had begun work on a large, isolated hill at the southern end of the eastern mounds (V.). Here have been found quite a number of inscribed tablets. To-day we began to plan the reduction of the diggings to a system by a trench through the graveyard, another through the Temple Hill, and a third through the hill where the tablets have been found. The weather has been fine, but the sun at mid-day is very hot, so that the temperature of the huts often goes above eighty degrees. We have had some trouble about workmen, and had to engage to pay Berdi to let us have men. The men themselves are eager to come. I have had to act as physician to all the country around. The female cases are very embarrassing. Two days since a green-turbaned descendant of the Prophet's family brought me his wife, suffering from some internal trouble, and expressed his readiness to have me examine her. I contented myself with feeling her pulse, asking her questions, and looking at her tongue. The latter was an ordeal. She had to be brought to my tent, where she unveiled herself for a moment, and put out her tongue in the most alarmed manner possible. As her digestion was out of order, I gave her some Warburg's tincture, whereupon, to my alarm, she fainted away. The skins of both men and women are so thick that I can scarcely find any pulse at all.

"February 14, 1889, Thursday. The Temple Hill is not accurately orientated north and south at the corners, but is twelve degrees off. Field has arranged to put the men in at the southern corner, both on the inner and the outer walls, and when the corner is found, the trench can be laid out. Mekota and the Mudir came, accompanied as usual by a host of followers. The former went uninvited into my tent. He is still begging for my pistol. He insisted on our coming to see him, and offered to take us to see Delehem, a mound reported to be of great interest. We had to agree to go, Noorian and I, next Sunday. Later, Nahab, a chief of the Sa'id, appeared.

He had treated the Wolfe Expedition with great kindness four years ago, and had hospitably received and brought to the mound our party two weeks since, therefore he also had to be hospitably received. He brought with him five or six men, and announced his intention of spending the night, and we had much ado in finding a place for him, and each of us had to contribute some article of bedding. He wanted to build a hut and furnish twenty men for the diggings, that he, too, might 'have a share in this work.' As this would cause trouble with Berdi and others, I had to refuse. Mekota is already very jealous of our relations with Berdi, and told us an Arab proverb about entering by the side of the house instead of by the door. He also complained of our giving Berdi a silk gaboon or gown. More tablets were found to-day, among them some case tablets. They have so far all come from the same place (V.).

"February 15, 1889, Friday. Day before yesterday, some Arabs, whom Noorian tried to send away, danced the war-dance, and cried 'Down with the Christians!'" hence, the Mudir's visit yesterday. The only two things of interest in the work have been, first, the finding of a tomb upon the Temple Hill at the digging at base of cone. This was made simply of mud bricks. There were found there a few rings and beads. [It was at this point that we found the only faint traces of Layard's brief excavations thirty-eight years before. I had written earlier to him for further information about Nippur than that published by him in his *Nineveh and Babylon*, and also for any advice which he might feel inclined to give about excavations in Babylonia. He replied that his connection with Babylonia had long ceased, and that he was ignorant of what had been done of late years. It will be remembered that his published impressions of Nippur were not favorable. He almost died of pleurisy and fever; the country was very unsafe, and, finally, his hosts wished to go to war, and he was compelled to leave. He found nothing but coffins and jars, and concludes (p. 562): "On the whole, I am much inclined to question whether extensive excavations carried on at Niffer would produce any important or interesting results."] The second thing was the finding of tombs in among the tablets at the southern hill (V.). A fire broke out in one of the Arab cabins, but was fortunately put out in time to prevent the destruction of the camp. We ordered the removal of the huts to a little distance from our camp. This evening came a despatch to Bedry from the Wali, refusing the map because not signed by me or by him, and also reproving us for not obtaining guards from Hajji Tarfa.

ARAB WORKMAN'S HUT.

"February 16, 1889, Saturday. They are still finding fragments of tablets at V., the southern hill. At I., by the columns of the building, we found another slipper-shaped coffin, and the attempt was made to get it out whole, but it went to pieces. There has been some fighting to the west of us, and to-day an Arab came and tried to persuade our Hamza Arabs to go and fight. Noorian ordered him away, and finally laid hands on him, whereupon he threatened Noorian with his gun and knife, but the rest took part against him.

"February 17, 1889, Sunday. Ten men arrived to-day from Nahab to work for us. We have allowed them to commence, and to build huts to the west of our camp. We gave the men thirty-eight piastres to buy a sheep to-day for what they call a sacrifice. Last evening and this evening they danced for us. Interest in the diggings has stagnated for the last few days, and the Temple Hill is a hopeless perplexity. The weather has become very warm. After three days' fighting the Hamza have killed three of the Behahtha. Hajji Tarfa was expected back last night to settle the dispute. The Mudir regretted that five hundred had not been killed, instead of three, and when I told him that we had been quiet because the Arabs had been fighting, he devoutly prayed that they might continue to fight for thirty days. He took lunch with us, and this time, unlike the last, heartily enjoyed his food, and ate pork and beans with a relish, although I am not certain that he knew what he was eating. It seems that the Temple Hill is called by the Arabs both Bint-el-Amir, and Kassl Bint (Castle of the Daughter), and the depression to the south of it is called Shatt-en-Nil.

"Yesterday, when we were riding to the north of the mounds, an Arab, whose sister I had doctored a few days before, came out on a mare and challenged us to race. He said that he could pass us, and snatch off our hats. I accepted his challenge, and Niffer easily distanced his mare. The sick still come in crowds. To-day the descendant of the Prophet, whose wife fainted the last time I doctored her, came again, and brought four chickens for a present. His wife was better, but wanted more medicine. A sheikh came from a distance to-day, and brought me a young man of distinction, son of a former head sheikh of distinction, to be physicked. They spread their beds in our reception tent, and propose to remain several days to have me 'look at the young man many times.' To-day I went through very absurd scenes, as men followed me everywhere, with their tongues lolling out of their mouths and their hands extended, to have their pulses felt and their tongues looked at. I have given out a great deal of sulphate of magnesia and quinine in the last few days. I am surprised at the number of people who come complaining that their urinary or genital organs are in a bad state. The way, too, in which they treat wounds and sores with red-hot irons is appalling. Yesterday a man came who was putting iron-rust into a wound. Saturday night the Arabs on the hill had a war-dance with some of the members of the expedition. We were to have gone to Mekota yesterday, but the Mudir brought word that he and all of his tribe had gone away, and that only the women were left behind.

"I am beginning to understand some things in the Bible better in consequence of my Oriental experience. The way these poor miserable wretches bring their sick to me reminds me of the story of Jesus, and oh, if I could only help them a little more! I never was so directly brought into contact with physical misery. And I am so powerless to relieve the really touching cases. Their lighter ailments alone I am able to remedy.

"The weather here is already becoming very warm. The sun is hot, and the winds overwhelm us with dust. Moreover, flies, fleas, and other vermin are beginning to abound. But the nights are wonderful. From our position on these high mounds, looking out over the flat plains, we can see everything that goes on. On all sides at night there are great fires, where the Arabs are burning the marshes so as to make sheep pasturage. We have had only one day of rain this month, and the moon seems to shine always. The heavens are wonderfully blue and far away. There is war just now close to us between our sub-tribe of the Affech and another sub-tribe, but it does not seem to affect us.

"Friday, February 22d. Night before last Harper reported that among the tablets found were some of Samsu-

A Deep Trench on Tablet Hill (V.), showing constructions of Xerxes's time above, and remains of 2000 B.C. below.

Iluna, Nabonidus, Cyrus, and Cambyses. This shows that Nippur played a great role longer than we had supposed, 2000 to 500 B.C. In the house of unburned bricks which Abbas is digging out close to the camp have been found a number of ordinary Hebrew bowls, and a couple in Arabic letters. Along with these bowls have been found millstones, playthings, and other utensils belonging to life, but so far nothing belonging to death. On the tops of the hills in all that region have been found fragments of these bowls, but none far below the surface. A satisfactory trench has at last been laid out on the Temple Hill, but each day shows us that we know nothing of what is there. We are always treated to new surprises.

"To-day Bedry went to see Hajji Tarfa, but the interview does not seem to have been satisfactory. Bedry is very homesick, and has showed me a letter from his wife. She had just been paid the salary due up to last August. How can Turkish officials live without bribery? Last night and to-day have been quite cold again. As to-day is Washington's Birthday, we had another war-dance this evening.

"February 24th. Two of the sub-tribes have been fighting, and our friend Berdi and the el-Hamza have been victorious, killing three of the el-Behahtha. The result is that the el-Hamza must pay the el-Behahtha about $75, and from three to six women. The former is blood money, the latter by establishing ties of blood is supposed to cement peace. Such is the practice in this country. The conquerors pay the indemnity. Hajji Tarfa, the great chief, was called home to settle the dispute, his son Mekota having failed to do so. A day or two after his arrival the Mudir of Affech arrived here with twenty zaptiehs, whom the Governor has sent to guard us. I protested, but was told that one hundred more were at our command, and an additional twenty on the march. I then refused point blank to quarter or feed them, as we had been compelled to do with the six already with us. The Mudir said that the Government was bound to care for them, not we; and that if they needed anything we could send them to him. We took him at his word, and the poor fellow has had to feed them out of his own pocket ever since. His salary, he says, is nominally seven and a half liras a month, and his expenses thirty-five. The zaptiehs are much mortified at their position, and try to make themselves as agreeable as possible. Accordingly, whenever they see the Beg, as I am called, they rise and give the military salute, or run to hold my horse, or render any service possible.

"Day before yesterday, Noorian and I went to call on Hajji Tarfa. His reception tent was a fine large hut of mats of grass spread on arched columns of bundles of reeds tied together, the universal house in this country. But this was the largest and finest I have ever seen, at least sixty feet long and fifteen high, the roof a rich mahogany color from the coffee fire constantly burning in the middle of the tent. There were eight coffee pots on the smouldering ashes of that fire. In the largest they cook the coffee first, then they drain it off into the next, and so on until they reach the smallest, or one of the smaller. It is slightly flavored with myrrh, and only a sip is given you, in the bottom of a tiny cup. But this sip is repeated at irregular intervals, so that one ultimately drinks a good deal of strong coffee. By the fire squats a slave who attends to the coffee. About the middle of the hut, where the light was vague, as there are no windows, and the door is so low that you must stoop to enter, sat the great chief, with his back to the wall, and along the sides of the tent squatted many other lesser chiefs, and innumerable other Arabs. Hajji received me with much friendliness and great honor, and I reclined, since I do not enjoy squatting, by his side. He

The Muthif or Guest House of an Arab Sheikh in Southern Babylonia.

insisted that we must eat with him, but as pious Shiite Mussulmans may not eat with Christians, our food was served apart. A round mat of straw was placed on the ground in front of us, on which was set a great bowl of rice, a smaller one of mutton, a couple of bowls of lebben, or milk soured by fermentation through leaven, and two of the great flat, unleavened, half-cooked barley cakes, which they call bread. For them was served in like manner. They ate with their fingers, but we used our lebben spoons for the rice also, reserving our fingers for the bread and mutton. It requires more skill than we possessed to eat rice with our fingers, without slobbering, to use an unpleasant but expressive word. After our party had eaten all they wished, others took their places, and so on until nothing remained. Everything was done decently and in order, for Hajji Tarfa maintained such order as I have not seen before among the Arabs, and, indeed, he is the first gentleman I have met among them.

"The Mudir arrived while we were there, but Hajji Tarfa absolutely ignored him, and afterwards insulted him by abusing the Turkish Government in his presence. The Turks have no authority over him, and stand in much awe of him. It is not many years since he killed the Mutessarif of Hillah and massacred a whole battalion of soldiers, and he appropriates regularly the taxes supposed to be due to the government. But all good Arabs are murderers, and even our nice little Berdi murdered two of his brothers while they slept. When we left, Hajji showed us the honor of accompanying us to our horses. The next day the Mudir came to tell us that he had resigned, and was about to leave. Hajji Tarfa had driven him away.

"The Affech were much irritated by the presence of the zaptiehs, and unfortunately Bedry increased this irritation by using zaptiehs as guards and spies in the trenches, thus forcing them before the Arabs, and at the same time asserting in a way peculiarly odious to the latter the government ownership of the mounds, which they called their own.

"Hajji Tarfa sent word that he was coming to call to-day, and we prepared to receive him; but, later, a messenger arrived to say that he would come to see us to-morrow. I have a suspicion that this was done because I treated Mekota, his son, in the same way.

"We are digging diligently with a force of one hundred and twenty men; but Nippur is an immense place, and it takes a long time to find what we want. We pay our ordinary workmen twelve cents a day, and the skilled laborers sixteen and twenty cents.

"Monday, March 4th. We have had two alarms this week. Berdi threatened to burn us out and murder Noorian, because we had not taken all our men from him, and because we had not paid him a salary for the men we had taken. All the soldiers were on guard one night, and we have been very careful all the time. Berdi murdered two of his brothers in their sleep, and is believed to be capable of anything. Another chief, some of whose men we employ, heard of it, and sent us word that he had told Berdi that if our camp were burned, he would make war on him. Yesterday and to-day Berdi has been here professing that he never said such a thing, and trying to win our confidence again. We are not afraid of a direct attack, but with the greatest care which we can exercise we could not be sure of preventing a man from stealing up these dark nights and applying a match to our inflammable straw huts before he could be detected.

"Our other alarm has been connected with Haynes. He has been sleeping in a bad atmosphere, as he insisted on having his horse at one end of his hut and his photographic workroom at the other. By day, too, he has been in a bad atmosphere, developing pictures, and taking little or no exercise. Sunday, there seemed to be serious danger of brain fever or typhoid. His temperature was over 104°, and he had not slept a wink for two nights, and the pain in his head and his back seemed to be beyond his endurance. By evening we succeeded in reducing the temperature to the normal, and relieving his head, but he could not sleep Sunday night either, in spite of heavy doses of laudanum. Harper and I sat up with him. To-day, however, he was able to get up. He was to have gone to Hillah to-day for money, and insists that he shall go on Wednesday.

" Mekota has sent us a number of workmen this week, more than we were ready to receive, although we have raised our force to one hundred and thirty men. He also sends me a good many sick people to be doctored. Among others, there came yesterday some negresses, slaves of himself and his father. One of them had a private request to make. She wished her master to love her, and she wished to become *enceinte*. Se'id Ahmed, one of our overseers, relieved me of this case. Indeed, he has undertaken to relieve me of a good many. He pretends to be my disciple, it seems. He begged an old *Saturday Review* a few days since. This he carries in his pocket and pretends to consult, as he has seen me consult a nurse book. He also feels their pulses, and makes them put out their tongues, as he has seen me do. One of his prescriptions to a man was like this: " Wash yourself in hot water; eat mutton, lebben, and milk; but avoid dates; keep warm, but do not go out in the sun." Nevertheless, in spite of his good offices, too many cases leak through to his ' master.' Among others, I have had one crazy boy brought to me, and one woman with tapeworm.

" The morality of the Arabs is very low, as we have had occasion to notice. As Haynes and Noorian were riding out the other day a young man offered them his sister for a few metalliks, and Bedry tells me that even in a city like Hillah, quite respectable Arabs will give their daughters for a beshlik.

"The heat this week has been excessive, reaching 98° in the tents, and the flies are almost beyond endurance. I have had the open lumberman's tent pitched in front of mine, so as to make a sort of selamlik in which to receive people. There has been little of interest found in the last week, but the holes are beginning to look very deep and large.

"Thursday, March 14th. One day last week in III., in the front room, underneath a mud brick wall, about two metres and a half below the surface, we dug out a live toad. He seemed torpid and inactive. Scorpions and snakes have begun to appear. The temperature one day last week reached 102° in my tent, and 105° in Field's. This, accompanied with high winds and clouds of dust, and swarms of flies, made that week a very trying one; but this week has been delightful, and at night and early morning even a trifle too cold. Haynes left Friday morning for Hillah. He was much improved, and felt that the trip would really do him good. I suffered the first part of last week from pangs of toothache. By Thursday the toothache became almost unendurable, the whole jaw and throat were sore, and I could scarcely eat. This continued Friday and Saturday. The latter day a violent sick headache set in, and I had to go to bed before dinner. Since then I have been regaining tone. Hilprecht is looking miserable, and feeling so, and this week both he and Harper have had fever very lightly. Field, owing to his out-of-doors life, is in splendid condition.

"This week we decided to increase our force by seven extra gangs on the City of the Living (V.), in order to lay bare as much of the mound as possible. Last week

Female Avocations. Arab Women pounding Grain to make Bread.

we had another visit from Mekota, who brought with him the new Mudir, one of the notables of Hillah, an Arab, of the Persian sect of Mussulmans. Mekota begged as usual. The Mudir asked me to write a letter to the Mutessarif, expréssing my satisfaction with his appointment. I excused myself from doing this. They have a very exalted idea of my importance.

"Saturday, the Kaimakam of Diwanieh arrived to pay us a visit, and stayed until Sunday afternoon. We treated him as well as we knew how, and I think that he enjoyed the visit. At first he would not eat with us, for fear of wild boars or pork, but on Sunday he changed his mind, after he had seen more of us. He asked permission to carry off ten of the new zaptiehs, and I told him he was welcome to all, but they are still here. They have built a little prayer platform beyond their tents. Sunday afternoon, when he was going away, Harper and I escorted him some distance, and then took a ride to the northward to search for the bed of the Shatt-en-Nil. As I was riding at a brisk gallop, Niffer's forefoot went down in the sand and he fell on his head. I held fast, but, fortunately, for it just saved Niffer from a somersault, the girths broke, and saddle and I were shot eight or ten feet forward into the soft sand, and Niffer rolled over on his side. I jumped up to catch him, but the wind was knocked out of me, and I fell over again, and Niffer ran away. Harper went after him, but Niffer charged him, and finally chased him into camp on a wild run. Arrived there, he demolished the captain's tent, the captain himself having a narrow escape. Then he attacked the other horses, but was caught, and Noorian had a saddle on him in a jiffy, and Kework on a spare horse, and was out on the gallop after me. Bedry ordered all the zaptiehs to follow, but Field and Harper managed to stop them before they had gone far. However, Bedry and a posse of armed Arabs joined the hunt. I was found wandering about with my saddle on my back, trying to avoid some suspicious-looking Arabs. On the way back we came to a large canal bed, which the Arabs said was the Shatt-en-Nil.

"Yesterday Harper and I rode out to two small mounds about an hour and a half away to the northeast, called Abu Jowan, or Father of Millstones. They seem unimportant. There are several large canal beds in the neighborhood. One we followed westward, but it disappeared about half an hour from Nippur. I think it originally went on and joined the Shatt-en-Nil to the north of the mound. We passed several cross canals on the way. The sandhills lie to the north and northeast of us, they are of fine sea sand, and constantly change shape as blown about by the wind. The Euphrates seems to be rising, and the water is approaching the mound on the south and west. Nothing of any importance has been found since my last writing. Constructions on the Temple Hill are becoming more interesting than ever, but also more perplexing. There are tombs found everywhere in the other trenches.

"March 18th. We are in the midst of the worst hurricane but one I ever saw; and that lasted only a few minutes, while this has gone on for hours. Yesterday, Sunday, the wind blew very hard and very hot all day, and the dust was suffocating. It continued all night, choking and burning one at the same time. This morning it blew a gale. By noon it was a hurricane. One could scarcely make head against the wind at all, and the air was so full of dust that the plain was not visible. You could not walk against the wind and see, and the amount of dust in the tents and huts was almost incredible. Shortly after noon the tents began to go. Harper's was the first, and three soldiers' tents followed suit, leaving twenty-one of our guard houseless. Then my ridgepole snapped. I had mine and Hilprecht's tents eased by throwing off the flies, and putting casting-ropes outside to support the poles. My ridgepole was spliced after a fashion, or rather the ends were fastened by a rope. In the meantime a number of men were put on to save the huts by refastening the mats and propping the poles within to windward. But the stables went to wreck, and the storeroom and dining-room are in a bad condition. Somewhere about 10 P.M., the storm was still raging, when there came a single lightningless thunderclap,—as though it had been a divine command, the Hebrew " voice of Yahweh," and the wind was still instantly. I had the camp aroused in a minute to rehabilitate the fallen tents, restore the flies, and get ready for rain in general; and now the rain has begun, accompanied by a stiff cold wind from the north, in refreshing contrast to the burning sirocco of the last few days.

" The storm has temporarily put a stop to a war between some of our neighbors. Sunday evening a village was burned in a war between two hostile sections of the Affech. The village was close to the mound, and the illumination was a fine one.

" Tuesday, March 21st. Wednesday morning of last week a boat arrived from Hillah, bringing Haynes's purchases, among which were fruit and green things, greatly needed by all. The water in the swamps is rising, and a boat can now come quite close to the mound. This boat was large, and a sloop. It was engaged to return April 25th to take us away. Going over the accounts, I found that we could increase the workmen by one hundred and ten men until the middle of April. I therefore arranged to put on as rapidly as possible twenty more gangs, five on the City of the Living, and fifteen on the Temple Hill. To-day thirteen of the twenty-four extra zaptiehs were recalled by the Government. Yesterday a piece of a wall fell on a man at the Temple Hill, hurting him quite badly. The workmen ran from the trenches on all sides, brandishing their tools. Bedry thought it was an attack by the Arabs, and was so frightened that he became ill. Nothing of any importance has been found of late. Interest, however, centres about the Temple Hill, where new and more perplexing constructions are constantly occurring, and the City of the Living. A great number of tablet fragments were found to-day at the latter place, more than were ever found before in one day. Tombs are still very numerous everywhere, and at all depths.

"March 24th. The thermometer in my tent is 92°, and there are at least ten flies for each degree of the thermometer. I do not remember the flies in America as having long stings, but these fellows bite worse than mosquitoes, driving what feels like the end of a sword right through my clothes.

"Thursday, March 28th. We are in the midst of another storm, almost burying us in the dust. It began suddenly about noon. One minute it was almost calm, and the next the dust was whirling so that one could hardly see. In a couple of hours the plain was invisible. I went out to ride and almost lost the mound, the air was so thick. While we were at dinner there came an alarm of fire. It turned out to be nothing but a fire lighted in one of the huts to cook by. A quarrel ensued among the Arabs, and I found that Bedry was meddling in it as usual. A little later some of them commenced a war dance, singing: 'The last day is come!' He was off in a moment, interfering again. Yesterday there was a quarrel between two families, and one woman wished to stab a man. Indirectly Bedry helped that on. A few days since an armed Arab came and asked for water at one of the huts. A soldier ordered him away, whereupon he told the soldier that he came to see the giaours, and did not estimate the soldier or the Turkish authorities as much as a ——. At this the soldier threatened him, and the Arab ran off a little distance and then turned and pointed his gun at the soldier. The latter fired at once, into the air he said, but the place where the bullet struck was suspicious. However, the workmen ran out of the trenches and threw stones at the Arab, and some of Hajji Tarfa's men are said to have followed him and given him a beating for causing a disturbance. It seems that what the Arabs sung the other night was that now the giaours had come the Wali could not come here. The Arabs all around seem to regard us with the greatest favor.

"To-day we obtained a wild boar which they had shot in the marshes. The flesh was very good, but more like beef than like swine's flesh. Of course, none would touch a hand to it excepting our own men. It is amusing to see how these dirty Arabs, whom to touch is to soil one's self, regard us as unclean. Field reports that they will not let him drink out of their tins of water in the trenches. Haynes has fever again to-night. His health is not satisfactory. Hilprecht also shows wear. Harper suffers from fleas and consequent loss of sleep. Field is in the best condition. The weather for the last few days has been intensely hot, but I suppose that this northerly storm will cool it. The flies are almost intolerable. In the last few days a large number of fragments have been found at the old place in the City of the Living. The Temple Hill continues to present curious developments in the line of constructions.

"Sunday, March 31st. After trying for some time to get off to Tello with Bedry, for the real purpose of having him away from the diggings for a while, we at last got off very suddenly yesterday late in the afternoon. We took a guide and a muleteer, and two soldiers. We rode down to the shore of the canal opposite Berdi's, or Berdan's, village, where we took boats for Affech. By the way, the last time Berdi called on me he politely offered to put Bedry out of the way if I would only say the word. Our boats were canoe-shaped, of twigs and reeds overlaid with bitumen. They were pushed with tamarisk poles, which were, of course, crooked and frail. The day, like those preceding, had been intensely hot, so that every one was discouraged and anxious to stop work, to which I would not consent before the end of April. On the canals it was lovely. They were full of white beds of fragrant ranunculus, through which we poled. Frogs croaked on all sides, buffaloes grunted, and birds flew up out of the high reeds through which we passed. Beyond Berdi's village we passed two more villages of the el-Hamza, the last being Mohammed el Berjud's residence. Both of these, especially the latter, had picturesque and refreshing-looking gardens of palms and almonds connected with their mud castles. People came to the bank to ask who was there, to which went back the answer, 'The men from Nufar.' 'Which?' 'The Sheikh.' Men were calling the cattle out of the marshes, and women were filling jars with water from the canal. Bedry told me that Hajji Tarfa's life had been threatened because of his friendly relations with the government, and that that was the main reason why he lived in the Shamieh. At this season, especially, he said, the Affech set the government at defiance, because, the water having filled their swamps and canals, their dwellings were practically inaccessible. There were but few mosquitoes in the marshes, the flies had gone to bed, and the atmosphere was delicious.

"We reached Affech after dark, and went to the muthif of Shamir, Hajji Tarfa's brother. Apparently he was not expecting us. There was no fire in his selamlik, no coffee, no guests, and only a miserable little lamp to give light. Pretty soon, however, guests began to assemble, but no supper appeared until half-past ten. At first we thought it was intentional, but this turned out not to be the case, and he was much mortified at the seeming lack of hospitality. When it came it was bountiful and good—chicken, rice, pilau, and lebben. As no one could pollute himself by eating with me, I had the good fortune to have a whole chicken, a bowl of lebben, and a dish of pilau to myself. We were not allowed to go to bed until about midnight, and then there were plenty of fleas, but I slept soundly. A cold wind arose during the night, and a little rain fell. There were nine coffeepots on the fire, which was burning when I awoke, and all our breakfast was two cups of coffee. Every one wished to be doctored before I left, and as we were riding out of the village a man left his work in the field, and came running to beg me to look at his sick wife. I was astonished at the activities of agriculture in the immediate neighborhood of the village. The fields were flooded, and men were plowing with cows, and one man even with a horse. This is the pasturage season, and it was very difficult to obtain any barley for our horses, which had been ridden down by the soldiers and a muleteer.

" At Affech, we increased our force by one guide and two beasts. I went somewhat out of my way to visit Delehem, which Dr. Ward so much regretted not having seen. He missed little, for it is only a grave mound, of the same general character as Umm-el-Akarib, but much smaller. Abu Erij was more extensive, but lower. There is a ziaret on the highest point of this. The day was delightfully cool, a refreshing breeze blowing all the time, and now and then violent gusts blowing over us, or flying by without touching us, but raising the dust in eddies. We spent about half an hour drinking lebben in an encampment of the el-Budeir, and examining the beads of the women in search of antiquities. We only secured a couple of small Sassanian seals, for which we paid three and a half piastres. The country was full of camels, sheep, and a few cattle, which Bedry says are driven in here at this season to avoid the taxes. He says, also, that they use the camels of this region for breeding with the shorter, thicker camels of Anatolia. A little before one we reached an encampment of es-Se'id, where we were forced to stop for the night, because we had reached the limit of the waters of the Euphrates, and there was said to be a journey of eight or nine hours before we could reach the Tigris water coming in by the Shatt-el-Hai.

"The name of the chief with whom we stopped was Hammadi. He was suffering from a severe trouble of the eyes, so that he could hardly see at all. He and a number of those who gathered in his tent demanded medicine. I had nothing with me but purgative pills and quinine, both of which I distributed freely, giving to Hammadi, according to my custom, a double dose to mark his rank as sheikh. Hammadi was somewhat afraid of the pills, but Abdan, our guide, established my reputation as a physician by narrating how I gave something to a man of Affech who was all swollen out, and it worked so well that it took almost everything out of him in one night, and left his belly quite small. The black goat's hair tent I found to be a very pleasant protection against the sun, and by raising the sides one obtains a refreshing breeze; but the party who gathered in Hammadi's tent were not a high class of Arabs. However, Bedry skilfully and kindly saved me from much annoyance through their inquisitiveness.

"Hammadi related a doleful tale of the corruption and oppression of the Turkish Government. Ahmed Bey, an official whom we had met in Diwanieh, came out to estimate the amount of land under cultivation. Hammadi told him that there were about six acres. He offered to return that amount on condition of receiving thirty liras. This Hammadi refused. The commissioner then said that he would return eighteen, and refused even to go and look at the land cultivated. Both Bedry and Mehemet, one of our zaptiehs, thought that our good Kaimakam was concerned in this. Later, however, we found a couple of hundred acres under cultivation by this encampment, which throws a somewhat different light on the matter.

"I went out for a little walk, and found the remains of quite an extensive mud village, and two mud forts. One of these was built solid for about six or eight feet, so that in falling into ruins it made quite a mound, as did also the mud village. From a small grave mound near by both Bismya and Delehem were visible I was much pestered by the lower Arabs of this village, who begged incessantly. I put them off by jokes, which they seemed to enjoy immensely. They played all sorts of childish antics to amuse me. Later, a man brought me his one-year-old daughter, and offered her as my slave, showing by expressive gestures what this meant. For a little money, these people would sell their daughters, or even the honor of their wives. Abdan offered me his fifteen-year-old daughter for a 'wife,' but on our return we found that she had eloped with a young man. One young man, who espied me from a distance, came running up to me with extravagant gestures of pleasure. It turned out that he had come to Nippur for medicine, and I had given him something which he thought had cured him. I am thankful that it did not kill him. While we were in the tent the cry of mad dog was raised, and I saw a poor creature beaten with sticks until he was injured in the backbone and his hind legs almost paralyzed, but their humanity did not allow them to kill the beast outright, although they mocked at and gloated over his misery.

"The eating here was like the eating at Affech. As the Shiites could not eat with me, Bedry and I ate together, and afterwards our Sunnite zaptiehs ate from the same dishes. We learned that this part of the country was suffering for lack of water, for they will not cut the canals above, nearer the Euphrates, as, owing to the low state of that river, the water is not more than sufficient for the Affech swamps. Formerly, they say, the swamps, and consequently the cultivated ground, extended far beyond Bismya, of which we had abundant evidence later. Last year the great flood in the Euphrates swept all of this country, and the large grain fields of Hammadi's camp, which we saw later on our return far beyond Bismya, were planted on the ground soaked by the flood. Going to bed was a trying operation, as a good part of the tribe stayed to witness it, and admire my bed and my clothing. Four men of the tribe were detailed to watch for us through the night, and it was necessary, for thieves prowled about a good part of the time. The guards set an old reed hut on fire to give light, and thus frighten off the thieves, and finally one of them was obliged to fire his gun.

"We were up long before dawn, and under way by five o'clock, our breakfast consisting of three small swallows of coffee. It was quite cold, so that I actually suffered from cold feet. Our course was south, sixty degrees east. We left Bismya on our left, and about six o'clock we passed quite a large ruined mud castle, which, I was told, Midhat Pasha had blown down with cannon in the Affech war. Had it not been for this information I should have supposed it to be a ruin of an earlier period, so extensive was it. We passed one or two low mounds of an insignificant character, and at 8.15 had on our left a long low line of little mounds, apparently a canal line, which our guide said ran all the way from Nippur. In the meantime we had shifted our course to the east to avoid the sand hills, which our guide said were to the south. At about half-past eight we crossed a low line of sand hills, which seemed to be bodily changing their place with the wind, which was fortunately behind us. To the south we could see immense tracts of sand and sand hills. The country was unspeakably barren, and entirely without water. There were no flocks of any sort. We met a few travelling Arabs and some wool merchants. The country is not regarded as safe, and for greater protection we had taken with us Hammadi's brother. Once a horseman from a party some distance to our right came galloping toward us, and Abdan called on our soldiers to unsling their guns and be ready for action. In that region every one seems to be regarded as an enemy and a robber.

"After crossing the sand hills we observed on the surface of the ground everywhere quantities of fresh water shells. Watching more closely on my return, I noticed that all the country subject to inundations from the Tigris or Euphrates, or their canals, is covered with similar shells, and most of this country seems to have been subject at one time or another to such inundations. At 10.40, close to a marsh caused by the overflow of the Mejidieh, a canal said to leave the Tigris near the point of departure of the Shatt-el-Hai, we found a camp of black tents of the Beni Temim. Here we rested and obtained something to eat. They seemed poor, although they possessed great quantities of sheep. They told us that a few days before the edh-Dhefir had plundered from them sixty she-asses and two mares. Here, as among some other tribes in this region, I thought that I noticed quite a different type of face from the markedly Semitic and rather handsome Arabs of Baghdad, Hillah, Affech, and the like. The faces were broader, the noses more inclined to turn up than down, and the eyes were neither so dark nor so liquid. We started again at 12.29, shifting our course to the southeast. Abdan is the first Arab I have seen who can go in a straight line, a thing I should suppose it very difficult for men unacquainted with the compass to do in a country without, or almost without, landmarks. Shortly after two we passed through a large camp of Sa'adun, the true Montefich. We passed several small mounds and canal beds, and at 3.05 could see to the south, twenty degrees west, the large low mound of Umm-el-Akarib, pronounced Ajarib. At five o'clock we entered the cultivated land irrigated by the Shatt-el-Haí. This was so intersected by canals that it proved necessary to obtain a local pilot from a camp on the edge, and by his assistance we reached an encampment of the Beni Rechab, on the banks of the Shatt-el-Haı, at 6.15.

"We found that we had reached the Shatt some distance above Tello, and Bedry at once set to work energetically to obtain a boat to take us down that night, while I fell asleep, being much fatigued. It was 9.40 before a boat was obtained from a village some distance below, and we were embarked. In the meantime we had been fed and refreshed, and I had been called on to play doctor to a number of the tribe. We left our horses, our muleteer, one zaptieh, and our Se'id guide here, taking, in place of the latter, the chief of this encampment. They told us that the trip down the Shatt would take a half an hour, but it was actually 11.55 before we landed. Our first boat was too small and rather dangerously frail, and we had to put ashore at the village from which it came and get another. Here the boatman attempted to desert, unless we would pay him a larger sum than that agreed on. The boats we used were long and thin, and brought, I think, at least the frames, from India. They are of wood pitched over. They were rowed with sticks, but there was a mast.

"On arriving at M. de Sarzec's camp, we received word from him that he was sick, but a very pleasant hut was placed at our disposal, and the next morning he was with us before I was dressed. As he was not well, the men were not working, but at Bedry's request a chief, whom he knew from having been commissioner there last year, sent four horses to take us to Tello, and the present commissioner, Mahir Bey went along. They tell me that he employs at the highest this year one hundred and fifty men, which is more than he ever employed before. De Sarzec's camp among the green fields on the border of the Shatt seemed more like a summer pleasure party than a rough hard-working camp like ours. His wife, his ten-year-old son, and a French maid are with him. But pleasant as his location is, it cannot be good for the work, for we found that it was a ride of over an hour to the mound. The latter is very uninteresting in appearance, low, and, in comparison with Nippur, not at all extensive. The diggings are not deep at any point, and I do not think, from what I was told, that the lower part of the mound has ever been touched. The two commissioners squabbled and contradicted one another so much that it was difficult to obtain any information from them, and M. de Sarzec did not wish to give me any, and would not even permit me to see what had been found. There were a few other small tels visible from Tello, the largest being the seven tels of Medain to the northeast.

"On our return, the chief who had lent us the horses invited us to stop and drink coffee, but we had scarcely arrived in the tent before the cry of war arose, and all the men of the camp were off in an instant, leaving us alone. There was some trouble about the canals, resulting in the burning of a hut belonging to a man of this village by another village of the 'Atab. The soldiers were called upon to interfere to prevent fighting, which they did. Bedry tells me that since the Montefich were chastised by the Turks some years since, this country is very obedient. In the meantime, my horse having been taken for the war, I returned on foot. After a while I heard the returning warriors singing a song of triumph, as though they had won a victory. This was my first experience of native saddles, and I cannot imagine how people succeed in keeping their seat upon them, or going faster than a walk.

"M. de Sarzec gave us an excellent European breakfast, and about the middle of the afternoon we started on the return journey. As we were going against stream, the boat was drawn by a rope attached to the top of the mast and pulled by two men on the shore. They were as frisky as two kids. Sometimes they stopped to dance, and then, when the boat had come to rest and the rope was slack, they would start at full speed, almost overturning us. One of them was in love with a maiden named Chorla, an inhabitant of one of the villages which we passed. The sight of this village led him to sing, 'Chorla, how I love thee, I cannot live without thee!' and much more of the same sort. We had the pleasure of seeing Chorla herself walking on the bank, but she was so wrapped up that her charms were invisible. I was surprised at the amount of cultivation along the banks of the Shatt-el-Hai, and the commerce on its waters.

"We reached the encampment where we had left our horses shortly after sundown. On the way the chief had spoken so enthusiastically of Yokha, or Jokha, that we determined to visit it, but when it came to the point, the Beni Rechab told us that it was in the territory of the predatory tribe of edh-Dhefir, and that we should have to take with us fifteen or twenty armed men. We tried to hire a guard of five, but money apparently would not tempt them to go. I even told Bedry to offer a good backsheesh to a man who would take a fast horse and go with me alone. Either he did not offer as I bade him, or not a man could be found to do it. As a guard of fifteen or twenty men would mean war, we could not accept that, and, for the time being, had to surrender the point. I had also wished to see Umm-el-Akarıb, but that was in the same region.

"Wednesday, April 3d, we started for home at 6.10 A.M. Our course was a little more northerly than that by which we had come, and we passed a few small mounds and canals which I had not observed before, neither was Umm-el-Akarib visible. At 10.25 we reached an enormous encampment of black tents, or rather a series of encampments, and at 10.45 we reached the selamlik of that encampment. On the rug at one end was a camel's saddle, which Bedry declared to be the sign of a great chief. Presently the chief himself appeared, and took his seat on the right of the saddle throne, I being placed on the left. It turned out to be an encampment of the Sa'adun, and the name of the chief to be Hamud-el-Bendir. They seemed to be rich, and their flocks of camels and sheep were countless. They were Sunnites, and Bedry told me that Hamud and his family stood on very good terms with the government, and that it was they who had furnished the government with guides, and otherwise assisted them in the war with the Montefich. He was very hospitable, and the impression made on my mind was extremely favorable. The respect shown to him by his tribe seemed great, and the order in the selamlik was in striking contrast to the mob-rule in Hammadi's camp. He asked us to spend the night, and I gladly accepted on the condition that he should send us to Jokha that afternoon. He gave us a delicious lunch of camel's milk and bread soaked in something, and at 1.05 we left for Jokha, accompanied by our guide, our zaptiehs, and five spearmen, one of them a negro slave of the chief. The latter did not himself accompany us, being in delicate health.

"Our course was south ten degrees west. We passed innumerable camels, but what they found to eat I could not see, and indeed they gave the general impression of being out for a walk merely. At 2.05 we entered some low sand hills, and at 2.18 we were on the other side of them, but there was still abundance of sand, and the ground was curiously worn and hardened by the constant passage over it of the sand driven by the wind. At three o'clock we reached Jokha. Our pace from the camp had been fairly good, and I should think we had covered a distance of ten miles or a little more. The mound was extensive, but low, and half-covered with the sand. To the west and south were sand hills, and the wind from the west whirled the sand over us in great quantities. The tower of el-Hammam was visible south seventy-five degrees west, but in the sand haze it was impossible even to guess at the distance. Umm-el-Akarib was said to be southeast, but was totally invisible. There were no glass fragments nor remains of glazed pottery on the surface of the mound. We found a couple of brick walls cropping out, and a double well of pottery, or such at least it appeared to be.

There were great quantities of stone fragments on the mound, some of them having worked surfaces; and one large piece we found on which the worked face had been destroyed intentionally, as though to efface something. The stone used was very various, and must have come from a number of different places. The bricks which we saw looked ancient, but were uninscribed. I picked up a few pieces of copper on this mound. The ruins seemed to me, so far as I could judge from the surface indications, ancient, and not built upon in later times; but it would be a place difficult to excavate, because, first, of the sand; secondly, of the lack of water. A third difficulty in the way of digging here is the insecurity of the region, and I should suppose that for the same reason it might be difficult to find workmen.

"We left the mound again at four o'clock, and reached

camp at 6.10. Our Arab guides had kept a pretty careful watch while on the mound, and on the return four of them rode off in war circles to the west, seeing, or pretending to see, suspicious characters. I was told at camp that the Shatt-en-Nil comes down from Nippur to this point, and is here lost in the sand hills. I wished to follow its course back to Nippur, but this was beyond the possibilities of my guide or any that could be found. We were entertained at a royal dinner, by far the best I have seen among the Arabs. There was a great dish of pilau, at least a yard in diameter, surmounted by a lamb with the head on. This was surrounded by a circle of smaller dishes containing some preparation of meat which I did not try, and these again by a circle of sweet dishes of milk, musk, etc. There was also a dish of chickens between me and the chief. The whole was set upon mats, and we ate with our fingers, of course. Being Sunnites, there was no difficulty about my eating with them, and our two Shiite guides and our muleteer, in view of the character of the meal, also found no difficulty in eating with us. We established quite a friendship with Hamud-el-Bendir. I could not give him the medicine which he needed, and he agreed to come to us in the autumn, when I should send for him, and I would try to bring it. He was then to send me through the Montefich country wherever I wished to go. I said that I should like to bring him a present from America, and, of course, he asked for a gun, which Bedry insisted on promising, saying that he would give it himself if I would not. Hamud also wrote a letter on our behalf to Hajji Tarfa's family. He made on my mind decidedly the impression of an Arab gentleman. I saw no firearms in the hands of this tribe, but only spears. The wool merchants were there buying wool at the period of our visit. The Arabs said that they received four piastres a sheep, and ten sheep out of every one hundred were thrown in for nothing. Bedry says that the annual government tax on each sheep is four piastres, and on each camel ten piastres. The tax on the government land cultivated by the Arabs is fifty per cent. A separate white Egyptian tent was pitched for us, and we spent a better night than usual. The next morning, in addition to our coffee, we had delicious milk, fresh from the camel.

"April 4th. We started at 6.05, our course northwest. At 7.04 we had reached the southern end of the marsh formed by the waters of the Mejidieh Canal. This already covered a great extent of ground, but we were told that in a month it would cover vastly more. As the waters retreat again, the Arabs sow the land in durra. About a half-mile to our left was the northern end of the Sa'adun camp, the southern end of which we had passed on the outward journey. The chief of this, Ferhan-el-Meshed, is a cousin of Hamud. The time of the retreat of the waters from the marshes is, they told us, September, and the waters begin to enter them in March. At 9.30 we had reached again the country of the el-Budeir. Their land, so far as it has any water, is supplied from the Euphrates. From 9.30 to 10.45 we passed through wheat fields sown on last year's inundated land. On the border of these we stopped to lunch on cold chicken and sugar-coated bread given us by Hamud-el-Bendir, and a bottle of M. de Sarzec's wine. At 11.28 we were under way again, and at 12.40 we were on the mound of Bismya, from the top of which we could see the country of the el-Budeir, and of the Affech beyond, dotted with mud forts, for the most part in ruins. Our guide said that this mound was on the Shatt-en-Nil, which he pointed out, but which I failed to see. The mound is very extensive, and a little higher than Tello or Yokha. It is a succession of long low hills with valleys between. It also gave the impression of an ancient mound, not built upon in later times. I saw no glass nor glazed pottery. Dr. Ward saw here the remains of walls. It would not be easy to conduct excavations on account of the lack of water, which at present comes no nearer than Hammadi's camp, two hours away. We left the mound at 1.15, and reached Hammadi's camp at 3.10.

"We left Hammadi's camp on April 5th, at 6.20 A.M., and took a direct course for Nippur, about northwest, but our direction and our speed were much interfered with after we entered the Affech country by large canals, which sometimes necessitated a circuitous course. The water in several of those which we crossed was considerably above our horses' bellies. At 7.27 the guide pointed out to the north, twenty degrees east, a long mound in the distance, which he said was larger than Bismya, but which we could not visit on account of intervening canals and marshes, at least so he claimed. The name which he gave to this mound was Tuweyhis. At 10.42 we caught sight of Nippur. At 11.15 we reached the old canal bed called Hayatt Jeheysh, which we followed, north seventy degrees west, until 12.40. The guide said that it came from Nippur, but, so far as I could see, it came from Mudeynah, or Abu Jowan, the low hills about two hours north of east from Nippur, which Harper and I visited one afternoon a month or more ago. We reached camp at 1.45 P.M.

"During our absence nothing of any great importance had been found. Much more of the temple had been laid bare, but the plan of the whole is no nearer explanation, apparently, than before. In uncovering a wall on the east side, a door socket of stone was found with an inscription of Kurigalzu, but the inscription was the same as that on the bricks. At V. what appeared to be a kiln was found, and a number of baked tablets of the Hammurabi dynasty, as fresh as if just made. On the day after we left Berdi had given a great feast to the camp. There had been trouble during the week with one of the

Affech workmen, in which the zaptiehs had thought that the workmen were threatening them and the camp. In reality, the men wanted to take a refractory workman out of the hands of the zaptiehs, beat him, and drive him off the mound.

"April 14th. During the last week some stealing has been discovered. In the bushes near the point at which we get our water was found a rag containing thirteen tablets and a brick stamp, the latter, which is very interesting, being the stamp of Naram Sin. Some of the tablets were of the late Babylonian and Persian period, such as are found generally near the surface at V.; some were of the Hammurabi dynasty, such as are found ordinarily in the same hill at a greater depth; and the brick stamp and a stone astronomical tablet were more like the few archaic fragments found on the Temple Hill. All the pickmen swore on the Koran that they knew nothing about it. Since then we have been trying in vain to ferret the matter out, and to-day the scrapers and basket-carriers of the suspected trenches, who came from this neighborhood, have been taken to a ziaret beyond Affech, which they regard as peculiarly efficacious, to put them through an oath. It has inflamed the jealousy between Birs Nimrud and Hillah, which was largely due to Bedry, and for the last few days there has been constant trouble. The men, moreover, have not been working as well as before, and we have so many that it is difficult to oversee them. Last night we had to discharge ten gangs for laziness. We had also to send for Mekota to take away some of his men who had been causing trouble. He inflicted himself on me most of the afternoon, and, as usual, begged for a gun or pistol. Last night four sheep belonging to our workmen were stolen. They were in a little space almost surrounded by huts, and directly behind the huts of our soldiers. One day not long since some of the neighboring Arabs beat and robbed a poor lad who was getting grass for us.

"While I was away the weather was quite cool, but since my return the heat has been excessive, and there has been an invasion of fleas. Berdi was here one night, and I had him sleep in my tent, which pleased him, but did not diminish the number of my fleas. The country around us looks beautiful now, with rich patches of grass and glimmering water, and palm-trees in the distance. Only to the east of us it is barren. The view is animated also, for great numbers of sheep and some camels have been driven into our neighborhood. There are a number of new camps about, and occasionally one sees the white sails of a boat on the marshes bound for Sukh-el-Affech. There are quantities of young gazelles brought to us, and Noorian has bought several, to the rearing of which he gives much attention.

"During my absence the permission arrived. I got Noorian to translate it, so that I might read it to all. It is even worse than I supposed.

"A few days ago from a house at I. was brought out an enormous, inscribed, Jewish bowl, which is, I believe, quite unique in size.

"Wednesday, April 17th. Sunday, our boat, which was engaged for the 22d, appeared, or rather it reported itself as being at Shkheyr, the Behahtha village, ready for us.

"On the way to the ziaret to swear, Hajji Mehemet was taken sick and came back. His halfa, or scraper, also failed to appear to take oath. In the swearing, two men testified that they had been told by two of the gang of Abbas-el-Jasim that he had offered them a reward if they would swear that Ziara was the thief. The men themselves testified that Abbas had offered them a reward if they would find out who did it, and that he had told them that he was sure that it was Ziara, and as one of them had a brother in Ziara's gang, he could find out through him. Ziara worked in X., and was a Birs Nimrud man. The other two worked in V., and were Jimjimeh men. Against all three we entertained more or less suspicion. On their return Bedry had Abbas, against whom he had a violent prejudice, arrested, and declared his intention to send him and Hajji Mehemet to the Kaimakam of Diwanieh the next day."

CHAPTER XII.

THE CATASTROPHE.

Shooting a Thief—Danger of Attack—Arab Allies—Parleying—Excavations Stopped—Useless Zaptiehs—Mekota—The Burning of the Camp—The Robbery—I Accuse Mekota—Our Departure—Evidence Against Mekota—An Arab Dinner—The Governor-General—His Suspicions—Resignations—Recalled—Emigrant Wagons—A Jewish Shrine—Variations of Route—A Hail Storm—Horrors of the Trip.

IT was about two o'clock in the morning of Monday, April 15th, that Abbas, the prisoner, heard a noise and waked Mehemet, the zaptieh to whom he was bound. Four es-Sa'id Arabs were trying to steal the horses and mules, and had actually untied one of the latter. Mehemet ran out and raised an alarm. They fled, and he fired and killed one of them. It is the ordinary custom to fire to alarm a thief only, not to kill him. Unfortunately, Haynes, annoyed by the thieving propensities of the Arabs, had, without my knowledge, promised the first zaptieh who shot a thief a mejidieh. At the first alarm, moreover, Noorian, half-asleep, ran out of his hut in his night-clothes, shouting out to kill the thief. Mehemet, therefore, thought that he was acting under orders. But no sooner was the deed done than he realized that he had put himself in peril. According to the notions of the country, he had committed murder, for which the dead man's tribesmen were entitled to exact blood revenge.

He wished to run away at once and try to get through to Daghara, from which place he hoped to escape to

Diwanieh; and Bedry, and even Mehemet's superior officer, Murad Chaous, were in favor of this as the best way to relieve us of responsibility. I would not consent, for the man had but obeyed orders, and I believed that the Expedition should stand by him. Murad Chaous, too, quickly changed his mind, recognizing that the man would be killed before he could reach Daghara. I went down with Noorian to look at the dead man, who had fallen in the bed of the Shatt-en-Nil. He seemed to have been shot through the heart. His body was carried off almost immediately by the nearest es-Sa'id, encamped just at the foot of the mound, within rifle range. The dead man himself, as we afterwards learned, came from a more distant camp to the east.

Within five minutes of the shooting, Noorian had very promptly sent Abbas to Berdi's camp to announce the occurrence, and for his good services that night, the matter of stealing in the trenches against him and Hajji Mehemet was dropped altogether. A messenger was despatched on Bedry's account to the Kaimakam of Diwanieh, nine hours away. We also stationed guards about the camp, and prepared to defend ourselves.

Then followed a period of anxious suspense. Soon the death wail sounded from a village close beneath us. Then a signal fire was kindled. This was answered by another and another, until the whole plain was dotted with little lights, while through the still night came the sounds of bustle and preparation for the attack, and still no answer from the Affech. At last, after two hours, Berdi arrived with a small party of spearmen and gunners. He reported that he had sent messages to the other Affech chiefs to come to our assistance, and also to the es-Sa'id to warn them that the Affech were on the hill, and that to attack us meant war with the whole Affech nation. Toward morning, young Mekota, handsome and sinister, Hamud-el-Berjud, most gentlemanly and most faithful of the chiefs, Abd-el-Hamud, a jolly Irishman of an Arab, and a considerable force of warriors arrived. Then commenced a series of parleyings. First it was proposed on behalf of the es-Sa'id that we should surrender the zaptieh who had done the shooting, for they had no quarrel with us, but only with the Turks. This, of course, I would not do. Then Berdi urged us to separate ourselves from the Turks, and descend to his village and become his guests, leaving the Turks and the es-Sa'id to settle the matter between them, for, after all, it was an affair of the Turkish Government, and not our affair, and why should we mix ourseleves in it ? This proposition, like the other, I rejected as dishonorable. We would protect the zaptieh, and stand or fall by the result. Seeing that we were firm in this, the Affech finally agreed to stand by us, although openly saying that they had little stomach for protecting a Turkish zaptieh against what they could not but feel to be the just resentment of a friendly tribe. That was the natural feeling of the country. Even Noorian, after the first moment of excitement had passed, felt sympathy with the demands of the es-Sa'id, and indignation against poor Mehemet for his crime.

Having agreed to assist us, the chiefs composed and sent a most arrogant letter to Sughub, head-chief of the es-Sa'id, summoning him to appear before them, ordering him to restore the sheep which had been stolen, to punish the thieves, and to give guarantees that no injury should be done to us or ours. In course of time the messengers—two of our es-Sa'id workmen, who had been loath to go because, as they said, they would be counted as belonging to our tribe—returned with torn garments and other evidences of a beating, and the answer that Sughub was busy. After some discussion, the chiefs next proposed that we should stop the excavations and return to Baghdad, leaving them to settle with the es-

Sa'id after our departure, and in the meantime, until we were ready to leave, they would remain on the hill with a force sufficient to guard us. This was the only course to be pursued, for we could get no work out of our men, there were continual alarms of attempts of individual es-Sa'id to steal up and get a shot at the zaptiehs, and the men of Affech were evidently at heart in sympathy with the enemy. The zaptiehs were obliged to keep within the inner camp enclosure, and the one who had done the shooting was disguised and kept in hiding. It had been our intention to leave in a very few days, and we actually had a large boat in waiting in the marshes. Under the circumstances, therefore, we decided to accept the proposition, the workmen were paid off, and we began to pack forthwith.

In the meantime more zaptiehs had begun to arrive. Six came from Diwanieh, and four from el-Budeir, and Tuesday, as we were at dinner, twenty men arrived by boat from Hillah, with a trumpeter, a captain, and six hundred rounds of cartridges. The Arabs on guard were much exasperated by this, saying that they were guarding us, and that the zaptiehs were not needed. In point of fact, the latter were an utterly undisciplined crew of wild Arabs, whom the government should never have sent. Monday and Tuesday, the selamlik in front of my tent and my tent itself were thronged by the chiefs, their men, and the zaptiehs, and I had to distribute a great deal of medicine, cigars, and tobacco. Mekota and his scribe pestered me a great deal. The former would push his way into my tent and explore everything. He found my gun, and insisted on being shown its mechanism. His scribe found that I could read and write Arabic a little, so he wrote a sentence saying that Mekota wished for my pistol. The soldier on guard at the door became very nervous, and tried to tell me something in Turkish. I sent for Noorian, but when he arrived the paper with the Arabic sentence had disappeared. I asked Bendir, the scribe, where it was. He looked sheepish, but finally produced it. I found that it was much what I had supposed it to be. I told Noorian to tell him that I did not understand Arabic now, but hoped to do so next year, implying that I might bring him a pistol then. I did not wish to give a pistol to Mekota, because we had lost so many that we could not afford it without leaving ourselves too defenceless. Moreover, if I gave one to him, it would occasion great jealousy, and lead to similar demands from others. It would also expose me to annoyance and misrepresentation on the part of the Turkish officials, to the effect, probably, that we were distributing arms among the Arabs.

Tuesday, Shamir, Mekota's uncle, came out to see me and get his present for having made arrangements for the Tello trip. I brought an abba into Bedry's cabin for him, but he dared not receive it openly, and said that he would send a man to fetch it quietly the next day. No sooner had he gone than Mekota came and asked if the abba he had seen brought in there were for Shamir. Bedry replied that it was for himself, that he had need of it, and had asked it of me. A little later, one of Mekota's confidential men came to him and said that Mekota would accept no present from me but a firearm. Bedry replied that, as a representative of the Turkish Government, he would forbid my giving and Mekota's receiving such a gift. Monday night Mekota borrowed of Noorian Prince's shotgun, representing that he had left his own gun behind. The next morning Noorian had great difficulty in getting the gun back again, and, when he finally surrendered it, Mekota said, "I am no Sheikh, if I cannot have a gun." Tuesday night there was an alarm of an attack by the es-Sa'id, and a great deal of shooting and running around on the part of the Affech. It turned out to be a mere ruse on Mekota's part to frighten the

Turks and increase his claims on us. It was very clumsily executed, and took no one in.

The next day, Wednesday, almost everything was packed and carried on board the boat. Even our tents were struck, and we retained only our beds and saddle bags. That evening we had war-dances on the hill, and Mekota sought to show us his importance, and that he was a great chief. One of the songs which his men sang was, "We are as the dogs of Mekota," while he cheered them when he led the dance by singing, "When this thing is done you will all be shirted," that is, when we have finished this business, we shall have made so much money, that each of you can buy a shirt. He was treacherous and unreliable, a most dangerous protector. Of all our guards of every sort, there were not more than half a dozen on whom we could rely in an emergency. We ourselves numbered only five rifles.

Thursday morning, our saddle-bags strapped, our beds rolled up, we sat prepared to mount, waiting only for the cook's things to be packed. Suddenly there was a cry of fire. Fire had been set to our huts of reeds and mats, while the zaptiehs, who should have been on guard, were busy enriching themselves with the old tin cans and other rubbish which we had thrown away. A scene of wild confusion ensued. In five minutes the camp was a smoking ruin. Three of our horses, including my own, were roasted to death. Most of our effects, saddle-bags, beds, and cooking utensils were rescued and piled together in a heap which zaptiehs were set to guard, while we sought to rescue more. But the zaptiehs were cowardly and demoralized, and the Arabs fell a-plundering. One rifle was lost, and two saddle-bags were stolen from under the zaptiehs' very noses, they being too frightened to defend them. One of these, Hilprecht's, was recovered, but the other, Haynes's, containing a sack of about two hundred liras in gold,—for he, as business manager, had charge of the cash,—was not recovered. Afterwards I learned that Bendır, Mekota's secretary, had come into the kitchen suddenly when Haynes was making a payment and observed where he kept the money. Every one seemed to think that the fire was an accident, but I was convinced from what I had seen that it was kindled by Mekota's men. He sat a little apart with a very suspicious appearance. Hamud-el-Berjud during the progress of the fire had sat upon the ground weeping and beating his head, and Berdi also was the picture of shame and despair; Abd-el-Hamud had left the camp the night before. The immediate adherents of these men took no part in the plundering.

Mekota, hearing that my horse had been burned, offered me his mare, which I refused. I called the Mudir, and bade Bedry tell him point blank that it was Mekota who had done this thing. He, however, insisted that it was an accident, and Bedry begged me not to show Mekota my feelings, or we were all dead men. He also asked me to tell Noorian to pretend that he thought it was an accident, and to show no suspicion that it was Mekota. I did not believe in such cowardice, however, and let Mekota and his followers see precisely what I thought.

There was now nothing to do but pack everything in the two boats, the men included, and start. Accordingly, with ten zaptiehs to accompany them, and Mekota and Berdi escorting them in separate boats, the rest of the party started for Hillah by water, while Bedry, Harper and I, with one servant and forty zaptiehs, set out for Sukh-el-Affech and Diwanieh. Mehemet went along disguised as an Arab, walking, by my direction, at my stirrup for greater security. Hamud-el-Berjud and the Mudir accompanied us. At Berdi's village, Hamud with some difficulty procured us a boat sufficiently large to carry our party, and the horses were sent around to meet us at Sukh-el-Affech. The last that we saw of Nippur, the es-Sa'id were dancing a war-dance on the ruins of our camp.

I watched Hamud closely on the boat, and his conduct confirmed my opinion that he had nothing to do with this treachery, and that to him it was a shame and a mortification. Before leaving the Sukh, therefore, I made Bedry tell him that I still had trust in him, and that I did not hold him responsible for the burning, which I knew was done by Mekota's men. To this he replied, " You know." Afterward he assured me that neither he, nor Berdi, nor Abd-el-Hamud had anything to do with it. Later, we learned that he knew of the plot, but did not dare to tell us for fear of Mekota.

During the first half of our march to Diwanieh, until we had crossed the Daghara, all seemed apprehensive of trouble. After that, our women, being no longer afraid, told of a conversation they had overheard between Mekota and Ri'a, his kinsman and confidential follower. Mekota asked Ri'a why he had "done this thing and put his (Mekota's) beard in our hands, and nothing would come into his hands." All the last part of the way the zaptiehs, brave when danger was passed, danced war-dances, shouted, and fired their guns. We reached Diwanieh after dark, and the whole population joined with our wild fellows in a mighty tumult and jubilation in front of the residence of the Kaimakam. From Diwanieh Bedry telegraphed his government, and I the American minister, that the Arabs had treacherously burned our camp.

The next day we spent resting, as we were to start for Hillah in the evening and travel all night. At sunset we went to dine with one of the notables of the place, who, after the fashion of town Arabs, did not eat with us, but served us. We sat on the floor around a low table. The chief dish was a lamb entire, stuffed with rice and I know not what else, which was very good. One of the guests was a white-turbaned imam, and, to our surprise, just as dinner was ready, he, the Procuror-General, and a major arose and performed a religious service. After dinner we were ferried across the Euphrates, our horses awaiting us on the other side. At four o'clock in the morning we had reached Imam Jasim, where we rested until six, and it was almost noon when we reached the serai of the Mutessarif at Hillah. He wished to know if I had telegraphed to Constantinople to make any complaints or demands. I told him what I had telegraphed, and that I did not make any demands, but simply left the matter in the hands of the government. He said that they would exact the double of our loss, and a heavy penalty in addition. We breakfasted with him and then went around to the khan, where the rest joined us before the day was over.

Sunday, the Wali Pasha arrived. Monday morning he sent an aide-de-camp to request to see me, just as I had sent Noorian to ask when he would receive me. I went to him at once. Like the Mutessarif, he also wished to know whether I should make any complaints. I told him that we were in his hands, and waited to see what he would do. He insisted that the fire was an accident, and reproved Bedry severely for having telegraphed to Constantinople that the camp was burned by the Arabs intentionally. Of course he promised reparation, and that it should be made practicable for us to return next year. In the afternoon he returned my call. He was very suspicious regarding our antiquities, and when we left the next morning he detailed an officer to follow us to Baghdad and watch us. Privately he expressed the opinion that we had lost no money, and I believe he thought that the whole thing was a plot between Bedry and ourselves to cover the transfer to us of the antiquities excavated, so bad was Bedry's reputation, and so unfortunate had been the Wali's experiences with archæologists of other nations.

It was two o'clock on Wednesday morning when we left Hillah, and noon of the same day when we reached Baghdad. On the way Harper handed me his resignation in writing. Field gave me his when we reached Baghdad. Haynes stated that he would resign, but did not put his resignation in writing. Hilprecht communicated directly with the Committee. Noorian, who knew better than any of us the feeling of the Arabs, handed me a written statement to the effect that he would under no circumstances return to Nippur, as he believed that his life would be endangered by doing so. In general, they all felt that the excavations had not yielded satisfactory results, and that Nippur was not a promising site for further work. Hilprecht, particularly, was of the opinion that whatever Nippur might originally have been, all vestiges of the ancient city had been destroyed, and that the buildings of which we had found remains were of the Sassanian period.

Our first year at Nippur had ended in failure and disaster. I had failed to win the confidence of my comrades. None of them agreed with me in my belief in the importance of Nippur, and the desirability of excavating down to the foundations. The Arabs had proved treacherous. The Turkish authorities disbelieved our story of Arab treachery, and suspected us of plotting with our Turkish commissioner to carry away antiquities. I was sick and nervous, having suffered for two months almost incessantly from severe facial neuralgia and consequent sleeplessness. In fact, I was on the verge of collapse, and the world had never seemed quite so black before.

I had come out originally with the intention of remaining one year only, for the purpose merely of starting excavations in Babylonia. I had hoped that at the end of that time some one else would take my place, and allow me to return home. But as it gradually became clear that the excavations of the first year would not be so successful as I had hoped they might be, I had reached the conclusion that it was my duty to remain a second year. I now felt that this was an absolute necessity, that unless I remained Nippur would be abandoned, and that the whole cause of Babylonian exploration would receive a serious set-back. I wrote to the Committee that in my judgment I should go to Constantinople, make arrangements with the Turkish Government and the Museum authorities, and return to Nippur in the autumn with Haynes and Noorian, who, I was confident, after they had had time to think the matter over, would be willing to go with me. But before I had had time to despatch this letter, I received a cable recalling me to America, and instructing Hilprecht to remain in Baghdad. This he, however, declined to do. Fortunately, at this moment Haynes received his exequatur as consul, which obliged him to remain. I therefore turned over the effects of the Expedition to him and started at once for America with Hilprecht and Harper. Field had already gone on. Noorian remained with Haynes to await developments.

It chanced that four emigrant wagons from Aleppo had arrived at Baghdad a few days before, conveying some wealthy Turk and his harem. I engaged two of these, and a Turkish pasha, Salih, who was returning from his post to Constantinople, secured the other two for himself and his harem. It was the 2d of May when we made our start, but it turned out that the two wagons of the Pasha were not sufficient for his party, and about an hour from Baghdad we came to a halt in the neighborhood of a Jewish shrine, said to be the tomb of Joshua, son of Jehozedek, the high priest, but which the Moslems claim as the shrine of St. Yusuf. Here we waited all that day for extra baggage animals for the

Pasha. I visited the tomb, which consisted of a court with a gallery above it. This swarmed with people of both sexes, amusing themselves, and with vendors of all sorts of edibles. At the western end was the shrine proper, quite highly decorated within in rich colors. In this was a large brass tomb, about which a crowd of people was constantly moving, devoutly kissing it. In an alcove to the north of the tomb burned little lights for the sick, a custom common to Christians, Jews, and Moslems in that region.

That evening began the fast of Ramadhan, which added to the difficulties of our journey, making it harder to obtain food supplies in the villages on the way. The next day we found the bridge across the Euphrates at Kal'at Feluja broken by the flood, and were compelled to delay there one day, which delay I utilized to make a more careful examination of 'Anbar. Hilprecht had been taken ill as the consequence of exposure the preceding night, when, awakened by a fight among the horses, in alarm, not knowing where he was nor what was happening, he started in his night-clothes for Baghdad, first falling out of bed and spraining his wrist.

Our route was almost exactly the same as that by which we had descended, excepting only that on account of the narrowness of the street, we were unable to pass through the town of 'Anah, and compelled to keep on the plateau, and in general our course was somewhat more along the plateau than on the descent. At one place we found the Anazeh engaged in a raid against the Shammar of Sheikh Faris. We were encamped among them, and had an interesting opportunity to watch their method of crossing the river by means of inflated skins. Salih Pasha sent for their chief, Fehid Bey, with whom we had quite an interesting conversation. I also saw somewhat more of the natives of the valley on the way up than I had done coming down, and they appeared even more miserable, ground down between the bedouin Arabs on the one side and the Turkish tax-gatherers on the other.

Between Meskene and Aleppo our route was slightly different from that pursued by us in December. We went farther to the south, spending a night at a place called Jedeyda, on the Nahr Dhahab, close to Lake Sabakhah. This occupies the place assigned to Jebre on Kiepert's map. It is a village composed partly of cone huts and partly of square mud huts. By the side of it there was a small natural hill of pebbles, and around it, irrigated by the stream, were pomegranate gardens and a mill. Jebbul, the ancient Gabbula, the largest town in that region, was within sight, on the shores of Lake Sabakhah, half an hour away, near the western end of the lake. Close to Jebbul on the lake shore was a large tel of curious shape, which the natives said was a haraba, or ruin, called Wastha. About a quarter of an hour away, north thirty degrees east from us, was a fair-sized tel called Saba'in. The principal industry of the neighborhood seemed to be the cultivation of licorice. Salt is collected at the lake in autumn and winter when the water is low.

From Jedeyda to Jebrin was a ride in our wagons of three hours and a half. From that point on to Aleppo, our road was the same as before. Scarcely had we entered the hotel, Saturday, May 25th, when a violent storm of rain and hail broke. The hail fell in enormous quantities, and the next afternoon people were still busy bringing horseloads of hailstones into the city to serve as ice, and I saw in the fields great masses of hailstones lying in heaps where they had fallen and been a little protected from melting by mud, or water, or grain stalks.

This trip from Baghdad to the coast remains in my mind as one horrible nightmare. A letter written immediately afterwards will give a sufficient idea of the general character of our journey:

"There has been a period which has been a sort of blank of everything but suffering, from the time I left Nippur until I reached Addalia, at the head of the Gulf of Addalia, or Pamphylia, two or three days since. During that time I had neither the physical nor moral strength to do more than was forced upon me by the actual necessities of the moment. I left Baghdad by wagon, accompained by Harper and Hilprecht, on the 2d of May. We had two wagons, and a pasha with his harem had two. The trip by wagon, it was supposed, would be shorter and easier than by horses, or mules and camels, and no boat was leaving for a fortnight. In reality, it proved to be a terrible trip, and instead of taking us twenty days to reach the coast, it took twenty-six. There is no road, and the ground cannot be called level. We stuck in morasses, we ascended and descended such precipices as I had supposed it impossible for wagons to overcome. Once my wagon upset, and one night we got lost, and a wagon containing six women and children of the good old pasha (for he was as good as gold, and we never could have gotten on without him) upset as he and I were walking just behind it. We travelled all day, and the perpetual motion and bounding and bumping of those springless wagons would result in a nervous rather than a muscular fatigue. The food was not very nourishing, and we suffered much from loss of sleep, partly owing to violent and frequent rainstorms, partly to sandflies,—an insect peculiar to the region, and combining all the worst features of the flea and the mosquito,—and partly to other disturbances incidental to the route. I think that if I had been in good condition to start with, I should have been able to make light of it all; but I was not in a condition to resist the strain, and day after day I suffered more and more from face-ache, showing an increase of nervous debility. This also interfered sadly with my rest. Moreover, both

Harper and Hilprecht were ailing. For the first half of the route the latter was the sick one, then Harper began to break up, and by the time we reached the coast he was quite ill. I finally got the fever by sleeping out in the rain to make him comfortable in the tent, for the poor fellow was in an awful state, and for three the tent was close quarters. Fortunately, we all found steamers at Alexandretta. Harper and Hilprecht started on a French steamer via Alexandria the day we arrived, and the next day I left on a Turkish merchant steamer for Constantinople."

APPENDIX A.

SUBSCRIPTION PAPER OF THE BABYLONIAN EXPLORATION FUND.

WE, the undersigned, subscribe the sums set opposite our names respectively, to be paid, as set forth below, to E. W. Clark, Esq., Treasurer, for the purpose of sending an exploring expedition to Babylonia under the lead of the Rev. John P. Peters.

These sums are subscribed under the following conditions :

(*a*) All finds which can be exported are to be brought to the City of Philadelphia and to become the property of the University of Pennsylvania, provided the said University furnish suitable accommodations for the same in a fire-proof building ; otherwise they shall be deposited in such place as may be hereafter decided by vote of the subscribers.

(*b*) No subscription shall be binding unless a sum not less than Fifteen Thousand Dollars ($15,000) be subscribed by the first day of March, 1888.

(*c*) The subscriptions are to be paid, one half upon our being advised that the sum required has been secured, and one half thereafter upon the call of the Treasurer, as the same is needed for the prosecution of the work ; or, in case the total sum subscribed amounts to Thirty Thousand Dollars ($30,000), one third to be paid upon our being advised that the sum required has been secured, and the balance in two payments thereafter, upon the call of the Treasurer, as required for the prosecution of the work

(*d*) The supervision of the Expedition to be entrusted to a committee of five to be selected by the subscribers.

The following tabulated statement shows the sums actually contributed during the years 1888-90 by thirty-two subscribers.

BAYLONIAN EXPLORATION FUND SUBSCRIPTIONS.

	1888	1889	1890	
C. D. Reed,	$500 00			
J. Lowber Welsh,	250 00			
W. G Warden,	500 00			
S. A. Crozer,	500 00			
Henry C. Lea,	500 00	$1,000 00	$500 00	
W. E. Garrett, Jr.,	500.00	500 00	1,000 00	
C. C. Harrison,	500.00	1,000 00	1,000.00	
W W. Justice,	50 00	50 00		
Jos. Wharton, Jr.,	125 00	125 00		
Geo. C. Thomas,	50 00	50.00	100 00	
Rev H. Clay Trumbull,	100 00			
E W. Clark,	500 00	1,000.00	1,500 00	
Allan Marquand,	25 00	100 00		
J. V. Merrick,	125 00	250 00	125 00	
Alexander Brown,	500 00	1,000 00	500 00	
Wm. Weightman,	250.00	750 00		
J. C. Strawbridge,	250 00	250 00		
Henry C. Gibson,	500 00	1,000 00		
Joseph Jeanes,	250.00	250.00		
Samuel Jeanes,	250 00	250 00		
Anna T Jeanes,	250 00	250 00		
H H. Houston,	500 00	1,000 00	500.00	
Stuart Wood,	250 00	250 00	500 00	
George W Childs,	250 00	250 00		
Jos. D. Potts,	500 00	1,000 00	500.00	
W. W Frazier,	500 00	1,000 00	1,000 00	
C. H. Clark,	500 00	1,000 00	500 00	
F. S. Kimball,	50 00	50 00	100 00	
Dr Wm Pepper,		1,500 00	1,500.00	
J. Hinckley Clark,		100 00		
Horace Jayne,		750 00	500.00	
Enoch Lewis,			50 00	
	$9,025.00	$14,725 00	$9,875 00	
For Antiquities .				
W. W. Frazier,		1,083.33		
C. C Harrison,		1,083 33		
C. H Clark,		1,083 33		
E. W. Clark,		1,083 33		
Stuart Wood,		1,083 33		
Dr. Wm Pepper,		1,083 33		
	$9,025 00	$21,224 98	$9,875 00	$40,124 98

The total amount received by the Treasurer was $40,124.98 ; but of this $6,500 was subscribed, not for the Expedition proper, but for the purchase of antiquities The antiquities purchased with this money through the agency of members of the Expedition included the two Shemtob collections of Babylonian antiquities, purchased in London ; the similar Khabaza collection ; a collection of Cappadocian tablets ; a considerable number of seal cylinders ; Palmyrene busts, and various other objects ; plaster reproductions of the Nippur mounds ; and a collection of plaster casts of Assyrian and Babylonian monuments ; all of which are now in the University of Pennsylvania Museum in Philadelphia. A small collection of Babylonian objects purchased for the University of Pennsylvania Museum, by Mr Prince, through Professor Hilprecht, is not included in this account, since the money did not pass through the Treasurer's hands.

APPENDIX B.

FIRST APPLICATION FOR PERMISSION TO EXCAVATE, MADE THROUGH THE TURKISH MINISTER IN WASHINGTON.

To His Excellency, Mavroyeni Bey, Envoy Extraordinary and Minister Plenipotentiary of his Imperial Majesty, the Sultan of Turkey.

SIR :—An Expedition under the auspices of the University of Pennsylvania has been organized to excavate some of the ruins of the ancient cities of Mesopotamia, in the present Vilayets of Baghdad and Haleb, provided that permission to do so can be obtained from his Imperial Majesty, the Sultan of Turkey. We therefore address ourselves to you to learn whether and in what form such permission can be granted.

The object of our enterprise is entirely scientific. We represent no religious body, nor have we any religious object in view in this excavation. Neither have we any commercial interests. The Expedition has solely scientific objects in view, and is conducted solely by scientific men, interested in the excavation of those ancient cities for the purpose of increasing knowledge. Of these facts we beg that your Excellency will assure yourself by the most careful examination.

Furthermore, we beg leave to call your attention to the fact that this Expedition will be under the control of, and sent out by, a private Institution formed solely for purposes of study and research. There is therefore no possible political motive in this Expedition, nor danger of political complications arising out of it, since we represent a scientific Institution disbursing the funds of private individuals for the sole purpose of advancing knowledge of the ancient world.

Further, we desire to call your attention to the fact that this Expedition goes out from a country which is in no way involved in European politics, and that the citizens of this country, comprising this Expedition, can have no interest in such matters; and that this country and its citizens have always stood in the most friendly relations to the empire and subjects of the Ottoman Porte.

It is our intention, if the permission of his Imperial Majesty be obtained, to conduct excavations for a series of years, employing workmen engaged in the country, and hence expending money there, to the manifest advantage of the people employed, and the increase, to that extent, of the resources of the region in which our explorations shall be conducted.

Inasmuch as it is impossible to determine beforehand the exact spot in which such excavations as we propose to make should be conducted, and inasmuch as this must often be determined after investigations conducted on the spot, or even after preliminary excavations have been made on a small scale, we would therefore ask that we be permitted to excavate within the Vilayets of Baghdad and Haleb, but more especially within the Vilayet of Baghdad, in such places as shall not be excepted by reason of grants to others; but that this permission constitute no claim on any ruins within the boundaries assigned other than those in which we shall actually conduct excavations

Inasmuch as a considerable period of time is necessary for the conducting of such excavations as are referred to above, we would ask that a permission be granted to us to excavate in the manner and in the regions above narrated during the period of ten years, beginning with this current year.

We should expect to take with our Expedition a photographer, and we should send to the Museum of his Imperial Majesty copies of all photographs taken, as also casts or squeezes of all inscriptions, as also copies of all publications issued ultimately in connection with the Expedition. On the other hand we hope to obtain permission to bring back to this country as considerable a portion of the inscribed bricks, stones, and other articles (exclusive of the precious metals, gold and silver) as it may consist with the liberality and generosity of his Imperial Majesty to permit. For this country is new and without Museums, and his Imperial Majesty would win the lasting gratitude of the scholars and citizens of this country at large, if out of the abundant antiquities of his Empire he would permit us to take such small part, now lying disregarded and unused, as should enable us to teach and show our coming scholars something of the history of the old world. We would gladly pack and send to the Museum of his Imperial Majesty all duplicates of articles found, of which there are always in fact very many, and especially of the most important.

We hope that his Imperial Majesty will be disposed to give a favorable ear to our desires, and pray your Excellency to present to his Majesty the request that a permission to excavate under the terms and in the territory and for the purposes above specified be granted to Rev. John P. Peters, Professor in the University of Pennsylvania, in the city of Philadelphia.

We hope that your Excellency will also show yourself favorably disposed toward a work thus undertaken for the advancement of knowledge, and will render us such assistance as may be within your power.

Signed at Philadelphia, Pennsylvania, this twenty-third day of February, 1888.

THE TRUSTEES OF THE UNIVERSITY
OF PENNSYLVANIA

By WM PEPPER,
Provost.

APPENDIX C.

IRADÉ GRANTING PERMISSION TO EXCAVATE.

IN behalf of the trustees of the University of Pennsylvania, the United States Legation at Constantinople has applied for permission to excavate for antiquities at Birs Nimrod, in the district of Hillah, and at a place called Tel Niffer, in the subdistrict of Divaniah, both belonging to the Vilayet of Baghdad ; and subject to the following conditions this permission is herewith granted :

(1) According to the laws relating thereto, all the antiquities discovered shall revert to the Imperial Museum.

(2) The objects found shall be kept in a safe place appointed by the Government, through the commissioner, and the excavators shall not touch or meddle with them

(3) Excavations shall not be begun until maps of the places to be excavated are approved by the Vali (governor-general) of the glorious city of Baghdad.

(4) Excavations shall not extend beyond the limits shown by the maps ; nor shall excavations be made in more than one place at the same time.

(5) If there be discovered any attempt to defraud the Government in any way and by reason thereof the excavations be stopped, the excavators shall claim no damages for losses accruing from the delay.

(6) If excavations do not begin, or if begun are not finished, during the period for which this permission is granted, the excavators are obliged to obtain a new permission before they can prosecute further excavations.

(7) If, at the end of the excavations or before, the Govern-

ment be duly notified and the excavators are proven to have walked according to the statutes of the law, the bond-money deposited by the excavators shall be returned.

(8) If without good reason excavations do not begin within three months after this permission has been passed over to the excavators by the Vali of Baghdad, or if without good reason the excavations shall stop at any time for two months, this permission is null and void.

(9) The permission can not be transferred to another party or sold.

(10) The excavators shall pay the salary of the commissioner appointed by the Minister of Public Instruction to accompany them.

Finally : the excavators shall strictly fulfil all the above conditions, then the excavators may purchase such part of the objects found as may seem superfluous to the Imperial Museum if, after the price has been agreed upon, the supreme court of Bab el-Aali consent to the sale thereof.

Therefore, for the period of two years to the above mentioned trustees this as a permission has been given.

                Grand Vizier
                    MEHMED KIAMIL BEN SALLIH.
            Minister of Public Instruction—Muniff.

Nov. 19, 1304 ; and First Spring 27, 1306

APPENDIX D.

TRANSLATION OF TURKISH LAW ON ARCHÆOLOGICAL EXCAVATIONS.

ART. 1. The remains left by the ancient populations of the States forming at present the dominions of the Ottoman Empire,—that is to say, the gold and silver and other ancient coins, and the inscriptions containing reference to history, and statues and sepultures and ornamental objects in clay, stone, and other materials, utensils, arms, tools, statuettes, ring-stones, temples, palaces, circuses, theatres, fortifications, bridges, aqueducts, bodies and objects in tombs, burying mounds, mausoleums and columns,—are regarded as antiquities.

ART. 2 In general, the right of ownership of all the antiquities is regulated by the present law.

ART. 3. All the antiquities discovered in the Ottoman territory, be it on the surface, underground or exhumed, picked up in the sea, the lakes, the rivers, the streams, or the valleys, are the property of the Government.

ART. 4. The monuments of antiquity which happen to be in the property or houses of private persons, either loose or built in the walls, cannot be moved by the proprietors of the property; and for the keeping of those antiquities in their original place the Government has inaugurated the following measures:

ART. 5. It is forbidden to destroy the antiquities which may be discovered on one's land, like buildings, roads, walls of castles and fortresses, baths, tombs, and other things; and in order not to occasion any damage to antiquities, they will refrain from establishing any lime-kiln at a distance less than half a kilometre from the spot where the antiquities are to be found ; or from the erection of any kind of building and works which would be injurious ; or to remove the stones of tumbled-down ancient monuments ; from measuring or taking moulds ; or of placing ladders on them for any purpose whatsoever ; from appropriating or restoring old buildings and making use of them in part or in all ; or to use them for deposits of grain, straw, or hay, or to use them as tanks, or for cattle, or turn them into fountains, or to use them for other purposes.

Art 6. The places on which the Government has decided to make excavations may be bought from their owners, if they are in the hands of private persons or societies ; if they refuse to sell, the regulation on expropriation for public uses shall be applied in order to buy that property.

Art. 7. No one is allowed to make excavations, to extract or appropriate antiquities in the Ottoman dominions without having previously obtained the official permit in accordance with the present regulation.

Art. 8. The exportation of antiquities found within Ottoman territory is absolutely forbidden.

Art. 9 The permit for the excavation and exhumation of antiquities may be granted to private persons or to any scientific society. The terms of that permit must be in accordance with the conditions of the present regulation

Art 10 As to the searches and excavations for antiquities, after the opinion of the administration of the Imperial Museum and the conclusions of the Council of Public Instruction have been obtained, and after the Ministry of Public Instruction has submitted the case to the Sublime Porte, the final permit will be granted in accordance with the terms contained in the third chapter of the present regulation.

Art. 11. A duplicate list describing the quantity and the quality of the objects excavated must be made on the printed blanks to be furnished by the Ministry of Public Instruction, which must be signed and certified ; then one of the copies will remain with the excavator and the other with the Board of Public Instruction ; where such Boards do not exist, they will be recorded in the books kept for the purpose by the local authorities and sent to the Ministry of Public Instruction.

ART 12. The antiquities excavated with an official permit belong to the Imperial Museum, and the excavators have only the right to take drawings or moulds.

ART. 13. The antiquities discovered without permit are confiscated; and if the excavator has already disposed of them, he will pay their value.

ART. 14. The antiquities which may be discovered by accident in digging the foundations of a building or of a wall or of a sewer shall be divided in equal parts between the owner of the property and the Government; and then at the division of those antiquities, as the Government had the choice of taking such as it thinks proper on paying their value, it may get from the land owner, out of those which have fallen to his share, such a portion as it wants.

ART. 15. Those who desire to undertake excavations of antiquities shall prepare a topographical plan showing the boundaries of the spot to be excavated, and present it at Constantinople to the Ministry of Public Instruction; and, if they are in the provinces of the Governors-General, with written request, and the Governors-General will forward it together with their report of their investigation of the subject to the Ministry of Public Instruction

ART. 16. The delivery of the permit of excavation appertains to the Ministry of Public Instruction after agreement with the direction of the Imperial Museum, but unless the necessary investigations are made and, according to Article 10, the consent of the Sublime Porte is obtained, this permit can not be given.

ART. 17. The permit for excavating antiquities can only be granted under the following conditions :

1. After having ascertained that it will cause no obstruction to the forts, fortifications, public buildings, nor interfere with public utility.

2. If the excavations are to take place in the landed property of a private person, to satisfy the owner.

3. The pecuniary security which will be agreed upon by

the Director of the Imperial Museum must be actually deposited.

After the fulfilment of those conditions the Ministry of Public Instruction, after having conformed to the prescriptions of the preceding article, delivers the permit.

But no permit can be granted for more than two years And if, before beginning the excavations, or even after having begun them, for some reason the period of the permit is allowed to pass and the explorer wants to continue his researches,—if there is no objection the Ministry of Public Instruction, after an agreement with the Director of the Museum, may grant a permit for an additional period not longer than one year.

ART. 18. The Ministry of Public Instruction will collect on the permits of excavation on account of the Museum: on a permit from one day to six months, 5 liras; on a permit from six months to one year, 10 liras; on a permit from one year to two years, 20 liras.

ART. 19. If, after having obtained the permit, the excavations are not commenced within the period of three months from its date, or after having commenced then they should be discontinued for two months, the permit will be annulled: and if the explorer wants to renew it the Ministry of Public Instruction, with the Director of the Museum, may continue or not the old permit; or cancel it and furnish a new one in its place.

ART. 20. The permit for excavation shall not embrace a larger area than ten square kilometres. If after the commencement of the excavations an objection is found on the part of the Government, on the order of the Ministry of Public Instruction the works shall be temporarily stopped, and the time of stoppage shall be accounted for in the period of the permit, and the explorer will have no claim for expenses or damages on account of that stoppage

ART. 21. At the place where excavations are to be made the Government will keep an able and capable official; and the travelling expenses and the salary of this official, after having been fixed by the authorities, will be collected from the excavators in full and paid to him monthly by the Treasurer of Public Instruction.

If the excavations are finished before the expiration of the permit and the researches abandoned, the surplus of the money paid for the salary of the official shall be returned to the excavator.

ART. 22. No permit of excavation shall be granted to officials of the Ottoman, or of a foreign, Government for excavations to be made within the district of their official post.

ART. 23. The transfer by the recipient of a permit of excavation is forbidden.

ART. 24. A person cannot have permits for excavation in more than one place.

ART. 25. Those who by accident discover antiquities are bound, if at Constantinople, to inform the Ministry of Public Instruction within five days, and if in the provinces, to inform the local authorities within ten days.

ART. 26. At the expiration of the permit or at the termination of the excavations, when the excavator gives notice of it, if it is found that he has fulfilled all the conditions of the regulations, the money he had deposited as security will be returned to him in accordance with the receipt.

ART. 27. The amount produced by seizures of antiquities, or, on condemnation, from sales at public auction in accordance with the rule by an official auctioneer, and the money accruing from divisions with the owners of antiquities, and also fines, and fees of permits, and the product of confiscations shall belong to the treasury of the Museum.

ART. 28. The importation from abroad of any kind of antiquities is free and exempt from customs duties, and all kinds of antiquities which are to be transported from one district to another within the Ottoman dominions are exempt from internal duties.

ART. 29. Permission for the re-exportation of antiquities introduced from abroad into the Ottoman dominions, and for the transportation from one district of the Empire to another of antiquities found within the Empire, can be obtained by drawing up a list of said antiquities by the owner and shipper and transmitting it to the Director of the Museum through the Ministry of Public Instruction ; and in localities where there are no such Boards or Commissions to the local authorities.

The owner of antiquities introduced into the Empire from abroad is bound within eight days to transmit a list of them, as before stated, to the administration of the Museum through the Ministry of Public Instruction, and in the provinces to the Board or Commission of Public Instruction ; and if there is no such Board or Commission to the local authorities.

ART. 30. In any case the re-exportation of antiquities imported from abroad, and the transportation from one district of the Empire to another of antiquities found within the Empire, is necessarily subject to an official authorization, which can be procured from the Ministry of Public Instruction, with the agreement of the Director of the Museum.

ART. 31. The antiquities exported without the special permit of the Ministry of Public Instruction shall, if captured, be seized or confiscated in the name of the Museum.

ART. 32. The granting of the official permission to export antiquities into foreign countries, though reserved to the Ministry of Public Instruction with the consent of the Director of the Museum, is subject to the following conditions :

1st. The Museum should possess already a duplicate of the kind.

2d. It should be established that the said antiquities have been imported from a foreign country.

ART. 33. Those who appropriate antiquities found on the ground or exhumed, on private or Government property, will be liable in accordance with Article 138 of the Penal Code to damages and a fine, and to imprisonment from one month to one year.

ART. 34. If those who have accidently discovered some antiquities do not give notice of it, they, after being deprived of the share to which they had a right, are punished with a fine equal to one fourth of the value of their discovery ; and if those antiquities are out of reach, besides the fine they will have to pay their total value

ART. 35. Those who, in transportation from one district to

another of antiquities found within the Empire, violate Article 32, will be subjected to a fine of from one to five Turkish pounds.

ART. 36. The lawsuits which may originate out of these regulations shall be heard in the ordinary courts of law.

ART. 37. The Ministry of Public Instruction is charged with the enforcement of the present regulations.

The 23 of Rebbi-ul-Akhir 1301, and 9th of February, 1299 : (*i. e.* Feb. 21, 1884, A.D.).

APPENDIX E.

THE GEOGRAPHY OF THE EUPHRATES.

GREEK and Roman geographers and historians differ materially in their descriptions of the Euphrates Valley and of Babylonia. The earliest account of the Euphrates which we have is that contained in Xenophon's Anabasis (400 B.C). He journeyed down the Euphrates on the Mesopotamian side, and reports no cities or towns between the river Khabor and the Median Wall, excepting the half deserted Corsote. But across the river during these desert stages was the large and wealthy town of Charmande. This was the city of Anatho, or 'Anah. From what Xenophon obtained the *Charm* in his Charmande, I do not know.

About the beginning of our era, Isidorus of Charax wrote his $\Sigma\tau\alpha\theta\mu o\grave{\iota}\ \Pi\alpha\rho\theta\iota\varkappa o\acute{\iota}$, an itinerary of the route from Antioch to Seleucia, on the Tigris. The road followed by him crosses the Euphrates at Birejik, and descends the Belikh to the Euphrates, which it reaches at Nikephorium. From Nikephorium onward, this route is the same as that followed by Xenophon. The first station, four schoeni beyond Nikephorium, was a deserted village, Galabatha. One schoenus beyond this was the village of Chubana. Four schoeni beyond this were Thillada and Mirrhada; beyond which were a palace, a shrine of Artemis, a building of Darius, a walled village, and a canal of Semiramis. The Euphrates at this point was walled in with stones, and at certain seasons it inundated the fields, but in summer, when the water is low, owing to this obstruction, ships were wrecked at this point. Manifestly Thillada and Mirrhada were in the gorge which the

Euphrates breaks through the el-Hamme range, and approximately in the position of Halebieh and Zelebieh.

Four schoeni beyond these was a walled village named Allan, and four schoeni beyond this, Biunau, where was a shrine of Artemis Then comes Phaliga, a village by the Euphrates, near which was Nabagath, a walled village on the Aboras Nabagath was situated about where the Roman fortress Circesium was built later, and Biunau must have been nearly opposite Deir.

Four schoeni beyond Nabagath was the village of Asicha, and six schoeni beyond that was Dura, the city of Nicanor, founded by the Macedonians, but called Europus by the Greeks. This must have been almost opposite the modern Mujawada

Five schoeni beyond this was Castle Mirrhan, a walled village. This castle stood, presumably, about on the site of el-'Irsi Five schoeni beyond this was a city, Giddan ; and seven schoeni beyond that, Belesibiblada. Six schoeni beyond that was an island in the Euphrates, where Phraates, " who cut the throats of his wives, had a treasury, which Tiradates the exile seized." Four schoeni beyond this was the island of Anatho in the Euphrates

The schoeni for this part of the route are evidently not the same as the schoeni for the part between the Belikh and the Khabor Like the parasang, the schoenus is an approximate measure by time, and the length of time occupied in traversing a mile in one part of the country may have been longer than the time occupied in traversing the same distance in another part. But, allowing for this difference, it seems impossible to insert all the places mentioned between the Khabor and 'Anah ; while below 'Anah the number of stations is insufficient.

The next station below 'Anah, twelve schoeni lower down, is the island of Olabus, "where was a treasury of the Parthians." Twelve schoeni below this was Uzzanesopolis ; and sixteen schoeni below this, Aeiopolis, "where are bitumen springs" Aeiopolis is evidently Hit. Now, between Hit and 'Anah there are four islands in the river, all of them, apparently,

ancient sites,—namely, Telbeis, Haditha, Alus, and Jibba.
Isidore, in his list of stations, mentions only two islands between 'Anah and Hit—Olabus and Izzanesopolis. The latter
of these is clearly Alus or el-'Uzz; and the former, from its
name, appears to be Telbeis. But the distances given by him
are not correct for these two places, nor, indeed, for any of the
island towns now existing. As there were too many places
between the Khabor and 'Anah, so there are too few places
between 'Anah and Hit. I am almost inclined to suppose
that the island with the treasury of Phraates mentioned before
'Anah, belongs after 'Anah, and that it is the island of Haditha,
the next station after Aeiopolis,

Twelve schoeni below Hit was Besechana, in which was a
shrine of the goddess Atargate. Twenty-two schoeni below
Besechana was Neapolis on the Euphrates. From there to
Seleucia on the Tigris, by the Nahr Malcha, was nine schoeni.
Neapolis was Nearda, or, at least, was situated in the same
general position as Nearda Besechana would have been
approximately opposite Ramadieh, but the length of the stages
given is excessive, especially the twenty-two schoeni from
Besechana to Neapolis

These Parthian stations of Isidore's give, not all the towns
on the route but, the stations on the road of the traveller.
Comparing Isidore's stations with Xenophon's Anabasis, it
will be seen that there is little in common between the two

About half a century later than Isidore, Pliny wrote his
Natural History. In the fifth and sixth books of this work he
gives some account of the Euphrates. According to him,
the main stream of the Euphrates flowed through the Nahr
Malcha to the Tigris, a smaller stream going southward through
Babylonia to lose itself in the swamps The point of division
was near a place called Massice. But earlier there had stood
at the point where the Nahr Malcha and the Euphrates
divided a very large city, named Agranes, which the Persians
destroyed. Pliny says further that the Persians destroyed
Hipparenum, that is, Sippara, which, like Babylon, was
rendered famous by the learning of the Chaldeans, and was
situated near the river Narraga. In the same district, toward

the south, was Orchemus, that is, Erech, a third place of learning of the Chaldees, which was also destroyed by the Persians. He states that in his day Thapsacus was called Amphipolis The only information which he gives in addition to this is that at no great distance from Sura on the Euphrates was Philiscum, a town of the Parthians.

Strabo, writing about the same time, gives us absolutely nothing tangible about the Euphrates.

Ptolemy's geography was written a century later. I have stated that it is of little value for the identification of localities. In some cases it is difficult to conjecture where or how he obtained his information. Nikephorium he places on the Euphrates above the bend of the river by Barbalissus. Khabora is located inland from the Euphrates, and both the rivers Khabor and Belikh are omitted altogether. On the other hand, a river, Saokoras, is represented as emptying into the Euphrates a little above the town of Hit (Idikara). It is possible that this may be the Tharthar, which is reported (where, I do not know) as flowing from ancient Hadr to the Euphrates Xenophon represents a river, Maska, as emptying into the Euphrates apparently near 'Irsi, that is, much higher up.

The towns mentioned by Ptolemy, like the stations of Isidore, are for the most part stations of travellers, having no more permanent a character than the stations in use at present. The names, therefore, are of little assistance; and the few which can be identified are strangely turned about and transposed from their proper positions, so that we cannot rely on Ptolemy's map for the identification of places not hitherto known.

Arrian, at an earlier date, tells of the Pallakopas Canal, which, from his description, was in about the same position as, or identical with, the modern Hindieh Canal. Ptolemy represents the Euphrates as having a channel running directly to the Persian Gulf from a point considerably above the junction of the Euphrates and the Nahr Malcha. This is evidently a reminiscence, at least, of the Saadeh Canal, constructed by Nebuchadrezzar, and which we found leaving the Euphrates at a point slightly below Hit. Ptolemy, however, represents it as branching off above Hit. That he is confused with regard to the position of Hit is evident from the fact that he locates that town in two different places. Like Pliny, he represents what is now the main channel of the Euphrates as a stream of comparative insignificance. The main portion of the Euphrates, according to him, flows across to the Tigris through the Nahr Malcha. At the point where this leaves the Euphrates, on the east side of the stream, he locates the city of Nearda, a location which accords in general with the information obtained from other sources. Farther down on the same stream was Sippara, the modern Abu Habba. Above Nearda, on the same side of the Euphrates, were Paccria and Teridata. What is now the main channel of the Euphrates, Ptolemy calls the River of Babylon, and describes it as flowing through Babylon. Below Babylon it is joined by another stream, the Marsares, which seems to be the Nahr Sar. These two streams united lose themselves in the swamps near Orchoe, that is, Erech.

Ammianus Marcellinus, in his account of Julian's ill-fated expedition against the Persians (363 A D), of which he was an eye-witness, gives us some information of a later date, part of which I have used in my text. One day's journey below Circesium stood, according to his account, Zaitha and the tumulus of Gordian. A day's journey beyond, also on the Mesopotamian side of the Euphrates, was the deserted town of Dura. Four days' journey beyond that was 'Anah. Near 'Anah, situated in the middle of the stream, was the island of Thilutha, which is Telbeis. Next, they came to Achaiachala, fortified by the flowing about it of the stream. Next beyond this was Parax Malcha, and going on from there they came to the bitumen city of Diacira, on the other side of the river. Achaiachala and Parax Malcha represent two of the three island towns,—Haditha, Alus, and Jibba,—presumably the first and the last. Diacira is identified by the designation of "the bitumen city" as Hit. Next beyond Diacira, on the other side of the river, they came to Macepracta by a ruined wall, the Median Wall. About this point the river divided, part flowing down into the interior of Babylonia, and part flowing through the Nahr Malcha to the Tigris by Ctesiphon.

It is evident from this description that Macepracta was somewhere in the neighborhood of the modern Sakhlawieh. Just about or below this point was Perisabora, that is, 'Anbar, which was almost surrounded by the river, as by a wall, so that its position was semi-insular. A little beyond this, following the general course of the Nahr Malcha, toward Ctesiphon, Julian came to a small city inhabited exclusively by Jews ; and still beyond this to the large and strong city of Maoga Malcha.

A comparison of these geographical notices will show, as I stated at the outset, a curious lack of agreement in the names of cities and towns along the river. A similar lack of agreement appears in the accounts of modern travellers separated from one another by a half-century or so. I found, for instance, that many of the places given on Chesney's map had disappeared completely, or had changed their names. There are a few towns, like 'Anah and Hit, which constitute permanent landmarks, and we are compelled to study the records of the old geographers from these as a basis. The majority of the names given by them are the names of insignificant towns of a temporary character,—mere stages on the itineraries, which have always changed place and name frequently One fact, however, in which all of these geographical notices agree, is the division of the Euphrates into two channels, one flowing southward through Babylonia, and one flowing into the Tigris through the Nahr Malcha, which left the Euphrates somewhere near the site of 'Anbar.

I may call attention further to the maps of the Tigris and Euphrates contained in the *Liber Climatum* of Abu Ishak, toward the end of the twelfth century A D In these he represents the Euphrates and the Tigris as joined together by the Nahr Isa, which is the modern Sakhlawieh Canal. Just below this another canal, the Nahr Sarsar, leaves the Euphrates, running toward the Tigris, which it does not quite reach. A little below this is the similar Nahr Malcha ; and on one of the maps still a fourth canal is represented, the Nahr Sura. The English surveys of Selby, Bewsher, and Collingwood show a number of canals starting out from the

Euphrates within a short distance of one another, not far from 'Anbar, which is substantially the same condition represented on Abu Ishak's map, excepting only that in his day these canals seem to have contained more water than at present. But between the time of Pliny and the time of Abu Ishak the channel of communication between the two streams seems to have been transferred from the Nahr Malcha to the Nahr Isa.

In the text accompanying his maps Abu Ishak says that the Isa Canal leaves the Euphrates near 'Anbar and empties into the Tigris within the limits of the city of Baghdad. The next canal below this, also navigable, was the Sarsar, on which was the town of the same name, three parasangs from Baghdad. Two parasangs below this was a large canal, called Nahr-el-Malk, on which was a city of the same name, the Maoga Malcha of Ammianus. Beyond this, in the neighborhood of the Euphrates, and opposite Kerbela, was Kasr-ibn-Kubeire, the most important city between Busrah and Baghdad. The next canal, and the largest of all, was the Nahr Sura, on which was the city of the same name.

Josef Černik, in his *Studien Expedition*, 1872–73, gives us the best map in existence of the terrain of the Arabic bank of the Euphrates, but adds nothing to our knowledge of sites. He heard for el-'Irsi the name el-Baus, and describes it as the "Balessi of the Bible," whatever that may mean. For the Sakhlawieh Canal he heard the name Feluja Canal, and by the side of this he found in existence the Wadi Isa. Černik heard of old wells and stations on the direct line from Salahieh on the Euphrates to Sukhne near Palmyra.

I have mentioned the island city of Alus, or el-'Uzz, as named after an Arab goddess. That goddess was properly el-'Uzza, or simply Uzza, known also as the "Morning Star," and the "Queen of Heaven." She was the great goddess of the Arabs from a time after the beginning of the Christian era until the time of Mohammed. She was worshipped at her great yearly festivals with human sacrifices. At one of her shrines was a grove of trees, which constituted the temple, and in one of these dwelt the goddess. There was also a sacred stone in connection with this sanctuary. She was identified by foreign writers with Beltis, Venus or Aphrodite. On conversion to Christianity her cult tended to go over into that of the Virgin Mary, and *vice versa*. Manifestly a shrine of this goddess existed at Alus, or el-'Uzz. The worship of this goddess among the Arabs followed and superseded that of Allat and Manat after the beginning of the Christian era. It is not probable, therefore, that the name Alus or el-'Uzz is very ancient, but, as I have already shown, it was known to Isidore of Charax at the beginning of our era, for he calls the town Izzanesopolis, or Uzzanesopolis, which being translated means "city of Uzza," and a little later in the same century Ptolemy calls it Auzara, which is a corruption of 'Uzza

APPENDIX F.

A PORTION OF THE DIARY OF WILLIAM HAYES WARD, DIRECTOR OF THE WOLFE EXPEDITION TO BABYLONIA (1884–85), INCLUDING SELECTIONS AND TOPOGRAPHICAL DATA FROM THAT PART OF THE DIARY WHICH COVERS THE TIME SPENT IN BABYLONIA.

MONDAY, January 12, 1885 Leaving Baghdad about 10 30, we went over the bridge and through a level country, by old canals, till we came in six hours to Khan Mahmudieh. This is the finest khan we have seen. It is said to be the pious work of one man, and is free to any traveller. The outside is an immense square blank wall, entered by a covered doorway in the middle of one side, which leads across an interior passage-way into the middle court, where the animals are gathered. On each side of the interior passage-way are chambers, open the full width, and raised three feet from the ground, which can be shut off by curtains if there are any women in the pilgrim party. The passage-way is filled with horses and camels or donkeys. About the inner open court are similar open chambers. There is a great crowd of pilgrims from India or Persia who carry with them dead bodies, swathed in cloth, to be buried in the sacred soil of Kerbela. The sick are also carried to die there. The sick, as well as the women, are carried in baskets swung either side of a camel or mule. As we came in, there were scores of camels outside of the khan, and

Dr. Ward's party consisted of Dr J R S. Sterrett, now Professor of Greek in Amherst, and Messrs J H Haynes and D Z. Noorian. Dr. Sterrett fell ill on the way to Baghdad and did not accompany Dr. Ward on his trip southward from that place. Among the servants of the Wolfe Expedition were Mustafa and Artin, who afterward accompanied the University of Pennsylvania Expedition.

the owners were feeding them. They were made to come up in squads and kneel before the driver, who had by him lumps of wet meal as big as his two fists He would give eight or ten to each camel. They are thus fed every one or two days, and depend on what they can forage for the rest of their sustenance. They were very eager, and had to be cuffed about to make them keep their turns.

Tuesday, January 13th. The khanjee offered to be our guide, and we went with him to Abu Habba We had a letter from Daoud Thoma to Sheikh Abdullah, and saw him and also Daoud's brother, Abd-ul-Ahad ("servant of Sunday," the day on which he was born). It appears to be the duty of Abd-ul-Ahad to protect the ground against depredations by others. It is said that a part of the property about Abu Habba has passed into the private possession of the Sultan, and it seemed to be the idea of the people that he was providing against the time when he might be compelled to move his capital from Constantinople to Baghdad. On our way to Abu Habba we visited Abu Shema ("father of wax"), where some exploring has been done by Daoud. It is a small, unimportant ruin. There is at Abu Habba a large encircling wall which we did not have time to explore, and other walls dividing the city into quarters. The principal ruins seem to be in one of these quarters, the others being empty. There is a perfect network of excavations, and scores of ruins, large and small There is scarcely any sign of stone, but plenty of burnt and unburnt brick The highest elevation is low, and a shaft has been put through it, finding nothing The deepest excavation is near it, by a square tower, but nothing was found there Abdullah and Abd-ul-Ahad showed us all about and pointed out where the stone was found with the figure on it of the sun-god of Sippara They called it the stone with Noah and his three sons on it, and we were told how Rassam killed an ox in honor of the discovery. They also showed us where barrels and tablets were found One is struck by the absence of stone There is little anywhere excepting pieces a foot square, used as sockets for doors, or for the fastening of bolts between folding-doors, perhaps The guardians of the place protest that absolutely no digging has been done there since Daoud dug for Rassam.

Wednesday, January 14th. Travelled to Khan Mahawil. Noticed on the way several round boats or coracles that had been left stranded at the last overflow of the river, during which period, for several weeks, we were told, men went to Mahmudieh by boat

Thursday, January 15th. Soon after crossing the bridge over the Mahawil Canal, we came to a small mound with pottery and black stone, and a square door socket. We found that Tel-el-Kreni had been pretty thoroughly explored by Rassam. I saw plenty of diggings and pottery, and some inscribed bricks, the writing nearly effaced. Tel Kreni lies just to the right of the telegraph and the road. It is about three hundred feet long, and shows tufa, bones, and a little masonry.

Babil appeared in the distance, and as we came opposite to it we sent the animals ahead to Jimjimeh, while we rode along the canal to Babil. The height disappointed me, but it has been sadly broken up by digging. Anyone can dig there freely, and so it seems to be all the way to Jimjimeh, and several parties were busy getting out brick for the Hillah market. The men carry the dirt out in baskets, and the donkeys carry the brick to the bank of the river, where the coracles take them to Hillah. We went over the hill, which is perfectly gutted with diggings. I was told at Jimjimeh that nothing is found there; but in Baghdad I was told that two small Nebuchadrezzar barrels which I bought there came from Babil. The Arabs stopped digging and showed us about, but we saw nothing except the holes which they were digging. It was impossible to discover the details of any buildings. They keep filling up after them. An Arab offered to show us a big stone lion " near by." We passed bullocks lifting water into canals to irrigate palm-trees, by means of a bucket made of bullock's hide, the Egyptian Shaduf. This method is generally in use where the current of the river is not strong enough to carry the great water-wheel which is in use farther up the Euphrates. The lion was found after a long ride. It lies in a deep hole dug long ago, and seems to have been rudely cut.

We then rode hastily past hills and diggings to Jimjimeh, where we had letters from Daoud Thoma to Sheikh Tamer and his son Obeid We were kindly received, for they had heard that we were coming, and impressively informed that Mr. Rassam occupied the room where we were entertained. The old Sheikh was dignified and courteous, and called on us in the evening, and we returned his call

Friday, January 16th We left the gate of Jimjimeh at 9 44 with Obeid as guide, and started for the wall, es-Sur The wall was not evident at first, remains being visible at but one spot for about half the length of the southern side. Then it became ten or fifteen feet high and broken by several gates. The rest had been entirely removed by the plow. We turned the corner and rode towards Babil. About every sixty seconds there appeared a minor gate, and about the middle a larger one Once or twice canals have been cut through the wall. In the wall we saw fragments of coffins of blue glazed ware and bones, presumably late Parthian burials. At the southeast corner the road crosses the canal, and near Babil disappears in the canal. Here the rain interfered with our pictures and observations. We rode to Hillah by way of Tel Ahmera, Mujellibeh, Amram, and Jimjimeh, and found that rooms had been engaged for us at the khan. Ours was a fine room with dirt floor, plastered walls, two shelves, and two nails We noticed that another room, which was held by a merchant abroad on a journey, was sealed up with pats of clay covering the cracks between the door and its casing, and on the lock, each pat of clay being marked with the owner's seal protecting his property stored within.

Saturday, January 17th We took a zaptieh and horses and went to Birs Nimrud. We left the palms of Hillah and struck a bare country, much of it overflowed; and had to make a detour to the left to avoid the Hindieh River. On reaching Ibrahim Khalil, the companion mound to Birs Nimrud, we found some ragged Arabs at the holy place, and after a while the man to whom we had a letter of introduction from Daoud Thoma made his appearance,—a decent, intelligent man, who had been in charge of a gang of sixty or seventy workmen when Daoud was excavating for Mr. Rassam. He showed us around, and said that no excavations had been made since then, and we saw no signs of any, merely a possible grave or two having been dug open. From the top of Birs we could see just below us the excavations of the building. Along the chambers about the central court every seventh layer of brick is laid on a pure white fibrous matter, apparently ashes of reeds. The tower of Birs astonished us with the immense broken masses of brick molten together, tumbled about the tower, and unaffected by the weather. The tower hill of Birs seems to have been pretty thoroughly explored, but Ibrahim Khalil has been very imperfectly worked. I was told at Birs that the French dug four tunnels into the hill toward the foot of the tower, and found the bottom of it in two of them. I went into the tunnels a distance of about sixty feet, and found bricks at two places. It was clear that the French had worked for architectural construction, the English for tablets. It would seem as if in Mr Rassam's digging there was no more care for architectural details than in the diggings of the Arabs.

Wednesday, January 21st. Left Hillah at 10 55. Our course was about 30°. At 12 13 we crossed a canal called Wardieh, and passed Ibn-el-Hasr half a mile to the left, having about thirty palm-trees and a tomb. We were in a network of canals At 1 24 we saw a large encampment to the left, also Abu Seid, a long, low mound a mile or more away. At 1 41 we crossed a very large old canal embankment, and at 1.48 another old canal At 1.52 we reached the encampment of el-Seid, where our party stopped with Sheikh Hawer. At 2.23, leaving our caravan, Haynes, Noorian, and I started with two guides for Tel Ohemir; at 2.35 crossed an old canal; at 2 41 reached Tel-el-Huzreh, or Shan-el-Huzrieh ("glory of the treasures"), a low mound covered with ordinary broken pottery, black stone, green and blue glaze, glass, bricks, and slag. Daoud had dug a little

---

Bearings from Tel-el-Huzra: Za'ru Seis, 249°; el-Ohemir, 96°; Bender, 107°.

way into the mound, but found nothing. Here we stopped ten minutes and then went to Ohemir

Close by Ohemir is Tel Hudhr. Behind it is Tel Bender, very little excavated by Mr. Rassam, and to the right En-'Urrah. Daoud dug here with twenty men for a year, but, they say, found nothing. Ohemir is a reddish hill, with many low elevations to the west and north On our way to En-'Urrah we passed what was said to be an affluent of the Shatt-en-Nil The top of El-Hudhr is irregular, about two hundred and fifty paces long, running north and south, with apparently a small ziggurat at the south end. I had no time to go to el-Bender. We returned to Abu Seid and were for the first time entertained in a tent. The men were anxious for backsheesh, and not very amiable, but they finally thawed out and we engaged a guide to Shameli and Niffer

Thursday, January 22d. We left Seid at 8 26. Three men had watched our baggage all night, and wanted to take care of our pistols, but were told that we could not sleep without them. At 12 00 our course was 140° to Ziaret On. We were in a region of drifting sand, like great snow-drifts everywhere about the tamarisk bushes. At 1 56 a line of palm-trees, hardly a mile off, appeared to the right, and telegraph poles. At 2 05 we reached old canal and telegraph, and at 2.15 the Euphrates, much to my disgust, at el-'Allak. An hour or so later we stopped for the night at the village of Hegan, a considerable village of mud houses, where the Kaimakam kindly provided for us at the guard house, with two large palm-stem divans for the men.

Friday, January 23d. We left Hegan at 8 05 At 8 21 we crossed the telegraph line. At 9 55 crossed Nahr Shemeli, a deep canal put in repair. At 10 15 reached a few tents, 5

Bearings from Ohemir Seid, 258° 30', en-'Urrah, 128°; Zibbah, 116°; el-Bender, 107°, Abu Hatab, 100°, with a long, low line, and two slight elevations just visible

Bearings from en-'Urrah Ohemir, 30°; Bender, 32°; Zibbah, 97°, Abu Hatab, 93°; Ibrahim, 1°.

Bearings from On Tel Ohemir 327°, just visible; Ziaret Resht, 32°, a mile or two off; Ziaret al-Dhahara, by palm-trees, 161°.

minutes southwest of Kal'at Shemeli, where we stopped twenty minutes. At 1.05 we passed to the right of the large deserted town of Horiya, with its mud walls. At 2.30 reached the quite large village of el-Seid Ibn Kerbul, or Kal 'at Ibn Kerbul. Here we were hospitably taken into his tent by the Sheikh, and coffee was made for us by a negro, in a series of seven copper coffeepots, arranged in a row according to their size. The process of pouring the coffee from one pot to another was extremely impressive. Ibn Kerbul is near the swamp Khor-el-Lisan, where are said to be lions. The Sheikh was not there, but his brother was in charge, a young man named Nahab. We were abundantly supplied with meat and rice. Sheikh Ibn Kerbul, Sheikh Hommar, and Sheikh Seid belong to the Zobeid tribe

Saturday, January 24th. The caravan went directly to Niffer, accompanied by Ibn Kerbul, Sheikh Seid, and Sheikh Nahab, while Haynes, Noorian, and I started for Ziblieh, accompanied by an Arab guide, and our soldier, Abbas. Ziblieh, with its conspicuous high point, lay in the direction of about 43°, as the angle was taken on horseback. At 9 40 we came across considerable pottery, and five minutes later a fragment of brick with an archaic inscription in four or five lines On the way we passed a long wall of drifted sand about ten feet high We reached Ziblieh about 11.30, and remained there two hours. We had been told that it was dangerous to go there during the feud between the tribes, and at first we had been refused a guide We found the tower of Ziblieh made of unburnt bricks, with layers of reeds still well preserved. There were several burnt bricks and masses of mortar, but no inscriptions. The whole hill was seamed by rain and there was no sign of any digging. We noticed certain curious cement slabs, perhaps for graves, although one seemed to be in situ on the bricks. An arch runs through the hill, a third of the way from the top, about six feet wide at the bottom, and

---

Bearings from Ziblieh Niffer, 147° 30', Estel, 99° 30', a very slight elevation, el-Hawal (4 low hills not half an hour off), two of them 51°, another 30°, another 27° 30', Tel Lasa, 304° 30', long and low, Ibn Kerbul, 223° ? Kal 'at Ibn Mohammed, 214°.

having the shape of a low segment of a circle. It makes an angle of about 25°. I saw also a part of a circular ornament of cement. There are low elevations about and the usual amount of pottery. We saw no evidence of very ancient construction. There is no water in the neighborhood, but some grass.

I set out for el-Hawal, but the guide objected, and I went alone. The rest started southward for Niffer, but Haynes soon followed me, overtaking me just as I had reached the top of the mound, which was of no interest, to tell me that there were mysterious horsemen about, disappearing behind the sand hills. We hastened to overtake the remainder of our party, without stopping to take bearings. We galloped and overtook them in half an hour, the horsemen following us. Some men began to appear, signalling on a ridge in front for others to gather to meet us They were armed with long flint-lock guns, their signal being made with a sort of banner, a red kerchief on a spear. We went forward to meet them, as it was impossible to avoid them, and found them Affech Arabs, fifteen in number, who had gathered from their flocks, seeing us come from a hostile territory, and fearing that we were enemies, of the el-Baij tribe. As we approached, they first concealed themselves behind bushes and thorns, and were ready to shoot from a safe place Noorian and the guide went ahead, and our zaptieh in the rear The guide waved his meshlah and made signs that we were friends They were as ready for peace as we were, and began to march and sing, as well as we could make out:

" Ya Beg, eshha bina el medani
Ya Beg, eshha bina el nesrani "

which would mean :

" O Beg, we long for the field of battle,
O Beg, we long to meet the Christians."

But it was not very easy to catch the words, and our guide, when asked, said that they were singing :

" O Beg, we are beating out nitre."

that is, to make powder for war. We stayed with them but a few minutes, and were glad to escape so peaceably, even though the song was not reassuring. We left them marching and shouting.

Our road was along a very ancient low-banked canal, not the Shatt-en-Nil of to-day, which is to the east, and which we did not see. The old canal looked like a road, and was lined with pottery. Our rendezvous was Chirfan, but the caravan had gone on to Niffer. There is nothing of interest at Chirfan, only low lines, hardly mounds. We passed through a vast herd of camels feeding, perhaps five thousand in number. We hurried on from Chirfan to Niffer, although our guide was too tired to walk, and Noorian and I had to take turns in giving him a ride, and reached the tents of the Affech about 4 30

Sunday, January 25th. A rainy day, and we remained in our tents, only going in the afternoon, in a slight drizzling rain, to the neighboring tel of Niffer. The hills looked immense when on them. There are two clusters of hills, less wide than long, separated by what we were told is the Shatt-en-Nil, covered with pottery for vast extents, steep and high, and difficult of ascent with horses. There is no construction visible, and only in a few places layers of unburnt bricks and remains of graves. As we took our bearings and pictures, a crowd of men and boys followed us. We stole a picture of them in a ravine, as they lay down wrapped in their cloaks, watching us in the cold mist, close by the camera, and unsuspicious what we did, or they would have angrily resented it. In the evening our host, Sheikh Awad, killed a lamb and gave us a supper, himself sitting with us on the ground, and tearing the meat into fragments with his fingers and giving it to us.

Monday, January 26th. Left Niffer at 9 30, guided by our host. At 10.40 passed three mounds of Abu Jowan, running lengthwise directly across our course. At 11.05 we were by Shan, or Nishan (boundary) el-Bed'a. At 11 20 passed Tellul el-Bed'a, with Tel Shan Hindi about an hour to the left. Came to Kal'at Ejhesh, a mud fort, at 12 05, and crossed the

Bearings from Niffer· Ziblieh, 328°; Estel, 352$\frac{1}{4}$°; Ammal, 335$\frac{3}{4}$–336$\frac{1}{2}$° (fourth hill not visible); Ibn Kerbul, 291$\frac{3}{4}$°, Tel Doran, 51$\frac{3}{4}$°; Tel Abu Zen, 69°; Tel Delehem, 130°, Suk Affej, 170° (large)

stream Ejhesh a few minutes later, where we were delayed twenty minutes by Haynes's horse falling with him into the water. During the day, under the guidance of our host, 'Adi, from Niffer, and two other mounted spearmen, we had skirted along the side of the great Affech marsh, and crossed innumerable small streams or canals. The servants that we had brought with us began to be afraid to go farther, and asked leave to go to Diwanieh, as also did our zaptieh. But 'Adi told him: "You go back, and they will report at Hillah that you left them, and then won't you be happy?" So he and the servants continued reluctantly. The marsh was not reassuring to any of us, remembering how we had been told at Baghdad that we could never bring out our caravan when the flood began to rise. Our stopping place for the night was Seid Firhan. We were most hospitably received by Sheikh Dhahar, son of Sheikh Firhan, after whom the village is called. The houses are made of reed arches covered over with mats.

After getting our drenched companion cared for we started for the little tel-Ubyadh southeast of the village to take observations. A crowd accompanied us to the top. Young Sheikh Dhahar encouraged us with promising information as to our future course, telling us that we would find villages in plenty, and not much water. He provided us a supper, an admirable meal of chicken and pilaf. He gave me big pieces in my hand, and then helped his father, giving him a special plate. We were invited later to see a dance. Several young folks sang a monotonous refrain, and four boys, two of them quite small, danced the same dance over and over. They would clap their hands and jump up and down on their feet in unison, and squat down, and one of them would put his hands in mine. Then came a youngster with a double reed flute, fitted with bitumen, and played on it. I exchanged my nickel whistle for it, and the boys were delighted to get each a new silver piastre. The night was cold, and the people built fires for the comfort of their great black buffaloes.

Bearings from Tel Ubyadh Niffer, 295°; Delehem, 156° (across the marsh), Tel el-Lehan, 125° (middle of the marsh near us); Kal'at Bed'a, 190°.

Sera-Soukh, or Serasoubli of Kiepert's map, is not known.

Tuesday, January 27th. Left Firhan at 9 35 with two Affech guides, and Sheikh Dhahar. At 3 05 we reached Bismya At times during the day we seemed to be passing along by an old canal, but were not certain. We were told we should reach the Shat-en-Nil at Dhahar. We spent the night half an hour beyond Bismya, by an encampment of eight tents of Beni Rechab Arabs, who had just come from the Tigris. These Arabs did not seem hospitably disposed, and would provide nothing for us. We put up an awning by our single tent for our men. It rained hard all night, and we and our luggage were wet through. Our soldier told them that we had been sent by the Government to see what could be done to control the irrigation of the country and make it productive At night, after sitting and talking, the Arabs danced about wildly, singing war-songs, and after we had retired we heard guns fired, and bullets passed near our tent. When we asked if they wished to frighten us, they replied that it was to frighten wild beasts and robbers.

Wednesday, January 28th. The storm passed, and the morning broke clear and windy. Before breakfast Noorian, Firhan's men, and I started to see as much of Bismya as possible, while our men were hurrying to get away from the Arab camp. We struck a corner of the surrounding wall, and five minutes later reached the hill from which the observations were taken. I looked carefully for relics, but saw only uninscribed bricks and pottery, little of it blue glazed, and some fragments of the compact black stone. It was a large city, and may have been the fortress of a swamp region. We crossed, Tuesday, a considerable swamp before reaching it, and were told it was the Khor el-'Ayla, which had till five or six years before been deep water, but that the water had been carried off by the breaking of the Hindieh Dam. It was said that Bismya had itself been three fourths surrounded by water. The walls of Bismya are very irregular, but generally quadran-

Bearings from Bismya· Delehem, 286°, Tel Abu Hatab, 239½° (another of the name); Tel Dhahar, 152°, Tel Abu Matabel, 257¾°; Tel el-Haidi, 33¼°, Tel el-Haudhliye, 71½°; Tel Abu Falas, 61¾°. Tel el-Bedh, 146½°, Tel Abu 'Ashuf, 160¼°.

gular, with the corners to the cardinal points. I had not time to go around it as I desired It is one of the largest tels. At the west corner is a considerable square and the principal elevation. There seem to be two chief squares, one quite extensive, and part of a third to the south There is in the second a hill which may have been a ziggurat, and which is used as a graveyard

We left camp at 9 30 and passed many ruined forts, deserted since the water was stopped At 10 00 passed el-Berash to the right and el-Umm Rawah, nearer to the left, very small All deserted. There were ditches around, and a few encampments of Beni Rechab Arabs At 10.15 passed an insignificant elevation of two to six feet, called Hemar At 10 40 struck the Nahr el-Bedhr, by a very small tel, el-Zerayish. At 10 52 passed Tel el-Bedhr, a fair-sized long mound to the left, and reached Dhahar at 11.35. The Shatt-en-Nil was reported to be behind Jidr The line of the Shatt-el-Kehr was to the left At 12 30 we crossed a small tel, el-Melha. A line of several small hills to the left seemed to indicate an old canal. At 2.52 we reached the Shatt-el-Kehr, a swift stream twenty feet wide and a foot and a half deep, with a shelly bottom. We crossed the Shatt, and in a few minutes reached Tel Hammam.

All day from Dhahar to Hammam, and thence to Sheikh Hashm, we had seen nothing living on the ground larger than ants, except two toads. All was barren, and yet there were old canals and castle granaries. We were told that there had been some population there, but that six or eight years before a governor had doubled the taxes, which the people could not pay, whereupon he had shut off the water which came through the Daghara and the Affech Khor, and now it had gone, they said, to the Hindieh and was lost to the Daghara Canal This lowered the Shatt-el-Kehr also, and famine, followed by plague, resulted, and the country was wholly deserted

We remained an hour or more at Hammam, taking photo-

Bearings from Dhahar Bismya, 332°, Bedhr, 341°; Tel Barsha, 313°; Hammam, 162½°; Ummel-Merba, 87°; Umm Zaffeta, 104°; Aub Hatab, 241°.

graphs. The ruins are not as extensive as those at Dhahar, and not impressive, except the single conspicuous tower of unburnt bricks, split from the top, which reminds one of Zib-lieh. The Arabs call this one of "the towers of Anter," and say they were built as towers for beacon fires. The tradition which connected them, not with Nimrod, but with the time of the Baghdad Caliphate, may have its value as indicating the age of these constructions of unburnt brick still standing upright. The large tels thus far are, Niffer, Delehem (Derehem, near by, is called its brother), Bismya, Dhahar, Fara, and Hammam.

Leaving Hammam, our guide took us directly back north up the Shatt-el-Kehr to find a place where we could get food and fodder. We had to travel two hours, and it was quite dark before we reached the ford over the Shatt-el-Kehr (Karaat Harhurre, or el-Seid), and the welcome village of Hashm, called, like so many, after the name of the Sheikh, or rather, here, Khaya He is a bright, pleasant young fellow, and the people thanked us for coming, regretting that we had not sent word in order that they might have provided better for us. We were received and lodged in the muthif, or public house of the village, a fine building, which much impressed us with its beauty and roominess. It was forty feet long, eleven wide, and eight high, and was made of a succession of round arches of reeds tied together, each arch being eighteen inches thick at the bottom, with an oval section, and about six inches thick at the top, with a round section. The reeds composing the arches were tied together at distances of six inches with two reed ropes. The sides were of horizontal fasces of reeds, tied together at distances of a foot, two inches in diameter, and four inches apart. The framework of these arches and their sides were covered with matting, and there was a single low door at one of the two ends. The impression of the whole from the inside was airy and graceful. Near the door was an open fireplace, and our beds and luggage were put in the farther end of this village inn The ample fireplace was four

Bearings from Hammam · Dhahar, 343° ; Djedr, 23¾° ; Djid (or Ede), 192° , Um el-Batush, 66½° ; Tel Harahe, 134½°.

feet across, with a low mud wall about it, and within it eight coffeepots of various sizes, besides the monster one in the corner. Coffee was made in the most elaborate way. Then we waited till 9 10 for supper, as we had come so late. Our host said that he regretted we were so few, and added that the day before he had entertained three hundred horsemen. We did not believe it, but accepted the hospitable intent, which was emphasized by the fact that they would take no money for the entertainment of our people or our beasts. The supper was the best we had yet enjoyed anywhere in Babylonia. First a great mat was laid on the ground near the middle of the muthif. Then there was laid upon it an immense tinned copper platter, over two feet in diameter, piled with rice pilaf, on the top of which were spread pieces of mutton. Around the platter were spread eleven big plates, some of willowware, some of tinned copper, and in them were put three kinds of sauce for the pilaf. One was a curious preparation of plums, another a meat sauce with balls of hashed meat,—both good, but peculiar. There was also a very nice sweetmeat, pekmes sauce, finely flavored, which would have been good anywhere. A servant stood and held the big, square Turkish lantern, with colored glass corners to its faces. We all squatted or reclined around the mat, which was our table, our soldiers and guides eating with their fingers, taking a quantity of the pilaf in their hands, rolling it into a ball, and tossing it into their mouths Our cook provided us with spoons, and then the host supplied more He brought in the dinner himself and cleared it off. The meal was delightful after the dreary breakfast of nothing but rice at the miserable Beni Rechab camp in the morning Before supper the people showed us their watches of Paris make, with Turkish dials After supper we stepped out to see our horses tethered about in the beautiful moonlight, and I sat up to write until 12.30, while the people still gossiped about the fire.

Thursday, January 29th. After an unusually comfortable night, and a breakfast of rice pilaf, Noorian and I, with young Seid's younger brother, Mohammed, and a servant, both mounted on Arab mares, started for Fara, a mound said to be three hours distant, although it took us four hours to reach it, with some galloping We left es-Seid at 10.20 and at 10 40 reached Tel Umm-'Amr. This is a longish, low tel. At 11 00 we started again At 12 37 we came to Nahr Saheim, which flows from and to the Shatt-el-Kehr, and is fifty to one hundred feet wide About 1.20 Fara came in sight. Tel Bruf, long and low, was a mile off to the right. At 2 00 we reached a plain covered with pottery, and a long, low tel was parallel to our course. At 2 30 we reached Fara, from which very few tels were in sight

Fara is about a mile in length, and nearly as wide, irregular and low, not high enough to be furrowed like Niffer, and has no evident ziggurat, but very many elevations. We reached there so late that I could not go around it or all over it, but it is like the others, showing no bricks in position as at Niffer There is ordinary slag, and not much sign of graves. It is the largest tel hereabouts. We saw tracks on the tel, said to be of lions. A hurried ride brought us back to es-Seid. Again we were handsomely entertained by the young Sheikh, or Khaya The pekme we had to-night is made of rice pounded, and the rice water separated from the starch. This is boiled with sugar, then with milk, and spice is added, probably cinnamon Another sauce is made of plums and figs cooked in some sort of a fluid, a little tart, with nut-meats in it. This time we had rice pilaf with boiled chicken. Seid's father is in prison in Mahmudieh because he refused to pay a tax of one part in five of the produce, in the way it was demanded. He did not object to the proportion, but wanted the tax-collectors to come at harvest time and measure, instead of guessing at the amount of the harvest and claiming the whole of the actual product. The people asked us many questions about our country, our mosques, our Sultan, our government, and our taxes When I was asked if we had to pay one part in five, I found it not wholly easy to reduce our taxes, direct and indirect, and levied on property, to the denomination of a tax on harvests A

Bearings of Um-'Amr Hammam, 109° , Tel Jid (Yid, also Ede), 147°; Warka, 184½°.

Bearings from Tel Fara Tel Elojez, 209° , Abu Hatab, 339°.

young, white-turbaned uncle of Seid's, who wanted my pistol as a present, asked about marriage and slavery. Slaves, he said, were obtained at Busrah at prices ranging up to two hundred dollars for likely boys for eunuchs. Great dissatisfaction was expressed towards the Government, and a wish that they were under as good a government as ours.

Friday, January 30th. A short thunder-storm began just as we were getting up at 5 A M, preparing for a start at sunrise. We started at 9 00 A M, in a light rain. Our guide did not seem to understand that we were bound for Yokha, and took us down along the Shatt-el-Kehr to Hammam, which we reached at 10.30. Not liking the direction we were taking, I got uneasy and told him we must go to Yokha, and he then turned sharp off to the left, and went through miles of water, covering the sand. The walking was not very bad, however and we made good speed, I forcing the pace. At 12.30 we reached the sand hills. Among these are intervening spaces of fertile but barren ground, which forms the real level under the shifting sand. It was the most desolate scene conceivable, with the contrast of the rummel, or sand hills, on such rich but bare alluvium, and the evidences of old fruitfulness and population at every step. At 1.15 we reached Yokha. It was a large tel, but low, and I could only gallop over it while the caravan was moving. There were many signs of graves, and we picked up a tripod, like those used in baking pottery, and a flint saw. The latter certainly indicated a very ancient site, but the hasty view could not decide the age of the graves. The low level of so large a mound, evidently a favorite place for burials, showed that it had been much worn down by time.

At 2.15 we reached Umm-el-Aqarib. This place, only an hour distant, appeared, superficially, to be more important than Yokha, although not so large It is not so much covered with sand-drift, apparently, for Yokha requires a guide to find it, while Umm-el-Aqarib shows two considerable elevations, a few rods apart, with solid masonry of burnt bricks set in bitumen. The bricks have no inscriptions, but on the upper side two

Bearings from Yokha: Hammam, $254\frac{1}{4}°$; Tel Jid, or Yid, $220\frac{1}{2}°$, Tel Abrete, $350\frac{1}{4}°$; Tel Umm-el-Aqarib, $137\frac{3}{4}°$; Dhahar (scarcely visible), $215°$.

depressions. They are of about the usual length, but only half the usual width At the top of the highest elevation there seems to have been a cist, like a grave of masonry, out of which the Arabs had dug the earth, and near by were fragments of two stone bowls, and I picked up bits of flint saws This seemed to indicate that although the graves might be later, yet the mound was one of high antiquity. The brick work extended beyond the cist over the hill, and there were long lines of brick walls on the lower levels, and many more signs of graves, making it a hopeful spot to dig I simply hurried up to this hill alone as the caravan moved on, and took bearings, and then hastened along

Our objective point was Shatra, but it began to be doubtful if we could reach it that night before nine o'clock, and the guide insisted that we should stop at an Arab encampment, where he declared he could get barley. At last we struck a level of beautiful green to our right. The water of the Khor could be seen beyond it We saw a lot of straw, which gave promise of tibn (chopped straw for the horses). As we approached, one or two men appeared in the distance. Then we came suddenly upon a man lying flat on his face behind a square of tibn scarce two feet high, through a hole in which straw fort he was training his gun on us. We laughed at him when we discovered him, and asked him about straw and barley. The answer was favorable, and we hurried on, passing a very odd field in a little valley. The clayey soil had been dug into deep holes about twenty feet across, which fill with water and occupy half the ground. The rest is cultivated with water from these holes. It was a very irregular field, and looked like the spots about a village where the Arabs pile together their ricks of rice—as we saw at last night's encampment—in great wicker, mud-lined baskets, sunk in the ground and covered with straw and dirt Passing by, we reached about sunset the encampment of Shulal, Sheikh of the Montefich and Beni Rechab tribes hereabout There were a thousand sheep and other animals about the encampment, which consisted of some fifty tents Shulal's tent was about sixty feet long. He received us courteously, spread two rugs on the coarse hair mat, and gave us coffee, the succession of coffeepots being in a big basket, each wrapped in a leg of sheepskin.

Saturday, January 31st I sent the caravan on to Shatra, and Noorian and I returned to see Umm-el-Aqarib again, accompanied by the Sheikh and one of his men They amused us with skilfully practising the qaiti 'a, crossing each other's tracks on the gallop, and brandishing their spears. The ground was thinly covered with bushes, the prickly, bushy herb jibjab, on which the camels feed Another plant is the eshnan, shrubby, and with portulacca-like leaves, used for soap, the name of which is in the Arabic translation of Isaiah · "Cleanse me with eshnan, and I shall be white as wool" After washing white clothes with soap, they wash them again in water in which has been soaked the sun-dried eshnan, which is said to be better than soap In an hour and a half we reached Umm-el-Aqarib ("mother of scorpions") We spent some time going all over the ruins, which impressed me as making a much more extensive tel than I had supposed the day before. The graves extended to a great distance, and are of the same character, great round pots, with some relics of bones, pottery, shells, alabaster and soapstone vases, also flint knives and saws. We gathered a hundred pieces of them, and one nearly complete vase, and a piece of an archaic shell cylinder. One piece of a vase seemed to have come from an alabaster burial vase of immense size. I think that some of the burial places are brick cists. We returned with our guide to the encampment, and sent a man around to ask of all the tents if any of the women had any "beads" (seal cylinders) The best was an alabaster cylinder belonging to the chief's son, for which we had to chaffer a long time, but at last bought it for two rupees, a kran, a cherek, and seven piastres. Shulal was ashamed to take any present, but at last accepted three mejids for his son. The guide went with us to Shatra, and we found that Haynes, who had gone on before us with the caravan, had been most hospitably received by the function-

Bearings from Umm-el-Aqarib Hammam, $275\frac{1}{2}°$, Tel-el-Jid (Tel Ede), 238°, Yokha 320°

aries of the town. The Kaimakam had sent word that he would call (he did not). His messenger was an officer, an intelligent man who knew all about guns. He insisted on bringing in an excellent supper of chicken, pilaf, sweetmeats (like a cake in sugar syrup), and the inevitable piecrust. An Armenian officer and other officers called and spent the evening. We had one room fitted up with matting and bedding, and a borrowed rug. We were informed by our captain that a statue, like those from Tello, exists somewhere at a distance, which I was determined to see.

Sunday, February 1st. This was a busy day at our rooms in the khan, receiving visitors. The captain came early and said that our cook must not prepare breakfast, as he had it all ready. We were not smart enough to know that he was lying, but supposed that we must accept it against our will, and it was nearly noon before it came. Meanwhile he stayed, and talked freely in Turkish about Turkey and the Government, and his longing to go to America and study machinery and then come back. With most impressive gestures he would explain how badly things went—the employment of incompetent men just to give them a place; how an attempt to build a road would drive the people off and leave the land to desolation; how money was extorted and retained by functionaries. The great trouble, he said, was dishonesty. He was determined to work here a year, and then go to America to study machinery and railroads. An Armenian doctor came and talked a long while about politics, speaking Armenian, so that others might not understand. He asked all sorts of questions about Egypt, the French in southern China, the Congo Conference, the opinion of people about Turkey, and what would be the likely upshot when war came,—whether a partition or a protectorate of Turkey. Although wearing the Turkish uniform, he has no love for Turkish rule. He does not want a Russian protectorate or rule, but wants English railroads, and an Armenian autonomy, like the Bulgarian. In the evening our Turkish captain came again, and to our surprise brought us a dinner. We found that we must put a stop to his hospitality.

I called on the Kaimakam, who wanted to know what he was to report about us, and who copied our passport received from the Wali at Baghdad. During the day and evening all the other officers in the command called They all feel like exiles from Constantinople, and despise the ignorant, uncultivated Arabs, who eat their pilaf with their fingers, rolling it into a ball and tossing it into their mouths They say the Arabs hate them and look upon them as Kafirs, and they repay hate and abuse for hate. In the evening the old fat second major called, and asked many questions about America They had much curiosity about what kinds of grain and cattle we had, and whether we had irrigation, and about the climate and weather. We got no information about local antiquities, but were told that very likely those of the Tello statues that went to Turkey in the division were still in Busrah, for who would take the trouble to send them to Stamboul? One man, who seemed to have especial means of information, told us that there were fourteen statues found at Tello, sitting and standing, besides numerous smaller things, as tablets, and four barrels. The latter were not in niches in the walls, and were small. M. de Sarzec found one head of a statue protruding from the ground, but broken from the body. He then dug and found others The man who was his subordinate is rich and lives in Nasrieh His name is Naum, and his representative in Shatra is Selman Jasm. Nasrieh is the name of a town that has sprung up within a few years at the junction of the Shatt-el-Amara and the Euphrates. It is the seat of a Mutessarif under Busrah, as is this place. We were told that while de Sarzec was absent the men found a well, and dug down very deep to the bottom, and there found a large empty room, with no earth in it. The workman was frightened, and was drawn up and would not go down again. De Sarzec went, so we were told, to Aqarib, but worked there only one day, being driven off, or frightened away by some Arab horsemen. He only dug a few bricks on the top of the highest elevation. There would be no difficulty from Arabs in digging anywhere now, and it could probably be done without interference from any one. Zerghul is not far off, and our captain went there to see if bricks could be quarried for building a station house here ; but there was no water, and he found it impracticable. They report a place called Debbu, which ought to be examined. We were told that at a certain place four hours off is a sitting statue, like those of Tello, in perfect condition, with head and hands, and writing on the shoulders. We sent out for coffee, and the kaffejee refused to send cups for a Christian. Our captain happened to hear him, and he cursed the man, his father, mother, brother, sisters, and all his relations.

Monday, February 2d. We started off with our captain and guides to see the black statue, which seemed to be a genuine thing. We passed the reed and mat houses, in the mud walls, for an hour and a half; and then met scores of women, bare-legged to the knees, with armlets, anklets, earrings and nose-rings, bearing huge faggots of brush on their heads. But after nearly two hours travel we found that they were taking us to Sinkara (Senkereh), and the stone was reported at Anek, not far from Hammam, in quite a different direction,—too far for us to go there,—and we turned back to Shatra, quite disappointed. On questioning them, we found that they expected to take us to Sinkara, Ehsem, Tel Id (Ede), and Anek, and back. But that would require several days, and was not feasible. It was a day wasted, and all the worse that they report the river rising, and tell us we shall be unable to get south with a caravan.

One of de Sarzec's overseers gave this description of the French explorer's work at Tello.

" First we found the tower (kash), and we dug around it till we found the door. Then we dug room by room, and emptied it, and at the bottom we found the statues. In the middle of one room was a column of bricks, on the top was a cover-like brick. We removed it carefully, and the column was hollow, and inside of it were bronze figures each between two stones,—one stone green and one white,—in a niche upright. The green stones all had writing on them, while the white stones were uninscribed. There were many of them. The male figures were seated and holding a stick upright; the female figures were standing, with a sort of umbrella, or plate, over their heads. On shelves in the room were marble or gypsum figures A white inscribed stone was under each figure, and an inscribed green one beside it There were green ashes under the white stone. The tablets were found about a foot under the bottom of the room, and several barrels in the earth at the bottom of the room The tablets were longer than this segar case, the barrels a hand long We dug twice as deep as this room. (Perhaps fifteen or eighteen feet.)'

Among the places we heard of on the east side of the Shatt-el-Hai are Medine, Sereifeh, 'Abba, el-'Assam, el-Mahaneh, Abres. el-Sifr, Mansurie, Zerghul, and el-Hibba

Tuesday, February 3d. We were to go to Tello to-day, and our captain proposed to go with us. So he helped Noorian engage a meshhuf,—a long narrow boat of teakwood, pitched with bitumen, with a mast, but which is propelled, not with a sail, but by poling and rowing, or by towing. We poled up stream for a while, then one of our boatmen got out and towed. Then a boy put his load aboard, and pulled by a straw belt about his arms and body, the rope being tied to the top of the mast. We moved against the current at a fast walk It took us three hours to get opposite Tello, and there we got out and walked. It was over an hour's sharp, hot walking to the mounds.

The tel has two principal elevations, the larger one to the south, and the smaller one, of nearly equal height, to the north. The latter is the palace excavated by de Sarzec It has a court with rooms about it We collected fragments of cones, and photographed bricks, both impressed with a stamp and written. There were few tombs, and no flint knives or saws. We saw one or two of the large sunken burial jars, as at Aqarib, and some brick cists. The bricks are of various shapes, some very old, judging from the inscriptions; and some very late, with inscriptions in debased Greek letters

We delayed until an hour before sunset, and then hurried back, reaching the boat as it was getting dark. Our Turkish captain was worn out. Only Haynes, who was not feeling well, had taken an overcoat. We shivered all the way back, although I, who had carried the camera almost all the way back, was warmer. We pulled a rug over us, and the hours were long before we got home at nine o'clock. Then I sat up till nearly midnight reading, and trying to plan what we can do, as the water is rising, and we have so much yet before us. We are told that Zerghul alone will take four days, and I must do something on that side of the river

Wednesday, February 4th. This was substantially another wasted day. It is very difficult to get information how to reach Zerghul. Finally we decided to start to-morrow, and went over the photographic plates, and made the discovery that those taken with the cabinet camera are worthless. This necessitates a second trip to Tello

Thursday, February 5th. We left Shatra Khan at 7 55 for Zerghul,—Noorian, Mustafa, two zaptiehs, and myself. At 9 25 we had been taken across the river, making two trips on the boat, and the horses swimming. After going a little way along the north bank of the Bed'a affluent, we struck to the left towards a small tel, named Sase At 10 15 we struck a cluster of straw and mat villages on the Bed'a, all bearing the name of Hosein el-Sahel At 10.55 we left the village roads, and our course was about east. At 10 20 we turned to the left, to avoid Khor 'Umuka, a lake a mile or two wide, with waves. At 11 30 Tel Debbu was in front, long and low. At 11 40 we again struck the villages along Shatt el-Bed'a. At 12 00 we attempted to strike for Debbu, but failed on account of a deep stream, so went north along the left of a deep canal. At 12 20 we escaped the canal, and our course was near a lake to the right, several miles wide To the right and nearer, were Benet el-Me'ede and Debbu To the left were Ishare, 'Ewena, and a tree. At 11 15 we passed a small tel, with blue glazed pottery and glass. At 2 00 we reached Tel el-Hibba

Bearings from Tello · Tel Ehmera-rume, 97°, Abu Huraz, 32°, Abu Hawan, 353°; Mahayet, 348°; Abu-Tufra, 148°, Umm el-Ak, 275°; Shatra, 176°.

Bearings from Tel el-Hibba Zerghul, 118°, Benet el-Me'ede, 249°; Debbu is behind Benet el-Me'ede, Abu Te'ebe, 275°, Tel 'Awena, 302 $\frac{1}{2}$°; el-Zija, 353 $\frac{1}{2}$°, el-Afweize, 59$\frac{1}{4}$°, not very far off

This is surrounded by water on all sides, except the northeast. The mounds, a line of tels more than a mile long, run about north and south, with high elevations on the north end, on the Khor 'Awena. There is a pile of inscribed bricks at the top of the hill. There is a principal elevation, and others about it several hundred feet to the northeast. There is a brick platform here, and another to the north, which ought to be explored. The graveyard is to the south, with burial pots and three brick cists visible. We saw no flint knives, one old bone, shells, and pottery. We left Hibba at 2 50 and reached Zerghul at 4.45. Three minutes before reaching Zerghul we passed a little tel, el-Ru'bai, and observed glass on it.

Zerghul is a considerable tel, higher than Hibba, but not so large. It is formed of a line of hills, with a high and sharp elevation at one end, and another line toward the south end, running at right angles. It has a considerable ziggurat, and I fancied that I could see near the top the line of a platform. This is too steep for horses to be ridden up, and is visible from a good distance I found a few uninscribed cones to the south of the ziggurat, also a few fragments of inscribed cones. On the steep ziggurat itself are no particular remains On the second hill are pieces of bones. The graves seem to have been in cists, with cement covers ; and big pieces of cement are to be found. The smaller hill north of the ziggurat has graves, and I found there a piece of an inscribed cone. A great field of graves to the northwest has been explored by Arabs, and there are burial pots also to the west and to the southwest. No flint saws were picked up, and only two small inscribed bricks were found here, badly worn, like the ones found on the platform, and apparently like some found at Tello, probably put in a grave Afterward another brick was found, complete, with inscriptions in two columns, the left-hand side having seven single lines and one double

Bearings from Zerghul Shatra, about 275°, not visible ; Hibba (large), 299¼° ; Tel el-Ashareyat, 342° (seven hills, or more probably a part of Hibba), Tel el-Baira, 63⅜° (two or three times as far as Hibba), el-Tel, 98° (as far as Hibba), Tel Kubr es-Sheikh, 246⅛°, Khor el 'Amuka, to the south line, and the right-hand side having five lines, of which all but the fourth are double. Another brick was found, not stamped, but *written*, from the extremest northern hill. This also was archaic. There were on this fragment five lines, each an inch and a half wide.

Our trip to Zerghul was taken in pleasant weather. There were flocks of white cranes on the water, also storks and ravens to be seen in abundance. Men were digging canals, and going to and from their work, marching and singing. We had to make long detours to get about the canals. There is not one of them straight. The people cannot make a straight ditch or a straight furrow. There is nothing straight in the country except the British telegraph line. There is an immense waste of labor on the canals. As we approached Zerghul an Arab there said that he could not give us barley, although we mentioned an extravagant price. We then went half a mile beyond Zerghul to a sheikh's tent, and were well entertained He gave us pilaf in a big dish, with mutton, which he tore with his hands from the bone and passed to us. He would roll up a ball of pilaf and hand it to our people. Some milk was very acceptable. We all of us slept very cold, on a single rug, in our clothes. I had on my meshla, but it was an uncomfortable night for us all. Our host was hospitable, and provided us in the morning with more milk and a large loaf of rye bread, and went with us to Zerghul. On the hill I bought of an Arab a piece of a monstrous worn marble cylinder, which may have been the top of a staff, engraved in archaic style with bulls, and said to have been found on Zerghul.

Friday, February 6th We left Zerghul at 9 A.M. and reached Shatra in the evening.

Saturday, February 7th. Haynes, Noorian, and I visited Tello again for photographs. We were three and a half hours going, and a little less returning. We spent most of our time in taking photographs of the ruins, and of bricks. The main direction of the hills and buildings at Tello is southeast and northwest. The chief building is at the northwest end, and is made of bricks bearing the two-column stamped inscription It is twenty-three paces long, and nineteen wide, the width running southeast and northwest. There are several walls with bricks arranged in different ways, one with bricks wedge-shaped, in sectors of a circle. One of these bricks had a written cuneiform inscription

There must be in the chief palace several different ages, as some rooms have the bricks written, others stamped with a two-column inscription, and others with a bi-lingual inscription in a late Phœnician or Palmyrene character of four lines, with the name of Adadnadin. Some bricks had a written inscription in one large column, coarsely written, and somewhat variant I tried very hastily to copy the written ones, after Haynes had started and it was getting late, but depended on the cabinet photographs, which again failed us. There is a maze of rooms about the sides of the hall, which has very inconspicuous entrances. There are graves all about.

Monday, February 9th. Left Shatra at 8.30 for Nasrieh, otherwise called Merkez. All Shatra came together to see us off We went down the right bank of the Shatt-el-Hai. In a few minutes we left it and struck a course about south. The ground is perceptibly greener, and the prickly shrub shows young leaves. We tried to ford the Shatt-el-Ishbebe, but failed, the water being up to the top of the horses' backs. This Shatt starts from the el-Hai and goes to the Euphrates. We turned to the right and crossed Shatt-el-Ishbebe by boat at Detche, where was a company of Turkish soldiers, and where we took a soldier for guide. The crossing took an hour and a half. We started again at 1.25. At 1.40 we passed a small tel, Medineh, and picked up a cone From this tel we saw Tel Khadi, and Tel el-Milah (salt). At 3 15 we crossed the Shatt-el-Kesra, and recrossed it at 3 55

We reached Nasrieh as much as an hour after sunset, and sent Noorian ahead with a zaptieh to find a khan. They returned, reporting that there was none, and I told them to go directly to the Government House, which is the headquarters of a Mutessarif. He received us most hospitably, and supper and room were given us, while the men tethered the animals in the court and set up the tent

But while the men were at supper a soldier stole Mustafa's bag of clothes, with which were two liras, and a little Aintab money, which is uncurrent here, Luckily Mustafa is a Moslem. Noorian told him to tell the soldiers that if it was a joke the things had better be returned, as he did not want the Bey (meaning me) to complain to the Mutessarif. So Mustafa spoke to the kaffejee, and he to the commander of the soldiers, and the worthless things were returned during the night. Our beds were placed in a room adjoining the hall of audience, which had books and bags of paper in it. An excellent supper of six or eight courses was provided for us We made inquiries about tels. One Selman el-Hamid-el-Ghazawi, who seemed more intelligent than the rest, said that the largest of all the tels of the region is Tel Sifr ; that Abla is larger than Yokha, but not so high. He mentioned Assam Beniye, Medeien, or Medineh, Bedhr, Umm Gheyar (Mughair), Warka, Enfeje, and Jid (Ede). He said that Beniye is middle-sized, that Medeien has three hills, and is two days from Merkez. Enfeje is not large and is near Sifr is the largest, then Warka, and Medeien next. Umm Gheyar is of middle size.

Tuesday, February 10th. We spent the day in making inquiries and laying plans to visit Mughair and Abu-Shahrein. We planned to start the next morning for the two places, and also to go to Quseyr, if possible with horses. Noorian whispered to the Mutessarif, telling him about the stealing He is a young man lately come from Baghdad. He was evidently mortified and called the kaffejee and an officer, and gave orders, and had Mustafa inquired of, and we awaited the result. We moved our tent to a vacant lot we had hired on the bank of the Euphrates, and Haynes and Noorian made up their bed in a corner out of doors, under rubber blankets. In the night there came a thunder-storm, and while they were not much wet, their clothes under the bed were considerably wet. Meanwhile the water or the barley bread which we had been compelled to eat on the journey had affected me seriously. This bread, so much used among the Arabs, is made of meal which has been ground, or powdered, with the thin husk not removed, and it is harsh to the mouth, and must be irritating to the bowels.

Wednesday, February 11th. It has been a miserable, wet day, too wet to travel. Everybody was uncomfortable, and I kept in bed all day, trying to conquer my illness, as we are, and shall be, out of the reach of any physician. In the afternoon it cleared up, and we had our clothes and bedding hung out to dry. Mustafa has recovered nearly all his things, except the two liras. The uncurrent coin was returned. They found the soldier, who had got an excuse to go out with a bag under his clothes, and had him bastinadoed until he confessed, but he would not return the money, one lira of which had been entrusted to Mustafa to make purchases in Damascus.

Thursday, February 12th. Our tent is on the very bank of the Euphrates, which is visibly rising. The bank is, of course, used by every one as a water-closet, which must, as we have often observed in passing streams or rivers, be productive of disease. Near Zerghul, however, we observed the more sanitary practice required by the Mosaic law. The day was very pleasant, and we started by 9.45, and walked very slowly up the river. At 10 45 we were near a small tel, Kura, and another to the right of it. We crossed the Euphrates at 'Arjeh, and started again at 11 13 At 12 50 we turned to the south, and reached the tents of Sheikh Me'eide, of a Ma'dan tribe, about 1.20, where we stopped for the night. Along this trip my notes are very imperfect, as my illness weakened me so that I could hardly keep on my horse, and had to be helped to mount.

Friday, February 13th. Left camp at 7.30 Reached Mughair at 9 00. At Mughair we were not more than three hours from Abu-Shahrein, and I would have gone there if I had been well, but I did not dare run the risk. It was with some persuasion that we got permission from the Mutessarif at Nasrieh to go to Mughair, and he thought it necessary to send five of his soldiers with us, under a sergeant, and said that if we went beyond to Abu-Shahrein it must be alone and at our own risk, as the Arabs were not friendly. The sheikh with whom we stopped over-night was at first willing to introduce us to other Arabs who would take us to Abu-Shahrein, but the next morning he refused to do so, as the letter of the Mutessarif only gave us safe conduct to Mughair, and I had been obliged to give the Mutessarif a letter relieving him from responsibility if I went any farther. Still, I should have gone but for my sickness. I was unable to go about Mughair as I wanted to, and had to lie down most of the time, while Haynes and Noorian were taking photographs. I went all around the tel on my horse, and nearly over and around the chief elevation on foot, but could make no notes. The buttresses described by Taylor are still visible. One corner of the mound has been dug down, and a hole dug in the centre.

I left Mughair at 11.00, and rode direct for the 'Arjeh crossing, through the Khor where it was narrow, with thickets of high reeds, and with the water deep enough in places, I fear, to wet the photographic plates. Coming from behind the thick reeds into an open space several rods wide, we came upon a great black wild sow, with three well-grown pigs. She faced us without the least fear. I was following next to the Arab guide, and noticed that he swerved suddenly to the right into deeper water, before I saw the reason. We all passed Indian file, each looking back, and leaving the immense animal mistress of her watery fortress. We reached 'Arjeh, half an hour above Nasrieh, at 1.35, where we crossed.

Saturday, February 14th. Mustafa's money has not been recovered. The Mutessarif feels badly. He says that hospitality is part of his religion, and that it now seemed as if they had received us to rob us. We heard that he told the soldier who stole it that we would make Turkey not worth a para to other countries when we returned and reported it.

Crossing the Euphrates at 'Arjeh, we started up the river on the west side at 11.58. I have no notes of the journey, except of a mound named el-'Abid, named after a tribe, and that at 5.50 we stopped at an Arab village, and occupied the muthif of Hosein, of the el-'Abid tribe, on the bank of the Eu-

Bearings from Mughair Abu-Shahrein, 211½°, Salahieh, 188½°; Nasrieh Minaret, 56½°, es-Saheri, 298¾°

phrates. Our Arab guide would not eat our food, and our soldier, Abbas, whom we had brought all the way from Hillah, abused him generally, saying that he could not eat good bulghur with butter, but would wait for bad bulghur without butter, made by Arabs. My health has improved somewhat.

Sunday, February 15th. On the beautiful Euphrates. There are many watering machines, and we find barley a foot high and can get green fodder for our animals, but no barley in the grain, and it seemed necessary to reach Samawa to-day. So we started at 6 40. We skirted the river for two hours, and then struck out over the level ground away from the river. At 4 52 we came to a considerable tel, called Abu-Berdi. We were very sorry to travel on Sunday, but we had little but green fodder for the animals, which were on short allowance of barley. Our animals were not well fed during all the past week. The Arabs encamped at Mughair, I am told, declared that they had nothing for the horses, but the soldiers threatened, and got their guns, when they yielded and supplied rice for the horses. It has been a most lovely day, and we have followed no path, and there has been little water to trouble us There have been patches of cultivated ground back of the Ma'dan villages, which dot the bank every mile or two, with their green patches of barley, and their fresh mud castles, square, with a little round tower at each corner Soon we left them to the right and struck out into the level, alluvial wilderness, a very rich soil, sandy enough to be rather light, and admirable for cultivation, with scarce a weed or plant upon it except here and there a crucifer, which makes a salad something like peppergrass, but not so clean-tasting. The horses' hoofs sank into the ground, which was thickly crusted by the drying rain, and this made it hard for the horses. Opposite Darajaan the guide said his orders were to go there. We told him that we had no business on the other side of the Euphrates and would not go there, but were going to Samawa. He yielded on our promising him a paper certifying our refusal. Then he wanted to go to el-Kudhr, said to be four hours from Samawa, and as it was two o'clock we would have yielded,

Bearing from Abu-Berdi Nowawis (a pointed tel), 191°.

but it was also across the river It grew dark and no Samawa (the word means Heaven) appeared About eight o'clock we struck a little Arab encampment, the dogs being our guide, and we were told that Samawa was half an hour off. We started off very much encouraged, but still Samawa seemed to recede. Never did heaven seem so far off At last, about ten o'clock, our guide told us that Samawa was too far off to reach it, and that we must stop at an Arab encampment near by. But had they barley? Certainly, said he. So we went there, woke up the dogs and finally the men, and settled ourselves. There was straw but no barley, and it was well after ten when we reached there. We set up our tent, got food, and our good soldier, Abbas, quarrelled frightfully, but unsuccessfully, for barley. The men were not very helpful at first, but thawed a little, and we got some half-cooked bulghur, not fit to eat; no chickens or eggs

Monday, February 16th The morning was pleasant, and Samawa in sight scarce half an hour distant. We had turned from it for this nearer encampment We actually got milk for breakfast, and I trust that I am none the worse for the hard day But I fear the horses are badly used up. We would not have made such a long day's march, but it was impossible to get information These Arabs do not know an hour from a day I asked "how many hours?" and they answered, "Just beyond," with a gesture There are no roads, no travel, no maps, nothing to calculate on.

We started leisurely, and came in less than an hour to Samawa, a town with mud walls, on both sides of the Euphrates, with a bridge of boats across. Samawa is not on the Ateshan, as our maps say We crossed to the east side of the Euphrates, which is here a narrow, very swift river. We found our horses in a sort of khan, a dirty yard with a shed for the horses, and we had to set up our tent. Scarcely had we done so before we had a call from a resident German, Dr. Blau, who introduced himself He had heard through the papers of our expedition, and was much interested to learn of us Soon it appeared that he had made a valuable collection of Babylonian antiquities, and I then guessed that he was Dr.

A Blau, who had written on Arab ethnology for the Z. D. M G. He acknowledged it, and was a great comfort to us while we were in Samawa. He had been a surgeon in the Turkish service but was now engaged in trade.

The Kaimakam sent for Abbas to know where he came from. When he learned that he was from Hillah and had not gone back to his command, he stormed and threatened him with six months in prison as a deserter, and to telegraph to Hillah ; and sent him back to us under guard for further information. We were absent, but our men blustered, said we had firmans from Stamboul and Baghdad, and told Abbas not to be afraid. Meanwhile an officer was sent to inquire about us. By this time we had returned and Dr. Blau with us, and he explained things and went with us to call upon the Kaimakam. He was very polite, and quietly dropped the matter about Abbas. I then went with Dr. Blau to his shop, and while seated on his bales of cotton a messenger came to say that the Kaimakam would call on us. I went back and we received him all serene. Dr. Blau deals in cloths, wool, leather, etc., which he buys in Busrah ; but gives his attention largely to the collection of antiquities. He showed me his collection of some costly cylinders and other valuable objects. He would not sell any, but intends in two years to return to Germany and dispose of them there.

Tuesday, February 17th It rained and we were obliged to lose another day. I took wax impressions of Dr. Blau's seals.

Wednesday, February 18th. Left Samawa gate on the west side at 8.05 for el-Khudhr We went back on the Shamieh road about four and a half hours. There we crossed the Euphrates in a meshkuf opposite el-Khudhr, where we slept in the muthif. A very disagreeable night, cold, wet, and hungry

Thursday, February 19th We left el-Khudhr at 7 30 for Warka, about three hours from the river. We were accompanied by the Vice-Mudir and a dozen of his men There are flint knives everywhere. The elevation Bouwarieh is of

Bearings from Warka , El-Jid, 22 ¾° , Senkereh, 100° to 104 ½° ; Hammam ?, 33° (very small) , el-Raheye, 83 ½° , Daraje, say 154°? ; El Khudhr, 210.°

unburned brick, with occasional layers of reed Wuswas is a crater-shaped elevation of bricks about a slight earthy depression. We left Warka without our escort, and crossed the Euphrates at another place by boat, returning the same night to Samawa. It was very late and the gates were closed, and we could not get them open, but our zaptieh led us along to a place where the wall was low and insecure, and there he kicked away the mud, and we thus broke our way into the city and to our tent.

Friday, February 20th. We left Samawa at 10.47, going along the east side of the river. At 12 30 we struck a ferry across the Shatt-el-Behar, which seems more a lake than a canal, being long and wide. It took us not less than two hours to cross. At six o'clock we came to a Turkish garrison at Hurumati, on the Euphrates, where there were probably fifty soldiers. We passed by and at 7 o'clock reached the comfortable village of Sheikh Ferhud, where we were very handsomely treated, and entertained in the finest reed mat muthif we have yet seen.

Saturday, February 21st. We left Ferhud at 7 05. As we were on horseback, ready to start, Sheikh Ferhud and his wife brought us their only child, about a year old, emaciated, flea-bitten, and evidently sick, and told me (they had probably heard me called "Doctor") that all their other children had died, and that they wanted me to give this child some medicine so that it should not die. Sheikh Ferhud had been so kind that I could not disappoint them, so I made a harmless preparation and gave it Then he wanted me to spit on the child, apparently to avert the evil eye. We rode along the east side of the river all day, but there was nothing of interest and no tels. The land was all uncultivated, but amazingly rich. We reached Diwanieh about sunset, crossing the bridge of boats, and went to a khan.

Monday, February 23d We left at 7 05 and made eight hours to Jasm, a small village with a considerable ziaret, and a few Ma'dan Arabs. Our men had better quarters than we, as they were supposed to be good Moslems. But we, undisguised Christians, were comfortable enough. The country to-day has all been uncultivated and barren, and yet this is the site of the Garden of Eden, and is of unsurpassed fertility, and would be teeming with population if there were a good government. What a region for colonization!

Tuesday, February 24th. Rode five hours into Hillah, and to our old khan. We passed thousands of palm-trees the last two hours. Noorian went with the soldier, Abbas, to explain his long absence, but he did not see the officer in command. Our old friends, the merchants, came to see us and bring tablets, etc, for sale.

Wednesday, February 25th. Abbas's wife came to us and reported that he had been put in prison for his desertion. Noorian went and threatened and scolded the men, but the officer was in bed still He went again about noon, and succeeded in having Abbas released, with a proper apology to us. Abbas came to see us, radiantly grateful. Toward night, Dr. Sterrett, to whom we had telegraphed from Diwanieh, made his appearance, his health completely recovered, thanks to the excellent attention of Dr. Bowman, the British Residency surgeon, and was warmly welcomed.

Thursday, February 26th. Remained in Hillah, purchasing tablets, etc, and sent a load ahead to Mahmudieh.

Friday, February 27th. Although the day was rainy and windy, we left in the middle of the forenoon and started for Kerbela. We travelled by way of Mahawil, and thence up the river to Museyib, where is a bridge, and where we rested in a khan.

Saturday, February 28th A ride of nearly six hours took us to Kerbela, where we went to the new Khan Spellal.

Sunday, March 1st. The servants, Christians and all, went to the great mosque, under the guise of being Moslems. I walked about the city, saw the Mosque of Husein, with its gilded dome and minarets, and also that of Abbas. Kerbela is surrounded by miles of gardens and palms Plums and quinces are in bloom. There are flowers by the roadside, one perhaps a geranium, and one like a rayless *Maruta cotula*. From this time I took pains to collect and press every plant that came into bloom, but when on reaching Homs, near the end of the journey I put the papers out to dry on the roof of the khan, every one of them was stolen and my whole collection lost.

Monday, March 2d. We left Kerbela, returning to Museyib, where we crossed the Euphrates on a bridge. That night we slept in the Khan el-Qadm, built as an act of piety for the comfort of pilgrims.

Tuesday, March 3d. While the caravan went its way to Baghdad, Noorian, a zaptieh, and myself started at 8 30 for Tel Ibrahim, the ancient Cutha. We could get no guide and I directed the course by compass. We reached Tel Ibrahim at 2 00 P.M, and spent an hour there. I took no bearings, having no guide, and our zaptieth was entirely ignorant of the region. The hill was not visible until we came within two hours of it, being concealed by mounds and sand hills, and being low. We could see it from the hills only. It is shaped like an amphitheatre, the open side being occupied by two hills, one of them with a ziggurat Perhaps a river or a canal ran along the wider edge. I looked carefully to see what excavations had been made. Of the dozen places that showed signs of digging, none were of importance, and none had apparently been successful in finding any constructions. In one place a brick wall was found below the general level of the digging, but it was not followed far enough to show what it was I saw some more brick work not excavated. The hill, where opened, seemed to be of sun-dried bricks. In one place a tunnel had been dug in for some twenty feet, and at the end a cross tunnel appeared to run at right angles to it; but as there was a part of a fresh carcass of a lamb by the entrance, and there were tracks of animals about, and the zaptieh said "arslan," lion, I did not venture quite as far as the cross tunnel, fearing to meet a hyena, or possibly lions The tel is large, and substantially unexplored; at least the slight excavations have afforded no clue to the system of construction. It is very much washed by rain and gullied, is low, and shows no sign of any ziggurat. I suppose that it should be dug into at a lower level, both in the hills and at their foot. A broad, deep well has tempted and occupied most of the labor, but I do not believe anything was found in the well. No flint was seen, and comparatively few signs of graves, except blue pottery, but it was not an ancient cemetery. We struck back, still by compass, across the dry Jezireh, with no water and few plants, for Khan Iskanderieh. Leaving Ibrahim at 3 00, we reached Iskanderieh at 6 50, where the loads with Sterrett and Haynes had preceded us. This is the most enormous khan we have seen, a triple one, and we have a magnificent room over a gate, where we put up our four beds four feet apart, and have plenty of room.

Wednesday, March 4th Left Khan Iskanderieh at 8 10. While the caravan went to Mahmudieh, Sterrett, Noorian, a soldier, and myself went by another route to visit Abu Habba. We reached Tel Kubr Faras ("horse grave"), an uninteresting mound. at 11 30. At 10 40, we passed Tel Hushm-edh-Dhib ("angry wolf"), and at 10 55 another tel, a mile to the right, said to have the same name. At 11 10 we passed a small tel, Jowab Hababi.

I spent two hours walking nearly all about the walls of Abu Habba, and over the ruins. I find it difficult to get a clear idea of the shape. It consists of a walled enclosure, of which the ruins occupy the middle third, more or less, while the other portions are unoccupied. I walked along the whole of the north, east, and south walls. I judge the width along the north wall to be about seven hundred yards I find that the excavations are chiefly about the southwest corner, and large spaces are yet undug. The same evening we reached Mahmudieh, and joined the rest of the party.

Thursday, March 5th. Noorian and I started early, in advance of the rest of the party, and in two hours reached Baghdad, in order to secure quarters.

Wednesday, March 11th. After a fortnight spent in Baghdad preparing for departure, we left the city at about 11 00 A. M., for 'Akerkuf. We had asked Consul Plowden to secure us a zaptieh, and he had sent his dragoman, but when we were ready to start no zaptieh had appeared. I left word for the zaptieh to follow us to 'Akerkuf On our way out several officers who seemed to be in waiting for us demanded our teskereh, which, after some delay, we showed on the bridge. We went on without a guide, and in three hours reached an encampment of Arabs, Beni Temim, near 'Akerkuf, and put up our tent.

Thursday, March 19th We had breakfast soon after sunrise, and then Sterrett, Haynes, and I walked over a mile to 'Akerkuf. There had been a hard frost, and we waded through herbage and barley, which had grown wonderfully, and with no signs of irrigation. The dock, melilotus, mallows, and geraniums were up to our knees, then to our middle, and we got thoroughly wet. The barley was up to our belts. 'Akerkuf looks 70 to 100 feet high. The top is quite inaccessible on all sides. On the top are nests of birds. On the northwest side is a deep recess half-way up, like an arched window. On the north corner is a projection like a very steep flight of stairs. The ordinary small holes pass through the construction, and there are the layers of reeds, that seem characteristic of late work, to every six to nine layers of bricks. No burnt brick is visible. It might be well to visit the top and recess. There are some small remains and ruins to the southeast, with two little excavations. The city could not have amounted to much. On our way to 'Akerkuf yesterday we saw a lion, not three hours from Baghdad, but too far off for a shot to reach it, as it trotted off slowly. Two holes in the bottom of the ruin of 'Akerkuf are the lairs of wild beasts, and we saw their tracks and quantities of bones about.

We left 'Akerkuf at 10.00, intending to make a short day on account of the animals But there was no place to stop short of Sakhlawieh, on the Euphrates, which we reached at 6 30 We passed a "station," with a little tent, and a dozen zaptiehs. Probably their regular quarters were at a square enclosure, khan, or mud fort, a mile or more off The land about now began to show signs of gravel, and gradually of larger pebbles, and finally a line of hills, marked with occasional outcroppings of gypsum The plants were a marigold, *Maruta cotula*, or something like it; twó yellow mayweeds (one rayless), some fleshy caryophyllaceæ, several cruciferæ, and a little weed like a polygonum, which covers large patches with a close carpet of pink   We found Sakhlawieh to be a mud village and a mudirlik

Friday, March 20th   Walked over to Sefeira. I had been very anxious to see Sefeira, hoping that it might preserve the name of Sippara. We crossed the Sakhlawieh Canal to go to Sefeira. It winds about and has a deep bed, but the water is shallow. The mound shows no signs of duality, such as is implied in the name Sepharvaim   The canal is on one side of it. It is not an impressive mound, low, 250 yards across, with Arab graves and no elevations, many pebbles, and a little pottery and glass. It was not worth photographing. A soldier rode up and asked us our business

In the afternoon Sterrett and I walked over to 'Anbar, which we had not found on our modern maps, and which the Mudir told us was much bigger than Sefeira, and so, indeed, we found it. It is three miles down the river and is a huge mound, larger by much than Abu Habba, and may be the Sippara of Anunit. It consists of a principal, or older city entirely surrounded by high walls, thirty to fifty feet high, the city on a level with the top of the walls. To the east of this city and wall is another city on a lower level, separated from the first by what seems to have been a canal or moat. The wall, or bank, on the east side is not always marked, but on the west side it is a marked feature. The west city is of irregular height and construction, and there are in it two large courts on a much lower level than the rest, of irregular shape, and surrounded by high walls, as if they were the open enclosures of great temples or palaces. Over a considerable portion the ground is covered very thickly with pieces of burnt brick, also considerable pottery and glass   No inscribed bricks were seen or reported. On a vertical side of what looked like a gate of the old city, on the east side, I saw a floor of brick laid in mortar above and below it. The eastern city is large, but on a lower level. At the eastern extremity was a space about 200 yards square, surrounded by walls of sun-dried bricks, and with a building projecting into the middle from the western side. A large bay runs in at the north, between the two cities, almost surrounded by walls   The two cities can hardly be less than a mile long. On the south side is an Arab village, and on the west a ziaret, but the mound has not been used much for burials. The western side seems to be irregular. There were several little outlying tels to the south or southwest. The walls were especially high on the north side, and on the northwest corner, and show, apparently, black ashes, etc., not much slag. We were told that brick was brought from here to Sakhlawieh.

In the afternoon we called on a Turkish doctor. He had an odd lot of broken bottles and medicine. He invited us to see his old stones, chiefly worn pebbles. He had one bead, and said that it was excellent to burn with a preparation and apply for diseases of the eye. He showed us with great satisfaction his mouse-eaten parchment diploma, in a tin box. He had studied medicine for fifteen years with a doctor, and when he was declared a skilled practitioner he received this diploma signed with about forty seals of government officials.

Saturday, March 21st. We crossed the Euphrates at 9 30. At 9.48 we crossed a canal, Nahal Mahlasieh, in a boat which reached half-way across it. This is a swift effluent of the Euphrates. The boat was one of the high, double-prowed kind. A couple of poles are stuck in the ground, one each side of the canal, and a slack rope runs from one to the other; and two men pull the boat along the rope, while the helmsman minds the stern end of the boat. It takes but half a minute to get a load across. At 10 01 we were all across. The road goes along the low alluvium, just below the bluff, a light loam, with a thin vegetation. At 2 22 we entered a broad valley, or plain, and the bluffs receded or disappeared. We reached Ramadieh at 4.15 and put up at the khan. It has a large public coffee-room, and a number of people stay here all day, and I hear them all night. The custom is, I believe, to pay for coffee and narghileh by the week. At Shatra the charge was half a Persian kran per week.

Sunday, March 22d. Slightly rainy, and rain is much needed. The frost has burned the figs, melilot, etc, farther south. We called on the Kaimakam, an intelligent man, who told us of a stone, perhaps Hittite, at Bazarjik. He is from Aleppo. He promised us a zaptieh. In front of the coffee-room there was a crowd and a fight. The man attacked was thrown down, and cried out convulsively to Noorian for help, saying that he would be a Christian if Noorian would help him, that the Christians have more mercy than Moslems Noorian had a whip in his hand and he went to the man's help, talking only in Turkish, as if he were an officer, and threatening to put the man in prison who made the attack, and who was actually trying to kill his victim with a knife. And yet the two were brothers-in-law. The man got up bleeding, but we did not hear of his becoming a Christian

Monday, March 23d We were compelled to remain here on account of the rain.

Tuesday, March 24th. Left at 7.25 A. M The village seems to have about two hundred houses, and is about a dozen years old. We passed by a young garden and crossed a miserable bridge and canal full of water. At 8.10 a narrow spur of hills approached to within about half a mile of the river. The general line of hills is low and two miles from the river. At 10.10 crossed a spur of hills. The last half, or more, of the road the foot-hills were close to the river, but very low. We reached Hit at 4 P. M. Found a half-ruined khan of charity, but put up our tent. Went immediately with Sterrett to see some furnaces of bitumen which we passed just before entering the town. The town is built on a hill, and of houses with good walls. The furnaces are used to melt the bitumen to pitch the boats in the shipyard The boats are oblong, with square vertical ends and sides, or slightly inclined inward ; thirty feet long, or more, and five feet high. There were also some of the small tub-shaped coracles These large boats are made by first tying together a flat bottom of grass or straw, which is covered with bitumen. This is then tied with bulrush strings to the bottom of the framework of the boat The framework of the boat is made of small branches, or roots, two inches thick, at the biggest, which are tied together at the ends with these strings, and the side pieces, the ribs of the boat, fastened to the bottom pieces by being set in tenons, as well as with strings and pitch. The joints are caulked with pitch. Then a layer of thick grass carpet is tied on outside, and this pitched all over on the outside, and rolled on. The hot pitch is prepared in furnaces close by. The furnace has three basins in which the pitch is melted and mixed with sand. A flue runs under the basins and has a chimney about two feet high. The fuel is plastic pitch, floating in water. Balls of it are picked up, torn apart with the hand, like molasses candy, and thrown into the fire, the water preventing it from sticking to the hand. The cords used to tie the parts of the boat, the sticks, and the grass, or reed stuff, together are very small, like twine, but the bulrush is very tough. After the frame of the boat is up they put across it the frame of a deck, and work on a gunwale, tied and pitched on. Everything is very primitive, a regular ark-yard. A boat costs five liras, very cheap. They are real arks, much like a canal boat, and are used only to float on the stream. Two full layers of bitumen are put on the outside, one full layer on the inside.

We met many flowers to-day, iris, a poppy-like red flower, a leguminous flower with bladder pods and spines; no blue flowers.

Wednesday, March 25th. We saw the workmen bring the bitumen from the springs in wet, sanded baskets, on the backs of donkeys. As we left Hit, Noorian, the zaptieh, and I galloped off the road ten minutes to the left, to see the bitumen springs. We crossed a clear, salt stream, and followed it up to a little hill In that hill, among the foot-hills, were two principal springs where the bitumen is obtained One was a fountain of warm, salt water, with bitumen rising to the top and floating in considerable masses, but not very abundantly This spring was less than twenty feet across. The other was in a depression a few yards away, and was a spring of cold water, boiling up a foot or so, apparently from the escape of gas, and I was warned that the air here was bad. This was said to produce the best bitumen. It is thick, stiff, moulded by the fingers, and carried in baskets. The amount seems small for the chief industry of the town. The water was very salt; and where the current was slow, and the stream wide, a flake of salty matter formed and floated on it. The salt stream seemed quite salt and pure

We left Hit at 8 30. At 9 45 we crossed a rather copious stream of salt water The road followed for some hours a fringe of cultivated fields, and then passed over the low line of gypsum hills which came close to the river. Occasionally there was a narrow line of vegetation. Reached the island of Jibbah at 4 40. There was a great flood more than forty years ago, lasting but one day, which swept all the houses off the island, and extended over the lower shelf of the foot-hills. An old man remembered it. The island is surrounded by a wall. The rock here shows bivalve shells. We encamped by the miserable khan opposite Jibbah and sent to the island for provisions, which made supper very late. Jibbah is the seat of a Mudir.

Thursday, March 26th. Another beautiful day. We left at 8 05, going back from the river to escape a big bend. The rocks and bridges are black with small grasshoppers, which we have observed for two days At 10 30 we reached the river again. We observed inhabited caves We left the river at 11 30 by a beautiful little island called Alus, and a little ruined castle. At 2 35 we reached Haditha and put up at a comfortable khan opposite the island I walked up on the hill and found caves in the soft limestone, and the hill honeycombed with rude old graves, in lines or rows, at all angles.

Friday, March 27th. In the morning I hired one of the boats to cross to the island with Noorian. It was a square-prowed boat, with two rude oars Just as we crossed, the morning ferry-boat was coming from the island. It was a pointed, high-prowed boat, and was crowded full of people, and low in the water, and was guided with skill through the swift current. Our boat was drawn far up the stream before starting. A woman pushed with an oar, while a man pulled. There is a wall nearly around the island, which is wholly occupied by houses, with very small plots of ground high-walled. The houses do not have the back protected against floods, but we often saw doors opening up-stream. The town has four mosques ; we visited three of them, one a mere rude room, the other two with steps for the reader, and some architectural pretensions inside That at the south end is long and very narrow, with heavy arches It formerly had a minaret, and we saw its foundations, but we were told that it had fallen perhaps a hundred years before The most interesting sight was a grist-mill. We saw women spinning, and people fluffing up cotton with a bow-string The island looks beautiful and cheerful. It has no school, but a mollah teaches the boys to read. No grasshoppers, such as we saw yesterday and day before, making the ground black, but very small ones which gather on rocks and promontories, when it is the least bit cool I am told that each water-wheel pays 12 okes of grain yearly for the support of the ferry

We left Haditha at 9 00, half an hour after the packs, and followed the river all the way, mostly on the lower shelf Near Haditha the alluvial valley was towards a mile wide, and there were water-wheels, sometimes four to one aqueduct, oftener two or three. It was an easy road Reached Fehemiah at 1.30. It is a mere soldier's station, or khan, a square enclosure, but so dirty that we set up our tent outside A long, low, uncultivated island lies near the shore No barley was to be had here, and we had brought barley with us ; but a family was living in the khan, and we got milk and yaort. Again we heard of the great flood of forty or fifty years ago. The water rises generally only some five or six feet higher than at present, and does not reach the level of the alluvial plain ; but in that high-water year it rose all over the alluvial plain, up to the first shelf of the rocks The people from the island below, which we are told has 400 houses, had to encamp on the hill, watching against their foes, the Anazeh Arabs, and they had only black, unground grain to eat. The flood lasted only one day and then retired, but it ruined the houses on the island. We saw ruins said to date from that flood. Our road to-day has been easy, for an hour or so in the bottom, then over white stone and earth with scanty herbage, irises and fringed hyacinths, and yellow and white tansy and other composites, including *Maruta cotula*, also catch-fly. I found forget-me-not, a fumariaceous plant, a woody asparagus, yellow star grass, matrimony vine (*Lycium barbarum*), poppies, marigolds, yellow daisies, yellow achillea, and plants like Lithospermum and Spergula.

Saturday, March 28th. After an uncomfortable night in the rain, we started at 9 25, after a full hour's detention caused by the vicious grizzly mule going out of the track in crossing the water, stumbling in the water, and losing his load of photographic and archæological boxes in the water The men got horribly muddy, and the boxes covered with mud, we hope not wet inside The rock is limestone, underlaid by a pebbly conglomerate. Uninteresting flowers, —no violets, anemones, roses, columbines, but humble pinks. At 1.50 we reached the first palm-trees and gardens of 'Anah, and arrived at the serai at 3 00, but there were so many soldiers that we pitched our tents just beyond under some palm-trees, but with no shelter for the men from the threatening weather. Apparently the people are suffering from oppression and are cowed. The women appeared with uncovered faces. We broke down a piece of the mud wall to make room to pitch our single tent. A crowd of soldiers came to see and help We received a call from the Kaimakam, a decent and honest-looking man. We tried to return it, but found that he had gone with soldiers and people to kill locusts. They drive them into ditches and cover them over.

Sunday, March 29th. Remained in camp and visited the town. There is a series of islands in the stream, a long one to the south, with ruins of houses, and a mosque with a curious series of windows in the minaret, which looks more like a tower. There is what looks like the remains of a bridge in the river, this side of the island, but it is probably the remains of an aqueduct, with a long series of water-wheels. It was a great work. The great flood destroyed the houses on the island. There are eight islands and many people live there. The flood is said to have destroyed also the houses on the river side of the main street of the town, but not on the desert side. It lasted one day. There are at 'Anah a thousand houses and from 300 to 400 soldiers, more than there used to be. We saw one boat painted white. There are very few shops at the northern end of the long single street. There are said to be from fifty to one hundred houses of Jews on the island. They are silversmiths, and have no shops, but sell things in their houses. They have two synagogues.

The great business of 'Anah is making cloth for abbas. There are said to be four thousand made in a year, worth from a lira down to twenty piastres. All the men use the spindle, and work everywhere in the street. I bought a spindle of a man for twenty paras. The women use the wheel for cotton, buying the thread at Baghdad. We visited two factories, where the heavy looms were set out under the palm-trees One had five and the other two looms. They use four shuttles to get one even color with the red-brown wool. They put in strips of white. The cloth is very strong. The weaving was done by women. One wore a wooden thimble with a wooden point to put the thread back so that it would not draw. We also visited a grist-mill, which has two wheels for grinding grain, and two for irrigation. There are nine millstones in the island, made of the black vesicular tufa, so commonly used for the smaller stones, of pieces ironed and bound together with skill. The water-wheels are of about fifteen feet radius, and the mill wheels of about nine feet. The spokes of the irrigation wheels have to be joined with wooden pins. On the wheels are floats of palm-leaf stems The aqueducts are beautifully covered with small ferns (Adiantum, if I remember, the specimens being lost at Homs), the first of any sort we had seen for months. The soldiers here seem to do some valuable service, and they report the native Arabs to be "bad," which I doubt, as they seemed diligent and quiet. The people do not know about burning locusts. They go out on the hills to drive them when small into deep ditches, and bury them. Otherwise they would, when larger, destroy palms and everything else. I saw a man knitting a stocking with hooked needles No antiquities were offered for sale, and none said to be found. A whole sheep, without the fat tail, pot-roasted in a huge copper pot, furnished our servants and ourselves with an unusual and welcome Sunday feast.

Monday, March 30th. A beautiful, cool morning. Left

camp at 7.56, attended by a gray-haired zaptieh, carrying food and barley for the camp to-night at Nahia. The long street goes up over aqueducts, past flourishing olive-trees. Saw two kinds of unfamiliar pink flowers on the rocks above the town. Good red-oak wood is brought from ed-Dhor, two or three days distant. The low, beautiful iris breaks into bloom almost exactly at noon. Reached the gate of 'Anah at 8 30, with steep limestone cliffs on the left, and walled gardens on the right. Near by was a cave for sheep. At 8 40 passed a large station on the hill across the river, built twenty years ago and never used. At 8 41, end of the valley, garden, and trees. A finely built square castle, or station, on the inner bend of the river. Turkish garrison. At 9 00, village of Rawa across the river. Reached the khan, or station, Nahia at 3 05 It is a comfortable place with three passable rooms over the gate. A man swept two of these out with a whisk of brush wood, and I swept one after him with the broom, then made my bed and went after plants and seeds.

Tuesday, March 31st. Left Nahia at 7.13. Reached el-Kaim at 2 50. On arriving at the station, I went to see the ruin It is from this that they call it el-Kaim ("the standing"). It is a hill formed by a shelf of harder rock making a butte. On one of the summits, separated by gullies, is a *standing* ruin of a tower, forty feet high, and nearly ten feet by eighteen at the base. A flight of steps wound around it for two thirds of the height, where it is divided, probably by the falling of what was an arch, into two walls. Some eight feet above the base a sarcophagus is worked into the coarse mortar rubble. It is four feet high and two wide, open at the end. People have dug about it for treasure. The wall on the northeast side has on the face projecting half columns. The winding stairs make the bottom larger. There is no pottery or sign of other antiquities on the hills. As I turned around the hill I saw a man on horseback on the west hill. He was not a robber, but a soldier sent to see that I was safe. It was cloudy all day, with occasional sprinkles threatening rain. El-Kaim is a mere station ; a khan and a house or two for the Mudir,—no tents, no milk.

Wednesday, April 1st   Left el-Kaim at 8 20. At 9 30 reached the great ruins of Sheikh Jaber, or Jabrieh. In the distance Jabrieh looked like seven artificial hills or buildings, in a row, two or three entirely broken down   As Sterrett and I rode up we found them to be parts of a long wall of a city.   They were most remarkable, as being the first I had seen of old brick walls standing partly upright.   I rode around the walls, while Sterrett took a rude measurement of the length.   The wall on the river side is hardly distinguishable, except as it joins with the corner hill. The wall is highest on the desert side, and there the bricks remain in part in perpendicular position.   The bricks are very large, thirteen inches square and six thick. There is on the northwest end a second wall, and at the corner a large tel, forty feet high or more, and 150 yards square, partly covered with Arab graves, covered with stone, partly alabaster, and some bricks, and a stick at each end of the graves, so that from a distance it looks like a military fortress   The top is gullied and shows some slight traces of walls, perhaps not very ancient, made of stone masonry.   Within the walls were remains of buildings, but very little pottery. Outside the wall, towards the desert, was a moat, and a low wall outside of it. Below the tel was a ruined building of brick masonry. Great masses were broken down, ten feet high. In the river wall was a gate with the alabaster stones yet in position   These stones do not rise more than a foot high.

The caravan had gone on, and Sterrett, Noorian, and I followed, reaching Abu-Kemal about two o'clock. The ride to-day was most interesting   The forage is better, the valley wider, not much cultivated, but near Abu-Kemal are good fields. The bushes are larger and more abundant, almost like trees, with great trunks and abundant branches, making a clump of matrimony vine or tamarisk. The soil often seems to hold water well, and the trees form big hillocks about them, sometimes making real hills ten feet high, as in the valley of the Wadi Ali. Our zaptieh was deaf and stupid, and we were separated from him most of the day, and learned little of the wadis. The valley has widened out as we travelled, and Jabrieh may have commanded a considerable extent of country, probably reaching into the interior on the Syrian side. To-day we saw a tribe of nomads on their travels, with separate flocks of lambs, kids, sheep, camels, donkeys, cows, and bulls, all loaded with tent stuff, matting, tent covers, poles, a donkey with a mill and stones, a woman carrying a young donkey with its head sticking out of a bag, a man balancing a sheep on a donkey, men carrying bare-legged and bare-bodied children before them on the saddle There were few horses, and women drove the donkeys. They stopped us and offered yaort to drink, and asked us for tobacco. At what I took for Wadi Ali was a square masonry building one eighth of a mile off, near the river, with sides inclined, buttress fashion, a ruin of some kind. The name of this is Suweih. Across the river, until the last half hour, has run a steep ledge, a high square declivity, certainly all the way from Jabrieh, and a stretch of small trees, close together, like willows The barley grows very strong, and I pulled up from the thick-growing grain one stool, produced by one grain, with eighteen stems that would produce heads, besides smaller ones. A sheikh in southern Babylonia told me " One grain produces a hundredfold "

Left Kemal at 8.55. Reached Tel Asheir at 9.57. Bricks a foot square, thin, no writing ; also broken bricks marked with cross lines. Asheir is scarcely a tel, it is so low. The Arabs have dug stones from it for their raising of water near by. There is a set of rooms, with two semi-circular projections in the front wall, looking like the foundations of a Byzantine church. A portion of another room and walls has been dug out nearer the river.

Left Asheir at 10.00, and at 10.30 reached Tel Harire. On a grave was a stone of black basalt, with a piece of the face polished, and ten inches of an ornamental feather pattern, fine cut, such as appears on some old Assyrian seal-cylinders. Tel Harire is said to be sand hills blown up. We first struck a square wall, small, evidently artificial. On the river side a wall ran off in a circular form and came around to a large hill of pebbles, pottery, alabaster walls, etc., with an Arab graveyard on the top, garnished with upright sticks or poles Harire was the site of a considerable city, but the hills with their gravel and pebbles seemed to be in part natural, as the plain is of fine clayey alluvium. Pottery is not very abundant. There were almost no bricks, but considerable alabaster. The walls did not go around to Medkuk, which is more than a mile away, and is chiefly a natural hill of gravel, a sort of island in the alluvium, apparently utilized, as if squared for a ziggurat, or defence, although the square sides were not very plain, and Sterrett doubted them. There were pottery, alabaster, etc, there, and large modern graves on the top. East-southeast from Medkuk is a large hill with graves, and beyond that is a moat running north-northwest, parallel with the farther side.

At 2.35 we reached Salahieh, a khan with tents about it The caravan had taken the direct road, and had been five and a half hours on the way. As soon as possible after reaching Salahieh I went to the top of the bluff. It goes off quite level with small stones. The face of the bluff is of layers of gypsum and clay In places it has tumbled down in enormous masses from the crumbling of the clay, and has rolled a great distance on the plain. From the bluff I saw Medkuk and Kan Kalessi, and returned to make inquiries I was told that the caravan load would not pass the latter, so I took Noorian and went to visit it. The distance was a mile and a half along the foot of the bluff, and then went up the ravine by the old city It consists of a long line of masonry fortifications, all of gypsum, running around two ravines, which themselves give a strong protection The walls follow the line of the ravines, and have square bastions It is an immense work. The wall on the Syrian side is thick and high, and strengthened with square towers, and the central gate is almost completely preserved. It is an arch, or succession of arches, with chambers over the gate, and its doors are one of them rectangular and the other pointed

Friday, April 3d. Left Salahieh at 6 18 Sterrett, Haynes, and I went to see and photograph Kan Kalessi. I went to

Bearings from Kan Kalessi Medkuk, 147½° ; Abu-Kemal, 146 °

the larger enclosure on the smaller hill. Inside were rooms about the walls The entrance was a round arch. I observed three round arches, two small doors with pointed top, and one castellated. As we came in to Meyadin we went to see Rehaba. It is a large mediæval castle, occupying an isolated hill left by the forkings of the mouth of a defile from the plateau. It is immensely strong. It has stone and brick foundations, and holes for arquebuses Behind the small front windows I found inside large pointed-arched recesses in a second wall. The inside is divided into spaces, and rooms, and substructures, and there are in the wall round holes for timber, and the ends of some beams are preserved There is a well inside sixty feet deep. Half-way down the well there seems to be a platform, perhaps connected with the substruction stones.

The valleys on our way were rich and wide The up-land exhibits flowers and thin grass and stones. English sparrows abound everywhere, such as we noticed at Eibil, clinging in multitudes to the inside vertical wall of the khan. There is an abundance of storks Saw one wild boar to-day, and abundance of signs of their rooting. The valley is wide here on the other side of the river. The ascent to Castle Rehaba is very difficult, and possible only in front The castle is full of towers, and re-entrant angles, and varieties of construction, and shows bricks laid in ornamental patterns Other buildings were not found, having been mostly removed to build Meyadin, which is more properly Meyadhin, meaning *scales* It has a little artificial hill Here we got accommodations in a clean, private house with an ample yard

Saturday, April 4th. Left Meyadhin at 8 00 The tops of the houses are used to store fuel, dung, and bushes, which makes them look as if they contained storks' nests A door of a mosque here is made of boards of the boxes which contain the large oil-cans, and is labelled very unecclesiastically, "Pratt's Radiant Oil, Guaranty Patent Can" The mosque had three pyramidal domes, and a yard with fig-trees 10 08 el-Buseira, and little Sle'a, and Tel Sheikh 'Isa well in sight 10.40 a little tel with pottery and bricks by the road. 10 52 another smaller, insignificant tel by the road, also one east of the road. At 10 40 Kara'at 'Asef ; 10 52 Abd-edh-Dhahar ; 11 00 Kariat Mohammed el 'Ssaf ; 11 45–12 00 a long line of hills a mile or two to the east, on this side of the river, called Ta'us el-Hubs ("sand heaps of the bread"?). They say there is no pottery there, but it looks artificial. At 12 20 another insignificant tel, just to the left of the road ; 12 30 long hill and ziaret Abu Nahud in the distance near the river ; 12 47 another similar tel to the right, and remains of a canal parallel to the road. Reached the city of Deir in 7 45 hours.

Sunday, April 5th Remained in the khan and took a walk across to the large cultivated island. Yesterday Noorian and I called on the Mutessarif He preferred to talk French, and was curt and sharp. To-day when Noorian went to engage zaptiehs he said that he could give us but two, and would not warrant our safety, also that we must not wear our suspicious white helmets, but should put on turbans I have given up my plan to go to the Khabor, and we start to-morrow for Palmyra

Monday, April 6th. Cloudy We had engaged three camels to carry water and barley to Sukhne, but later reports tell of plenty of water, and we have given up the camels and hired two horses at a mejid a day for the two to Damascus. Left Deir at 2.00. Took a farewell view of the Euphrates at 2 15 from the hill. Struck out southeast into the undulating plain There are flowers and sparse grass. A slight rain. Stopped at 3 58 by a little stream, Wadi Melha ("salty"). It is somewhat brackish. We saw some signs of petroleum. Wherever you dig you find brackish water.

Tuesday, April 7th. Started at 7.25, a threatening day. At 2 25 reached an old deserted station with a well and no inhabitants. At 1.50 we had begun to strike a series of ridge swells, with ledge faces. The station is by one of these ridges showing lime and white gypsum. Went to look for plants. Found the curious red and orange thistle head from which the people get the gum they chew to relieve thirst. I cut off one of these thistles near the ground, and waited a moment for the thick juice to gather, and put it in my mouth, and was surprised to find in a minute a piece of caoutchouc. The people clear away the earth about the root, cut it off five inches below the surface, and put a clean stone by the cut to catch the juice. A vigorous plant will produce a piece of two square inches, and nearly half an inch thick. The gum has a soluble, bitter element, which tastes like that in spruce gum. It is brittle, and when put in water the bitter element dissolves out, leaving what appears to be a sort of white rubber. Perhaps it might be profitably cultivated. The head is compound, composed of a number of heads, with a number of thick seeds about a central one. We met nearly a dozen donkeys loaded with sacks of truffles for the Deir market. They grow as large as a smallish potato, and are very tender and tasteless, and have no signs of attachment anywhere. They were brought from beyond Sukhne, and are found in the desert by searching for places where the ground is raised by the growing truffle. We bought some as an addition to our desert cuisine. The station bears the name of Bir Kabajub, or Kabakub. The walls of the inner rooms are all broken down. Besides the well there are some pools in the valley of the Wadi Kabajub up the stream, in a wide defile. The water is brackish.

Wednesday, April 8th. Left Kabajub at 5.55. After a few minutes we had the level plain. At 9.05 crossed the Daijeh hills; 9.25 reached the top of the plateau. The ground is generally light reddish, cultivable, not many stones, undulating, and occasional ledges crop out. We saw in the distance a longish mountain, Jebel Dhahak ("laughing"), the top white, almost like snow; also in the distance the separate hills, or high mountains, el-Menshar, two hours from Sukhne. Reached a pool, in a low piece of ground with hills to right and left, at 1.47. The pool is some twelve rods long, and is called Ebweb.

Thursday, April 9th. Yesterday we saw a plant consisting simply of a large crimson spadix, said to be a food plant; also met over a dozen donkeys with truffles. Started from Ebweb at 7 20. Rode through a broad valley; no stream or wadi; clayey; patches of pink vegetation, stock and the prostrate Polygonum—like the plant I had seen in Babylonia. In front is what I suppose to be Dhahak, with its white declivity. At 9 35 we reach the white cliffs, to the right of Dhahak. It looks like a white talus of clay below the reddish-white layers of limestone, but it is all a soft rock, clayish to the taste, and soft in the mouth, worn like clay. Stopped ten minutes to water the animals in a sink-hole, called 'Adi el-Zeir. Went up out of the basin, and over a long watershed, and started down into another fine basin, with flints. 12.00 conical white hill to left, and several smaller buttes; ground of white clay. Reached Sukhne at 1.00.

Just west of Sukhne, half a mile off, is the edge of a ridge of limestone, Sheikh Wasl, with two domes of a tomb on it. Thence the ridge ascends, and runs off E. N. E. to W. S. W., high, narrow, on both sides a clay plain. The long succession of white bluff cliffs to our right ended here in a succession of three. In front a line of hills crossed my view from southwest to where they were lost behind the jutting white cliffs in the northwest. A fine lot of new flowers on the hill, and petrified shells. Flint and chalcedony in masses on the top. I found the rock on top of the hill a calcareous conglomerate with small pebbles, sharks' teeth, and shells. The top of Sheikh Wasl is full of shell fossils, a hard limestone with much flint. Near the bottom of the hill comes out the white, clayey rock, which seems to be without fossils, and with considerable crystalline segregations, and here and there a thin layer running across vertically.

We went to see the springs to the southwest of the town, along the road to Tadmor. There are perhaps five or six of them, some warm and sulphurous. They have one for the men to bathe in, and one, with earth piled high about it, for the women. The business of the people of Sukhne is not agriculture, but they are catajis, doing the carrying trade to Aleppo, Damascus, Deir, etc. Twenty or thirty years ago there were 400 houses, but the Anazeh Arabs attacked them, and now there are but forty or fifty.

Friday, April 10th. Left el-Sukhne at 6.30. Stopped to see springs and bathe. 6 55 a solitary white hill to our left.

The nearer range of hills on the right begins here. It is lower, and of the undulating soft rock. The hills to the left are the same, and look like bluffs. At 9.45 another wide basin. Passed on the left the site of an old town,—said to be Kafrein,—a well, and a square cistern, the latter not in sight from the road. At 10.55 we had risen to the table-land. Two ridges of parallel hills to the right,—the nearer white, the farther irregular and higher. In front to the left, near, is a short line of isolated hills; and in the blue distance to the left a horizon of apparent hills. At 11.25 passed a ruined town two miles to the right, called Karas. We have risen higher to the level of the white rock, and immediately descend. At 11.38 a Roman milestone; 12.25 water in two holes on a high level, in thin gravel; 1.00 down a sharp pitch from the plateau.

Reached Erek at 1.30. Here a spring comes out of a hill and runs through a deep cut, largely artificial, partly covered with bridges of the upper layer of the natural rock. The water is good, slightly sulphurous. The stream is not copious. A few maiden-hair ferns grow in the deep cut. The stream empties into a small black pond, out of which several canals run, of which only one can run at a time. The fields are larger and better than at Sukhne, although there is much less water. They grow barley and a little wheat, and durra from the same fields in summer, with all sorts of vegetables. The Khaya gave me specimens of the durra, which is the tall millet, in foliage like the Indian corn, and in the head like broom-corn. He said there are twenty or thirty houses in Erek. There is beyond the spring a natural hill of white stone and clay, with old graves, and many artificial flint chips about it. No "antikas" in the town. I observed fragments of fluted columns.

Saturday, April 11th. Left Erek at 6.50, and immediately rose to a table-land. At 7.40 began to descend. At 7.52 a vast plain, limited by a line of low hills just visible on the left, with mountains in front and to the right; 7.55 a Roman milestone to the right, with a few letters visible on the under side; 9.00 a very little tel, with walls of a small, arched, mud-brick house, partly standing, and well; 9.20 a standing milestone with inscription:

D. N.
CONSTANTINO.

Also two fragments of another, of which one had the legible inscription :

D N
CONSTANTINO NOB
C. S
STRATA
DIOCLETIANA
A PALMYRA
ARACHA
VIII.

Sterrett and I spent some time galloping over the plain in search of other milestones Reached Tadmor soon after noon.

Remained in Tadmor from Saturday, April 11th, till Thursday A.M., April 16th. This time I devoted to search for Palmyrene inscriptions, while Sterrett worked over Greek inscriptions, and Haynes took photographs. I had hoped to leave Tuesday, but we had too much to do photographing and copying. We were all kept most busy, and had scarcely time to note the ruins. Not having made any study of the work of Waddington and others, all was new. Sterrett found two aqueducts coming from the hills. There are two good fountains, one near the town, which occupies the old walled Temple of the Sun, and the other, a copious warm spring, up by the hill. There is a hot bath by it, covered with a little dome, which I did not happen to see till just as we passed it, leaving Palmyra. I went all over the ruins and the tombs, looking for Palmyrene inscriptions, and on one occasion, when at the extreme edge of the place, visiting one of the fine, tall tombs, quite unarmed, I was threatened with a gun pointed at me by one of a party of Arabs going out into the desert. I spent most of my time over the octroi edict by the temple of Osiris, which it identifies, as it mentions that it is set up near this temple The man who found this magnificent inscription told me that the previous Mudir had put him in

See Vol III. of the *Papers of the American School of Classical Studies at Athens.* pp. 436-438.

prison for finding it, and would not let him out until his friends had paid 450 piastres. He wanted to know why he was finding things to show to strangers. We had him dig out the sand from before it. He said no traveller had seen and copied it, and we thought we had discovered a great treasure, and hastened to copy and translate it, but on reaching Damascus we learned from the French Consul that it had just been published, and our labor thus anticipated. The Mudir showed us some thirty Palmyrene heads, which he had piled up, mostly with Palmyrene inscriptions, generally in good condition, of which we took photographs. We took squeezes of this octroi inscription, but they were stolen from the stone before they were dry. This immense inscription is on a single slab of marble, and is on four panels, each of two columns, one Palmyrene and the other Greek. Unfortunately large portions are illegible, but the two columns supplement each other, and the whole gives a clear understanding of the source of the wealth of Palmyra, from the duties which every caravan and every traveller paid for the privilege of the fountain.

Some of the high tower tombs have a cave tomb connected with them. One tomb is of fine marble, mostly in good condition, with paintings on the carved ceiling The writing is often in red paint The tombs have great stone doors, generally broken to pieces. We saw one with the cross panels and wreaths, probably seven feet high, four wide, and one thick, with big dowel projections for sockets There are a number of these stone doors still in use, one is in the hole in the wall of the temple by which one goes to the Mudir's office, another opens to a garden The plan of everything would be easy to make out and reconstruct. The walls, as in the case of the temple of Osiris (Rabasira), were thrown outward by an earthquake, and lie there in their exact orderly arrangement. Across them a French explorer of note had left his name in large letters, quite in contrast to the minute penciled names of Messrs Irby and Mangles, which I was so fortunate as to find inconspicuously recorded with their date on a lintel in one of the tombs.

Thursday, April 16th. Left Palmyra at 8.50, and ascended the hills, past the high tombs, to the plateau, with chalk hills to the right, and ragged limestone hills to the left. At 10.00 we passed a number of wells called Abu Fuaris, two now in use, and at 10 45 an Arab camp. The soil is clayey, no stones, on the level of the chalk rock. At 11 35 the ragged line of high limestone hills, called Jebel Abyad, which we have had on our right for an hour, begins to fade into chalk; on the right are the high limestone hills, Jebel Hayin, both about two miles distant. We learn that the hills about Palmyra are el-Muntar to the right, to the left Umm Melkis. We are pointing due west to Jebel el-Teyas. 12.30 a Roman milestone with name of Antoninus. No time to work out the rest. Another soon after, in its regular place. About fifteen minutes later, another, the XIII. mile, also Antoninus; then another, the XVIII. 5.15 by the big range of mountains to the right which we had been aiming for all day. At 6.45 we reached water at Teyas, and a beautiful wide valley of white heavy soil, clayey, which holds good water. A magnificent vast extent of grass, knee high. We pitched our tent in the high grass, but nearer the head of the valley was a good place which we did not find in the dark. We found eight milestones during the day, four in position, three in order. They inform us that Antoninus Pius made the road, and mention Septimius Severus, and Marcus Aurelius. Several had the distances from Palmyra. The Roman road ran to the north of the big mountain we were aiming at, and we had to leave it We would not have struck it, perhaps, if we had not gone out of our regular caravan road, the guide being about to take us by a longer route that gave us longer days and shorter time.

Friday, April 17th. Started at 7.30. The snow of Lebanon just visible in the southwest through the mist. On our left on a distant hill was a tall building, like a tomb of Palmyra. As we rose on the plain, a few remains of ruins at the edge of the valley. At 1 30 ruins on the distant hill to the right; 5.10 an inconspicuous ruin; 5.15 a well of water; 5.22 a small valley of grass, not as good as last night, and a dozen wells of water, with scum on top. Pitched here at Feraklus. It had been an uninteresting day, except as Lebanon had been constantly in sight, the northern line covered with snow, and that to the south streaked on the top with snow Mostly a fair soil, not very strong, and the mountain ridges at right and left more receding. We saw more signs of the ruins of the outlying important towns of Palmyra

Saturday, April 18th Left Feraklus at 7.38. At 8 25 considerable ruins of a city with low walls of unhewn, or decayed stone. Buttercups. At 10 30 a valley and wells or pits; anemones; 11.10 plowed fields; 11.30 a cone (kubab) village, —the Syrian Christian part kubab, the Mohammedan stone and mud, both good,—called Abu Deli. At 12 30 village of Sukara, or Sakhra; 1.45 village of Zeda, all Christian, 100 houses; 2.30 Homs. Here we reached the black trachyte. Heard of a stone representing a man hunting a lion, which was found near here, and sold and carried off.

From Homs we went to Damascus, and thence to Beirout, by a route that needs no description.

END OF VOL. I.

POPULAR ARCHÆOLOGY.

Primitive Man in Ohio.—By WARREN K. MOORE-HEAD, Fellow of the American Association for the Advancement of Science, author of "Fort Ancient, the Great Prehistoric Earthwork of Warren County, Ohio." 8vo. Fully illustrated . . $3 00

This book which is a companion work to Nadaillac's "Prehistoric America," is the result of the observations of the author and his collaborators in Ohio during a number of years; their deductions are made from the testimony of the burial-places, village sites, and fortifications marking various epochs in primeval man's existence It is a comprehensive statement of their discoveries related without ornamentation.

Prehistoric America. By the MARQUIS DE NADAILLAC. Translated by Nancy Bell (N. D'Anvers), author of "History of Art" Edited, with Notes, by W. H Dall. Large octavo, with 219 illustrations. Popular edition $3 00

"The best book on this subject that has yet been published, . . . for the reason that, as a record of facts, it is unusually full, and because it is the first comprehensive work in which, discarding all the old and worn-out nostrums about the existence on this continent of an extinct civilization, we are brought face to face with conclusions that are based upon a careful comparison of architectural and other prehistoric remains with the arts and industries, the manners and customs of 'the only people, except the whites, who, so far as we know, have ever held the regions in which these remains are found.'" —*Nation*

"His book is one which no anthropologist should be without. It gathers into one critical and incredulous volume all that is most solid, sure, and trustworthy in the whole realm of American archæology."—*Pall Mall Gazette*

The Customs and Monuments of Prehistoric Peoples. By the MARQUIS DE NADAILLAC. Translated with the permission of the author, by Nancy Bell (N. D'Anvers). Large octavo. Fully illustrated $3.00

"To the student of archæology and anthropology this book is invaluable, to the class interested in the knowledge and speculation concerning the primeval races it will be a rare book for the library, for the world at large it will be a contribution to scientific literature not to be forgotten."—*Columbus Despatch.*

G. P. PUTNAM'S SONS, NEW YORK AND LONDON.

POPULAR ARCHÆOLOGY.

Rome and Pompeii.—Archæological Rambles. Translated by D Havelock Fisher. With maps and plans. 8vo $2 50

"Gaston Boisser is a refreshing writer with whom to travel . . . He gives us ideas and improves our knowledge, while improving his own, and adds to the treasures of his memory what can be gained by direct contract with events and even with ruins; . . . particularly interesting and valuable are the notes to be found in his archæological rambles "—*Paris Correspondent of N. Y. Evening Post.*

A Manual of Archæology.—Containing an Introduction to Egyptian, Oriental, Greek, Etruscan, and and Roman Art. By TALFOURD ELY, Author of "Olympus: Tales of the Gods of Greece and Rome" With 114 illustrations, 8vo . . . $2 00

"For a brief yet comprehensive account of the earliest art, we know of nothing better . . . After a careful examination, we say that Mr. Ely's statements are scholarly and trustworthy "—*Christian Union.*

Egyptian Archæology. By G. MASPERO. Translated from the French by AMELIA B. EDWARDS. With 229 illustrations. 8vo, gilt top . $2.25

"A rich and enjoyable book in every way satisfactory and fascinating. It is delightful to find frankness, accuracy, and scholarship united in the production of this work, which makes the humanity of vanished Egypt live again "—*The Critic.*

A Manual of Oriental Antiquities. Including the Architecture, Sculpture and Industrial Arts of Chaldea, Assyria, Persia, Syria, Judea, Phœnicia and Carthage By ERNEST BABELON. Translated and enlarged by B. T. A. EVETTS, M.A. With over 250 illustrations. 8vo, gilt top . . . $3 00

"The work is of a high class, and Oriental students, as well as students of the history of civilization and of art, will be grateful to M Babelon for his excellent treatise "—CYRUS ADLER in *The American*

G. P. PUTNAM'S SONS, NEW YORK AND LONDON.

www.ingramcontent.com/pod-product-compliance
Lightning Source LLC
Chambersburg PA
CBHW071139300426
44113CB00009B/1020